The Kabbalistic Words of Jesus in the Gospel of Thomas

Recovering the Inner-Circle Teachings of *Yeshua*

Lewis Keizer M.Div., Ph.D.

Copyright Lewis Keizer 2009

ISBN 978-0-578-02140-9

Contents

PREFACE:
The True Meaning of the *Logia*

I have written this book because the many scholarly translations of *The Gospel of Thomas* available in books and online do not correctly interpret the *logia.* Neither literal translations nor attempts to clarify through paraphrase have been adequate. As a result, readers blissfully create their own interpretations of the sayings oblivious to which are Gnostic interpolations, which are authentic, and what the original Aramaic *davarim* of *Yeshua* really taught.

This book is for people who want to know what the sayings really meant to *Yeshua,* and what they can mean for twenty-first century people.

The key to understanding the teachings of *Yeshua* is familiarity with the thought-world of Jewish messianic mysticism upon which they were based. These included the Jewish wisdom tradition, prophetic and apocalyptic schools, and *Merkabah* mysticism. Much of this was transmitted orally and in private to close disciples by a *Rav* or Master of Israel.

Oral transmission of mystical knowledge or *manda* (Greek *gnosis*) concerning the inner meaning of Scripture was known as *kabbalah* (קבלה), "receiving" that which was spoken from the mouth of the teacher into the ear of the disciple. Although little of it was written until the medieval period for the sake of initiatic secrecy,[1] scholars can restore much of the kabbalistic tradition of *Yeshua's* era through sources like the *Sepher Yetzirah, Sepher Ha-Razim,* and the *haggadah* preserved in the *Mishna,* Babylonian and Palestinian *Talmud,* and the vast literature of the intertestamental period known loosely as the Apocrypha and Pseudepigrapha of the Old Testament. These were the Holy Scriptures of Essenes, Zadokites, and other messianic Jews of the period, including *Yeshua* and his disciples. The Psalms they chanted in worship and *Shabbat Seder* were not just those of our Old Testament, but the messianic *Odes of Solomon* and others preserved in Enochian and

---

[1] *Kabbalistic* knowledge was committed to preservation in writing when medieval Christian pogroms against Jewish communities decimated so many Jewish men that family lineage became matriarchal instead of patriarchal. That is why even today membership in Israel is traced through mothers instead of fathers. The son of a Jewish man married to a non-Jewish woman is not considered to be Jewish in orthodox circles, but the daughter of a Jewish woman married to a non-Jewish man would be not only Jewish, but able to carry on Jewish family lineage—very different than in ancient Israel.

apocalyptic scripture. A study of this forgotten literature allows modern scholars to reconstruct the oral *kabbalah* of *Yeshua's* period.

A comparison of what can reliably be accepted as authentic historical teachings of *Yeshua* with the messianic mysticism of his era clarifies many things. For example, his messianic understanding was rooted in the tradition of the large diaspora community in Babylon. He taught not the Palestinian *Messiah Ben-David* or *Messiah Ben-Joseph*, but the Son-of-Man *Messiah*, or Aramaic *Bar-Enash*, of the Babylonian school of Daniel. He relied upon Babylonian scriptural schools such as Deutero- and Trito-Isaiah, the Enochian apocalypses, and wisdom traditions we know from the Babylonian *Talmud*, which preceded the Palestinian. He practiced and privately transmitted forms of *Merkabah* meditation *(shaqad)* and ascent developed in Babylon. The "lost years" of Jesus? Probably in Babylon.

The Gnostic Prologue to *The Gospel of Thomas* promises that whoever discovers the true interpretation of these sayings "will never taste death"—an Aramaic idiom meaning that he or she will achieve the *Qimah,* which is the conscious after-death state of a living *tzadik* or realized saint. Concerning the *Qimah,* which was taught by the Pharisees but not accepted by the Sadducees, *Yeshua* (Jesus) said that those who achieve it "neither marry nor are given in marriage [are no longer male or female] but are like unto the angels [androgynous divine beings]." The *Qimah* of the ancient Jewish mystics lies at the historical root of the *Anastasis* (Resurrection) phenomena as they were perceived and understood, visions of the Risen Jesus, and the Christian cult of saints.

Here is a hymn about the *Qimah* of the righteous from the first-century Pharisaic Apocalypse of Baruch, contemporary with *Yeshua*. It may have been one of the hymns sung by *Yeshua* and the disciples during his *Shabbat Seder,* which was a mystic participation in the Marriage Banquet of *Messiah*. Note the kabbalistic terminology and the parallel to *Yeshua's* statement about "like unto the angels:"

> But those who have been saved by their works,
> And to whom the *Torah* has been now a hope,
> And understanding *(Binah)* an expectation,
> And wisdom *(Hochmah)* a confidence,
> Shall wonders appear in their time.
> For they shall behold the world which is now invisible to them,
> And they shall behold the time which is now hidden from them:
> And time shall no longer age them.
> For in the heights of that *'Olam* shall they dwell,
> And they shall be made like unto the angels,
> And be made equal to the stars,
> And they shall be changed into every form they desire,

From beauty into loveliness,
And from Light *(Aur)* into the splendor of glory. [2]

No one can truthfully promise that if you understand the true meaning of the sayings, you will achieve the *Qimah*. Certainly, however, by examining the *logia* of *Thomas* with the aid of Aramaic-based translation, along with commentary illuminated by the Jewish messianic mysticism that informed the understanding of *Yeshua* and his *talmidim,* you will gain an understanding of the sayings—many of which preserve *Yeshua's* historical inner-circle, kabbalistic, or "secret" teachings.

But the Master taught that hearing[3] alone was not sufficient. The key was in doing or practice.[4] So here is a promise I can truthfully make: If you understand the kabbalistic teachings of *Yeshua* that we will reconstruct from the *Gospel of Thomas*, put them into practice, and walk the rest of his *Halakah*, you will be on a path to achieving the *Qimah*[5].

---

[2] I Baruch 51.7-10, edited R.H. Charles, online at
http://www.pseudepigrapha.com/pseudepigrapha/2Baruch.html
[3] Hebrew-Aramaic "understanding." The root *shamar* meant both to hear and to understand, so the idiom "Hear *(Shema)*, O' Israel," for example, means not merely to have audible perception, but to deeply understand. *Kabbalah* demanded a deep "understanding" of the inner meaning of Scripture. That is what was meant by *Yeshua* when he spoke a *davar* or prophetic oracle and said, "Let those who have ears to hear, hear!"
[4] Matthew 7.24; Luke 6.47 from Q Material. Cf. James 1.22 :"Be ye doers of the Word, and not hearers only."
[5] As Paul said, you will become a spiritual athlete *(asketes)*, putting on the Perfect Humanity to compete in a race *(agon)* against the old Adam of your nature (I Corinthians 9.24-27 *et al.*)

CHAPTER ONE:
Origin of the *Gospel of Thomas*

Let me begin by explaining how the *Gospel of Thomas* seems to have come into being and the basis I use for translation and interpretation of the *logia*.

The oldest sayings in *Thomas* were remembered and dictated in Aramaic by a disciple of *Yeshua*—possibly the Apostle Judas Thomas himself. Aramaic was the dialect of Hebrew spoken by *Yeshua* and the language in which he taught. The scribe who first recorded these memorized Aramaic *davarim* or revelatory teachings was multilingual. He translated what was dictated into a written collection of Koine Greek *logia*.

The Hebrew and Aramaic Alphabet as used at the time of *Yeshua* who, like the Jews of Palestine and Babylon, spoke and wrote Aramaic, but read scripture in Hebrew. The relationship of Hebrew to Aramaic could be compared to that of Chaucer's English to modern English.

By the Second Century, Aramaic was written in the Syriac alphabet, which resembled later Arabic script. The common tongue was still Aramaic. Tatian's *Diatessaron* or Syriac gospel harmony was translated from the four Greek Gospels back into Aramaic in late 2nd century when Aramaic-Greek equivalencies were still understood. The Syriac *Diatessaron* is useful to scholars trying to recover the original Aramaic vocabulary of *Yeshua*, but it depends upon the Greek New Testament and is not, as some have claimed, the "original Aramaic New Testament!"

Tet	Chet	Zayin	Vav	He	Dalet	Gimel	Bet	Alef
(T)	(Ch)	(Z)	(V/O/U)	(H)	(D)	(G)	(B/V)	(Silent)

Samech	Nun	Nun	Mem	Mem	Lamed	Khaf	Kaf	Yod
(S)	(N)	(N)	(M)	(M)	(L)	(Kh)	(K/Kh)	(Y)

Tav	Shin	Resh	Qof	Tzade	Tzade	Fe	Pe	Ayin
(T/S)	(Sh/S)	(R)	(Q)	(Tz)	(Tz)	(F)	(P/F)	(Silent)

It is vital to understand that the Hebrew-Aramaic *davar* was a powerful teaching or "word" of God delivered by a prophet. It was mysterious and dynamic. It could be compared to a seed that must be germinated, unfolded, and its fruit ripened by a wise hearer. *Davarim* might have the force of divine law (as in the Book of Deuteronomy or *Devrim*), mandate new requirements for *mitzvoth,* admonish unfaithfulness to the ways of God, or transmit the *razim*, "secrets, hidden mysteries" of Heaven including foreknowledge of the future. But they were always forms of divine revelation from the Throne *(Merkabah)* of God.

By contrast, a Greek *logion* was the Saying of a wise teacher or philosopher. It might be a "dark Saying," like one of the cryptic verses attributed to Heraklitos regarding his *panta rhei* oracle describing the mystery of all phenomena in flux: "On those stepping into rivers the same, other, and other waters flow." Such a *logion* was directed to insiders of a philosophical school. It demanded keen understanding and interpretation, often best served by allegorical paraphrase, in this case: "One cannot step into the same river twice."

But a Greek *logion* might also be aphoristic and directed to all hearers, like one from the collection of *Golden Verses* attributed to Pythagoras: "Never suffer sleep to close thy eyelids, after thy going to bed until thou hast examined by thy reason all thy actions of the day. Wherein have I done amiss? What have I done? What have I omitted that I ought to have done? If in this examination thou find that thou hast done amiss, reprimand thyself severely for it; but if thou hast done any good, rejoice."[6]

These latter forms of *logia* were collected from oral and written sources and recorded by the chroniclers of the Jewish wisdom schools like *Qoheleth* (Old Testament Book of Ecclesiastes) and *Yeshua Ben-Sirach* (Intertestamental *Wisdom of Jesus Ben Sirach*). Collections of non-attributed Jewish wisdom sayings are found in the canonical Book of Proverbs. In the Hellenistic Greek translation of Jewish scripture known as the Septuagint, these proverbs would be called *logia.*

But it is vital to understand that the core sayings preserved in *Thomas* were not *logia.* They were *davarim* concerning the *razim* or mysteries of Heaven revealed by the Master *Yeshua* to his closest circle of disciples. The original Greek transcription from which *Thomas* developed might be best described as the Secret Sayings Source, or Secret Q. Like Mark's sources for the Secret Gospel, Secret Q was reserved for private instruction of advanced *talmidim.* It amplified the meaning of public parables and allegories that we find in Q[7] of the Gospels of Matthew and Luke.

After these divine revelations were dictated, translated into Greek, and recorded as written text, they assumed the literary form of Greek *logia.* As the text of this secret collection was copied and circulated among gentile Christian churches, the *davarim* were understood as "dark sayings" like those of Heraklitos.

That is why Clement of Alexandria wrote, "Thus he [Mark]...brought in certain sayings of which he knew the interpretation would, as a mystagogue,[8] lead the hearers into the innermost sanctuary of truth hidden by seven veils."[9]

---

[6] The practice of evening contemplation is done in many spiritual traditions worldwide.

[7] The lost source document for much of the Gospels of Matthew and Luke.

[8] An Initiate of the mystery religions who assumed the powers of Egyptian Thoth or Greek Hermes to lead an initiand through the process of initiation. In the early church a Bishop gave a "mystagogical homily" to

The Prologue to the *Gospel of Thomas* (Logion 1) also attributes the function of a mystagogue to a correct interpretation of the *logia* : "Whoever discovers the interpretation of these words will not taste death." In the case of *Thomas* in its final form, however, the initiation occurs through private reading and understanding, since the original Gnostic *cultus* had suffered persecution and may no longer have survived to operate.

Thus the *Gospel of Thomas,* which was a Gnostic redaction based on an original Koine Greek text of the *logia,* presents them much in the same way as the Neo-Hermetics presented the dialogues of Hermes Trismegistos—as what Professor Dieter Georgi liked to call a "reading mystery." The initiatic cult of Trismegistos had long ago ceased to operate because of persecution by the proto-orthodox Athanasian Christians of Alexandria, but some of their writings were hidden away and preserved at Nag Hammadi. Others were Neo-Platonized and transmitted in the form of what would be later known to the medieval European Hermetic Renaissance as the *Corpus Hermeticum.*

Logion 1 is not a *davar* of *Yeshua.* In fact, it claims to be a saying of the disciple Didymos Judas Thomas[10] who, in this Gnostic tradition, was honored as the greatest and most beloved disciple of *Yeshua.* But let us paraphrase the essential parts of Logion 1 to demonstrate what it would mean as hypothetical Prologue to a secret collection of Aramaic *davarim* given by *Yeshua:*

"These are the heavenly mysteries *(razim)* which the immortal *Yeshua* revealed...Whoever understands and puts them into practice will likewise become an ever-living saint."

Indeed, this is the Prologue I provide for my translation of the core authentic *davarim* in this book.

The authentic *davarim* or Aramaic sayings of *Yeshua* were recorded in Greek between the years 30 and 50 C.E. That was during the era of Apostolic discipleship and messianic communities immediately following the crucifixion of *Yeshua.* In other words, it was before the development of second and third generation Greek-speaking Christian churches. This was the non-literary era before Paul had dictated his epistles or the Gospels had been

---

catechumens at the last stage of preparation leading to baptism. A Lodge Master or appointed Master of the Freemasons often delivers a special lecture with the same function during the raising of a Master Mason. In the Alexandrian and Thomas traditions, the Risen Christ was considered to live and operate as Mystagogue through a correct hearing (or in *Thomas,* reading) of the initiatic Words of Jesus. This was also probably the intent of the *Corpus Hermeticum.*

[9] Morton Smith, *Clement of Alexandria and a Secret Gospel of Mark* Harvard University Press, 1973; see history of the Secret Mark controversy at http://www.gnosis.org/library/secm_commentary.htm As the reader will note, I agree with Profs. Helmut Koester, Hans-Martin Schenke, and others about the authenticity of Secret Mark. Prof. Hans Deiter Betz remarks, "It is my opinion that Smith's book and the texts he discovered should be carefully and seriously studied."

[10] The original Apostle was Judas (not Iscariot, and not the brother of *Yeshua*), known in Aramaic as *Tau'ma* ("Twin'), which was transliterated as Greek *Thomas,* then translated as *Didymos,* the Greek word for twin.

compiled. In other words, the sayings of the original kernel of *Thomas* are older and more authentic than the earliest writings of the New Testament!

Sometime in the second century, the Greek collection of the kernel sayings was reworked by ascetics Syrian Gnostics who claimed to derive their tradition from the Apostle Thomas. They added their spin to the existing sayings of *Yeshua* and created new ones of their own.

Greek fragment from the Oxyrhynchus papyri.

The Coptic Gospel of Thomas discovered at Nag Hammadi is mostly intact.

The Gnosticized Greek version is what we find preserved in fragments from the Oxyrhynchus Papyri #1, #654, and #655, dating the Greek version of the *Gospel of Thomas* to at least 200 C.E.

Scholars didn't know what document the Oxyrhynchus fragments represented until the mid-twentieth century, when a Coptic version of *Thomas* was discovered at Nag Hammadi. This Coptic version of the *Gospel of Thomas* was translated from the earlier Greek *Thomas*. It is the only full and complete version of the secret sayings that we have. But since it represents yet another translation cycle into a completely different language, it is thrice removed from the original Aramaic.

Coptic is a late form of the Egyptian language. The written form uses Greek uncial or capital letters augmented by several other alphabetic characters derived from Demotic glyphs. The text looks somewhat like Greek, but has absolutely no relation to the grammar, syntax, and vocabulary of the Greek language. Coptic, in fact, in fact is more similar to Semitic languages of the ancient Near East.

Below are examples of Greek uncials compared to the fourth-century Coptic alphabet use in the Nag Hammadi manuscript of the *Gospel of Thomas*. The Egyptian glyphs added to the Greek letters are the sixth letter *so* and the final seven letters. *Thomas* is written in a dialect of Coptic spoken on the Upper Nile known as Sahidic.

The Coptic alphabet incorporated 24 Greek capital letters plus 8 characters derived from Demotic glyphs.

A	B	Γ	Δ	E	Z
Alpha	**Beta**	**Gamma**	**Delta**	**Epsilon**	**Zeta**
(al-fah)	(bay-tah)	(gam-ah)	(del-ta)	(ep-si-lon)	(zay-tah)
H	Θ	I	K	Λ	M
Eta	**Theta**	**Iota**	**Kappa**	**Lambda**	**Mu**
(ay-tah)	(thay-tah)	(eye-o-tah)	(cap-pah)	(lamb-dah)	(mew)
N	Ξ	O	Π	P	Σ
Nu	**Xi**	**Omicron**	**Pi**	**Rho**	**Sigma**
(new)	(zie)	(om-e-cron)	(pie)	(roe)	(sig-mah)
T	Y	Φ	X	Ψ	Ω
Tau	**Upsilon**	**Phi**	**Chi**	**Psi**	**Omega**
(taw)	(up-si-lon)	(fie)	(kie)	(sigh)	(oh-may-gah)

The Greek uncial alphabet letters used by the scribe who translated the kernel *davarim* of *Thomas*.

ⲁ	Ⲃ	Γ	Δ	Ⲉ	Ϛ	Z	Ⲏ
a	b v	g	d	e	s	dz	e i
alpha	oida	gamma	daida	ei	so	zita	ita
Θ	Ⲓ	Ⲕ	ⲗ	Ⲙ	Ⲛ	Ⲝ	O
th	i	k	l	m	n	ks	c
thita	jauta	kapa	laula	mri	ni	ksi	c
Π	Ⲣ	Ⲥ	Τ	Υ	Φ	Χ	Ψ
p	r	s	t	u	ph	kh	ps
oi	ro	sima	tau	he	phi	khi	psi
Ⲱ	Ⲯ	Ϥ	Ⳉ	Ⳅ	Ⳉ	Ϭ	†
ô û	š	f	x	h	dž	tš	t
au	šei	fei	khei	hori	džaudžia	tš ma	t

Although Coptic was a late form of the Egyptian language entirely different from Greek, in a polyglot society where Greek was the international second language, Greek words were taken whole into native vocabularies. There were so many Greek loan words in Hellenistic Coptic that a dictionary must include two lexicons—one for Egyptian (Coptic) words, and another for the Greek loan words. Consequently, our Coptic version of the *Gospel of Thomas* preserves many loan words from the earlier Greek version of the Gnostic gospel.

The good news is that by identifying the Greek vocabulary from which Coptic *Thomas* was translated, a scholar can work backwards to the Aramaic vocabulary that underlies the original oral dictation. That is because we have an abundance of Hebrew-Aramaic literature that was translated by and for Greek-speaking Jews of the Diaspora, such as the Septuagint or Greek version of the Hebrew Old Testament.

The abundance of Greek loan words embedded in the Coptic text of the *Gospel of Thomas,* when taken with the fragments of the earlier Greek version of *Thomas* preserved in Oxyrhynchus Papyrus #1, 654, and 655, provides a scholar with solid clues to recover the Aramaic vocabulary and concepts of the authentic historical *davarim* of *Yeshua.*

Who had access to the Greek version of *Thomas* and translated it into Coptic? Probably a fellowship of ascetic men who migrated from Syria as part of the early desert father movement. The third and fourth century monastic movement that developed in the Egyptian wilderness along the Nile River drew men, and eventually women, from all over the Roman Empire. Many were from Syria and Asia Minor, where Greek *Thomas* had been produced. It was probably carried into the Egyptian wilderness by Syrian monks and their devotees.

Greek *Thomas* may have provided a model for the genre of the original Coptic *Philokalia,* known to westerners through Thomas Merton's *Sayings of the Desert Fathers.* The *Philokalia* was collected from memorized oral aphorisms, *logia,* and instructional stories from the great "solitaries" who laid the foundations of Western monasticism in the Egyptian desert alongside the Nile. Instead of "Jesus said," many of the oldest sayings of the *Philokalia* begin with a format such as "*Apa* Abraham used to say."

In fourth-century Alexandria, violent persecutions arose against non-orthodox Christians, Gnostics, and Neo-Platonists. These were fueled by Bishop Athanasius, an intransigent ideologue whose zealous followers drove pagans and heretics out of Alexandria. It was charged that Athanasius hired thugs to intimidate, beat, kidnap, and imprison his theological enemies. Alexandrian records show that he was tried many times for bribery, theft, extortion, treason and murder, but always managed to beat the rap.

Later the brilliant woman philosopher Hypatia, head of the Neo-Platonic Academy and a teacher of other Christian Bishops, was violently pulled from her chariot by an Athanasian mob, stripped naked, dragged through the streets by horses, and then murdered by literally being torn to pieces with sharp shells. Many historians lay the burning and total destruction of the Library of Alexandria, and with it most of the written archives of the ancient world, at the feet of Athanasian anti-pagan zealots.

While Christians know "Saint Athanasius" as author of the Anthanasian Creed and the political enabler for Constantine's state church, his intolerant Christian orthodoxy drove the non-orthodox away from Alexandria and far up the Nile where the Sahidic dialect of Coptic was spoken. This may have been what initiated a Coptic translation of Greek *Thomas* into the Sahidic dialect. Whatever the case, we can be more certain that the Athanasian persecution finally extended its influence even into the Upper Nile. It would have been then when the Nag Hammadi Coptic-Gnostic library was copied into codices, stuffed into pottery jars, sealed, and hidden in an obscure cave near Chenoboskion (modern Nag Hammadi). We can only speculate about the fate of those who preserved this literature for posterity.

The cave near Chenoboskion where *Thomas* was hidden is also the location of the first Christian monastery founded by Pachomius about 320 C.E.—contemporary with our Coptic version. It may have been zealous Orthodox Pachomians who drove away the Gnostic monks and forced them to hide their extensive library of forbidden books. The Gnostics would probably have migrated up the Nile to Panopolis (modern Achmin), where the alchemists and Neo-Pythagorean expatriates from Alexandria had created a city safe from Athanasian and later Byzantine Orthodox Christian rule.

In any case, what we have of Greek *Thomas* is only fragmentary. All Greek copies seem to have been destroyed in the persecutions, which may be why we find only fragments of them in the Oxyrhynchus garbage heap. But we do have one surviving manuscript of the Coptic version, and that is the starting point for our work to recover the original *davarim* of *Yeshua.*

As I said, it is relatively simple to recover the *Aramaic* vocabulary that underlay Greek translations. But what if we have only a few Greek loan words and mostly Coptic text, as we do in *Thomas?*

Fortunately, Crum's monumental Coptic Dictionary is a kind of Rosetta Stone that catalogues Greek equivalents to Coptic-Egyptian words. Because a great body of Hellenistic Greek literature was translated into Coptic with both versions still extant, a scholar can recover Greek words underlying a Coptic version, then get back to Aramaic equivalents through the Greek equivalents. However, this is a bit more dicey than working from a Greek text because there are usually many possible Greek words referenced for one word root in a Coptic dictionary. One needs to be familiar with the multi-denotational uses of Egyptian triliteral roots, carefully examine the options for a likely Greek translation-equivalent, and do this in the light of the likely Aramaic basis for an original *davar.*

Let us summarize. Over a period of about three hundred years, the sayings now preserved in the full Coptic version of *Thomas* from Nag Hammadi were translated from Aramaic into Greek, then from a Gnosticized Greek collection into the Sahidic dialect of the Egyptian language known as Coptic. If our goal is to properly understand the teachings of *Yeshua,* rather than those of the Gnostics, we need to recover the Aramaic language, word roots, and concepts that are native to the *davarim* of *Yeshua,* and use that as our basis to interpret the mysterious *logia* of the *Gospel of Thomas.*

Can scholars do this by analyzing the fourth-century Coptic-Gnostic text of the *Thomas?* Can scholars dig back through the Coptic and the Greek languages to recover the original Aramaic key terms and ideas in the historical teachings of *Yeshua?*

As Obama says, Yes we can! And that's what we do in this book.

CHAPTER TWO:
Recovering the Original Inner Circle
Davarim of *Yeshua*

The Gnostic *Gospel of Thomas* is an evolution of a literary process that began with private notes and memorized oral tradition circulated among messianic communities headed by disciples of *Yeshua* in the first generation after his crucifixion.

The sequence in which the sayings of *Yeshua* were dictated followed mnemonic, not literary, order. The only organizational principle that linked the sayings together was memory. Therefore the order of the sayings, while seeming at first glance to be random, begins with a summary of the path of a Jewish saint (Logion 2) and proceeds with each subsequent saying following a mnemonic clue in the previous one—a key word, concept, or format such as a *mashal* or parable reminding the speaker of another related saying. As we will later see, the last *davar* in the originally dictated collection was probably the ultimate revelation presented in Logion 113, "The *Malkuth* is spread out upon the Earth, but men do not see it."

This originally dictated sequence of sayings survived later Gnostic redactions as the foundation text into which other Greek *logia* attributed to Jesus were interpolated. The original collection, however, is identifiable by Aramaisms taken wholesale into the Greek, whereas the later *logia* are purely Greek, or some of them Coptic, in construction and employ specialized Gnostic philosophical vocabulary.

Many original disciples like *Shimone,* to whom *Yeshua* gave the initiatic Aramaic name *Cephas,* known in the New Testament writings as "Peter," were not illiterate, as earlier scholars have assumed. The letter of Clement of Alexandria discovered recently by Prof. Morton Smith in the archives of the Mt. Athos monastery, which preserves words from the Secret Gospel of Mark,[11] tells us that Mark carried with him to Alexandria not only his own notes taken as a disciple of Peter, but the notes that Peter himself had written in order to remember and organize the teachings of his Master *Yeshua.*

---

[11] Cf. note 6

Clement also reveals that Mark wrote two Gospels—the one in the New Testament for the general public, and another for "those who are being perfected" that contained initiatic teachings and revelations given only to *Yeshua's* inner circle of disciples. Clement says that when Mark came to Alexandria after Peter's martyrdom, he relied upon both his own notes and those of Peter to compose the Secret Gospel, which was eventually stolen by the Gnostic Carpocrates and revised to provide authority for his homosexual initiations. Thus the inner-circle teachings came into the possession of Egyptian Gnostics.

Many Gnostic groups claimed to possess secret teachings of *Yeshua,* but their sources are second and third century visions of the Risen Christ recorded as long, Hermetic-like philosophical monologues. *Thomas* alone seems to offer credible sayings of *Yeshua* that can stand up to the critical standards of authenticity demanded by modern scholarship. Let us look more closely at why this is true.

The *Gospel of Thomas* claims to represent these inner circle teachings through the Apostle Thomas. It is clear that the *logia* preserved in *Thomas* derive from a source independent of Q, which we will discuss below. Q itself seems to have been independent of Peter and Mark since it is not found in the Gospel of Mark and probably not in the Secret Gospel of Mark. It is reasonable to assume that the *logia* of *Thomas* were transmitted through an independent Apostolic tradition deriving from the historical Apostle Thomas. Why would that be so?

Lineage traditions in both the Hellenistic world and Asia were greatly valued and transmitted from generation to generation. However, many writings under the name of a lineage founder are pseudepigraphic, that is, composed in the founder's name by priests and prophets of his school many generations later. For example, the Book of Deuteronomy, which claims to have been written by Moses, was probably written by the High Priest Hilkiah (possibly the father of both prophets Jeremiah and Ezekiel). He claimed to have discovered a scroll of Moses in the archives of the Temple, then used it to influence King Josiah to reform the religion of Israel and return to Mosaic Law.[12]

The Pastoral Epistles of Paul, the Book of Daniel, and all the magical and apocalyptic writings from the intertestamental and New Testament eras preserved under such names as Moses, Baruch, David, Solomon, and Enoch are pseudepigraphic. They were composed by later generations who incorporated legends and oral traditions about the founding saint into their writings. They considered themselves to operate under his "channeled" guidance. It was considered legitimate in the Hellenistic world for a lineage holder or disciple to speak, teach, and write in the name of the founding saint of his school.

---

[12] Most objective scholars recognize Hilkiah as the author of Deuteronomy, which is written in the style and language of his era, reflects a settled agricultural society rather than a nomadic one under martial law, and tells the story of Moses' death—something Moses would have been hard-pressed to do if it were his own composition!

Aside from the editorial freedom its writer-translators have taken with sayings attributed to Jesus, the *Gospel of Thomas* is not pseudepigraphic. However it is clear from the Gnostic redactions of the Greek *logia* that the editors adhered to and promoted the same ascetic ideals found in other Syrian Thomas literature—the *Acts of Thomas, Thomas the Ascetic* ("Athlete"), the *Infancy Gospel of Thomas.*[13] Therefore we can reasonably speculate that the *Gospel of Thomas* in its current form derives from historical traditions and possibly even disciples or Apostolic successors of the unmarried Apostle *Judas Tau'ma* (Thomas).

The Syrian Gnostic Sect of Thomas

We can learn much about the Gnostic tradition that produced the *Gospel of Thomas* in its current form by studying the extant Thomas literature. Like many other Gnostic traditions, it was elitist, ascetic, and regarded its followers to be among the very few chosen ones— "one in a thousand, two in ten thousand."[14] The adherents were unmarried, monastic and separated from the rest of society—not unlike the sect of the Essenes that probably raised John the Baptist, but with affinities to the second-century gentile encratitic movement. They may originally have been exclusively male: "Let Mary go out from among us, because women are not worthy of the Life."[15] The appearance of the *Gospel of Thomas* in Egypt as a Coptic translation from Syrian Greek may indicate that it was translated by the same Gnostics who wrote the lost *Gospel of the Egyptians,* from which one fragment has Jesus declare, "I have come to destroy the works of woman."[16]

In the *Acts of Thomas,* the Apostle Judas Thomas is chosen by lot to evangelize the people of India.[17] He travels there as a freemason with the merchant Abbanes to the court of King Gundaphorus. The Lord Jesus appears in the bride chamber in the form of his twin brother Thomas to convince the newlyweds not to have sexual intercourse or breed children, but to become ascetic.

> "And the king desired the groomsmen to depart out of the bride-chamber; and when all were gone out and the doors were shut, the bride groom lifted up the curtain of the bride-chamber to fetch the bride unto him. And he saw the Lord Jesus bearing the likeness of Judas Thomas and speaking with the bride; even of him that but now had blessed them and gone out from them, the Apostle; and he saith unto him: Wentest thou not out in the sight of all? how then art thou found here? But the Lord said to him: I am not Judas which is also called Thomas but I am his brother. And the

---

[13] The stories told in the *Infancy Gospel of Thomas* about the miraculous child Jesus are comparable to the Hindu legends of the child-god Krishna. These romances were described by church fathers as *The Gospel of Thomas.* However, the *Protoevangelium* or *Infancy Gospel of Thomas* is of an entirely different origin and genre than our *Gospel of Thomas.*

[14] *Thomas* Logion #23

[15] *Thomas* Logion #114

[16] Clement *Strom.* iii. 9. 63.

[17] A name also used for Ethiopia. In another version Jesus has him shanghaied and taken by caravan to India.

Lord sat down upon the bed and bade them also sit upon chairs, and began to say unto them:

"Remember, my children, what my brother spake unto you and what he delivered before you: and know this, that if ye abstain from this foul intercourse, ye become holy temples, pure, being quit of impulses and pains, seen and unseen, and ye will acquire no cares of life or of children, whose end is destruction: and if indeed ye get many children, for their sakes ye become grasping and covetous, stripping orphans and overreaching widows, and by so doing subject yourselves to grievous punishments. For the more part of children become useless oppressed of devils, some openly and some invisibly, for they become either lunatic or half withered or blind or deaf or dumb or paralytic or foolish; and if they be sound, again they will be vain, doing useless or abominable acts, for they will be caught either in adultery or murder or theft or fornication, and by all these will ye be afflicted.

"But if ye be persuaded and keep your souls chaste before God, there will come unto you living children whom these blemishes touch not, and ye shall be without care, leading a tranquil life without grief or anxiety, looking to receive that incorruptible and true marriage, and ye shall be therein groomsmen entering into that bride chamber which is full of immortality and light."[18]

Some of us with teenage children may, at times, agree with this negative assessment of childbearing, but it is certainly the opposite of a life-affirming philosophy! However, there were many sects who would have agreed with the saying put into the mouth of Jesus in his dialogue with Salome from another *Gospel of the Egyptians* quoted by Clement of Alexandria: "The Lord said to Salome when she inquired: How long shall death prevail? 'As long as ye women bear children.'"[19]

Both Jewish and gentile sects existed as separated communities in second-century Palestine and Syria. One sect of Essenes had both male and female ascetics, but they adopted and raised children rather than procreate them through sexual intercourse. As earlier observed, John the Baptist may have been one of these children. There is no evidence I can find that the gentile Syrian Thomas ascetics raised children, however, and the extremely pessimistic words about children from the *Acts of Thomas* seem to preclude that possibility.[20]

In Asia Minor the Johannine churches founded by the Apostles John and Mary *Magdala* took a dim view of the ascetic Syrian Thomas devotees. That is why in the Gospel of John, special

---

[18] *Acts of Thomas* translated M.R. James, #11-12.

[19] *Strom.* iii. 6. 45.

[20] Authentic and well-known teachings of *Yeshua* reveal an extremely positive and life-affirming view of children that contrasts starkly with Gnostic pessimism.

pains are taken to marginalize Thomas as the "doubter," the least of the disciples. In Johannine tradition, John is the "beloved disciple," just as in the Petrine based Synoptics Peter is the "rock upon which I will build my church."[21] Just so, Thomas in his tradition is the Twin of Jesus, the greatest initiate of all the disciples.

The writer of Luke's massive two-part epistle to Theophilos (the Gospel of Luke and the Book of Acts) tells us that many others have written accounts about *Yeshua,* and that he has relied upon these accounts in framing his own narrative (Luke 1.1-4). Two of these sources were the Gospel of Mark and what scholars have identified as Q.

The *logia* of the *Gospel of Thomas* seems to represent, in their earliest form, another pre-New Testament written sources not available to the writers of Luke and Matthew, but resembling Q.

Thomas and Q

Notes taken by Peter, Mark, and others are not extant and we have no methodology for recovering them. However, the first generation of the Jewish messianic movement that would later be called Christianity did produce two collections of the sayings and parables of *Yeshua* that we can recover, even though none of the manuscripts have survived. They were both translated from Aramaic into Koine Greek, written down, copied, and circulated roughly between the years 30 and 50 C.E.

The first has been hypothesized to have existed by scholars since the advent of biblical criticism in the early twentieth century. It is known as Q, from the German *quelle,* "source." Scholars recovered its content by comparing the Greek texts of the Gospels attributed to Matthew and Luke.[22]

Both Gospels present a large number of common parables and sayings of Jesus. When we compare the Greek texts side by side, we find that they are almost identical—not only in wording, but in order and sequence. Originally scholars thought that one Gospel writer had copied the other. In the attempt to determine which was primary—Matthew or Luke—it became apparent that neither had copied from the other, but they had both used a common written source. This Q Source, as scholars sometimes refer to it (redundantly), was a primitive collection of sayings or *logia* and parables of Jesus that pre-existed the Gospels, which were late first-century writings.[23]

---

[21] Although a very good case has been made that the "beloved disciple" was actually Mary *Magdala.*

[22] The late 1st-2nd century Bishop Papias is quoted as having written that "Matthew compiled the logia (τὰ λόγια) in the Hebrew language, and each person interpreted them as he was able." This is speculated to be the origin of Q. Did the Apostle Thomas compile the kernel now preserved in the *Gospel of Thomas*?

[23] Religious fundamentalists and their biased biblical scholars present convoluted arguments against the existence of Q because they fear its existence violates the principle of biblical infallibility. As long as the

Matthew	Luke
δων δε πολλους των	ελεγεν ουν τοις
φαρισαιων και σαδδουκαιων	εκπορευομενοις οχλοις
ερχομενους επι το βαπτισμα	βαπτισθηναι υπ
αυτου ειπεν αυτοις	αυτου
γεννηματα εχιδνων τις	γεννηματα εχιδνων τις
υπεδειξεν υμιν φυγειν απο	υπεδειξεν υμιν φυγειν απο
της μελλουσης οργης	της μελλουσης οργης
ποιησατε ουν καρπους	ποιησατε ουν καρπους
αξιους της μετανοιας	αξιους της μετανοιας
και μη δοξητε λεγειν εν	και μη αρξησθε λεγειν εν
εαυτοις πατερα εχομεν τον	εαυτοις πατερα εχομεν τον
αβρααμ λεγω γαρ υμιν οτι	αβρααμ λεγω γαρ υμιν οτι
δυναται ο θεος εκ των λιθων	δυναται ο θεος εκ των λιθων
τουτων εγειραι τεκνα τω	τουτων εγειραι τεκνα τω
αβρααμ ηδη δε και η αξινη	αβρααμ ηδη δε και η αξινη
προς την ριζαν των δενδρων	προς την ριζαν των δενδρων μη
κειται παν ουν δενδρον μη	κειται παν ουν δενδρον μη
ποιουν καρπον καλον	ποιουν καρπον καλον
εκκοπτεται και εις πυρ	εκκοπτεται και εις πυρ
βαλλεται	βαλλεται

This selection from Q in Gospels of Matthew and Luke describes a fiery sermon by John the Baptist. Like the many other Q sayings and parables, the text varies only when the Gospel writers introduce a new section or stitch two sections together. Otherwise the text is identical (red type).

But with the discovery of the *Gospel of Thomas,* which contains much of the content of the Q sayings, scholars realized that they had stumbled upon a second, but uniquely different, primitive source like Q. Most scholars conclude that the earliest kernel of the collection of sayings preserved in *Thomas* was contemporary with Q. Q was a Greek document that represented translated notes or memoires of Aramaic-speaking disciples. It did not survive as a document, but was preserved in the Gospels of Matthew and Luke.

For one thing, *Thomas* is not just another second or third century philosophical discourse in the form of revelations from a Gnostic Heavenly Redeemer. Nor was it a narrative of the ministry of *Yeshua* that gave a story line and context to each teaching, as we find in the New Testament Gospels.

Rather, it was simply a collection of sayings beginning, "Jesus said."

Even more significant, many of the *logia* and parables of Jesus familiar from Q in Matthew and Luke are, in *Thomas,* riddled with Aramaisms—idioms and usages native to Aramaic rather than Greek or Coptic. This indicates they might be more original than those of Q, which appear somewhat paraphrased in idiomatic Greek. The Q sayings were also worded quite differently, often with unexpected emphasis or conclusions, and not just in a way to editorialize or alter them with Gnostic spin.

---

fundamentalist doctrine of biblical inerrancy persists, their denominational spokesmen will continue to dilute biblical scholarship with doctrinal apologetics that oppose the rational conclusions of despised "liberal" scholars. The fundamentalists have inundated the internet and Christian bookstores with their tortuous arguments. Consequently it has become very difficult for lay persons to distinguish pseudo-scholarship from the real thing. But the tip-off is this: At the end of the day, is this scholar spinning his arguments to defend the doctrine of biblical inerrancy? Creationism? Anti-abortion and anti-gay agendas? If the answer is yes, write him off. And by the way, it will be a him, not a her. By contrast, some of the best so-called "liberal" biblical scholarship is now being done by women scholars.

The process of oral dictation for recording by a scribe was the convention used by a disciple of a Jewish prophet to record his teachings. In contrast, sages of Jewish wisdom schools like Jesus Ben-Sirach wrote down their own teachings which were recopied and survived to modern times. But Apostles and original *talmidim* of *Yeshua* relied upon their students to render dictated teachings to writing. Even Paul dictated his epistles. Like other peripatetic Apostles of the early churches (who were known as *prophetes*), he had disciples and devotees who served him.

A Jewish prophet dictates visions to his disciple.

As opposed to Q, which in its pre-gospel form seems to have been a Greek literary document compiled from apostolic notes and recorded memories, the *Thomas* collection seems to have been dictation from a disciple to a scribe fluent in Aramaic and Greek.

Recovering the original sayings source is a multi-stage process. In its current Coptic form, the original kernel of *Thomas* has been amplified and editorialized to support ascetic Gnostic doctrines. Greek philosophical terms like *anapausis* (usually translated "rest") and *monochos* (usually translated as "a single one," but meaning a Gnostic ascetic) are interpolated into *logia* exhibiting Aramaisms and other evidence of historic authenticity. What is more, inauthentic Gnostic *logia* have been composed and inserted into the collection. In spite of all this, the authentic portions of *Thomas* are not usually difficult to identify.

In Q, Hebrew idioms and other Aramaisms were often paraphrased so as not to compromise the Greek translation, but in *Thomas* the translation was so literal that Aramaisms remained embedded in the Greek translation. That implies the kernel sayings of *Thomas* were dictated by an Aramaic-speaking disciple of *Yeshua,* while the Q sayings came from Koine Greek notes written by a disciple of an original disciple—such as Mark was to Peter. Many of the kernel sayings of *Thomas* are parallel to those of Q, but differ so much that most scholars agree they represent two independent sources.

Together Q and the oldest layer of *Thomas* are closer to the original historical teachings of *Yeshua* than what is preserved one to two generations later in the Greek texts of Paul's letters and the Gospel of Mark, or even later in the three other Gospels—all of which were composed late in the century in Greek for the use of early gentile (non-Jewish) churches.

Recovering the Original Kernel of *Thomas* and the Historical Teachings of *Yeshua*[24]

The original foundation of sayings upon which *Thomas* was constructed is known to a scholar like Prof. April De Conick, author of *The Original Gospel of Thomas in Translation,* as the Kernel Gospel—the original pre-synoptic Aramaic substratum that dates to the period 30-50 C.E. I agree with her general methodology, though less with her translation and interpretation. Here is a chart of Prof. De Conick's theory about the developing accretion of the various *logia* of *Thomas.*[25]

De Conick's Chronology

Kernel Gospel, 30-50 CE					
2	21.10	38.1	61.1	74	96.1-2
4.2-3	21.11	39	62.1	76	96.3
5	23.1	40	62.2	78	97
6.2-3	24.2	41	63.1-3	79	98
8	24.3	42	63.4	81	99
9	25	44.2-3	64.1-11	82	100.1-3
10	26	45	65.1-7	86	102
11.1	30	46.1-2a, c	65.8	89	103
14.4	31	47	66	90	104
15	32	48	68.1	91.2	107
16.1-3	33	54	69.2	92	109
17	34	55	71	93	111.1
20.2-4	35	57	72	94	
21.5	36	58	73	95	

Accretions, 50-60 CE
Relocation and Leadership Crisis
12
68.2

Accretions, 60-100 CE					
Accommodation to Gentiles and Early Eschatological Crisis					
(with shift to mystical dimension of apocalyptic thought)					
3.1-3	18	37	51	60	88
6.1	20.1	38.2	52	64.12	91.1
14.1-3	24.1	43	53	69.1	113
14.5	27.2	50	59	70	

Accretions, 80-120 CE					
Death of Eyewitnesses, Christological Developments and Continued Eschatological Crisis					
(with incorporation of encratic and hermetic traditions)					
Incipit	11.2-4	23.2	56	84	108
1	13	27.1	61.2-5	85	110
3.4-5	16.4	28	67	87	111.2
4.1	19	29	75	100.4	111.3
4.4	21.1-4	44.1	77	101	112
6.4-5	21.6-9	46.2b	80	105	114
7	22	49	83	106	

[24] We cannot know much about the historical Jesus, but we can reconstruct his historical teachings. However, we can do this accurately only by looking at them through the lens of his Aramaic language and the context of contemporary Jewish mysticism out of which he taught. It has been only recently that Christian biblical scholars have paid attention to the fact that *Yeshua* was a Jew. Only lately have scholars started to study the background of Jewish mysticism that informed his messianic teachings. The key to this is study of the intertestamental literature that, in effect, served as a Bible for the Essenes, the wisdom schools, and *Yeshua* and his disciples. When scholars do these studies, they find that *Yeshua* was not a simple "apocalypticist" who expected the immediate end of the world and forceful in-breaking of God's Sovereignty on Earth. He was a Master of Israel steeped in Galilean and Babylonian wisdom—prophet, *kabbalistic* sage, exorcist, healer, and Merkabah adept.

[25] *The Original Gospel Of Thomas In Translation: With A Commentary And New English Translation Of The Complete Gospel* (T & T Clark Library of Biblical Studies)

I don't agree with all of her chronology, but most of all I disagree with her criteria for selecting the kernel sayings. She rightly uses parallelism with Q sayings as one criterion. But she also considers eschatological content to be another characteristic of the kernel sayings. That is quite incorrect. Let me explain why.

She, like many scholars since the days of Schweitzer's *Quest of the Historical Jesus,* understands the historical *Yeshua* to have been what Prof. Bart Ehrman describes as a failed "apocalypticist." Perhaps a better term would be "eschatologist," since like Schweitzer, they assume that *Yeshua* expected the imminent intervention of God in human affairs and violent end of the old world. In other words, they believe that Jesus shared a common eschatological vision with not only the Palestinian world, but the Roman-Hellenistic world.[26]

Schweitzer based his idea that *Yeshua* expected the immediate, catastrophic end of the world on the words attributed to Jesus in New Testament narratives introducing the periscope of the so-called Transfiguration (which seems to reflect a *Merkabah* experience). Jesus said "There are some standing here who will not taste death until they have seen the Kingdom *(Malkuth)* of God come with power." [27]

To Schweitzer that meant Jesus expected the heavenly cavalry to come charging down to Earth to destroy the old world order and establish God's Reign. Any minute now, the old world would come to a sudden end and the new world order would take its place. This was the same messianic expectation held by the Essenes, the Galilean Zealots, and most of the Pharisees, who expected the warrrior *Messiah Ben-David* to lead armies of angels to reinforce Jewish freedom fighters in warfare against the Romans and to empower Israel to rule the gentiles.

Yeshua's words about the *Malkuth* or Sovereignty (wrongly translated "Kingdom") coming before this generation of disciples dies were considered by Schweitzer to be authentic because they were from the Marcan source, which was copied by Luke and Matthew to

---

[26] Hellenistic astrologers observed that the spring equinox Sun was moving gradually out of the constellation of Aries into that of Pisces. Many feared the world had rolled off its moorings and would come to an end. Stoic philosophers expected the Age of Aries to end in fire *(ekpyrosis)*as part of their theory of cosmic renewal *(apokatastasis,* and a new Age of Pisces to come into being. Both educated philosophers and superstitious priests of the Roman-Hellenistic period expected some kind of cosmic event to destroy the old world and bring about a new world order under the "fire" of Zeus. Roman apocalypses like *Scipio's Dream* (Cicero) show how deeply the astrological perspective had penetrated Roman-Hellenistic thought. Later the Christian philosopher Origen would develop a Christian theology of a final Apokatastasis, which even Satan would be reconciled to Heaven and redeemed.

[27] Mk 9:1

introduce their accounts of the Transfiguration.[28] Scholars of Schweitzer's era recognized that Mark was the earliest of the Gospels, used as a source document by Matthew and Luke, and thus a prime resource for authentic teachings of Jesus.

But the same Marcan source material tells us that *Yeshua* clearly opposed the eschatological *Messiah Ben-David* theory that is essential to an "apocalypticist." In a confrontation with Pharisaic *Ravs,* he pointedly asks this question: "Why do your scribes claim that *Messiah* is David's son *(Messiah Ben-David)?* For David himself said in the Holy Spirit *(Ruach Ha-Qodesh,* "Spirit of Holiness"), 'The LORD [God] said to my Lord [the *Messiah*], Sit on my right hand until I make your enemies into your footstool.' If David [in the Psalm] called him Lord, how can he [the *Messiah*] be his son *(Messiah Ben-David)?*"[29]

This demonstrates clearly that the Jesus of history was not in agreement with the common messianic expectation of his age—so-called "apocalypticism." In fact, a careful examination of what remains of the apocalyptic prophecies of John the Baptist reveals not an emphasis upon eschatology, but upon what messianic mystics called the Birthpangs of *Messiah*. This coming period of tribulation was also prophesied by *Yeshua,* and was the reason later messianic communities were forewarned to escape from Jerusalem before the holocaustic siege of 70 C.E. *Yeshua's* prophecy was not an expectation of the end of the world, but of the persecutions that would arise before *Messiah* and the *Malkuth* of God could appear on Earth.

In fact, *Yeshua* did not teach an eschatological end-of-the-world *Messiah Ben-David,* but a coming *Bar-Enash* or so-called "Son of Man" rooted in the Babylonian schools of Trito-Isaiah, Enoch, and Daniel. He prophesied that the forces of darkness would be defeated by the coming *Bar-Enash*—the scion or offspring of humanity foreseen at the Throne of God by the prophets Daniel and Enoch. Daniel described him as "one like unto a son of mankind," *k-bar-enash,* but Enoch simply named him the *Bar-Enash. Yeshua* referred to the coming *Messiah* as the *Bar-Enash* or Son of Man(kind).

Although the Gospel writers spun *Yeshua's* Son-of-Man sayings to refer to himself, in fact several of them make it clear that *Yeshua* considered the *Bar-Enash* or *Messiah* to be separate from himself. For example, in Mark 8.38 *Yeshua* says, "Whoever is ashamed of me and my *davarim* in this adulterous and sinful generation, of him the Son of Man also will be ashamed when He appears in the glory of the *Abba* with the holy angels."[30] In this Saying, *Yeshua* clearly distinguishes between himself and the *Bar-Enash.*

---

[28] Luke 9.27; Matthew 16.28
[29] Mark 12.35-37 (Luke 20,41-44; Matthew 22.41-46)
[30] Inserted into Luke 9.26 independent of Marcan context; does not appear in Matthew in Marcan context.

What is more, the so-called "Kingdom" of God that *Yeshua* proclaimed was not an earthly kingdom (Greek New Testament *basileion*). It was Aramaic *Malkuth,* Divine Sovereignty of Godhead on Earth, which shall explain in a later section.

We must note that the earliest Christian communities emphasized pneumatic "Holy Spirit" experience—something never taught by *Yeshua.* In fact the *Ruach Ha-Qodesh* or Holy Spirit is mentioned only twice in the teachings of *Yeshua.* Paul, the founder of New Testament gentile Christianity, emphasized belief in *Iesous* the *Christos* or *Messiah*—something never taught by *Yeshua.* But the coming of the *Malkuth,* which was central to *Yeshua's* proclamation, was never understood. It was shoe-horned into prevailing Jewish and Hellenistic eschatological expectation.

The Teachings of *Yeshua* and the Epistles of Paul

We can get more insight into the teachings of *Yeshua* by examining how they were reflected in the epistles of Paul, which along with Q and the *Thomas* Kernel are the earliest extant Christian writings. Paul has been accused of twisting the gospel preached by *Yeshua* into his own gospel about Jesus Christ the Savior of all mankind. Paul, who was never a disciple of *Yeshua* or even heard him teach, refers to what he preaches as "my Gospel." He boasts that his Gospel came to him in personal revelations, and not through human transmission.[31]

But on closer examination we find something quite different. By his own account he spent three years in Damascus and the desert areas ("Arabia") after his conversion experience.[32] Damascus was the location of a large Jewish messianic community headed by disciples of *Yeshua* like Ananias, who healed Paul's blindness. That was undoubtedly the community in which he, Saul, was baptized and given the Christian initiatic name Paul. To prepare for baptism, he would have been taught the sayings and parables of *Yeshua,* the legends of his life, death, and resurrection, and many biblical passages foretelling *Yeshua* as the *Messiah.* Direct disciples of *Yeshua* in Damascus and messianic wilderness communities certainly would have transmitted the entire Christian tradition *(paradosis)* to Paul before he went to Jerusalem after three years to sit at the feet of Peter and James.[33]

In spite of Paul's passionate declaration that he learned everything from personal revelation, he admits in many places that he had received the oral tradition from disciples of *Yeshua.* In First Corinthians 15 he states: "For I delivered unto you first of all the traditions *(paradoseis)* that I also received..." His familiarity with the historical sayings of

---

[31] Galatians 1.12
[32] Galatians 1.17-19
[33] Ibid.

Yeshua is also evident when he is quoted in the Book of Acts delivering a saying of *Yeshua* that is not found in the Gospels: "Remember the *davarim* of *Mar Yeshua,* how he said, 'It is more blessed to give than to receive.'"[34]

Paul (as Saul) had been a student of *Rav Gamaliel.* He was accustomed to strict rabbinic memorization, scholarship, and study. He carried those skills over into his life as a Christian, as his epistles demonstrate. But in his role as a missionary, Paul had to be, as he said, "all things to all men." His gentile hearers, being acculturated to Hellenistic mysteries and ecstatic spirit-*cultus* now transformed into Christian Holy-Spirit religion, considered personal divine revelation to be far more authoritative than Jewish oral transmission. That is why Paul presented himself both ways—as a prophet who received everything from the Holy Spirit, but also as a true Apostle of the tradition "born out of due season." His basis for Apostleship was that he, like the historical Apostles, had seen the Risen Christ.

However, it is precisely because Paul did receive oral teachings from original disciples that we can use his epistles as an entrée to recovering the authentic teachings of *Yeshua.* For example, on the level of personal piety Paul preached the Christ *(Messiah)* as a Second Adam that must be birthed in the heart of each person to overcome the old nature of the First Adam.[35] Theologically, Paul described the Church (congregation of the saints) as the Body of Christ, and Jesus Christ as the Head.[36] What did this mean in rabbinic and kabbalistic terms? The Christ as *Bar-Enash* was the new *Adam Kadmon* who sits at the right hand of God's authority. Paul developed his mystic ideas from historical *davarim* of *Yeshua* like those among the secret sayings of *Thomas.*

Paul understood the Heavenly archetype of the *Bar-Enash* or Christ as a corporate being whose body is comprised of the saints *(tzadikim),* at the head of whom is *Yeshua* as the first-begotten *(monogenes)* and guide of the New Humanity. We must recognize Paul's understanding of the *Bar-Enash* as one of our most reliable resources, once we take into consideration the biases of what he calls "my Gospel" as opposed to that taught by other Jewish disciples.

Although Paul and the early Christians identified *Yeshua* as mysteriously fulfilling the advent of the *Bar-Enash* and identified him as the *Messiah* or Christ, it seems clear that *Yeshua* had a different vision. Paul's transmission of ideas like "putting on" the Second Adam, and the Body of *Messiah* as a collective being, point to historical teachings of *Yeshua* about spiritual rebirth and the Son of Man(kind) as a collective heavenly archetype whose

---

[34] Acts 20.35
[35] Romans 6.6; I Corinthians 15.47
[36] I Corinthians 12.11ff;

body is comprised by spiritually reborn *tzadikim.* In *Thomas* disciples are called the "newly- borns."

This implies that for *Yeshua,* the Son of Man(kind) *Messiah* will be manifested on Earth through the spiritual transformation of mankind—soul by soul. The advent of the Christ will be a process, not a sudden event in time. Again it must be said, *Yeshua* was not an "apocalypticist." He was a messianic mystic who envisioned the gradual sanctification of humanity and the Earth.

By the same token, the "Kingdom" taught by *Yeshua* was not an invisible walled New Jerusalem suddenly descending from the skies, as the gentile Christians thought. The "Kingdom" was not "Lo here! Lo, there!" It was not a place. It did not appear as an event in history. Rather, it was invisibly and mystically "within" *(entos,* inside of*)* even the enemies of *Yeshua.*

Then what was the "Kingdom?" The Aramaic word used by *Yeshua* reveals the answer: *Malkuth,* "Sovereignty." It does not mean Kingdom, but "Kingship." It designates not a place, but the divine exercise of ultimate spiritual authority—the Sovereign Rule or Omnipotence of God. Most scholars translate it as Sovereignty.

Yeshua taught that God's Sovereignty on Earth is invisible to the eyes of men because dark forces rule the souls of humanity. But the day is coming when mankind will be liberated from bondage to *Shaitan* and God's Sovereign Rule will be manifest within and before the sight of all. A new, sanctified world will operate under the principles of God's divine *Malkuth:* Wisdom, Justice, Mercy, Love, Truth, Beauty, and all the other kabbalistic Names or divine qualities of Godhead.

Again, the Marcan Parable of the Mustard Seed, found independently in *Thomas,* makes it quite clear that the coming of the *Malkuth* is like the slow but faithful growth of the tiniest of all seeds into the greatest of all desert bushes. An independent version of an authentic *davar* of *Yeshua* preserved in *Thomas* tells us that God's *Malkuth* is "spread out upon the Earth, and men do not see it."[37] That is quite the opposite of an eschatological view. DeConick and other scholars who classify *Yeshua* as an "apocalypticist" consider that Logion to be among the latest of all Gnostic interpolations. I, however, consider it to be an original inner-circle revelation of *Yeshua.* My commentary on Logion 113 will explain why I take that view.

---

[37] *Thomas* Logion 113.

Significantly, Paul says little about the *Malkuth* of God. Rather, he understands Jesus Christ as reigning invisibly over the world. He refers to this as the Kingdom *(Basileon)* of God's beloved Son (Colossians 1.13), which was from the beginning, is now, and ever shall be. Clearly, even though Paul spoke Aramaic, he thought in Greek. His Gospel owes a great deal to the traditions handed down to him, but it also clearly breaks from the historical teachings of *Yeshua* in many ways. Paul was one generation removed from the historical *Yeshua* and never saw or heard him in person.

The New Testament writers of the later first century, however, were separated not only from the Jesus of history by three generations, but from the Jewish messianic mysticism of *Yeshua's* thought-world and culture. A huge gulf of language and religious phenomenology divided Greek and Jewish cultures.

The original Jewish messianic communities established by the Apostles refused to recognize the validity of Pauline gentile churches. The Hellenists had been persecuted by the Hebrews (which included Greek-speaking Jewish Christians of the Diaspora), and the Jewish Christians or *minim* excluded by their own synagogues, for two generations. There was much dissention among factions in the early churches, especially between Jewish and gentile Christian communities.

Consequently, the writers of the Christian Gospels wove the *logia* of *Yeshua* into church documents supporting the views held by late first-century gentile Christianity. They injected the idea that the Jews in general (not just the Jerusalem Temple establishment) had rejected their own *Messiah*. They interpreted the *davarim* of *Yeshua* about the coming Birthpangs of *Messiah* as prophecies of the end of the world. They did not grasp the rabbinic the subtleties of Pauline soteriology, instead portraying *Yeshua* as a god. Since for them as non-Jews, much of Christian orientation was indoctrination into Jewish theological ideas—a process of creed and belief—they misunderstood the *emunah* or faithfulness taught by *Yeshua* as "faith," meaning belief. They misunderstood *Yeshua's* teachings on the *Malkuth* as political and therefore mistranslated and confused Hebrew Sovereignty with the Greek concept *Basileion,* which means a royal kingdom, a monarchical government.

This misconception of *Yeshua's* teaching about the coming Sovereignty of God on Earth was probably what led to early gentile church interpretations of the Christ (*Messiah*) as a Son of David—the very idea that *Yeshua* opposed in his rhetorical question about David's son! The idea that the *Messiah*, by scriptural interpretation, was to be a descendant of King David was, in turn, why the Gospels of Matthew and Luke both took pains to trace *Yeshua's* genealogy back to King David—one on his father's side, the other from his mother.[38]

In one of the early Pauline epistles, the *Messiah Ben-David* eschatological theory is presented as the Second Coming of a victorious warrior Christ.[39] In fairness to Paul, that section of the epistle may be a later Pseudo-Pauline redaction, since most of what is said in the authentic Pauline epistles does not characterize the advent of the Christ *(Bar-Enash)* in terms of Davidic warfare. But if it is Pauline, it was offered to "comfort" those whose loved ones had died without seeing the coming of *Messiah,* whom Paul may have considered to be "children in understanding."

"Brothers," he declares in one place, "I could not address you as spiritual but as worldly– mere infants in Christ. I gave you milk, not solid food, for you were not yet ready for it."[40] Paul was not an "apocalypticist." Nevertheless, he is responsible for twisting the *Bar-Enash* of *Yeshua* into the Davidic *Messiah* that *Yeshua* clearly repudiated. Perhaps Paul saw himself as reconciling the popular *Messiah* with that of the Jewish mystics. But whatever his intentions, he decisively associated messianic advent with Davidic interpretation, thus opening a Pandora's Box of inauthentic doctrines like the Second Coming and the Rapture that in the next generation would be woven into the Christian Gospels.

If Dr. Schweitzer had access to the resources of modern biblical scholarship, he would have realized that the "Kingdom" was the *Malkuth,* or mysterious Sovereignty and Omnipotence of God as understood in the Wisdom schools, for whom God was present everywhere. For *Yeshua* the appearance of the Sovereignty of God on Earth would come through the rebirth and manifestation of the coming *Bar-Enash* or "Second Adam" within human souls. That is why the advent of God's *Messiah* and His *Malkuth* would be manifest on Earth before some of his disciples had "tasted death."

Yeshua was a messianic mystic, not an eschatological apocalypticist. But the early churches and their prophets were radically eschatological. They operated on all the end-of-the-world assumptions of apocalypticists. That was the framework in which they interpreted the teachings of *Yeshua* and spun them into the New Testament Gospels, along with anti-Semitism, marginalization of women's leadership, a Greco-Roman mystery-school mentality, and other cultural artifacts of the Hellenistic world.

---

[38] Since the two genealogies are contradictory, Tatian simply leaves them out of his 2nd century Syriac Gospel harmony known as the *Diatessaron.*

[39] I Thessalonians 4.13-18
Messiah Ben-David..

[40] I Corinthians 3.12

As we progress through the *logia* of *Thomas,* we will find that the oldest and most original core sayings in *Thomas* are not eschatological. They are focused on sanctification and sainthood—not on an imminent end of the world. Eschatological sayings are scribal insertions that probably accumulated after 50 C.E., and the ascetic sayings are probably polemics created in the second century when the Greek collection came into the possession of a Gnostic editor to compose his Prologue, "The Secret Words that the Living Jesus spoke and Didymos Judas Thomas Wrote."

Messianic Midrash and Kabbalistic *Manda*

The inner-circle *davarim* of *Yeshua* were based on messianic *midrashim,* or rabbinic interpretations of biblical passages. These were not specifically halakic or haggadic as found in Talmudic literature after the destruction of the Temple, but revelatory. They revealed the *razim* or hidden secrets of Heaven—*manda* transmitted orally concerning mystical interpretation of Scripture about the coming *Malkuth* (Sovereignty) of the *Bar-Enash* (Son-of-Man Messiah) on Earth. In Hellenistic terms, it was *gnosis.* This was the secret knowledge claimed by Gnostic movements, such as the Thomasian community. In Jewish terms, it was an ancient form of what many centuries later would be called *Kabbalah.*

There is so much similarity between Hellenistic Gnostic and kabbalistic doctrines that many scholars consider them to have been mutually interdependent. My observation is that the two are quite different, that pre-kabbalistic traditions in Judaism are to be found in the intertestamental literature far earlier than the advent of Gnostic literature, and that the ascetic and negative attitudes toward the world that characterize many of the Gnostic schools totally contradicts the family and world-affirming views of pre-kabbalistic Jewish wisdom schools. Kabbalah did not derive from Gnosticism. It was clearly the other way around. The Gnostics philosophized the "secret" or kabbalistic teachings of *Yeshua* however they were able to gain possession of them, as they do here in the *Gospel of Thomas* or as Carpocrates did with the *Secret Gospel of Mark.* They borrowed terms based on a shallow familiarity with the Jewish wisdom schools (*Achamoth* from *Hochmah,* etc.), and with the help of divines like the Alexandrian Valentinus, syncretized all these elements into various systems of Gnosis. In the case of the *Gospel of Thomas,* however, they left us a valuable document with minimal redaction from which we can recover historical kabbalistic sayings of *Yeshua.*

In this book, I refer to *Yeshua's* inner-circle teachings as kabbalistic to differentiate them from other forms of midrashic tradition. Many scholars would refer to them as pre-kabbalistic or proto-kabbalistic, since *Kabbalah* describes the later European movement in Jewish mysticism in which the oral tradition was written and circulated in books.

Kabbalah (Qabbalah) was a term first used in ninth-century rabbinic schools based on Aramaic (Chaldaean, Babylonian) קבל meaning "to take, receive." Jewish oral tradition was conservative. It added, but did not subtract, in its transmission through the centuries. For example, kabbalistic oral traditions from the era of *Yeshua* such as creation, death, purgatory, the kabbalistic soul, and the *'Olam ha-Ba* were preserved in the medieval *Bahir*, which is attributed to the first-century Rabbi *Nehuniah ben- HaKana.*

In addition to the later European writings of the *Kabbalah*, we also have ancient literary sources reflecting what are known as pre-kabbalistic traditions of the Hellenistic period. These include the *Sepher Yetzirah, Sepher Ha-Razim, The Hekhaloth, haggadah* preserved in the *Mishna*, the Babylonian and Palestinian *Talmud,* and the vast literature of the inter-testamental period known loosely as the Apocrypha and Pseudepigrapha of the Old Testament. A careful reading of these documents, many of which were considered by *Yeshua* and the earliest Christian to be Holy Scripture, reveals underlying kabbalistic oral tradition. An oral kabbalistic tradition was an interpretation of the inner meaning of Hebrew Scripture by a Master *(Rav)* of Israel, such as Jesus *ben-Sirach*. It was given privately to an inner circle of *talmidim*. When the teachings of *Yeshua* are examined in the light of Hellenistic and wisdom-school kabbalism, they become far more accessible.

The source of oral messianic *midrashim* in *Yeshua's* day seems to have been the large and creative Jewish community in Babylon. *Yeshua's* Son-of-Man(kind) Messiah reflects the view of Babylonian apocalyptic revelation—specifically Daniel, Trito-Isaiah, and the Enochian school. The only rabbi *Yeshua* paraphrased was Hillel, a Babylonian. His school was established in Palestine and produced two brilliant students whose teachings are preserved in Talmudic literature and can be used to illuminate those of *Yeshua: R. Yochanan ben-Zakkai,* founder of Rabbinic Judaism, and *R. Akiba,* saint and martyr, student of *ben-Zakkai.* Philo of Alexandria, a prolific Jewish author and mystic contemporary with *Yeshua*, leaves us a library of literature that is also extremely helpful in explaining such kabbalistic allusions as the Five Trees in Paradise of Thomas Logion 19.

As Scholem and other scholars have observed, pre-kabbalistic tradition had roots in the Hellenistic diaspora, not in Palestine. Babylon and Alexandria are the most likely origins. *Yeshua's davarim* in the *Gospel of Thomas* include pre-kabbalistic traditions from both cities, some of which were known to the Palestinian Pharisees *ben-Zakkai* and *Akiba*.[41]

---

41 The earliest Jewish Christians adapted the simplest methods of messianic midrash—typology and allegory—to create the "proof texts" of the Passion Narrative and the Gospel narratives. If a messianic text reads, "Out of Egypt I have called my Son," then Matthew creates a scenario in which the holy family flees to Egypt to avoid Herod's slaughter of the innocents (which never happened), then returns when it is safe. The

The messianic *Kabbalah* of *Yeshua's* era was quite unlike the complex diagrams and letter-numerology of contemporary Hollywood *Kabbalah*, which is rooted in the Lurianic and other medieval Jewish schools. Modern kabbalistic schools are as far removed from the *Kabbalah* of *Yeshua's* era as contemporary so-called Gnostic churches are from second-century Gnosticism. We can find survivals and transformations of the ancient knowledge in modern schools, but the resemblance ends there. So when I use the term kabbalistic, I refer to the ancient messianic mysticism that informed the *davarim* of *Yeshua*—not medieval or modern forms of Kabbalah.

Biblical scholars have developed tools to penetrate the veil of the Greek New Testament and recover the historical teachings of *Yeshua,* which are not the doctrines of Christianity. The *Gospel of Thomas* now offers us a new entrée into that long-hidden treasury. Most important, it represents an ancient oral tradition that not only pre-dates the New Testament writings, but preserves what I have called the inner-circle or initiatic teachings of *Yeshua.*

With this understanding, let us examine the *logia* of the *Gospel of Thomas.*

Christian Gospels are not historical documents, but midrashic narrations preserving sayings of *Iesous* redacted to reflect third-generation gentile church issues without regard for what they meant to *Yeshua.*

CHAPTER THREE: Logia 1 and 2

The key to understanding the original *davarim* is a full exposition of Logion 2, which summarizes the path of an initiate. Therefore I have devoted an entire chapter to it, as well as a few comments about the Gnostic redactor's prologue in Logion 1. After this chapter we will examine each saying in order

It is vital to **read my footnotes** if you want to fully understand the sayings. This kind of commentary is excursive. It requires many side-branches. The some six hundred footnotes contain a massive amount of necessary information that allows me to keep the main text coherent while still being able to expand it with vital details.

Also, the original Greek redaction of *Thomas* often links independent sayings with phrases like "therefore, thus," implying that the second or third saying in a series is a conclusion or commentary on the previous one. Sometimes these conclusions are Gnostic interpolations, for example Logion3.b, "When you discover your true nature, you will know that you are children of the Father of the All..." At other times they are authentic independent sayings of *Yeshua,* such as Logion 21.b.2, "When the fruit splits open with ripeness, one comes quickly with sickle in hand to harvest it." The Nag Hammadi scholars who originally published the text of *Thomas* left these independent *logia* linked in series to preserve the redaction. Thus, for example, Logion 21 is actually two or three independent *logia.* In such a case I divide them as Logion 21.a and 21.b.1 and 21.b.2., where 21.a is clearly independent, but 21.b.1 may have been followed by 21.b.2 as a conclusion in the original Aramaic *davarim* of *Yeshua.*

Logion 1: PROLOGUE [Gnostic Redaction]

1.a These are the heavenly mysteries *(razim)*[42] which the immortal[43] *Yeshua* revealed. 1.b Whoever understands and puts them into practice will likewise become an ever-living saint.

---

[42] Coptic ⲉⲑⲏⲡ [ϩⲱⲡ] for Greek *apokrypytos* (reconstruction from lacuna) doers not translate original Aramaic *razim* or "mysteries" used by *Yeshua* and his disciples. The Gnostic editor considers the Greek *logia* themselves to be oracular mysteries.

[43] Coptic ⲓ̅ⲥ̅ ⲉⲧⲟⲛϩ for Greek *Iesous ho zoon,* from an Aramaic expression meaning "immortal saint *Yeshua.*" He lives the Life of the *'Olam* of God, which is the spiritual existence of the *tzadikim* after death at the Throne of God. In the English New Testament the phrase is usually translated as "eternal life," which is deceptive as divine life was not understood in terms of infinite length, but divine quality, like the highest *loka* in Hinduism or the *Ogdoas* of the Hermetics.

COMMENTARY

What translators designate as Logion 1 is a prologue written about 200 C.E. by the original Gnostic redactor who edited the *Gospel of Thomas* into its current form. It claims to be copied from a collection of secret sayings of Jesus written by the Apostle Thomas. The Aramaisms of many of the Logia indicate that the original source document was either dictated in Aramaic or transcribed from Aramaic notes written by a disciple of the inner-circle (i.e., an Apostle). If so, Logion 1b would have been an oral or written saying of Thomas or another eyewitness disciple. It would have read as I have translated it above in light of the original Aramaic language and messianic mysticism.

The synoptic gospels transmit public sayings of *Yeshua* entitled "mysteries" of the *Malkuth*, but they understand them as allegories and *mashlim* (parables) needing interpretation even for the inner-circle of disciples. These are the "Mysteries of the Kingdom of God" in Matthew and Luke that were transmitted in public, non-initiatic form through the Q document. In the Gospels, they are understood as parables about the Jews rejecting their own *Messiah*, or the salvific power of belief in Jesus, or in other ways congruent with early gentile church teachings.

In Gnostic *Thomas,* however, the *davarim* of *Yeshua* were understood as oracular *logia* that, when properly interpreted, would yield salvational *gnosis.*

To the Gnostic editor of *Thomas*, the sayings of Jesus are like those of Secret Mark, concerning which Clement wrote, "the interpretation would, as a mystagogue, lead the hearers into the innermost sanctuary of truth."[44] Thus the Greek noun *kryptos* and adjective *apokryptos* are used in *Thomas* to describe the sayings as "hidden, secret." But if this were based on an original Aramaic expression, the Greek word would be *mysteria,* which was used to translate Hebrew-Aramaic *raz-, razim,* "divine, heavenly mysteries."

Raz is the term used in Daniel and Enoch to describe messianic and other sacred knowledge that could be revealed to mankind only through the intermediation of angels. The "Mysteries of Christ" is the phrase we find Paul using many times in his epistles. *Razim* is also used to describe the fourth-century Jewish collection of magical spells and theurgical ritual found in Cairo *geniza* by Margalioth entitled the *Sepher Ha-Razim* or Book of the Mysteries.[45]

---

[44] *Op. cit.* Note 8
[45] See *Sepher Ha-Razim and its Traditions: An Inquiry into the Interrelation of Jewish, Greco-Egyptian, and Chaldaean Magico-Mystic Practices in the Roman-Hellenistic Period,* Lewis Keizer; privately published as an e-book at http://wisdomseminars.org/Catalogue.html.

It is reasonable to conclude, then, that *Yeshua* revealed the "heavenly mysteries" or *Razim* of the *Malkuth* (Sovereignty, Omnipotence) of God to his inner-circle of disciples. These were not limited to discursive teachings, but also transmitted as dynamic experiences. Advanced disciples were taken in small groups and initiated into various levels of *Merkabah* practice, like the so-called Transfiguration. Secret Mark and the *Gospel of Mary* point to what would have been the highest level of initiation into the *Razim* that *Yeshua* transmitted—an all-night, white-robed transmission of the *Razim Ha-Malkuth*[46] given by *Yeshua* privately to an advanced disciple—not unlike the Hermetic ritual of Rebirth (CH 13 and Nag Hammadi Tractate 6, Codex VI).

To summarize, the first part of Logion 1 is Gnostic redaction, but the second part (Logion 1b) may reflect an original Prologue to the Aramaic *davarim.*

Logion 2

Yeshua said, Let the seeker keep on seeking until he finds,[47] and when he finds, he will experience the divine awe of God,[48] and in that consciousness he will ascend,[49] and he will share Sovereignty[50] with God over all things.

COMMENTARY

This is the first *davar* or revelatory saying of *Yeshua* in the original collection. It describes the initiatic path of a *tzadik* or saint. It is rooted in the path of a Jewish *hakam* or seeker of wisdom under the tutelage of *Hochmah*, Wisdom, the feminine face of God. She was with God in the beginning and knows all His works.[51] She was known also as the *Shekinah*, the immanence, radiance, and glory of God in nature and all that manifests. To the philosophers both Greek and Jewish-Hellenistic She was known as *Sophia.*

---

[46] "Mysteries of the Sovereignty"

[47] ⲙⲛ̄ⲧⲣⲉϥ ⲗⲟ ⲛ̄ϭⲓ ⲡⲉⲧϣⲓⲛⲉ ⲉϥϣⲓⲛⲉ Aramaic idiom "seeking seek" meaning "keep on seeking" rendered "let him not stop seeking" [cf. Gr. NT Q present tense Koine Greek expression idiomatic for persistence, fidelity]; "until he finds." This *davar* is independent of Q "seek and ye shall find, knock and it shall be opened," wrongly linked to the parable of the importunate neighbor in Luke 11 but not in Matthew. Note the "and...and...and," a Hebrew-Aramaic construction ו...ו...ו indicative of the original Aramaic language.

[48] Gr. loan word *thambeo* is equivalent for Aramaic *baet*, sense of fear or awe of God. The Wisdom tradition stressed the experience of divine *baet* as the "beginning of wisdom."

[49] Gr. Loan word *Thaumadzein*, "to be amazed by a miraculous event" for Ar. *nasa* "to lift up, ascent; be lifted up." This is a reference to *Merkabah* ascent to the Throne of God, the *Ma'aseh Merkabah* or Work of the Chariot.

[50] This is in reference to the Divine *Malkuth* or Sovereignty inherited by the *Bar-Enash*, "Son of Man," *Messiah*, New Adam, or New Humanity that *Yeshua* taught must be born within each soul. In the *Qimah*, each individual *Tzadik* is part of the corporate Body of the *Bar-Enash*, who reigns sovereign over all things at the "right hand" of God's power. Those worthy of the ascent while still in flesh participate mystically in the *Malkuth* of God.

[51] *Wisdom of Solomon* 9.9

In the wisdom schools, *Hochmah* first engages the aspirant as an Instructress who demands discipline and loyalty under all forms of trial. When the student has proven steadfast, She dwells with him and imparts Her *razim*. Here are two examples of the path:

- *Wisdom of Jesus Ben Sirach, 4:17,18:* "She [*Hochmah*, the "Holy Spirit" and immanent Face of Mother God] walks with him as a stranger, and at first She puts him to the test; Divine awe and fear She brings upon him and tries him with Her discipline; With Her [God's] precepts she puts him to the proof, until his heart is fully with Her. Then She returns to bring him happiness and reveal Her [God's] secrets to him."

- *Wisdom of Solomon, 6:17-21:* "For the first step toward discipline is a very earnest desire for Her; then, care for discipline is love of Her; love *[hesed]* means the keeping of Her laws; to observe Her laws is the basis for incorruptibility ["eternal life," spiritual immortality, the divine Life of the *'Olam* of God]; and incorruptibility makes one close to God; thus the desire for Wisdom leads up to a Sovereignty *[Malkuth]* ...honor Wisdom, that you may reign as Sovereigns forever."[52]

The path of the *hakam* or wise saint is fourfold:

1. Desire Wisdom and seek Her
2. Endure trials and testing by keeping faithful *hesed* (covenantal love) with Her laws
3. Receive Her revelations of God's *razim*
4. Draw close to God and participate in His Sovereignty

The initiatic path taught by *Yeshua* in this *Davar* follows the same sequence:

1. Seek God persistently and faithfully through all trials
2. Find and awaken the "fear of God" or awe of God's Presence
3. In that consciousness, make a [*Merkabah*] ascent [into the Throne of God]
4. Participate in the divine Sovereignty of God

This initiatic saying requires a great deal of commentary. First I will explain the background and role of the Path of Wisdom *(Hochmah)* in advanced discipleship. Then I will see how it was probably applied in the advanced messianic teachings of *Yeshua*.

'Olam עולם and the Sovereignty or *Malkuth* מלכות

The Hebrew word *'olam* has two basic meanings: 1. Most ancient is "hidden, that which was concealed long ago, the concealed future;" and in later Aramaic and rabbinic usage

---

[52] In about the year 200 B.C.E., Jesus the Son of a Jewish scholar named Sirach compiled the wisdom he had gained during his life. He wrote in Hebrew, and his son passed on the manuscript to his own son. In 132 B.C.E., this grandson took the manuscript with him from Palestine to Alexandria, where he later translated it from Hebrew to Greek, "in order that it might be studied by his fellow believers [Hellenistic Jews] in Alexandria and elsewhere who spoke and read only in that language." http://www.humanistictexts.org/

contemporary with *Yeshua,* 2. "the world" equivalent to Greek *aion* (aeon) or *kosmos.* The oldest meaning was interpreted in the kabbalistic eschatology of *Yeshua's* day as an original spiritual world or state of existence that was created by Godhead before the *'olam ha-zeh* or our visible world, whose creation was described in the first chapter of Genesis. This concealed *'Olam* of God lies at the very head, root, and beginning of all reality, yet it is also the concealed future goal of all reality. Today kabbalistics will speak about this world as the *'olam ha-zeh,* and the future messianic Age as the *'Olam Ha-Ba,* the World to Come.

In the first-century *Sefer Ha-Bahir* ("Book of the Brightness" or eternal Light) attributed to *Nehunya ben ha-Kanah,* who was a contemporary of *Yochanan ben Zakai,* founder of rabbinic Judaism after the Seige of Jerusalem, the sage declares:

> "In Aramaic, the World to Come ['*Olam Ha-*Ba] is translated 'the World that Came.' [53] And what is the meaning of 'the world that came'?

> "We learn that before the world was created, it arose in thought to create an intense light [*Ain Sof* Aur] to illuminate it. He created an intense light over which no created thing could have sovereignty. The Blessed Holy One saw, however, that the world could not endure [this light]. He therefore took a seventh of it and left it in its place for them. The rest He put away for the righteous in the Ultimate Future. He said, 'If they are worthy of this seventh and keep it, I will give them [the rest] in the Final World.'

> "It is therefore called 'the World that Came,' since it already came [into existence] from the six days of creation. Regarding this it is written (Psalm 31:20), 'How great is Your good that You have hidden away for those who fear You.'"[54]

Thus in kabbalistic understanding at the time of *Yeshua,* the messianic Age was established in the primal past before the foundation of this world, and lies as well in the eschatological future. It is both the World that Came and the World to Come, as in Logion 18. In other words, it exists in all times and places, but is concealed and unmanifest to our eyes. It lies "spread out upon the Earth, but men do not see it," as *Yeshua* declares in Logion 113.

The *'Olam Ha-Ba* translates literally as "The World, The One Coming." It designates the eternal six-sevenths of all reality that transcends time and space where God's Sovereignty or *Malkuth* was, is, and will be fully manifest. *Yeshua* declared in his *Basor* that God's *Malkuth* was now becoming manifest on Earth within and unto humanity. The Greek word used in the New Testament to translate "coming" was *erchomai,* but it did not have the past and future sense of Aramaic *ha-ba.* For this reason the Greek phrase "come into the Kingdom," which is found usually as "enter into the Kingdom," entirely distorts the original

---

[53] Remember that the ancient meaning could refer to archaic past or eschatological future, or both simultaneously. The *'Olam* of God transcended time and space. It was "beyond," as we will see in Logion #3 with parallels in Logion #18 and others.
[54] Passage 160, *The Bahir.*

meaning. Greek *Basileion* "Kingdom" misunderstood Hebrew-Aramaic *Malkuth,* Sovereignty—which is not a "king-domain" or place—and "enter" misunderstands the mode of becoming by which a person "comes into being" in the Sovereignty of God. It means to be found in, come into, inherit, or even be born into being, in the *Malkuth*—not to "enter in" as through a gate into a place. Depending upon context I will translate the Aramaic word מלכות as Sovereignty or simply transliterate it as *Malkuth.*

A vital key key to understanding *Yeshua's* teachings about afterlife and the messianic Age or "Kingdom" (*Malkuth,* Sovereignty) of God lies in the Aramaic meaning of *'olam* and the *'olamim.* As we come upon the many other ramifications of this concept in our examination of the *davarim,* I will use footnotes to explain them.

Wisdom and the Holy Spirit

In the scripture of the Old Testament, a *ruach* or spirit of God was personified in prophetic tradition as the Spirit of God or the Spirit of Prophecy. The later wisdom tradition personifies the Spirit of God as *Hochmah* or Wisdom. She is the immanent aspect of Godhead that interacts with those who seek her.

Where is *Hochmah* in the later messianic mysticism of *Yeshua?* By the first century before the Christian era, she has become the spiritual Guide of Jewish saints *(tzadikim)* under new personifications of God's *Ruach.* We find her in the *Testaments of the Twelve Patriarchs* and other intertestamental scripture as the *Ruach Ha-Qodesh,* Spirit of Holiness, Holy Spirit, or *Ruach Ha-Emeth,* Spirit of Truth. For *Yeshua,* she is the immanent aspect of the Father-Mother *(Abba)* who guides and instructs faithful seekers.

In the historical teachings of *Yeshua,* we find only two references to the Holy Spirit. Most important is the pericope in Q where he declares blasphemy against the *Ruach Ha-Qodesh* to be an *'olamic* sin.[55] However, this reveals his reverence for her. We have an extant *davar* of *Yeshua* about Wisdom sourced from Q in Matthew 11.19 and Luke 7.35: "*Hochmah* is proved right by her actions." In the messianic mysticism of *Yeshua,* Wisdom and the Holy Spirit are different names for the Spirit of God that guides individual seekers.

In the writings of the New Testament, references to the Holy Spirit are everywhere. She has become the voice of God to the community. Why does the Holy Spirit appear only twice in the *davarim* of *Yeshua,* but everywhere in the writings of the early churches?

Yeshua's execution by the Romans left his disciples without guidance other than the apostolic leadership of his closest disciples. Beginning with Mary *Magdala,* however, they experienced *Qimah* visions and appearances. Mary's was in Jerusalem at the tomb, and the others occurred in the Galilee where many of the Apostles had returned to their homes,

---

[55] Not meaning eternal, but in the *'olam ha-zeh* or this temporal world.

according to one early tradition. The story in Luke-Acts, however, has many of the Apostles and disciples remaining in Jerusalem and Peter receiving angelic aid, healing powers, and in Antioch the vision about all foods being clean—critical for the inclusion of gentiles.

In the wake of Resurrection appearances experienced by all the Apostles and "about five hundred disciples" over six weeks according to Paul, the early churches arose as charismatic movements dependent upon spirit guidance. Phenomena like "speaking in tongues"[56] competed for authority in the gentile congregations with the historical teachings of *Yeshua* transmitted by eyewitness disciples and Apostles.[57]

By the late first and early second centuries when the Gospels of Matthew, Luke, and John were written, the feminine *Ruach Ha-Qodesh* was understood as the neuter Greek *Pneuma Hagios.* The Holy Spirit was no longer recognizable as the *Hochmah* of *Yeshua.* Instead it (no longer she) guided the churches through its "prophets." In the Gospels she (it) had become a kind of *deus ex machina* that moved the narratives from situation to situation. In Johannine tradition the *Ruach* of God became the *Ruach* of Christ as the (Greek masculine) *Parakletos* or "Comforter."[58]

Since the Holy Spirit appears everywhere in New Testament writings, but only twice in the historical teachings of *Yeshua,* it appears that he did not teach spirit-channeling or other pneumatic practices. They developed in the early churches. Paul discouraged glossolalia, but it was only in the second century after much abuse that proto-orthodox Christianity rejected pneumatism in favor of received tradition.

---

[56] Paul was an opponent of glossolalia and the excesses of gentile spirit possession. He understood the *Ruach Ha-Qodesh* as *Hochmah.* "I would rather speak five words under the inspiration of divine mind *[nous]* than babble ten thousand in tongues." I Corinthians 14.19 To that extent he carried on the understanding of *Yeshua* about the Holy Spirit as rational guide of the saints. Paul fought a losing battle with gentile charismatics and was forced to write detailed explanations of why "prophecy" (inspiration of the spiritual mind) is superior to unintelligible "tongues." Even though the story in Acts presents the "tongues" phenomenon of Pentecost as disciples preaching the gospel (of the churches, not of *Yeshua*) in many different native languages to Jewish pilgrims in Jerusalem, it is clear from Paul and other sources that "speaking in tongues" in the early churches was unintelligible—rationalized as the "language of angels." But the phenomenon of glossolalia is well documented outside of Christianity in tribal and trance religions. It results from hypnotic stimulation of the preliterate cerebral cortex and has no connection with language, communication, or spiritual guidance. Most important, it has absolutely no basis in the historical teachings of *Yeshua.*

[57] It is likely that oral tradition versus spirit trance divided Jewish and gentile Christians more than any other single issue. With the demise of Jewish Christianity, the historical teachings of *Yeshua* lost their religious and cultural context, and charismatic phenomena dominated. By the end of the second century, however, the proto-orthodox churches renounced Montanism and other Holy Spirit heresies in favor of creed and theology.

[58] To add insult to injury, the neutered Holy Spirit appears as the masculine Paraclete in John's Gospel. He still has the function of the *Ruach Ha-Qodesh* in that he guides and exhorts disciples to strengthen them. The final sex-change operation was completed when St. Jerome translated the term Holy Spirit for his Latin Vulgate Bible that became standard for a thousand years. In keeping with the marginalization of women's leadership in the Church, he made the Holy Spirit masculine *Spiritus Sanctus.* That worked especially well with Trinitarian theology—Father, Son, and Holy Ghost, or the Three Guys.

The Wisdom Path of *Yeshua* and *Merkabah* Ascent

Let us more closely examine the path that is revealed in our recovered *Davar* on *Yeshua's* path of initiation.

STAGE ONE: Seek God persistently and faithfully through all trials

The parallel to Q found in Matthew 7 and Luke 11 is a promise that faithful persistence in spiritual goals will be rewarded. *Yeshua* said, "Keep on asking, and it will be given to you; keep on seeking, and you will find; keep on knocking, and it will be opened to you."

This saying was not about fulfillment of material desires. It is clear from the other Q reference to seeking that *Yeshua* was speaking about spiritual goals: "Seek first the *Malkuth* of Heaven and its righteousness."[59] Asking and knocking were part of the same spiritual quest.

Yeshua's hearers were seeking a *Messiah* who would liberate Israel from Roman oppression and establish a reign of justice and peace in their land. His *talmidim* (disciples) were hearers who had committed themselves to following his *halakah* or spiritual guidance and practice.

Luke 11.46 tells us *Yeshua* criticized the Judean rabbis by saying, "And you experts in the law, woe to you, because you load people down with **burden**s they can hardly carry, and you yourselves will not lift one finger to help them." The "burdens" are the heavy halakic requirements that official interpreters of *Torah*[60] had laid down for their disciples and hearers.

In contrast, *Yeshua's Halakah* was not harsh and ascetic, like that of John the Baptist, or legalistic and complex, like that of the Judean Pharisees. According to Matthew 11.28-30 he said, "Come to me, all you who are weary and burdened, and I will give you rest. For my yoke is easy and my burden is light." The "yoke" was his interpretation of *Torah*, and the "burden" was the *halakah* or life-practices he imposed upon disciples to fulfill divine laws of love and justice.

Discipleship with *Yeshua* did not involve complex ritual, extensive taboo avoidance, and expensive tithing that seemed disconnected to the simple requirements of love and justice. Rather, his *halakah* internalized love and justice in everyday thought and action. His *halakah* was in keeping with the common-sense approach of prophetic scripture rather than the priestly Pentateuch. *Yeshua* quoted mostly from the Psalms and Prophets in his disputes with the *Ravs*.

---

[59] Matthew 6.33 with parallel in Luke 12.31
[60] Divine Law as revealed in the Pentateuch or first five books of the Old Testament.

The basic outline of *Yeshua's* halakic teachings is preserved in Q through Matthew and Luke. It includes the Sermon on the Mount (Sermon on the Plain in Luke) and a great many of his parables. His *halakah* struck a deep chord with all who heard him, and it was public knowledge. It still is.

Practice of *Yeshua's halakah* is burdensome only for those who find honest self-examination, self-control, and willingness to forgive others difficult. Perhaps that is why the alternative—ritualism, taboo avoidance, and tithing—became so ingrained in institutional Christianity.

The *davar* of *Yeshua* that underlies Logion 2 in the *Gospel of Thomas* indicates that faithful practice of his spiritual *halakah* was the form of advanced asking, seeking, and knocking that comprised the foundational first stage of initiation into God's *Malkuth.*

STAGE TWO: Find and awaken the "fear of God" or awe of God's Presence

What do Peter, James, and John experience when they accompany *Yeshua* to a wilderness hilltop and witness the so-called Transfiguration event described first in Mark, then in Matthew and Luke? They experience the classic "fear of God" that the Wisdom literature tells us is the "beginning of wisdom." In Mark there is no mention of fear, but in Matthew they were "afraid" (Hebrew *yara,* to fear, be in awe, tremble with joy), and in Luke's account they were "heavy with sleep." All of these can describe the experience of the "fear of God," which is a response to awareness of divine presence that is well-documented in many cultures.

In Greek legends, when a human comes in contact with a god, his hair stands on end—an autonomic nervous reaction to an encounter with the otherworldly. The Oracle at Delphi knew she was being possessed by Apollo when her hair stood up and the leaf she held in her hand began to tremble. In Lucan's account of the shepherd girl forced to deliver an oracle by being dragged deep into a cave. Terrified by forced entry into the divine underworld, she faked possession to satisfy her captors. But they knew she was lying because her hair didn't stand on end, her pupils were not dilated, and she wasn't trembling uncontrollably. So they dragged her deeper into the volcanic cave until she was totally spirit-possessed and delivered an oracle revealing where her captor's enemies could be found.

In Semitic legend, when one stumbled upon a place where a deity had appeared or spoken, the shoes must be removed. If the epiphany of the god was witnessed, then a stone altar must be built and, depending upon what was seen or experienced, a shrine with regular rites of the god might be established. For example, the sacred ground where Jacob experienced his dream of the great ladder between heaven and earth with angels ascending and descending, and where Jacob saw and heard God speaking to him, was memorialized as *Beth-El,* the House of God, and later became the location of the royal Temple of Israel.

In the Transfiguration account, Peter asked whether they should build booths or temporary shrines to the living *tzadikim* Moses and Elijah, whom they had witnessed speaking with *Yeshua* in a "cloud."[61]

The Transfiguration event seems to have been an introduction to *Merkabah* experience that *Yeshua* provided for three of his most promising male disciples. If the *Gospel of Mary* and Secret Mark have a basis in fact, then we can assume that *Yeshua* transmitted even more advanced *Merkabah* experience on a hilltop at night to a single disciple who was able to receive it.

Awakening the *baet* or transformative awe of God in such a way as to shake a disciple to his core comprised the stage beyond *halakah*. It was probably achieved in many different ways by different disciples. Experiencing the Resurrection appearances after *Yeshua's* death probably served this purpose for many of them. It was only after this that powerful leaders emerged in the early churches. But it seems that during his ministry, *Yeshua* probably transmitted the experience of *baet* privately to his most advanced disciples.

STAGE THREE: In that consciousness, make an ascent [unto the Throne of God]
Logion 2 gives us the passive form of the Coptic root *shtortr* ("to be shaken") for the passive form of the Oxyrhynchus Greek word *thaumadzein* ("to be amazed"). But this Greek word is commonly used to translated the original underlying Hebrew-Aramaic word *nasa,* which means to "lift up, ascend." The stage in the initiatic path that follows *baet* is not just more "amazement" or "being shaken." It some kind of ascent or being "lifted up." Aramaic *nasa* is a term associated with the ascent to the Throne of God in *Ma'aseh Merkabah,* the Work of the Chariot, or *Merkabah* mysticism.

What little we can learn about the "riders of the Chariot" is found in the literature of Isaiah, Ezekiel, Enoch, the second-century sayings of the Rabbis collected in the *Mishnah* and *Tosefta,* and later traditions of the Jewish mystics. We are told that the fruits of *Merkabah* ascent included foreknowledge of events (prophecy), psychic powers like knowing the thoughts and motives of others, divine retribution against those who harm or insult the mystic, and the respect of all invisible beings from angels to demons.[62]

---

[61] The Hebrew word *anan* translated into Greek *nephos* "cloud" does not refer to meteorological clouds. It means literally a "covering, hiding place." God always appears from within an *anan*. The Son-of-Man *Bar-Enash* will come to Earth in an *anan*. That means "in a hidden and mysterious way." The "cloud" in which the disciples saw *Yeshua* speaking with Moses and Elijah (or whoever) was not physical or meteorological. It might be best described as the mysterious environment of a divine vision.

[62] "Said R. Ishmael: [What are the rewards to] one who desires to contemplate the mysteries of the chariot, to enter upon it in peace and return in peace? The greatest of his rewards is that it brings him into the celestial chambers and places him before the divine throne and he becomes knowledgeable of all future events in the world: who will be thrust down and who will be raised up, who will be weakened and who will be strengthened, who will be impoverished and who will be made affluent, on whom will be decreed death and on whom life, from whom will be taken away an inheritance and to whom will be given an inheritance, who

All the powers of a *Merkabah* mystic were attributed to *Yeshua,* and more. Gospel narratives reveal that it was his practice to retreat into the wilderness for private prayer and divine communion, often taking a select few of his disciples with him. The Transfiguration story can be understood only as a form of *Merkabah* experience, as I will show. The *Gospel of Mary* tells a story of initiatic ascent that *Yeshua* transmited to Mary *Magdala,* and the Secret Gospel tells of another one-to-one initiation into the Mysteries of the *Malkuth* that *Yeshua* transmitted at night on a mountain top near Bethany of Judea. All this, taken with Logion 1 of *Thomas,* suggest that *Yeshua* initiated his closest disciples into what might be called *Merkabah* experience and possibly even the *Ma'aseh Merkabah.*

See Appendix One for a summary of what is known about the *Ma'aseh Merkabah.*

By the second century C.E. the practices of the Jewish *Merkabah* mystics had developed into the complexities of *Hekhaloth* visualization of the hallways and sanctuary leading to the Throne of God. But at the time of *Yeshua* the practice was modeled upon the ascent of Enoch through the Jewish form of ten astrological heavens.

I reproduce a chart of the Enochian Heavens below[63] summarizing his *Merkabah* ascent in the *Secrets [Razim]of Enoch.*[64] Examine the Heavens in order of ascent.

---

will be endowed with Torah and who with wisdom. Greater than this is that he becomes knowledgeable of human behavior. If a person commits adultery he knows it; if a person commits murder he knows it; if he is suspected of having relations with a woman during her menstrual period, he knows it. Greater than these is the fact that he becomes a savant in the arts of magic. Greater than this is that whoever should raise his fist at him and hit him would be covered with leprosy. Greater than this is the fact that whoever should slander him would be smitten with wounds and growths which produce festering boils on the skin. Greater than this is that he becomes distinguished among all people in his behavior and is honored among higher and lower beings. Whoever should inadvertently injure him will suffer injury; and misfortunes will descend on him by heavenly decree, and whoever should raise his hand against him will suffer retribution from the heavenly tribunal." (*Pirkei Hekhalot Rabbati* 1:2-5)

[63] From *The Alpha and the Omega* - Chapter Two by Jim A. Cornwell, Copyright © 1995, all rights reserved "*The Book of Enoch and his translation into heaven*" on http://www.mazzaroth.com

[64] For internet access to *II Enoch* and most of the recovered Jewish Apocrypha and Pseudepigrapha of the intertestamental period, go to http://www.sacred-texts.com/chr/apo/index.htm. Much of this literature was considered to be sacred scripture by *Yeshua* and his disciples.

Heaven	Planet or Name	Description
First	possibly *Saturn*.	Here he sees a very great sea, greater than the earthly sea.
Second	*Jupiter*	Transported on "clouds that move," Enoch saw a place that includes those angels who had rebelled against God. Two hundred angels ruled the stars.
Third	*Mars*	This is where Enoch beheld the Garden of Paradise, and in the center the Tree of Life, or Knowledge. It is guarded by 300 glorious angels. When the Apostle Paul was caught up (2 Cor. 12:2) 'the third heaven" is the same as in Rev. 2:7, where the 'tree of life," the figurative antitype of that in Eden, in Gen 2:8. Ecclesiasticus 44:16 (not in the KJV) identifies paradise (2 Cor. 12:4) with heaven into which Enoch was translated. It also included the Terrible place where the wicked are tortured.
Fourth	*Earth*	Here he saw legions of Spirits, dragons, luminaries and wondrous creatures such as the fabled phoenix flying around the earth. Also here was the Host of the Lord.
Fifth	*Venus*	Here he met many soldiers ("host"), the *Egregoii*, with the appearance of men taller than the giants of the earth, those angels of the Fall, who mated with the daughters of men. (The Biblical Nephilim or Anakim, Sumerian Anunnaki). Here they are bound for their transgressions for ten thousand years are finished.
Sixth	*Mercury*	Here they had (*bands of*) luminous Angels with radiant faces, and they taught him the motions (*revolutions*) of the stars, the phases of the Moon, the revolution of the Sun. He met Archangels, Phoenix and the Cherubim.
Seventh	*Sun*	This is where he beheld Cherubim, Serafim, and Thrones. Angels with many eyes, nine legions and the Ophanimm (*Auphanim*, or *Wheels*) and the Ionait. Two winged men on clouds place him at the limits. From here he could see the Lord from afar siting on a throne. The archangel Gabriel came to Enoch to take him to the next place.
Eighth	Called *Muzaloth*	It is a place of the changing of the Season. Similar to the Hebrew *mazzaloth* in 2 Kings 23:5, RSV, "*constellations*", as a reference to Mazzaroth.
Ninth	Called *Kuvachim*	This is the Houses of the Signs of the Zodiac.
Tenth	Called *Aravoth*	Here Enoch recognized the constellation whence came our first ancestors, the star Altair (in *Aquila*). The countenance of the "*Lord*" was seated on a lofty throne and Angels who constantly approached Him to receive orders. His bodyguards were the Cherubim, Serafim (*beings with six wings and many eyes*). The Archangels: Michael, Uriel, Raphael and Gabriel, Prawil (*excelling in knowledge*). Enoch became Metatron.

The Chariot-Throne or *Merkabah* of God is in the Tenth Heaven. That was where Isaiah and Enoch stood in the presence of God, and that was the ultimate goal of *Merkabah* ascent. But the more attainable goal was the Third Heaven of Paradise—the Talmudic *Pardes*[65] where the immortal trees of life and knowledge always stood in full leaf. In *Yeshua's* unknown kabbalistic tradition (Logion 19 of the *Gospel of Thomas*), five trees stand.

The Transfiguration story was left unexplained in all three Gospels because, like the Lazarus narrative, it was the public version of a complex discourse and teaching reserved for initiates. If Secret Mark is ever recovered, it will probably have a summary of the initiatic version of the Transfiguration story in its narrative.

The so-called Transfiguration story could derive only from Peter, James, or John. It appeared in Mark's Gospel, and then was retold by Matthew and Luke. Mark was Peter's

---

[65] The Hebrew word *gans* means a garden with different fruit trees; the Babylonian (Aramaic) word *pardes* (Paradise) refers to an orchard with only one kind of tree—the pomegranate. In the Septuagint, both words are rendered with the Greek *paradeisos,* Paradise. In proto-kabbalistic and Talmudic tradition, the word used to refer to the spiritual garden of mystic knowledge where Jewish divines carried on their researches into the *razim* was Aramaic *Pardes.*

disciple. Therefore the story must have been told by Peter. It is likely that the event represented one of Peter's most vivid memories.

Recall that the initiatic sequence of Logion 2 begins with (1) faithful *halakah*, then (2) awakening of the *baet* or divine awe, then (3) the ascent. In the Transfiguration event, *baet* was awakened in the disciples, but the ascent was made only by *Yeshua*. It was witnessed by the disciples, but not achieved by them. Peter, James, and John did not speak with the saints of the *Pardes,* but saw them speaking with *Yeshua* from a distance and within a "cloud" (*anan*, mystic covering) of light.

"His face shone like the sun, and his clothes became dazzling white. Suddenly there appeared to them Moses and Elijah, talking with him." Matthew 17.2,3

According to Matthew 17.1-9, *Yeshua* took the three disciples up to the mountain "after six days." In Secret Mark, the young man[66] who is taken to the mountain for initiation was given a six-day period of preparation.[67] Both the Transfiguration and initiation events occur at night on a "mountain" near Bethany of Judea.

Yeshua allowed them to witness by means of *mishqad,*[68] a form of single-pointed meditation kept in Christian tradition only as an all-night Easter Vigil. The Aramaic term is translated *gregorein,* "to watch." Many times in the Gospels *Yeshua* tells his disciples to "watch." But the Aramaic term used by *Yeshua* meant to "meditate, keep a spiritual vigil." It was a mindfulness practice such as might be held in consciousness through *mantra, mudra,* and *yantra* visualization in Buddhist or Hindu spirituality. In kabbalistic practice it might be done with silent prayer or quiet intoning of *niggunim.*

---

[66] The term "young man" is initiatic. In his poem about descent into the Divine Underworld, Parmenides is led by an immortal *neoteros* or "youth," the same term used for the young initiand in Secret Mark and by *Yeshua in Luke 22.26:* "let one who would be great among you become as a *neoteros."* In *Thomas* the disciples are described as "young children" or "newly-borns."

[67] In Secret Mark, the young man was first raised from his tomb as in the Lazarus story of John's Gospel. This may be allegorical for a ritual of rebirth. It may also explain the term *neoteros* (ibid.).The nameless youth is a model or archetype of the secret Initiand who has experienced spiritual rebirth and ready to be taught the *Razim Ha-Malkuth.* Paul compares baptism to death (going under the water) and rebirth in Christ (being raised up out of the water), which seems a curious view of *mikveh* unless it is rooted in received *paradosis* about initiatic *palingenesis.*

[68] From Hebrew *shaqad,* "to keep watch."

According to the various descriptions in the synoptic Gospels, *Yeshua* had instructed the disciples to keep a silent *mishqad.* This could have been as simple as a single-pointed meditation on light, or as complex as mental recitation of Psalm, prayer, or scripture. In any case, Luke tells us they fell asleep. But when they "became fully awake,"[69] they were able to witness *Yeshua* conversing with the physically dead saints. Matthew and Luke both say that *Yeshua* charged the disciples with secrecy.

What did Peter, James, and John witness in their vigil with *Yeshua?* The conversation between *Yeshua* and the other saints identifies this as a *Merkabah* ascent to the Third Heaven of the *Pardes* or Paradise—the same Third Heaven that Paul described in II Corinthians 2.4. It was in the *Pardes* that the great *tzadikim* of Israel like Moses and Elijah dwelt. This was the "Life of the *'Olam*"[70] or eternal life, as it is inaccurately rendered in the New Testament.

In other words, because *Yeshua* was conversing with Moses and Elijah, the implication for a messianic Jew of that culture would have been that he had ascended to the *Pardes* or *Gan Eden* of the Third Heaven. But knowledge of the *Merkabah* ascent was part of the initiatic *Razim Ha-Malkuth* that were eventually lost to gentile Christianity.

What the three disciples witnessed in a vision was not full ascent to the *Merkabah* or Throne of God. They would not have been capable of sustaining that level of vision because the most dangerous part of *Merkabah* ascent was the attempt to enter *Aravoth,* the Tenth Heaven, to stand in the direct presence of God upon His Throne. Only the most pure of heart could stand before the Face of God without being utterly destroyed.[71]

But even the ascent to the Third Heaven was not without its dangers. The *Tosefta*, a 2nd century Hebrew and Aramaic compilation contemporary with the *Mishna,* warns of the consequences for impurity in the ascent to the Third Heaven: Death (inability to return to the physical body); Madness (ability to return, but with a broken mind); or Spiritual Separation from Israel ("heresy," idiomatic "cutting the shoots").[72]

In the so-called Transfiguration event, *Yeshua* seems to have both catalyzed and facilitated the vision of his ascent to the Third Heaven for his disciples by means of *mishqad.* They were pure of heart, sincere, and without guile. That was their protection. They were able to safely witness the result of *Yeshua's* ascent and descent through preparation, meditative vigil, and inner vision, but were not exposed to the dangers of actual practice.

---

[69] Out-of-body experiences often begin when a person realizes he is asleep and awakens within sleep.
[70] Meaning the plane or *loka* of divine life where the saints dwell.
[71] *Yeshua* said, "Blessed are the pure in heart, for they shall see God." Matthew 5.8 "Sermon on the Mount." (But not in Luke, so possibly not in Q.)
[72] *Tosefta Hagigah* 2:3-4

Did Paul really make an ascent to the Third Heaven, as he claimed in II Corinthians,[73] and return safely like *Yeshua* and Rabbi Akiba? Even a cursory reading of his epistles reveals a brilliant mind, but also one that employed manipulation and guile to be "all things to all men." I have some doubts about his claim. Interestingly, Paul avoids attributing the experience to himself, instead saying "I know a man who…" But since his motive is to impress readers and hearers with his apostolic credentials, he nevertheless implies that he is speaking about his own private *Merkabah* ascent to the *Pardes*.

There are two things that don't ring true about Paul's claim. First, he speaks about being taken up, as though the experience simply came upon him. But *Merkabah* ascent was a focused practice involving the use of will, intoned prayer, and visualization.[74] Second, it was absolutely forbidden to speak about *Merkabah* experience to even one student, let alone an entire congregation![75] But Paul, a one-time rabbinical student of Gamaliel well acquainted with proto-kabbalistic tradition, blithely lay out his claim to be published widely and read to the churches. That was, to say the least, an extreme measure to defend his apostolic authority from the attacks of Jewish disciples.

Whether he experienced it or not, there can be only one reason that Paul made his claim to *Merkabah* ascent. It would be interpreted by the gentile churches as evidence that Heaven had granted him the same authority as an Apostle, even though he had never been a disciple of *Yeshua* or even heard the Master speak.

The historical Apostles had seen and spoken with the resurrected *Yeshua* during the forty-day period after his crucifixion.[76] Paul had originally based his claim to apostolic authority

---

[73] 12.2ff.

[74] However, Paul's initial experience of the Risen Christ was also an involuntary epiphany. Jung has observed that those rational and critical minds who predispose themselves against spiritual experience are often the ones most vulnerable to it through unexpected experiences. Paul would have been a good candidate for involuntary experience.

[75] "The Work of the Chariot may not be expounded unless it is to one who is a sage who has already developed intuitive *gnosis* of it." (*Mishnah Hagigah* 2:1)

[76] In Jewish *kabbalistic* tradition, the personality or *nephesh* of the deceased lived in the astral-sidereal world parallel but invisible to the earthly world for seven weeks before it dissolved in a second death and released the *neshamah* to ascend and dwell in the Third Heaven. That *'olam* contains both a place of temporary purgatory *(Yeshua's Gehenna)* and the *Pardes* or Paradise. *Yeshua*, being the greatest of the saints, was able to make himself visible and audible in his *nephesh* body to those who loved him. This was possible for a period for seven weeks after Passover (preceding the Feast of Pentecost) before ascending in his *neshamah* body— not merely to the *Pardes,* but to the very Throne of God. There he sat Sovereign at the right hand of divine power as the first-born (Greek *monogenes*) of the corporate Son-of-Man(kind) Messiah, *Bar-Enash,* or Pauline *Christos.* Therefore Paul's encounter with the Risen Christ on the road to Damascus would have been of an entirely different nature than the so-called Resurrection appearances. In fact, however, according to Johannine teachings which show strong evidence of traditional Jewish messianic and *kabbalistic haggadah*, *Yeshua* tell his disciples in advance that he is going away (will die) and "you will see me no more," but he will send them a *Parakletos* (masculine form of the Holy Spirit/Spirit of Truth) to guide them. In Johannine terms, a Post-Ascension appearance of *Yeshua* himself (after the seven weeks of Resurrection appearances) would therefore have been impossible. Such a claim as Paul's encounter on the road to Damascus would be

on having received a personal vision of the Risen Christ on the road to Damascus. Like the other Apostles, he had seen the Risen Lord.[77] Now he sought to strengthen his apostolic credentials with a claim to *Merkabah* ascent. This indicates that many leaders of the early churches must have known that the Apostles had been initiated by *Yeshua* into the practice of *Merkabah* ascent. That would have been the most secret of the *Razim Ha-Malkuth* (Mysteries of the "Kingdom") that he transmitted to his closest *talmidim*.

So Paul has unintentionally provided us with more evidence that *Merkabah* experience was a vital part of early Christian initiatic tradition.

STAGE FOUR: Participate in the divine *Malkuth* or Sovereignty of God

It is important to distinguish between the coming "Kingdom" or Sovereignty of God that *Yeshua* proclaimed as part of his public *Basor,* and which he compared to the slow but mighty growth of a mustard seed, and the mystic Co-Sovereignty that the initiated *tzadik* would share with God. The first is non-initiatic, but the second is the goal of the initiatic *razim*.

Before we examine the mystic *Malkuth* of a saint, we must understand the public *Basor* that *Yeshua* proclaimed.

The Gospel and *Messiah* Publically Proclaimed by *Yeshua*

The Gospel proclaimed by *Yeshua* was not the one later taught by the New Testament and gentile Christianity.

Yeshua's self-consciousness was that of a prophet sent to Israel with a message directly from the Throne of God, like the message of Isaiah. His message was messianic—a proclamation of the advent of God's *Messiah* and the *Malkuth* or Sovereignty of God on Earth.

This was a special kind of proclamation known as a *Basor.* In Near Eastern secular terms, when a king wished to prepare his people for the eventual rule of his heir, he sent forth messengers to publically proclaim the son's birth, then sometime later his royal marriage

---

considered fraudulent or delusional. It may have been on this basis that Paul's claim to apostolic authority was challenged by Jewish disciples, and that he therefore had to refute them by the extreme measure of revealing that he had personally experienced the same *Merkabah* ascent that Peter, James, and John had witnessed in the so-called Transfiguration.

[77] This same claim by second- and third-century Gnostic visionaries was their basis for authority. The Nag Hammadi Coptic Gnostic library is full of long revelatory visions and theosophical tractates dictated to a Gnostic founder or scribe by the Post-Ascension Risen Christ. Paul set a precedent that would later result in nothing but trouble for proto-orthodox Christianity.

or enthronement as a prince in line for succession. The king did this to ensure a peaceful transition of power and to protect his heir from the inevitable attempts of others to take power during the transition. The people of the kingdom would support the legitimate heir.

The *Basor* proclaimed by *Yeshua* was the advent of the *Bar-Enash* or Son of Man(kind) *Messiah* prophesied in the visions of Daniel and elaborated in the apocalyptic *Merkabah* ascent of Enoch. From a recently discovered codex in the Qumran library we are fortunate to have recovered the messianic text of Enoch's revelations that would have been known to *Yeshua*. The New Testament quotes from Enochian apocalyptic literature, treating it as scripture in the Epistle of Jude 14-15. It was, in fact, Holy Scripture to *Yeshua* and his *talmidim*.

I reproduce a translation of Enoch's revelation of the coming *Bar-Enash*[78] as he stands before the *Merkabah* Throne of God to illustrate the concept of *Messiah* that *Yeshua* proclaimed.

> And there I saw One who had a head of days, and His head was white like wool, And with Him was another being whose countenance had the appearance of a man, And his face was full of graciousness, like one of the holy angels.

> And I asked the angel who went with me and showed me all the hidden things, concerning that *Bar-Enash* ("Son of Mankind," New Adam or Humanity), who he was, and whence he was, and why he sat with the Head of Days? And he answered and said unto me: This is the *Bar-Enash*, who hath righteousness, with whom dwelleth righteousness, and who revealeth all the treasures of that which is hidden *(razim)*, because the Lord of Spirits [messianic designation for God] hath chosen him, and whose lot hath the pre-eminence before the Lord of Spirits in uprightness for an aeon *['olam]* of aeons *['olamim]*[79]...

---

[78] *Bar-Enash* is Aramaic for Hebrew *Ben-Adam*, literally the Son of Adam or Mankind. "Son" means Heir, and could represent a daughter as well as a son, so is not gender-specific. "Adam" was androgynous, containing both male Adam and female Eve before the separation of sexes, and means Humanity. The *Bar-Enash* appears in Paul's Epistles as the Second Adam, a new humanity that must be born and raised within each soul. The First or Old Adam must be "crucified" or allowed to die from the exposure of self-examination. The Second or New Adam must be nurtured from childhood into mature Christian adulthood. We must "put on" the Perfected Humanity. This idea points back *Yeshua's* original teachings of rebirth paralleled in the Johannine Gospel.

[79] Aramaic expression meaning "forever." However, most of the teaching of *Yeshua* rendered as "forever" in the New Testament do not mean forever in Aramaic, as there are many different expressions in which Hebrew-Aramaic *'olam* is used. An *'olam* of *'olamim* means "forever," but an *'olam* means a conditional state of existence; The *'Olam* means the Divine World of God; this *'olam* means the visible and phenomenal world. *Yeshua's* statements about suffering in *Gehenna* (Jewish Purgatory later interpreted as Christian Hell) are described as lasting for "an *'olam*," implying temporary, not "eternal," suffering in keeping with Jewish *kabbalistic* teachings, which considered one year to be maximum. But Christianity, in a remarkable display of uncharitable attitude toward its enemies, assigned them the fate of eternal, everlasting damnation.

> And this New Humanity *(Bar-Enash)* whom thou hast seen shall overturn the kings and the mighty from their seats, and the strong from their thrones, and shall loosen the reins of the strong, and break the teeth of the evil ones...

> Because they do not extol and praise the Ancient of Days, nor humbly acknowledge whence their sovereignty was bestowed upon them. All their deeds manifest unrighteousness, and their power rests upon their riches, and their fidelity is to the gods which they have made with their own hands, and they deny the Way of the Lord of Spirits, and they persecute the houses of His synagogues, and those who keep faith with the Way of the Lord of Spirits."

The advent of the Anointed One (*Messiah*, Christ) as *Bar-Enash* would result in the establishment of God's Sovereignty[80] on Earth. God was already Sovereign over all, but mankind had blinded itself to divine realities. Humanity was like the Prodigal Son who, in a quest for the illusion of independence and personal happiness, demanded his financial inheritance, left the wisdom of his home and parents behind, and made a mess of his life.The human world (Johannine and Pauline *kosmos*) had willingly accepted self-created bondage to the *qlippoth* or dark forces mediated by fallen angelic archons and principalities under the rule of the fallen Archangel *Shaitan.* That bondage was the cause of disease and injustice in the human world. The *Messiah* would free humanity from the bondage of *Shaitan,* ripen, transform, and rebirth it into the maturity of spiritual adulthood, and lead it back to its true home and spiritual inheritance.

The messianic *Basor* proclaimed by *Yeshua* was similar to that proclaimed by his teacher,[81] the great prophet known as John the Baptist. It was also similar to the messianic expectation of the Qumran Essenes and other separated desert communities opposed to the Temple establishment in Jerusalem who had capitulated to Roman rule. It was also conformed in general terms to the popular messianic expectations of Zealots, Palestinian Jews, and Hellenistic Jews of the Diaspora throughout the Mediterranean, Asia Minor, and stretching along trade routes from Egyptian and Ethiopia to Babylon and eastward along the Silk Road deep into Asia.

But there were many variations on the messianic theme. The *Messiah Ben-David,* a "son" or royal descendent of King David, would lead Jewish fighters reinforced by angels to drive the Romans out of Palestine and make Israel great over the gentiles. He was the militant *Messiah* of the Essenes, Zealots, and Pharisees.

Yeshua spoke against this concept of the *Messiah* when he said, "Why do the Pharisaic interpreters of *Torah* say that *Messiah* is the son of David? David himself, inspired by the *Ruach Ha-Qodesh*, declared: 'The Lord said to my Lord: Sit at my right hand until I make

---

[80] *Malkuth,* wrongly rendered with Greek *Basileion* or "Kingdom" in the New Testament.
[81] And elder cousin, according to Christian tradition.

your enemies your footstool. If David himself calls him Lord, how then can he *[Messiah]* be his son *[ben-David]*?"[82]

This saying of *Yeshua* was transmitted to Mark by his teacher, the Apostle Peter. Mark's Gospel has no infancy stories of *Yeshua* or any genealogies. It begins starkly with a summary of the *Basor* proclaimed by John the Baptist and the inauguration of *Yeshua's* public ministry. Mark is one of our earliest and best sources for the teachings of *Yeshua*, and it was used as a source by the redactors of Matthew and Luke, who wrote a generation later.[83]

Then, one must ask, why do Matthew and Luke present Jesus as the *Messiah Ben-David?* Each of them begins with a genealogy—one through his mother Mary, the other through Joseph—designed to show royal lineage from King David. [84] The answer is that the popular view of *Messiah* that *Yeshua* specifically disputed was enthusiastically adopted in gentile Christianity, probably thanks to the influence of what Paul called "my Gospel." Paradoxically, the Greek translations of the sayings of *Yeshua* were used to bolster Christian theology that often ran totally counter to the original teachings!

In Paul's "rapture" vision of I Thessalonians 4.13, he addresses the concerns of those whose Christian friends and relatives have died without the "Kingdom" appearing on Earth. Other beloved deceased have been ritually baptized after their death to "save" them. What will be their fate?[85]

Paul, or a later redactor, comforts them with a vision of Jesus Christ as the militant *Messiah Ben-David:* "The Lord[86] himself will come down from heaven, with a loud command, with the voice of the archangel and with the trumpet call of God, and the dead in Christ will rise

---

[82] Mark 12.35-37

[83] But Mark's Gospel reflects the Pauline theology and Christology of the early gentile churches. Thus the teachings of *Yeshua* are employed or "redacted" by the writer in the light of second-generation gentile Greek Christian interpretation—rather than the original Jewish messianic context. Many of the sayings have been interpreted wrongly to reflect contemporary church issues, and the original context and meaning of the *davarim* has been lost.

[84] The two genealogies are mutually exclusive, by the way, and constitute one of a multitude of "contradictions" among the Gospels that biblical literalists go to extreme lengths to rationalize out of existence!

[85] I use quotation marks around Christian terms and doctrines that represent misunderstandings of *Yeshua's* teachings (Kingdom, faith, rapture, save, repent, etc.)

[86] Paul's word for Lord is Greek *Kyrios,* which in the Septuagint Old Testament read by all Greek-speaking Hellenistic Jews like Paul translated the Hebrew word *Adonai.* This was a title used only of God. By contrast, *Yeshua* as a Master of Israel would have been addressed with the Aramaic *Mar,* which meant "Lord" in the sense of a guru or spiritual master like Lord Buddha, or even Lord Chesterfield. The title is still used of Bishops in Syriac and other Christian orthodoxy. But it does not mean *Adonai Elohim,* Lord God, as Paul used it in the divine title *Iesous Kyrios,* Lord Jesus. Also, when the English word LORD is found in capital letters in the KJV, it translates the Tetragrammaton יהוה or unpronounceable Name of God, which was made into a substitute name by taking the vowels of *Adonai* and placing them between the consonants of YHVH to create the hybrid name Jehovah—a favorite of medieval Protestants.

first. After that, we who are still alive and are left will be caught up together with them in the clouds to meet the Lord in the air."[87] This may be the earliest Epistle of Paul and by internal evidence has been dated 50-51 C.E. Thus within a generation after *Yeshua* taught, his opposition to the concept of *Messiah Ben-David* had been forgotten. Only the one pericope in Mark about the *Messiah* not being the son of David points us to his authentic teaching.[88]

The coming *Messiah* of the Hellenistic Jewish wisdom schools was another variation. He was designed as the *Messiah Ben-Joseph,* a spiritual descendent of the great seer and interpreter of dreams who was elevated in the court of Pharaoh after having been persecuted and left for dead by his brothers. The *Messiah Ben-Joseph* was an archetype of the Jewish saint, the Suffering Servant of Trito-Isaiah.[89]

The School of Isaiah[90] was transplanted to Babylon in the Captivity, and it was there over generations that Deutero- and Trito-Isaiah (the later visionary and messianic parts of Isaiah) were written. It was also there that the Enoch literature was produced, and in Babylon also that the School of Daniel came into being. Indeed, that may be the scribal tradition that transmitted and added to the literature of Isaiah and, later, Enoch.

The historical Daniel was a great Jewish saint, martyr, and interpreter of dreams like Joseph. He found favor with the King, whose dreams he successfully interpreted, and saved the Jewish community from persecution.[91] His students and their lineage produced what we know as the Book of Daniel—the only scripture of the Old Testament produced late

---

[87] I Thessalonians 4.16f.

[88] This is why Scripture must be carefully examined. The ancient writers included every source they had, even if they contradicted themselves. For example, the story of Noah and the Flood in Genesis conflates two separate versions. In one, Noah brings the animals onto the Ark in pairs. In the other, he brings them on in groups of seven. By noticing that the Hebrew Name of God used in each account is different, scholars were able to start unraveling the separate sources used by the writers to compose Genesis—one an Elohist, one a Jahwist, etc. By the same token, Mark includes *Yeshua's* criticism of the Davidic *Messiah* because it was in his source—probably notes from Peter—even though it contradicts the early Christian doctrine of Jesus as the *Messiah Ben-David.* The Gospels contain clues within them to look back into their sources for more authentic and less redacted material that helps us recover the historical teachings of *Yeshua.*

[89] Isaiah 53ff.

[90] The disciples of Isaiah and their disciplic lineage that first wrote what the historical Isaiah dictated, then transmitted the prophecies with expansions and eventually new revelations by prophets we call Deutero- and Trito-Isaiah.

[91] Indeed, Daniel was probably the model for the Priestly stories of Joseph in the court of Pharaoh in the Pentateuch, which was redacted in Babylon after the Captivity. It is important to note that previous to the Babylonian Captivity in the 6th century B.C.E., Passover—with all its Egyptian Captivity legend as we know it—was probably not celebrated. The precursor seems to have been a barley grain festival of unleavened bread *(matzoth)* that was common in the ancient Near East to ward off a fungus or smut that attacked the ripening grain crops. Many of the legends of *Pesach* or Passover may have been inspired by the dilemma of Babylonian Captivity and Jewish advocates like Daniel. Nevertheless it continues to stand as a great celebration of freedom and release from bondage. Ultimately it is a kabbalistic and messianic celebration. The Cup of *Elijah,* the open door, the future hope ("Next year in Jerusalem") exhibit origins in the messianic Babylonian School of Daniel.

enough to be written in Aramaic.[92] Daniel was the last and youngest book recognized by the first-century council of rabbis at Jamnia *(Javne)*[93] to be validly inspired Scripture for inclusion in the canon of the Old Testament.

It was undoubtedly in the prophetic schools of the large Post-Captivity Jewish community at Babylon that the apocalyptic figure of the *Messiah Ben-Joseph* developed. Later Palestinian apocalypses envisioned the *Messiah* as a saint whose powerful teachings would slay the enemies of Judaism. But he finally would be slain as well. He would be a suffering *Messiah*, like the Suffering Servant of Isaiah 53 whose death would be sacrificial and salvific, like those of the Jewish martyrs such as legendary *Taxo* in the *Assumption of Moses*.

Yeshua drew upon the legends of the *Messiah Ben-Joseph* in his teaching. He framed the Jewish prophets as martyrs and prophesied that retribution for the shedding of their blood will fall upon the Jerusalem Temple establishment, "from the blood of righteous Abel to the blood of Zechariah son of Berekiah."[94]

But the *Messiah* proclaimed by *Yeshua* was neither the *Messiah Ben-David* nor the *Messiah Ben-Joseph.* It was the Babylonian concept reflected in the title he uses through his teachings, wrongly rendered as the Son of Man. His most authentic sayings from Q speak about the coming of the Son of Mankind, i.e. Son of Adam, or *Bar-Enash.*

When we look back from the perspective of Paul's Second Adam, which undoubtedly derives from the messianic teachings of *Yeshua,* we find something very important. The *Messiah* proclaimed by *Yeshua* was not a single individual, but a *corporate being,* like the First Adam, known to the Kabbalists as *Adam Kadmon,* an androgynous heavenly archetype of humanity who, as primal Mankind, was divided into male Adam and female Eve.

But the *Bar-Enash* was the coming heir of the First Adam or old humanity. Unlike the First Adam, the Son of Mankind was spiritually mature, a perfected form of humanity. He/She was worthy to inherit—meaning to share and apprentice—God's universal Sovereignty in

---

[92] The Aramaic language dates our current version to second or third century B.C.E.

[93] Graetz introduced the idea that the Pharisees under Ben-Zakkai made such decisions at *Javne* or Jamnia, where they were allowed by the Romans to continue their school after the Seige of Jerusalem 70 C.E.. It was accepted by scholars for almost a century but has been recently questioned. The Wikipedia article on Jamnia is a good summary of the issue http://en.wikipedia.org/wiki/Council_of_Jamnia.Quoting: lbert C. Sundberg, Jr. wrote in "The Old Testament of the Early Church" Revisited 1997: Are there alternatives to Jamnia (or later Usha)? As we have seen, it was at Jamnia that the tradition says the Hillelites gained the ascendancy after Lewis in his attack upon Jamnia in order to foster his belief in a Hebrew canon from pre-Christian times. But that case, as we have seen, is confounded by numerous difficulties. With the time of canonization of the Hebrew tripartite canon now probably fixed between 70 and 135 C.E., and as a triumph of the Hillelite Pharisees in post-destruction Judaism over the house of Shammai, what alternatives are there to Jamnia as the venue? It was the school at Jamnia that became a substitute for the Sanhedrin of Jerusalem. It was at Jamnia that the third section of the Hebrew canon [The Writings] was first named. It was the Jamnia decisions that, while not "official," came to be generally accepted in post-destruction Judaism…"

[94] Historical *davar* of *Yeshua* sourced from Q in Matthew 23.35 and Luke 11.51.

Daniel's Son-of-Man *Messiah* vision. Christians and Gnostics are often exhorted to "put on the Perfect Man," which they have the right to do by virtue of their baptism or initiation. Originally, however, as we find in *Thomas* and Johannine tradition, the metaphor was divine rebirth.

Paul represents the Christ or *Messiah* as a corporate being, with Jesus as its head (meaning chief ruler) and the Church as its body.[95] For Paul, Jesus sat in the place of pre-eminence at the messianic table, and the saints (all members of the church) sat with him in a congregational body. But for *Yeshua,* all *tzadikim* who had been reborn as part of the New Humanity in the *Bar-Enash* were united in one mystic body of divine Sovereignty. He was merely the first-born of this Sovereignty.

The theme of the congregation of saints as one body made of innumerable individuals was common in first-century Christian literature. Perhaps the best-known example outside of Paul can be drawn from the *Shepherd of Hermas,* which at one time was included in nearly all collections of the New Testament. Here the church is compared to a Temple and the members to the stones with which the Temple is built.

The Church as Body of Christ survives in of modern Christianity. However, instead of Jesus as the chief ruler of the messianic Corpus, he seems to have swallowed the whole thing!

Many members, one body.

With the rise of Pauline gentile Christianity, the historical *Basor* proclaimed by *Yeshua* was replaced by another Gospel declaring that Jesus Christ is the Son of God and Savior of mankind. That has remained the basic Gospel of Christianity to this day.

But the Gospel proclaimed by *Yeshua* declared the advent of a new *Malkuth* or Sovereignty on Earth. God's invisible Sovereignty would become visible to mankind, who had suffered long ages under self-created bondage to *Shaitan.* It would be shared by a community of saints whom God would anoint progressively and collectively as the archetype of a new humanity—the heavenly Son-of-Mankind *Messiah.* Their activities would bring about the manifestation of Divine *Malkuth* and the implementation of Divine Will on Earth, visible and manifest to all.

---

[95] The Hebrew and rabbinic *rosh* had a much broader meaning than the anatomical head. It referred to the first and pre-eminent place of order, like *Rosh Ha-Shannah,* the Jewish New Year's Day or Head of the Year.

Yeshua's Mystic Advent of the *Bar-Enash* Interpreted as the Christian Second Coming of Jesus and the Pauline Rapture

The early Christians understood *Yeshua* to be the incarnate *Messiah* or Christ. Since his first advent had ended in crucifixion, was interpreted as the *Messiah Ben-Joseph* who was prophesied to teach and reform, but finally to die. Since the *Basor* of *Yeshua* proclaimed the immanent appearance of the *Malkuth* or Sovereignty of God on Earth in fulfillment of prophecy, they associated this with a future advent of *Messiah*, whom *Yeshua* called the *Bar-Enash* or Son of Mankind.

In the Greek translation of Daniel's vision, the "Son of Man" was seen approaching the Throne of God in the "clouds" of Heaven so that he could be presented at Court and anointed as Co-Sovereign with God. Thus, it was concluded, when Jesus Christ returns to Earth as the victorious and conquering *Messiah Ben-David,* he will descend from the sky riding on the physical clouds.

What were the "clouds" of Heaven in Daniel? Aramaic עֲנָנֵי־שְׁמַיָּא *anni-shmia* is from the Hebrew words *anan,* a covering, and *shamyyim,* the (day and night) heavens. From the sense of a covering or obscuring *(anan)*, the Hebrew word was used to designate divination (Latin *augurans, divinans*), hidden arts taught by the fallen angels, sorcery, magical arts. But by the same token it was the word used to describe the covering or "cloud" that God dwelt within to obscure the fiery glory of his primordial light, and to protect humans from instant death. "The glory of the LORD appeared in the 'cloud' *(anan)*."[96] "And the LORD said unto Moses, Lo, I come unto thee in a thick 'cloud.'"[97] "For the 'cloud' of the LORD was upon the tabernacle by day, and fire was on it by night, in the sight of all the house of Israel, throughout all their journeys.[98] When Job was confronted with the mysteries of God, he was asked, "Hear this, O Job...Dost thou know when God...caused the light of His 'cloud' *(anan)* to shine?"[99] Logion 83, "His *Tzelem* (Image) will remain concealed by His Light."

By the late Hellenistic period when Daniel's *Merkabah* visions were written, the 'cloud' of light described by Ezekiel covering the Throne of God was understood to be something quite different from a storm cloud flashing lightning, as it is still understood by modern translators. The *annani*[100] of Heaven were metaphorical veils surrounding not only the *Merkabah* or Throne-Chariot of God, but concealing the mysteries *(razim)* of the *'Olam* of God. They were comparable to the seven veils that separated the Holy of Holies from the rest of the Temple sanctuary. They were not physical "clouds."

---

[96] Exodus 16.10
[97] Exodus 19.9
[98] Exodus 40.38, *et al.*
[99] Job 37.15, usually paraphrased to mean lightning coming out of the *anan* that conceals God's glory, but kabbalistically understood as the *Ain Soph Aur* or limitless primordial Light of God.
[100] Hebrew *anan* became Aramaic *annan* in the Roman-Hellenistic period.

Daniel described the Son of Mankind as "coming, arriving" with, within, near *('im)* the *Annani* of the Heavens as he approached the Throne to be presented to the Ancient of Days. The language of that approach is what we find later interpreted in Marcan and Pauline tradition to describe the advent of the Son-of-Man *Messiah* on Earth—the Christian Second Coming of Jesus Christ.

Mark narrates *Yeshua's* trial before the High Priest and the Sanhedrin. Caiaphas asks him if he is the *Messiah*, the Son of God. "And Jesus said, 'I am: and ye shall see the Son of Man sitting on the right hand of power, and coming in the clouds of heaven.'"[101] This is, without doubt, pure Marcan fiction or creative story-telling. None of the disciples were present as eyewitnesses to the trials. Even in Mark, the *Messiah*-ship of Jesus is concealed throughout his ministry—the "Marcan secret." There is no historical basis for knowing what transpired or was said in the privacy of either the Jewish or Roman trials of *Yeshua*, who never declared himself to be the *Messiah* in his historical teachings.

But it is clear that by the fifth decade of the first century, when the Marcan narrative was probably redacted, Christians had interpreted the Son of Man vision to prefigure the return of Jesus to Earth as the triumphant *Messiah ben-David.* He would return to Earth just as he had approached the Throne to receive Sovereignty—"in the 'clouds' of heaven," meaning a descent from the sky riding physical clouds.

As we said, this interpretation appeared by mid-century in I Thessalonians 4.16. The Lord himself (Jesus Christ) will descend from the sky. An Archangel [probably Michael] will shout the command, another [probably Gabriel] will blow the ram's horn, and all the dead will arise for judgment, with the faithful awakening first. Then the faithful still alive on Earth will be "snatched up" into the clouds along with the risen faithful to meet Christ in the air. Whether this originated with Paul, as some think, or was already present in Christian tradition as it appeared in the earliest Gospel by Peter's disciple Mark, we probably cannot know.

But we can surmise that this was a Christian interpretation of *Yeshua's davar* about the advent of the *Bar-Enash* in the very early Q material,[102] which is contemporary with the source of *Thomas* and earlier than either Mark or Paul's first Epistles. *Yeshua* teaches that the coming of the *Bar-Enash* will occur when he is least expected, like the flood of Noah or a thief in the night. At his advent, the Lucan and Matthean redactions of Q declare that two will be in a bed; one will be received *(paralambanein)*, the other left behind.

But the Greek *paralambanei* translated Aramaic *laqach,* meaning to "receive knowledge." The original meaning was, "One will receive knowledge, the other will not." This is a very

---

[101] Here the Greek term *nephele* means the physical clouds, but the phrase is quoted directly from Daniel's Aramaic description.
[102] Matthew 24:40-41; Luke 17:34; independently in Logion 61

different kind of "rapture" than the Synoptic versions, which have been redacted and interpreted in the light of the Pauline opinion expressed in I Thessalonians 4.16.

Yeshua's understanding of the advent of the *Bar-Enash* was that it was associated with a moral and spiritual judgment (*mishpat* or "division") within humanity, as in the Matthean Parable of the Sheep and the Goats. It would also come when least expected, like the flood of Noah or a thief in the night. All humanity would be involved in this *mishpat*—not just the Jews. Humanity would be divided or separated by the *Bar-Enash* or New Sovereign Humanity according to the deeds of each one.

Yeshua also used the "when least expected" phrases to describe unpreparedness for personal death—the rich man who cared only for his wealth and possessions, *et al.* His view of the advent of the *Bar-Enash* was therefore not eschatological, but personal. The coming of *Messiah,* like the advent of the *Malkuth,* was not "Lo, here; lo, there." It was soul by soul—a personal eschatology fully "realized" not at some historical time, but only after death. The Son of Mankind or New Adam had now, in his eternal advent, become the standard by which the moral and spiritual quality of each soul will be measured after death.

The Mystic *Malkuth* of Apostles and Initiates

Logion 2 summarizes the path of spiritual mastery that *Yeshua* taught to his close disciples and those whom he found whose souls were already prepared to receive the *Razim Ha-Malkuth* (so-called "Mysteries of the Kingdom"). The many *davarim* memorialized in the *logia* of *Thomas* address finer points of his spiritual *halakah.* The final goal of the seeker, according to Logion 2, was mastery not just of self, but collective mastery or sovereignty over the universe itself. This seems to have been adapted into messianic mysticism from the teachings of the Jewish wisdom schools, as we have seen in previous commentary on Logion 2.

In the future, the New Humanity would wrest control of the Earth from *Shaitan,* the Accuser. They would apprentice and carry out the works of God, seated as an anointed heir at the right hand of divine power. The Coming One would be spiritually generated soul by soul in fiery trial through the Birth Pangs of *Messiah.* The *Malkuth* would grow slowly, like the development from tiny seed to fully fruited tree. It was not "Lo, here; lo, there," but "within you (all)." The coming *Bar-Enash Messiah* is a future New Humanity.

But here and now, a saint who had successfully undertaken the path of interior sanctification that *Yeshua* taught in his *halakah* could draw near to God's Throne and be transformed in spiritual rebirth. For the *Malkuth* is "spread out upon the Earth, but men do not see it."[103] It is "within you, and beyond you."[104] An initiate would personally experience

---

[103] *Thomas* Logion #113

the fiery trials that all humanity must pass through—the Birth Pangs of the *Messiah*. The (feminine) *neshamah* (soul) of the saint would be worn like an outer garment by the (masculine) *yechid* (spirit) of the *Bar-Enash* (New Adam).[105] In that divine identity he or she would become spiritually *shalem* or whole (neither male nor female, but androgynous) like the angels,[106] and participate in the universal Sovereignty of God.

It is important to understand that sainthood of itself did not constitute initiatic rebirth into the *Bar-Enash*. Sainthood in life resulted in what might be understood as continuity of consciousness after death in the *Qimah* or resurrection-state. One might say that the personality or *nephesh* had become imprinted with the spiritual qualities of one's individual *neshamah* through the righteous activities of life in flesh.

But sainthood did qualify one for spiritual initiation or rebirth in the *Bar-Enash*, which was a new evolution of humanity that now sat at the right hand of sovereign power in Heaven at the Throne of God. Because of the righteousness and suffering of countless saints throughout history, a new human archetype—a New Adam—had presented itself at the Throne, and God had accepted and anointed this "son" of mankind to inherit and share Divine Sovereignty. [107]

Unlike rabbis to whom young men applied for acceptance as *talmidim, Yeshua* selected and called each one—male and female—who would become an inner-circle disciple. In both public and Secret Mark the writer says of one whom he chose, "and *Yeshua* loved him." That means he recognized the signs of spiritual readiness that could develop with halakic training. It was to the chosen one that he privately taught the *Razim Ha-Malkuth* and transmitted spiritual rebirth in the *Bar-Enash*.[108] Many clues from the canonical Gospels, Secret Mark, and the gospels of Philip and Mary, indicate that this was done in an all-night session on an isolated hilltop, and probably included an anointing later developed as the Gnostic Sacrament of the Bride Chamber.[109]

---

[104] *Thomas* Logion #3

[105] Cf. *Gospel of Mary* 9.9 where Andrew chastises Peter for doubting Mary and says, "Let us...put on the Perfect Man *(Anthropos Teleios),*" a Greek expression for the "Son of Man" (5.1) meaning the *Bar-Enash*. To think and act with what Paul called the "Mind *(Nous*—Higher Intellect*)* of Christ" was for the "man to eat the lion" (see *Thomas* Logion 7), empower the *Yetzer Ha-Tov* or Divine Impulse (Image) within the heart, and rise above the fleshly limitations of the Old Adam.

[106] Mark 12.18ff.; Matthew 22.23ff.; Luke 20.27ff.

[107] "And I beheld, in the Hidden Mysteries *(Razim;* metaphorically for "clouds"), of Heaven there came one like unto a *Bar-Enash (i.e., in human form rather than the form of a beast)*, and he came to the Ancient of Days, and was presented before him. And to him was given dominion and glory and *Malkuth (*"Sovereignty"), that all peoples, nations, and languages should serve him. His dominion is for the entire *'olam* of the messianic Age on Earth (an "everlasting" dominion), which dominion shall not pass away, and his *Malkuth* is one that shall never be destroyed." Daniel 7.13-14

[108] The legend of Lazarus being raised from the dead may allegorize this initiation of rebirth.

[109] The divine "marriage of *Messiah*" from *kabbalistic haggadah* was the basis for *Yeshua's* sacred meal, which was a mystical participation in the Heavenly wedding banquet that celebrated the union of saint (bride,

While *Yeshua* taught his *halakah* to guide disciples on the path of sainthood, he also came upon anonymous Jewish saints whose lives and interior development had already prepared them to receive the *Razim* of spiritual rebirth such as Nicodemus, a Pharisaic *Chazzan* or Synagogue Leader in John's Gospel to whom *Yeshua* explains the Birth from Above. Such disciples required only a short preparation, such as the one-week period given to the anonymous initiand of Secret Mark.[110]

The distinctions between disciple *(talmid)* and Apostle *(mebasar)* made traditionally in Christianity reflect—albeit inaccurately—historical categories of *Yeshua's* disciples. The Greek New Testament terms *mathetes* and *apostolos* are usually used interchangeably in the Gospels, but in Paul and Acts the term Apostle is of great importance. The Apostles are the successors of Jesus as church leaders and teachers. Other church members are called *hagioi,* "saints." But most of these would not have qualified as *tzadikim* in the thought-world of *Yeshua.*

I would suggest that the original Apostles, of whom at least 17 are referenced in the canonical Gospels and many others by name or anonymously in Paul and Acts, were those who had been initiated into the *Razim Ha-Malkuth* by *Yeshua.* They were mostly men, but clearly *Miriam Magdala,* a woman, was one of the most advanced of these.

The "Sovereignty" shared by the Apostles while yet incarnate as human personalities was manifested as the powers of what was known to the Greeks as a *Theios Aner,* or Divine Human like Apollonius of Tyana. These included healing, exorcism, divine vision, and all the charisms of the Holy Spirit described by Paul. The saints of the church each had some small share in this Sovereignty through the "gifts" of the Holy Spirit as part of the Body of Christ, but in gentile Christianity the initiatic *Razim* had been lost.

---

yechidah) with the *Bar-Enash* (groom, *yechid*). In Valentinian Gnosticism this became a ritual of associating the initiate with a "bride groom" angel in the giving of the Christian name.

[110] This was probably a reason for jealousy on the part of longer-term disciples, and possibly allegorized by the parable of the laborers in the vineyard in Matthew 20.1ff. "For the kingdom of heaven is like a landowner who went out early in the morning to hire laborers for his vineyard. Now when he had agreed with the laborers for a denarius a day, he sent them into his vineyard. And he went out about the third hour and saw others standing idle in the marketplace, and said to them, 'You also go into the vineyard, and whatever is right I will give you.' So they went. Again he went out about the sixth and the ninth hour, and did likewise. And about the eleventh hour he went out and found others standing 1idle, and said to them, 'Why have you been standing here idle all day?' They said to him, 'Because no one hired us.' He said to them, 'You also go into the vineyard, and whatever is right you will receive.'"So when evening had come, the owner of the vineyard said to his steward, 'Call the laborers and give them *their* wages, beginning with the last to the first.' And when those came who *were hired* about the eleventh hour, they each received a denarius. But when the first came, they supposed that they would receive more; and they likewise received each a denarius. And when they had received *it,* they complained against the landowner saying, 'These last *men* have worked *only* one hour, and you made them equal to us who have borne the burden and the heat of the day.' ...

We find evidence of gentile distortions of initiatic Sovereignty in Paul's admonitions to the Corinthian pneumatics. His opening chapters in First Corinthians deals with the factions that have arisen through different Jewish and gentile teachers, and especially with those who claim to have the secret wisdom of initiatic tradition. In I Cor. 4.8 he rails against the Pneumatics, who taught that there were three spiritual levels—the fleshly *(sarkikos)*, the baptized Christian *(psychikos)*, and the initiated Christian *(pneumatikos)*. He writes, "Now ye are full, now ye are rich! Ye have reigned as kings without us! And I would to God ye did reign, that we also might reign with you!"

Here "full...rich...reign" are terms of Sovereignty or *Malkuth*. In the language of *Yeshua*, the Pneumatics were claiming to be *shalem* or perfect like Godhead, who lacks nothing and reigns omnipotent. It is their spiritual inflation that Paul condemns, not the idea of Soveregnty, which he understands as a future state.

It is probably at this point in church history—soon after 50 C.E.—that the initiatic *Razim* of *Yeshua* were corrupted by Gnostic teachers. We are told in the Book of the Acts that the Gnostic Simon Magus (probably *Megas*, "the Great," pejoratively renamed by Christians as "the Sorcerer") sought to purchase the initiatic powers transmitted by *Yeshua* from Peter.[111]

There is much evidence in the fragmentary teachings of Pantaenus, Basilides, Isidore, Clement, and Origen that a more authentic form of the initiatic *Razim Ha-Malkuth* was transmitted in the Alexandrian churches perhaps as late as the fourth century. If Clement's letter about Secret Mark is authentic, as I believe it is, then the theft and corruption of Christian initiatic material by the Gnostic Carpocrates is a continuation of an ongoing attempt by sectarians to gain access to the inner-circle teachings of *Yeshua*.

We can then speculate that there were understood to be three aspects of Divine Sovereignty *(Malkuth)*. The first was public—the advent of the *Bar-Enash* and his Sovereignty on Earth. This was a long, slow process that would eventually transform all humanity and its institutions. It came into manifestation soul by soul.

The second was the goal of sainthood that would be realized after a sanctified life or many lives of sacrificial service in the *Qimah*. In that state, the Life of God's *'Olam* would be experienced in the *Pardes*, followed by eventual union with the *Bar-Enash*. From here the *neshamah* of each *yechid* would participate in the telepathic guidance of incarnate human souls, analogous to the *Ogdoad* of Hermetic saints.

The third aspect of divine Sovereignty was experienced by an initiate while yet incarnate on Earth. This included participation in the Heavenly Marriage Banquet (*Yeshua's* sacred

---

111 Acts 8.9ff.

meal *seder* that Paul transformed into the Christian Eucharist) and the development of various psychic and spiritual charisms (Pauline "ministries") to be exercised for the benefit and liberation of humanity.

I have given a detailed commentary on many aspects of Logion 2 so that the reader will have a basis for understanding the rest of the *logia* of *Thomas* and the reconstructed *davarim* of *Yeshua* in the following chapters.

CHAPTER FOUR: Logia 3-11

For each reconstructed *davar* of *Yeshua,* I have indicated the traditional Logion number assigned by translators to the saying referenced in the *Gospel of Thomas.* I present the sayings in the order they appear in *Thomas* and comment on authenticity and meaning. However, in an appendix I reorder them by topic such as *Malkuth* (Sovereignty) and *Bar-Enash* (Son-of-Man *Messiah*) to reveal the larger context of meaning. Then I further comment on the initiatic implication of each topic.

Logion 3

3.a[112] If those who try to exert spiritual influence over you[113] say, "Behold, the *Malkuth* will descend from the sky," then the birds of the sky will be greater than you in the *Malkuth.* If they say to you, "Behold, the *Malkuth* will arise from the sea," then the fish will be greater than you.[114] But the *Malkuth* is within your heart and beyond your understanding.[115]

---

[112] Logion 3 consists of two sayings, the first of which (3.a) is an authentic *davar* of *Yeshua.* However, the editorial expansion (3.b) uses Gnostic terms and concepts. Its juxtaposition with *Yeshua's* teaching about the spiritual nature of the *Malkuth* reveals that the Thomas Gnostics understood βασιλειον "Kingdom" to be part of the "true nature" of the soul—not unlike the Buddha Nature of all sentient beings—which was discovered through individual *gnosis.* By contrast, *Yeshua's Malkuth* was a corporate community that grew and manifested on Earth over time. It was not part of the true nature of the Pauline First Adam, but of the reborn *Bar Enash* or Second Adam. In that sense, the Pauline and Christian concept of Βασιλειον as the true Church (Community of Saints) held more closely to *Yeshua's* original inner-circle teachings about the "birth from Above," as reflected in the *palingenesis* of John 3.

[113] I.e., rabbinical and synagogue authorities.

[114] There were two popular views of the *Messiah:* the *Messiah ben-David,* who according to apocalyptic writings would descend from the sky with angels; and the *Messiah ben-Joseph,* who would arise from the sea to gather his armies for the conquest of evil.

[115] Coptic **ⲤⲘⲠⲈⲦⲚⲂⲀⲖ·** The Greek reconstruction *ka'ktos* done by scholars for the lacuna in the Oxyrhynchus Greek fragment is based on translating the Coptic as the contrasting "outside of you," then using this to construct a rare and non-Koine Gr. word *katektos.* Since there not enough space, so the reconstruction is contracted into *ka'ktos* to make it fit. But in my opinion the Coptic might be better translated as "far beyond you," so a Gr. word like *ametro* that we find in the writings of Paul is more likely. Most translators opt for the contrasting "within-without," but *Yeshua's* description of the *Malkuth* in Logion 113 as "spread out upon the earth" and invisible to mankind indicates a transcendent reality that is not merely "outside," but "beyond."

3.b[116] When you discover your true nature,[117] you will know that you are children of the Father of all spiritual life.[118] But if you do not discover your true nature, then you remain spiritually impoverished, and indeed you are the epitome of spiritual poverty.[119]

COMMENTARY

The first part of the Logion (3a) is an authentic inner-circle teaching given by *Yeshua*. The second part (3b) is a Gnostic expansion.

Yeshua spoke this *davar* to counter other messianic views that were advocated by Essene, Zealot, and Pharisaic schools. All messianic speculation was promulgated privately for fear of the Romans, not in synagogues, but was also publically rumored as common Palestinian and Babylonian haggadic tradition.

Here *Yeshua* takes a tongue-in-cheek potshot at the two main views concerning the *Messiah Ben-David* and the *Messiah Ben-Joseph,* who would respectively descend from the heavens or arise from the sea with armies of angels to restore Israel and make it pre-eminent among nations. For *Yeshua,* the appearance of God's *Malkuth* on Earth is identified with the advent of the Son-of-Man *Messiah,* so his *davar* begins, "If [they]…say, 'The *Malkuth* will descend from the sky…'" rather than "If [they]…say, 'The *Messiah* will descend from the sky…" They are one and the same future event.

---

[116] A Gnostic expansion—not part of the original *davar.*

[117] The Gnostics referenced the Greek proverb inscribed above the entrance to the Temple of the Oracle of Delphi, which admonished those seeking personal prophecies: Gnothi Seauton, "Know for Thyself." This became the mantra of the Greek philosophers.

[118] *Yeshua's* familiar term for God *Abba* translated "Father" did not imply male patriarchy, but the primordial Source from which all spiritual reality (which underlies physical manifestation) is begotten. Godhead is the Father-Mother Begetter in a *kabbalistic* system that did not teach creation by a Platonistic Demiurge, as did later Christianity and Gnosticism, but emanation of the *'olamim* from the divine fountainhead. Wisdom or feminine *Hochmah* (later Johannine masculine *Logos* "Word") was the architect of formation and manifestation *(Shekinah).* However, this Gnostic extension emphasizes the masculine paternity of Godhead, just as does Logion 114—also a Gnostic composition. Pythagoras distinguished two forces: masculine, which ruled even numbers, changeless divinity, immortality; and feminine, which ruled odd numbers, mutable corruptibility, and mortality. In a fragment from the Gospel of the Hebrews, Jesus says, "I have come to destroy the works of woman." The male was source of a living seed, the female was merely a receptacle, like the soil. Thus the Gnostic God of Thomas as Begetter of the All is a Father—not a Father-Mother as would be found in true Jewish Kabbalism of *Yeshua's* era..

[119] The "poverty" theme found in many of the Thomas *logia* seems to be a Gnostic development of *Yeshua's* "treasure in the heart/in Heaven" teachings.

Then he declares the true understanding of *Malkuth:* "But the Sovereignty of God is within you and beyond your understanding."[120] Note that this is not given in the future tense, and that the Aramaic idiom "within you" means literally "within your heart."

The physical heart stored virtues and vices from activity in life. The physical heart was understood to be the hub of the physical body connecting all channels and systems. It was the center of consciousness (which we now consider to be the brain). The "thoughts of the heart" was a common Hebrew expression. Below an Egyptian storage vessel for precious fluids and ointments was modeled upon the physical heart.

The kabbalistic teaching about the heart is a key to understanding the initiatic teachings of *Yeshua* and was well known to disciples. It was rooted in the Egyptian concept of the physical heart as a jar *(leb)* used for storage of precious ointments, perfumes, and other "treasure." The Egyptian word for the heart was *ab, leb,* from which the Hebrews derived their word for heart, which was *lab, lebab.*

The heart was the source of good and evil within a person, like the Hebrew *lab,* which contained the *yetzer ha-ra* (evil image or impulse) and the *yetzer ha-tov* (divine image of God given at the emanation of mankind). The heart wandered from the body in sleep or trance, as the *Ka,* and could either dwell with the gods as a *Sahu* after death or be devoured by the beast *Ammut* if it failed to weigh equally against the feather of Ma'at in the Court of Osiris at the judgment after death (see note below).

The heart had weight because it was a storage vessel for the essences of good and evil deeds. Good deeds were spiritual and added no weight to the heart, but evil deeds were gross and caused the heart to accumulate weight that prevented it from entering the spiritual realm of the righteous after death. Thus it was weighed against a feather after death in the Court of Osiris to determine its fate.

In the process of Egyptian mummification, all human organs were removed and placed in canopic jars except the heart. The *leb* was regarded as the seat of consciousness and spiritual vessel containing all the many dimensions of the soul. Leaving the heart in the mummified body allowed the *ka* to remain with the *khat* (corpse) for forty days before dissolution, releasing the *ba* to soar upward into the Heavens. The *ba* was to the *ka* as soul

---

[120] The usual Greek reconstruction of this lacuna is *ka'ktos* is based on translating the Coptic as the contrasting "outside of you," then using this to construct a rare and non-Koine Gr. word *katektos.* But there is not enough space, so the reconstruction is contracted into *ka'ktos* to make it fit. But the Coptic ⲤⲘⲠⲈⲦⲚⲂⲀⲗ is better translated "far beyond you," so a Gr. word like *ametro* that we find in the writings of Paul ("beyond, transcending our understanding") is the more likely reconstruction. Thus WITHIN AND BEYOND (OUR UNDERSTANDING) is the original meaning.

is to body. Beyond that were many gradations of the human constitution, both mortal and immortal. In the cosmogony of Hierapolis these totaled nine in all, perhaps reflecting the Egyptian emanation of the Ennead of gods.[121]

Apparently, in the Old Kingdom process of mummification for a Pharaoh, priestly rites were performed to preserve the life of the *ka* beyond its normal forty days. The *ka* was the lowest astral or sidereal aspect of what we call a soul—the human personality and intelligence of Pharaoh. By extending its life through symbolic sacrificial offerings and construction of a symbolic door on the tomb through which it could enter, exit, and communicate, a psychic priest could remain in communication with Pharaoh for advice and divination concerning state matters while the young Pharonic heir matured into his office. During the period of the Middle Kingdom the concept was extended to family members of the royal court and priesthood, and eventually to all who could afford tombs and priestly services.

The tripartite body-soul-spirit found in the New Testament is a Greek simplification of the human psychic constitution known in Jewish wisdom schools. This kabbalistic understanding was based on Egyptian Priestly thanatology but organized as a series of six increasingly subtle gradations through physical, psychical, and spiritual realities.[122]

---

[121] "**Khat (Kha)** - The physical form, the body that could decay after death, the mortal, outward part of the human that could only be preserved by mummification; **Ka** - The double that lingered on in the tomb inhabiting the body or even statues of the deceases, but was also independent of man and could move, eat and drink at will. (There was both a higher, guardian angel like Ka and lower Ka that came from knowledge learned on earth); **Ba** - The human headed bird that flitted around in the tomb during the day bringing air and food to the deceased, but travelled with Ra on the Solar Barque during the evenings; **Khaibit** - The shadow of a man that could partake of funerary offerings and was able to detach itself from the body and travel at will, though it always was thought to stay near the **Ba**; **Akhu (Akh, Khu, Ikhu)** - This was the immortal part, the radiant and shining being that lived on in the **Sahu**, the mind, intellect, will and intentions of the deceased that transfigured death and ascended to the heavens to live with the gods or the imperishable stars; **Sahu** - The incorruptible spiritual body of man that could dwell in the heavens, appearing from the physical body after the judgment of the dead was passed (if successful) with all of the mental and spiritual abilities of a living body; **Sekhem** - This was the incorporeal personification of the life force of man, which lived in heaven with the **Akhu**, after death; **Ren** - The true name, a vital part to man on his journey through life and the afterlife, a magical part that could destroy a man if his name was obliterated or could give power of the man if someone knew his **Ren** - naming ceremonies in Egypt were secret, and a child lived his whole life with a nickname to avoid anyone from learning his true name." *The Ancient Egyptian Concept of the Soul*, Caroline Seawright, from Lionel Casson, *Ancient Egypt* www.touregypt.net/magazine/mag05012001/magf3.htm

[122] Second Temple Jewish mysticism was syncretistic. It drew from many spiritual contacts made in the Diaspora including not only the Babylonian, but priestly Hermetic and Pythagorean knowledge. This included astrological and Platonic concepts. Jewish astrologers, diviners, healers, exorcists, magicians, and alchemists were employed by rulers and wealthy citizens well into the Middle Ages. The twelfth-century rabbi-philosopher Maimonides warned Jews to disavow esoteric practices to avoid inciting gentile pogroms against perceived witchcraft. Since that time rabbinic Judaism has disassociated itself from occult knowledge and arts which, however, continued to be practiced by Jewish sages like Nostradamus and the legendary Abramalin. *kabbalistic* writings (an oxymoron, since *kabbalah* means initiatic knowledge transmitted only orally) surfaced in the 16th century with Rabbi Isaac Luria. However *kabbalistic* tradition began several centuries before the era of *Yeshua,* Secret books like *Sepher Yetzirah* and written collections of incantations and theurgical evocations such as those found among the Greek and Demotic magical papyri and Margalioth's

Kabbalistic descriptions of the subtle constitution of man survive through intertestamental pseudepigrapha and apocrypha such as the *Testaments of the Twelve Patriarchs* and clues from the wisdom school writings such as the biblical *Ecclesiastes,* which speaks metaphorically of the "silver cord" that connects the *nephesh* to the body.[123]

The later kabbalistic writings preserve the Jewish mystical understanding of the six vessels subsumed under the New Testament categories of *soma* (body), *psyche* (soul), and *pneuma* (spirit). They are:

- *Basar* (בסר): Flesh, "meat," physical body that decomposes after death.

- *Nefesh, Nephesh* (נפש): Personality, lower animal nature, astral-sidereal body composed of subtle ethers that survives death for about forty days then dissolves back into its subtle elements in a second death. Contains the mortal mind, perception, personality and gender individuality of the deceased. Probably derived from Egyptian *Ka and Khaibit.*

- *Ruach* (רוח): Spirit that is released and ascends when the *Nephesh* disintegrates at the second death. No gender. Probably derived from Egyptian *Ba.*

- *Neshamah* (נשמה): The "soul" that is incarnated at birth and survives death for Purgatory and Paradise (there is no eternal Hell in kabbalistic teaching). No gender. It is capable of limited understanding concerning God and the highest *'olamim.* Probably derived from Egyptian *Akhu.*

- *Chayyah* (חיה): The spiritual *Nous* (Hermetic Greek term) or Understanding of the *neshamah* that can experience the Vision of God. Pauline "Mind of Christ." Probably derived from Egyptian *Sahu.* Androgynous like the angels.

- *Yechidah* (יחידה): The highest aspect of the human subtle constitution through which a *tzadik* or realized saint achieves divine union with God. Possibly derived from Pythagorean Greek *Monas.*[124] Unlike Monad, which was a neuter term

---

reconstruction of a *Sepher Ha-Razim* can be dated to the early second century. They appeared during the Talmudic period after the failed *Bar Cochba* messianic revolt and the expulsion of all Jews from Jerusalem as a means of preserving oral *kabbalistic* tradition. They were not copied in Jewish scribal schools like the scriptures, but transmitted privately.

[123] *Qoheleth* warns us to remember God before "the silver cord be loosed, or the golden bowl be broken, or the pitcher be broken at the fountain, or the wheel broken at the cistern." Ecclesiastes 12:6

[124] The Egyptian *Ren* or true Name was the probable *kabbalistic* origin of the name written on a white stone in Christian baptism. In *Yeshua's* inner circle, he renamed a disciple after he/she had shown evidence of receiving the second "birth from Above." For example he gave the name *Cephas* to *Shimone* or Simon, whom we know as Peter. *Cephas* means rock or stone in Aramaic. That was translated into Greek as *Petros,* from which "Peter" is given in English. The renaming of an initiate was an ancient tradition in many mystery religions, but usually the name was kept secret. In medieval European schools it was sometimes used as a *nom de plume* to guard anonymity. The naming of Bishops and even Christian children after Christian saints, as well as the Christian name given at baptism, reflect a survival of the originally esoteric institution of the *Ren* or the Hebrew *Shem.*

synonymous with Godhead, *Yechidah* is a Hebrew feminine term. The individual being at its highest expression is feminine to Godhead, who is masculine *Yechid*.[125]

Now let us look again at *Yeshua's* assertion that the *Malkuth* or Sovereignty of God "is within your heart and beyond your understanding."

First, "within you" is the Aramaic idiom "within your heart." When *Yeshua* speaks of interior realities, he is invoking the kabbalistic understanding of core being, which is centered within the heart. What lies within the heart? Two formations or impulses: the impulse, motivation, or motion of the Divine Image *(yetzer ha-tov)* given at the emanation of a human soul, and the evil motion *(yetzer ha-ra)* which entered into the heart of mankind as a kind of necessary reaction.

The Hebrew text at Genesis 2.7 reads, "And *Yahweh Elohim* formed Mankind *(Adam)* out of the dust of the earth *(adamah)*. However the Second Temple scribes spelled the verb *yetzer* "formed" with a double *yod*, so it read *yyetzer*. Why? Because the kabbalistic explanation for the origination of evil in *Adam* or Archetypal Mankind, who was formed by the good and perfect Godhead, is that it was a consequence of the creation process[126] and evil in the form of *qlippoth* or shattered sephirotic shells was necessary to animate and set the universe into motion. In one of his *davarim, Yeshua* said, "It is necessary that evils will arise; but woe to the man by whom they come!"[127] Evil is necessary in the world, but it does not originate from God. "For from within—out of men's hearts—come evil thoughts, sexual immorality, theft, murder, adultery, greed, malice, deceit, lewdness, envy, slander, arrogance and folly."[128]

The Jewish wisdom schools developed this kabbalistic theodicy to explain the origin of evil. To summarize, in order for the primordial *sephiroth* to communicate as a system, their vessels had to be shattered, which produced "shards" known as *qlippoth*—the dark and negative forces of reality. By the same token, the very act of incarnation requires an equal and opposite reaction that, in the heart of Mankind, manifests as an image or impulse *(yetzer)* of evil.

Thus every person is dual in his heart. He or she must struggle against evil impulses and strengthen good impulses. Simply put, this is the process of sanctification and self-

---

[125] The Pauline reference to the Church as Bride of Christ reflects the *kabbalistic* understanding that union of a saint with Godhead is like that of *Adonai* and *Matronit*. It is the mystic union of lover and beloved.
[126] Specifically, the shattering of the Vessels or *Sephiroth*.
[127] Matthew 18.7
[128] Mark 7.20-22 and parallels.

perfection that *Yeshua* taught in his *halakah.* All the sayings in the New Testament and in *Thomas* about making the "mind" or heart single refer to this interior spiritual struggle.

As the redactor of *John's Gospel* said, *Yeshua* knew "what was within mankind," meaning the good and evil within each heart. "Strait [strict] is the path and the gate that leads to Life [God's *Malkuth*]," he warned, "and few are they who find it."[129]

So when *Yeshua* says that the *Malkuth* "is within your heart and beyond your understanding," he reveals that both the coming *Messiah* and his Sovereignty are already resident in each heart in the Divine Image or *Yetzer Ha-Tov.* They have been there from the beginning as an image or pattern. The work of sanctification is to grow into that image, just as a mustard seed develops into a tree.

Not many in a given generation will become *shalem* or attain full spiritual maturity. In fact, the work of sanctification is so demanding, and the gateway into divine Sovereignty so narrow, that only a few will achieve it in a given lifetime. Yet it is incumbent upon us to make the attempt, because the "treasure" that we accumulate in our hearts will be carried forward into future lives and bring us closer to the goal.

The kabbalistic doctrine of reincarnation and the heart has many parallels with Hindu teachings concerning the *jiva* or *jivatma.* The "soul" is a tiny thin filament at the core of the heart. It accumulates karmic patterns of virtue and vice according to how one's life was conducted and leaves the body at death. After a period it forms the core for a new incarnation both bound by karmic chains that have been previously forged, and partially liberated by virtues that carry forward. Similar doctrines were probably current in Jewish Mandaism, and are later found in the Manichaeism that survived long after in the medieval European Gnostic communities of Bogomils and so-called Catharii.

Logion 4
4.a A spiritual master of Israel will not hesitate to ask a newly-reborn[130] saint of the *Malkuth* about the *Razim*[131] concerning the Abode of the Living Ones,[132] and he will also become a Living One.

---

[129] Matthew 7.14 Here the Greek word for "find" is equivalent to the Aramaic word מצא *matza,* meaning "to attain through effort." It does not mean "discover, stumble upon" as it is often rendered in *Thomas.*
[130] One who has achieved the Birth from Above or spiritual rebirth in the *Malkuth.*
[131] The *kabbalistic* secrets and mysteries of the *Pardes*—the profound inner gnosis known and discussed only by the spiritual masters of Israel.
[132] Those who have achieved the *Qimah,* Resurrection, or immortality in the Divine World.

4.a [Literal Translation] An old man[133] will not hesitate to ask a newly-born child of seven days[134] about the 'Olam[135] of Life, and he will become alive.

4.b Many who are regarded as masters of Israel will take the lowest seats at the Marriage Banquet of Messiah.[136] But they [all] shall become a single being [the Bar-Enash].[137]

4.b [Literal Translation] Many who are greatest[138] shall become least.[139] And they shall become a single one.

COMMENTARY

Logion 4 is a redaction of two *davarim* contrasting culturally perceived spiritual status in the present age with true spiritual status in the coming *Malkuth* or Sovereignty of God on Earth. The Gnostic redactor adds "and they shall become a single one" to 4.b.

The kabbalistic Place of Life referenced in Logion 4.a was the spiritual *Maqom* or the *Pardes* (Paradise) of God in the Third Heaven. This is the abode or highest level of existence of the Standing Ones—those who have achieved the *Qimah* or Life of the *'Olam* after death. They serve as saints guiding those human souls who are able to attune to them. Moses and Elijah were Standing Ones who appeared with *Yeshua* as spiritual guides in the so-called Transfiguration event.

The Coptic term ⲕⲟⲩⲉⲓ means not just a young child, but a newly-born infant. *Yeshua* initiated his close disciples into what in John's Gospel is described to Nicodemus as spiritual birth "from Above" *(ano)*. This is in reference to the divine birth of *Messiah* in Psalm 2.7: "I will declare the decree: the LORD hath said unto me, Thou art my Son; this day have I begotten thee," which is quoted often in early Christian literature.[140] Those to whom *Yeshua* had transmitted spiritual rebirth were the "newly-born ones" of the *Bar-Enash* or

---

[133] A spiritual elder of Israel.

[134] Boys were circumcised and the mother purified on the eighth day, so this seven-day-old child is uncircumcised (not yet acknowledged as a member of Israel) and not yet cleansed by *mikveh*—the "least" one in Israel.

[135] Greek/Coptic *topos* for Aramaic *maqom*, the "standing" or immortal place of saints who have achieved the *Qimah*.

[136] Spiritual and social status in Israel was acknowledged by seating order at a banquet. *Yeshua's* reference to greatest and least in the coming *Malkuth* implies seating order at the Marriage Banquet of *Messiah*.

[137] All those of the *Malkuth* or Sovereignty, from greatest to least, constitute the corporate New Humanity.

[138] Copt. "early" for Gk. *Protos* "primary, first" = (probably) Ar. *Qaram* "chiefmost person."

[139] Copt. "be late" for Gk. *Eschatos* "last" = Ar. *Achrit* "final, very last."

[140] Acts 13.33; Hebrew 1.5; 5.5

Messiah. Spiritual rebirth was not for just one individual, but for all members of the Body of *Messiah.* We see clues in the interpretation later offered by Paul. Christian baptism symbolized dying and rising with *Messiah* as a new Adam. This conflates *Yeshua's* Birth from Above with John's baptism of water.

But messianic rebirth was not the same as John's *mikveh.* The water baptism of John symbolized a re-crossing of the Jordan into the Promised Land, as the ancestors had done after wandering in the wilderness of Judea for forty years. The new crossing of the waters symbolized many things—a *mikveh* of purification and preparation for the coming of *Messiah,* immersion into the waters of a new Creation, gateway into the coming *Malkuth* of God.

According to John's Gospel, *Yeshua* himself did not baptize, but his disciples did.[141] It is clear from all sources, however, that after the martyrdom of John the Baptist, *Yeshua* continued John's baptism of submission to God *(nacham,* wrongly rendered as "repentance" in New Testament Greek). It was perpetuated in the gentile churches, who regarded themselves to be the New Israel, as a substitute for circumcision—the rite that symbolized admittance to Israel. But despite the fact that later second-century Christianity treated baptism as an initiatic rite done only once a year at Passover, and for which long study and preparation was required, water baptism was not the initiatic rite used by *Yeshua.*

Instead, he transmitted an initiation of spiritual rebirth *(palingenesis* in John's Gospel), in which one advanced disciple came to him alone high on a hilltop at night. He or she wore only a white linen robe, possibly modeled after the seamless priestly robe used by *Yeshua* as a *cohen* or priest.[142] In an all-night session, *Yeshua* transmitted the *Razim Ha-Malkuth Ha-Shamayyim* or Mysteries of the "Kingdom" of Heaven. As part of this, the heavenly Name was conferred (i.e., *Shimone* became *Cephas*).

Christian initiation after baptism is implied in Paul's exhortation about the Corinthian Pneumatics who claimed the power of divine Sovereignty.[143] The third chapter of John's Gospel reveals more. It is made even more explicit in what Clement of Alexandria says about "those who are being perfected" in his discussion of *Secret Mark.* But as the gentile churches cut off their Jewish kabbalistic roots, the *razim* were lost and water baptism (an admission rite) alone remained.

---

[141] Although this may be pious editorializing to further distance Jesus from John the Baptist.
[142] *Yeshua* and his brother *Iakob* (James the *Tzadik*) were of priestly lineage and had the right to serve as priests and even High Priest in the Temple. A seamless white linen robe was the vestment used by Jewish priests.
[143] I Corinthians 4.8 "Now ye are full, now ye are rich, ye have reigned as kings without us: and I would to God ye did reign, that we also might reign with you."

Logion 4.b is an original *davar*, but independent from *Yeshua's* teachings in Q that the spiritual children in the *Malkuth* are of higher status than the greatest prophets of this age (John the Baptist), or that the poor and beggars of Israel will enter the *Malkuth* before the self-righteous Pharisees.[144] I have paraphrased it into an unequivocally messianic *davar* because the Q logion may reflect not just anti-Temple establishment hyperbole typical of *Yeshua,* but an incipient marginalization of John the Baptist, such as we find later in John's Gospel. However, *Yeshua* could have used this kind of hyperbole to emphasize the greatness of the *Malkuth.*[145]

Logion 5

5.a Know what is in your sight, and the *Razim* will be revealed to you.

5.b There is no *Raz* that will not be brought into the light.

COMMENTARY

Again we find two *davarim* connected by an editor. The common theme is revelation of the *Razim* of Heaven, but the first concerns a way of being taught by God (as *Hochmah*). This is a kabbalistic *davar* reflecting the Jewish wisdom tradition. The second is an apocalyptic *davar* about the coming *Malkuth.*

The term *raz* (or *radz*) does not occur in the Hebrew of the Old Testament, but is first used in the Aramaic of the Book of Daniel. From the 2nd century B.C.E. on, it becomes an important apocalyptic term. Indeed, the Greek word *apokalypsis* "apocalypse, revelation of Divine secrets or mysteries" is a translation of Aramaic *raz.*

The term literally means "coverings" and is used by extension to mean the "clouds of Heaven." Daniel's prophecy was that the future *Messiah* would come "in the Mysteries of Heaven," but the idiom was misunderstood to mean "in the clouds of Heaven." Thus we find the Pauline description of Christ coming in the clouds, and the further Christian misunderstandings leading to doctrines of the Second Coming of Jesus and the Rapture.

---

[144] Luke 7.28b; Matthew 11.11 "I tell you, among those born of women there is no one greater than John; yet the one who is least in the kingdom of God is greater than he."
[145] As in "you must hate your father and your mother" in comparison to your love of God—not an exhortation to hate your parents!

The *razim* consists of prophecies about the coming *Bar-Enash* ("Son of Man," *Messiah*) and the divine sciences of the angels (magic, theurgy, exorcism, alchemy, etc.) which, in Enochian tradition, are taught to humans by the fallen angels of *Shaitan*. *Yeshua* was accused of being in league with *Shaitan* when he performs exorcisms and replied, "How can Satan cast out Satan?" He showed the absurdity of the accusation by remarking that a house[146] that is divided against itself must fall.

The *razim* (or *radzim*) are the Mysteries of God ("Mysteries of the Kingdom of Heaven") that *Yeshua* transmitted initiatically to his closest disciples. Here he reveals that the *razim* can be discovered, for they are encoded into the visible world, and in the coming *Malkuth*, all of the divine sciences will be discovered and understood.

At first reading, this seems to reflect Hermetic thought: As above, so below; study Nature, and she will make an obeisance to you, and reveal all her secrets to you. Can it be an authentic *davar* of *Yeshua?* Does it look more like Gnostic editorializing?

But when we examine other teachings of *Yeshua,* we find him always drawing lessons about divine realities from observable human behavior and natural phenomena—the growth of seeds, the raiment of lilies, the sun shining and rain falling equally upon the just and the unjust. The ways of God are revealed in the myth and allegory of daily life, if only we learn to observe and interpret them.

What is more, the lessons *Yeshua* draws from these phenomena are halakic, that is, moral and spiritual. The Hermetic applications of divine world being reflected in physical nature are astrological and alchemical. They are proto-scientific. But when *Yeshua* reveals that we should "know what is in your sight," he is referring more to a way of *manda* or spiritual knowing than of observing physical phenomena.

Yeshua declared that he taught to his disciples what the *Abba* revealed to him.[147] God as *Abba* would seem to refer to *Merkabah* revelations from the Throne of God. But there was another form of divine instruction—that of *Hochmah,* or God's immanent feminine form, the divine instructress of sages in the wisdom schools. She was known to *Yeshua* as the *Ruach Ha-Qodesh* (the "Holy Spirit"). When he speaks of the Son [probably *Bar-Enash*] doing what he sees the *Abba* doing,[148] the reference must include the *Ruach Ha-Qodesh* as an aspect of the *Abba,* for she was the instructress.

---

[146] I.e., a sovereign princedom; *Yeshua* referred to *Shaitan* as the "Prince of this world."
[147] John 5.19 "The *Bar[-Enash]* can do nothing on his own accord, but only what he sees the Father doing, What the Father does, the *Bar[-Enash]* does likewise."
[148] Ibid.

That is borne out by another saying attributed to *Yeshua* in John's Gospel: "It is written in the prophets, And they shall be all taught of God. Every man therefore that has heard and **learn**ed from the *Abba* comes unto me."[149] Since it is unlikely that all those who sought to be disciples of *Yeshua* had ascended to the Throne of God and been taught by the transcendent *Abba*, it seems clear that instruction from God was considered to have come to those who rigorously sought it by way of His immanent *Shekinah,* the feminine *Ruach Ha-Qodesh* or Wisdom. That is probably the meaning of "know what is in your sight, and the *Razim* will be revealed to you.

Logion 5.b seems to be an independent version of the Marcan *davar,* "There is nothing [sinful] hidden that will not be made known, and no *razim* that will not be revealed."[150] It appears quite differently in Mark and Luke, which may indicate a third independent version. This is a good indicator of authenticity.

In *Thomas,* the independent logion declares that every *raz*[151] will be "brought into the light." The Greek word reconstructed by scholars in the Oxyrhynchus papyrus fragment is from *egeirein* and translated " will be aroused from sleep." But the lacuna is so large that all clues to the Greek word are missing, and I fail to see how the Coptic of *Thomas* could indicate that verb. In fact, the Coptic ⲉϥⲛⲁⲟⲩⲱⲛ︤ϩ ⲉⲃⲟⲗ points to the Greek equivalent *phainein,* which would translate an original Aramaic expression from Hebrew *aur,* "light." Assuming the logion does represent an independent Aramaic *davar,* the translation must read, "be brought into the light." This is consistent with the metaphorical language used by *Yeshua* and perpetuated in Johannine Greek.[152]

For a *raz* to be brought into the light[153] is a semitic idiom meaning that a science or body of knowledge previously unknown to humanity will be discovered. It might be read in the context of Daniel 12.4, a passage that *Yeshua* would have known well, where the angel of revelation tells the prophet to seal up the scroll until the end times, for as time passes "many will go forth to increase knowledge."

Yeshua. had a great respect for what we know today as science.

---

[149] John 6.45
[150] Mark 4.22 paralleled Luke 8.17
[151] The heavenly *raz* is not a "secret" or something that has been hidden, but a science or body of knowledge not yet understood or manifest on Earth.
[152] I.e., *Yeshua* uses "light" as a metaphor for good works ["let your light shine before men"] and knowledge ["see to it that the light within you is not darkness"].
[153] Not to be confused with Divine Light, or the *Ain Soph Aur.*

6.a His disciples questioned him and asked,[154] Do you want us to fast? and how should we pray,? and should we give alms? and what diet should we observe? Jesus answered, Do not fabricate a lie, and do not do what you hate others doing. For all deeds are manifest before the Face of God.[155]

6.b [Redactional Comment] For (just as) there is no *Raz* that shall not be brought into the light, (so) there is nothing hidden that shall remain without being revealed.

COMMENTARY

Either logia 5 and 6 were originally dictated in sequence because of the "nothing hidden that shall not be revealed" mnemonic device, or the Gnostic redactor has added the comment. There is nothing in Logion 6.b to identify as Gnostic—it is, in fact, a well-known authentic *davar* of *Yeshua*. But this appears to be redactional, not original to the *davar*.

It is common editorial technique to append a saying like this as an interpretation of the previous logion. This is done throughout the Gospels of Matthew and Luke in their redaction of the Q material, all too often twisting the original meaning to fit their own bias. Prime examples are *Yeshua's* prophecies against the Jerusalem Temple establishment, which are twisted into wholesale anti-Jewish propaganda that have provided fodder for Christian anti-Semitism throughout the ages.[156]

Here the *davar* "there is no *raz* that shall not be brought into the light" is incorrectly cited to amplify "all [evil] deeds are manifest before the Face of God." In fact, the *davar* that would properly amplify the meaning would be "there is no evil deed hidden that shall not be made known." This is referenced in the second half, but the first part would not have been mnemonically connected in a original dictation. So I have not rendered the translation

---

[154] The idiom "questioned and asked" along with the sequential connective *vavs* (וֹ...וֹ...וֹ) indicate original Aramaic structure.
[155] Literally **"Heaven," which is a semitic reference to Godhead.**

[156] Also to emphasize early Christian doctrine, such as the priestly sacrifice of Christ, as in Matthew 20.28b. Here the authentic *davar* is first given: "Whoever would be chief among you, let him be your servant, even as the *Bar-Enash* comes not to be ministered unto, but to minister." Then the Matthean doctrinal interpretation is added: "and to give his life a ransom for many." The term "ransom" is Pauline language comparing the execution of *Yeshua* to an expiatory Temple blood sacrifice to appease an angry god. It has nothing to do with the teachings of *Yeshua*.

6.b in boldface type, even though it is a conflation of two original *davarim,* because it does not appear to have been part of the original dictation.

The answer to "do you want us to fast" is that of the messianic prophets—a true fast is not to cover your body in sackcloth and ashes, but to fast from sin. In this case, *Yeshua* answers, "Do not fabricate a lie." He taught that his disciples should be single-souled (meaning to act only on the impulses of the *yetzer-ha-tov*) and without guile or double intentions. The goal, expressed in Aramaic idiomatic language, was to make oneself single-minded, single-hearted, single-intentioned; to look not to the right or left, but proceed straight ahead; to make the eye single; let your yes mean yes, and your no mean no. That was the true fast from sin.

What diet to "observe" (rabbinic term for keeping a religious obligation)? *Yeshua* did not prescribe a diet. He and his *talmidim* ate whatever they were served on their travels from village to village, notwithstanding later ascetic fabrications like the so-called *Essene Gospel.* Early Christian travelling "prophets" followed the same rule.

As for the rest of the questions, which are addressed in later logia, his answer was a variation on Hillel's famous adage, "Do not do unto others as you would not have them do unto you." He said, "Don't do what you hate to see others doing." He knew that it is much easier for us to identify evil behavior in others than in ourselves,[157] so he told them to use their dislike of sinful behavior in others as a standard to measure their own behavior.

Logion 7

Happy is the lion whom the man eats, for the lion will become man; but utterly destroyed is the man whom the lion eats, for the lion will become man.

COMMENTARY

This logion has never been properly understood. It has nothing to do with man-eating lions, but with controlling the violent impulses of the *yetzer ha-ra.*

Yeshua characteristically employed paradox and hyperbole. Here he uses the metaphor of eating and being eaten—a motif we will see in other inner-circle teachings found in *Thomas.* He also employs a paradox using the phrase "the lion will become man" in two opposing ways.

---

[157] Matthew 73 and parallels "Why do you see the speck that is in your brother's **eye,** but do not notice the log that is in your own **eye**?" See *Thomas* Logion 26.

Shaitan is often described in idiomatic Aramaic apocalyptic as a "raging lion" on a rampage through city streets when great evil is unleashed, such as Roman troops pillaging a Jewish town. In this metaphor, the "lion" is the force of rage and anger that arises from the *Yetzer Ha-Ra* in one's heart.

It was said of one of the Egyptian desert saints that "he never allowed anger to rise up beyond the throat;" he swallowed it and sanctified himself. By the same token, if the provoked man "eats" the lion by refusing to empower his rising anger with evil words or deeds ("beyond the throat"), then his lower animal nature is tamed, transformed, and sanctified into that of the Perfect Man (New Adam, *Bar-Enash*). The lion becomes man.

But if he is consumed and ruled by his lower nature such that the lion rages uncontrolled, he can eventually lose his human soul. It is one thing to recognize anger rising, but quite another to allow it to be expressed in violent words and actions. The lion becomes man, and the man is consumed.

This is not advice to suppress anger such that eventually it is not felt or recognized, yet continues to wreak psychological havoc. The inner *halakah* of spiritual transformation requires that anger and all other negative impulses arising from the *yetzer ha-ra* be recognized and acknowledged. Rather, it advises that once the destructive impulses arise, they must be sublimated and transformed. That is what the metaphor of "eating" means.

How is this done? First by holding the impulses in check while they can be analyzed. Simply looking at them is transformative.[158] Self-examination was the *sine qua non* of *Yeshua's* halakic advice to his disciples.

Logion 7 represents insight into *Yeshua's* transmission of practices for interior purification of the heart and soul. Compare the practice of "eating" the lion to that of "shadowboxing" found in Logion 98. His *halakah* was not merely a collection of ideas. It was rooted in practice. This *davar* was given to his disciples as one of many spiritual practices that must be accomplished not in desert caves, but in the trials of daily living.

Yet the spiritual practices taught by *Yeshua* did survive in deserts and caves. *Yeshua* emphasized *halakah* in daily living, but he also retreated into the wilderness for private devotions and practices. This Logion reflects the interior spirituality that he and his disciples practiced, which was perpetuated by Christian Egyptian Desert Fathers and

---

[158] Krishnamurti advised people to contemplate their day before sleeping—to examine their good and bad behaviors. Then instead of castigating themselves with guilt or taking up extraordinary ascetic remedies for their failures, they were advised to simply go to sleep. Their behavior would change over time just through the process of self-examination. This is similar to the wisdom found in the Golden Verse of Pythagorus quoted in Chapter One. But to that *Yeshua* added a further suggestion. Do self-examination in the very midst of action! The only remedy required was to take a breath and stop long enough to look at it. That itself would begin the transformative process of spiritual digestion ("eating").

Mothers. Like Buddhist monks, they developed early monastic techniques of sanctification in wilderness retreat, creating special practices to focus the mind, such as weaving reed mats and then unweaving them to develop non-attachment.—another initiatic teaching of *Yeshua* we will examine later on. It is through their traditions preserved in the *Philokalia* that we are able to understand *davarim* like Logion 7.

Logion 8 [An Authentic *Mashal*]

The *Bar-Enash* is like a wise[159] fisherman who cast his net into the sea and pulled it up full of small fish. Among them he found one good, large fish. That wise fisherman threw all the small fish back down into the sea without regret, but chose to keep the large fish. Whoever can understand my *mashal*,[160] let him apply it to his own life.

COMMENTARY

Bar-Enash: "The Man"

A depiction of Primal Adam
Kadmon *(Qadmon)*

Here Coptic ⲡⲣⲱⲙⲉ translates Greek *Ho Anthopos* (The Ανθρωπος) for Aramaic *Ha-Enash*. When the word "man" is used with the definite article, as here, it means mankind, humanity. The Aramaic *Ha-Enash* translates Hebrew *Ha-Adam,* meaning archetypal androgynous humanity, just as *Ho Anthropos* meant in Hermetic philosophy.

In early kabbalistic thought *Ha-Enash* was known as *Adam Kadmon[161],* the Primal Mankind who was a microcosm of all the worlds *('olamim),* and was later divided into man and woman. It paralleled the Hermetic myth of *Ho Anthropos,* who was the "Son of God."[162] In the *Poimandes* he/she bent down through the planetary spheres, became fascinated with his/her reflection in physical nature, and was trapped into

---

159 Coptic "man of good heart."
160 Aramaic term for a parable or allegorical story.
161 From Hebrew *qadam (kadam)* meaning "before."
162 Plato's term for the macrocosm.

incarnation.[163] He/she was divided into two sexes along with all other animal life in the universe. Then the planetary spheres were set into motion and time (growth and change) appeared.

The rabbinic or wisdom school understanding of *Ha-Adam* in the Book of Genesis current with *Yeshua* was influenced by Pythagorean and Hermetic concepts of Primal Humanity, just as the 1st-2nd century kabbalistic *Sepher Yetzirah* grew out of contacts between the Jewish wisdom schools and Pythagorean communities.[164]

In messianic Judaism, the *Bar-Enash* was the new Adam or humanity who would redeem and replace the old fallen Adam.[165] We find the Aramaic term *Bar-Enash* translated in the New Testament as "Son of Man." The *Bar-Enash* (Aramaic form of Hebrew *Ben*-Adam) was the cosmic *Messiah* that first appeared in prophecies recorded by the Babylonian school of Daniel. In order to grasp the initiatic teachings of *Yeshua*, we must understand his proclamation of *Messiah* as "Son of Man" or *Bar-Enash,* rather than the popular *Messiah Ben-David* or *Messiah Ben-Joseph.* Here I offer a brief explanation.

It was in the Jewish community of Babylon that the second and third additions to the Scroll of Isaiah were made (Deutero- and Trito-Isaiah), with their revelations concerning the messianic Age. This implies the existence of a school of Isaiah or priestly lineage that preserved and added to his prophecies. Indeed, Deutero- and Trito-Isaiah form the main bulk of what we know today as the Book of Isaiah. The same process developed with the disciples of Daniel. This legendary prophet lived in sixth-century Babylon and was able to protect and preserve the Jewish diaspora community by serving as royal seer and

---

[163] Parallel to the myth of Narcissus, who saw her own reflection in a pool of water and fell in love with it. The "sin" of the *Anthropos* that resulted in incarnation was self-love and *eros,* Empedocles' cause for growth and change in the universe, depicted as the primordial *logos* of Hesiod's Theogony.

[164] All mystical traditions in the history and phenomenology of religions are eclectic and syncretistic, thus theosophical, including Hellenistic Jewish mysticism which adapted to itself the best of other mystic traditions in its contacts with other religions in the Diaspora. Prime examples are the first chapter of Genesis, which was adapted from the ancient Babylonian *Enuma Elish,* and the legend of Moses hidden in a reed basket floating on a river and being rescued by the royal family, which is told millennia earlier of King Sargon. The great Jewish scholar Gershom Scholem recognized long ago that the letter-number mysticism of *Sepher Yetzirah* developed from Pythagorean numerology. Most scholars today recognize that Hellenistic Jewish thought, like Christianity, was deeply influenced by Chaldaean cosmology and cosmogenesis (e.g. Book of Genesis), Platonism (e.g Philo), and all important spiritual and intellectual streams that were syncretized in the Roman-Hellenistic world. Plato, as an initiate of the Pythagorean schools, also explored proto-Hermetic cosmogenesis in his *Timaeus*—an Egyptian Priest of Hieropolis (i.e., a Hermetic initiate) who tells basically the same cosmological myths as found in the Hermetic *Kore Kosmou,* the *Virgin of the World.* All these views were cross-culturally shared, known to Jewish *kabbalistic,* and amplified their own *kabbalistic haggadah.*

[165] Paul refers to them as the First Adam and the Second Adam. In the *Gospel of Mary* and other important early Christian texts, the new Adam is called the Perfect Man (from Aramaic *Enash,* Hebrew *Adam*) which is "put on" like a garment as a template for the thought and actions of a saint. Paul says, "have the *Nous* (Higher Intellect, Mind) of Christ."

interpreter of the King's dreams, just as Joseph is said to have functioned for Pharaoh a thousand years before.[166]

But the Book of Daniel, original of the Son-of-Man *Messiah*, was composed in Aramaic, not Hebrew like Isaiah. It is the only book of the Old Testament written in Aramaic, which was a late form of Hebrew spoken by Jews in the last two centuries before *Yeshua*. Scholars usually date Daniel to the second century before the Christian era. The Jewish sages at the Council of Jamnia considered it to have been the last revelation given before the Spirit of Prophecy left Israel. But like Deutero- and Trito-Isaiah, the Book of Daniel was not written by the prophet. It is pseudepigraphic, like the later messianic apocalypses of Enoch, which were also written in Babylon in Aramaic, but not accepted into the Old Testament canon because they were later than Daniel and relied upon heavily by messianic Jews and Christians.

In Daniel's visions, the Earth is ruled by "beasts" with many horns (i.e. nation-states whose kings and their princes) operated under Satanic forces. These were Hellenistic patriarchal dynasties built on blood, slavery, and conquest. The prophet sees visions about the future rise and fall of the Greeks, Medes, Persians, Romans, and other "beasts" motivated by evil. But he also sees God anointing[167] "one like unto a son of man" who will sit Sovereign at His right hand of power to bring divine justice to Earth and free humanity from bondage to Satanic powers. In subsequent kabbalistic interpretation, "one like unto a son of man" became the divine figure of the Son of Mankind *Messiah*, meaning the New Adam or spiritually perfected heavenly archetype of a new humanity—Paul's Second Adam.

Recent discoveries at Qumran ("Dead Sea Scrolls") have given us one of the most important scriptures sacred to *Yeshua* and the messianic Jews. It is an Aramaic scroll of the ascent of Enoch to the Throne of God and his vision of the *Bar-Enash Messiah* from the late second century. I reproduce a translation of the *Sefer Razim Hanokh* below.

> And there I saw One who had a head of days, and His head was white like wool, And with Him was another being whose countenance had the appearance of a man, And his face was full of graciousness, like one of the holy angels.
>
> And I asked the angel who went with me and showed me all the hidden things, concerning that "Son of Man" [*Bar-Enash*, meaning literally "Son, Scion, Future Heir of Mankind, Humanity, Future or Coming Humanity, New Humanity"], who he was, and whence he was, and why he sat with the Head of Days? And he answered and said unto me: This is the Coming Mankind *(Bar-Enash)* who hath righteousness, with whom dwelleth righteousness,

---

[166] It was during the Babylonian Captivity that the legends of Joseph and the Egyptian Captivity first emerged, the Genesis creation story was developed as the Jewish answer to the Babylonian Creation Epic, and that messianic ideas of universal liberation first appeared—as opposed to simple political aspirations for a Jewish king.

[167] I.e., enthroning. The Greek Christ is a translation from Aramaic *Messiah*, which means Anointed One.

and who revealeth all the treasures of that which is hidden *(razim)*, because the Lord of Spirits [messianic designation for God] hath chosen him, and whose lot hath the pre-eminence before the Lord of Spirits in uprightness for an *aeon* of *aeons...*

And this New Humanity *(Bar-Enash)* whom thou hast seen shall overturn the kings and the mighty from their seats, and the strong from their thrones, and shall loosen the reins of the strong, and break the teeth of the evil ones. ..

"Because they do not extol and praise the Ancient of Days, nor humbly acknowledge whence the kingdom was bestowed upon them. All their deeds manifest unrighteousness, and their power rests upon their riches, and their fidelity is to the gods which they have made with their own hands, and they deny the Way of the Lord of Spirits, and they persecute the houses of His congregations, and those who keep faith with the Way of the Lord of Spirits.[168]

The *Bar-Enash* was said to pre-exist the creation of the heavens:

From the beginning the Son of Man *(Bar-Enash)* was hidden,
And the Most High has preserved him in the presence of His might,
And revealed him to the elect."
   - 1 Enoch 48:3-5, 62:7

This is probably the source of the early Christian interpretation of Christ and the Elect pre-existing from the beginning.[169]

In the New Testament Gospels, the messianic title "Son of Man" was always made to refer to the individual man *Yeshua.* That is because post-Pauline churches identified *Yeshua* as the conventional *Messiah Ban-David/Ben-Joseph,* and thus as the incarnate Christ or *Messiah.*

But this was a misunderstanding of the *Bar-Enash* proclaimed by *Yeshua,* which was a corporate, androgynous, and heavenly archetype of the pre-existent and future new humanity. While *Yeshua* clearly identified himself as a member of the corporate *Bar-Enash,* he regarded himself as essentially the first-born of this new spiritual generation. He must have regarded Simon Peter *(Shimone Cephas)* as another member, since he gave him the initiatic name *Kephas.* He named James and John, the sons of Zebedee, "Sons of Thunder," which in Greek was *Boanerges.[170]* They too were members of the Body of *Bar-Enash.[171]* It is

---

[168] Book of Enoch, Book of Parables XLVIII

[169] "For He [Christ] was **foreknown** before the foundation of the world, but has appeared in these last times for the sake of you." 1 Peter 1:20 ; "...even as he chose us in him before the foundation of the world..." Ephesians 1.4

[170] A Syrian (Aramaic) translation shows *Bnay Ra`mâ* for Greek *boan* (Aramaic *bene-* "sons of") and *erges* (Aramaic *rama* "thunder"). The older James was martyred but John, youngest of the disciples, eventually travelled to Asia Minor with Mary *Magdala* and Mary the Mother of *Yeshua* to found the churches of Ephesus and many others.

not unlikely that Mary *Magdala*'s initiatic name was *Magdala*.[172] She was also a member of the Body of *Messiah*.

In other words, Christ is not any one individual, but the heavenly archetype of a second, regenerated, or new Adam. *Yeshua's* disciples aspired to become worthy of the *Qimah*, in which they would exist as saints partaking in the Divine Sovereignty of the *Bar-Enash*. They each aspired to become Christ-like as was *Yeshua*, so to speak. The monastic ideal of the *Imitatio Christi* has ancient roots. *Yeshua* encouraged his disciples to imitate God and "be the children of your *Abba* which is in heaven: for he maketh his sun to rise on the evil and on the good, and sendeth rain on the just and on the unjust."[173]

As in *Yeshua's* better-known parables, Logion 8 draws from familiar human activities to illuminate divine realities. "The Man" is the *Bar-Enash*, who is compared by *Yeshua* to a shoreline fisherman in the Sea of Galilee. He wades out among the reeds and casts his net, then pulls it back in. Net fishermen sorting through their catch and throwing back undersized and trash fish were a common sight along the inland seashore in *Yeshua's* day.

This parable describes the *Bar-Enash* choosing among human souls (fish) after death. The process of divine selection is also what Paul called "election." [174]

---

[171] Probably derivation of the Pauline concept of the Church as Body of Christ (*Messiah*) with many members (saints).

[172] We are not told Mary *Magdala*'s initiatic name, unless it was indeed Aramaic מגדלא *Magdala* from Hebrew מגדל *Migdal*, meaning "Tower." Scholars have always assumed that the name *Miriam Magdala* means "Mary from Magdala, a small fishing town in the Galilee. But the phrase appears in the same grammatical structure as *Shimone Cephas*, Simon Peter (birth name + initiatic rebirth name). It doesn't translate from Aramaic as Mary of Magdala, but Mary Magdala—like Simon Peter. That may have been her initiatic name— Mary the Tower of Strength, parallel to Simon the Strong Rock. We know that she was an Apostle because she travelled extensively proclaiming the *Basor* after *Yeshua's* martyrdom and was revered as the greatest of *Yeshua's* woman disciples. But she was systematically marginalized in the New Testament writings after Paul and by later generations of male church leadership, who finally excluded women from their primary positions of leadership in the post-resurrection communities and, in the fourth century, identified her as a repentant prostitute. This provided a symbol of church redemption that endured through the ages, but is historically false and, in my view, one of the lynchpins of Christian antifeminism and sexual guilt.

[173] Matthew 5.45

[174] Εκλεγειν, "to choose, pick out." Saints (early church members) were called "elect" or chosen. This had both a sense of being chosen by merit, and having the merit of making the choice oneself. In Greek the concept is also associated with voting in an election using black and white stones. In Aramaic the association is with Hebrew *bahar, bary* as in the chosen people of God.

Yeshua is said in the New Testament Gospels to have selected and called forth his disciples—quite unlike rabbis, who were petitioned by potential disciples to be accepted. By the same token, the New Adam, who shares God's Divine Sovereignty in Heaven, judges[175] and selects[176] human souls as they arise after death from the sea of existence in mortal flesh. Most of them He returns to the sea "with no regrets" (allows to them reincarnate)[177] so that they may have another chance to mature into "good large fish," *tzadikim,* or great souls. But when the *neshamah* of a saint ascends into the Son of Mankind's presence after death, He chooses, accepts, and makes it a part of His Body. How? By "eating" or absorbing the perfected soul. Thus the *tzadikim* achieve *Qimah* and merge with the body of the perfected and sovereign New Humanity.[178]

Logion 9 [Authentic *Mashal* Altered to Reflect Gnostic Views]

> Behold, The Sower went forth, filled his hand, and scattered seeds. Some fell on the road, but the birds came and ate them. Some fell on stone, could not strike root into the earth, and did not produce ears of grain. And a few fell on thorns. They choked the seedlings and the worms ate them. But some of the seeds fell onto good soil, and it brought forth good fruit. It bore from sixty to one hundred per measure.

COMMENTARY

This is a Gnostic retelling of the Marcan Parable of the Sower, where "a sower" is comparable to *Yeshua* or one of his *tzadikim* proclaiming the *Basor.* That is how it is explained in the Gospels. In the New Testament, the intent is to sow the seeds into good soil, and the vast majority of them fall on good soil and grow. That is indicated by the Greek sequence *allos...allos...alloi,* "a few...a few...many."

---

[175] As the "Son of Man" does in the Parable of the Sheep and the Goats.

[176] Cf. Logion 23, where the redactor identifies *Yeshua* as the incarnate Gnostic Redeemer calling the "elect" ones.

[177] Reincarnation was one of two Jewish *kabbalistic* views about the issue of reincarnation current at the time of *Yeshua* .Individual reincarnation such as we find here was the view that became standard in later *kabbalistic* communities, but there was also a view that parents lived on in Israel through their offspring. For more, see John 9.1ff. concerning the man born blind. *Yeshua* is asked whether the man was born blind because of his own sins (in a previous incarnation) or because of his parent's sins (in a previous generation).

[178] A shared "eating" motif is probably the mnemonic thread that sequences Logion 8 after Logion 7.

The Coptic of *Thomas* preserves the idiomatic Aramaic *vav* sequence through ⲘⲈⲚ…ⲀⲨⲰ…ⲀⲨⲰ…ⲀⲨⲰ, and introduces the variation, "and the worms ate them." This points to a probable underlying independent Aramaic version of the Parable of the Sower.

In *Thomas,* however, it is "The Sower," implying perhaps Godhead casting souls into incarnation. *Yeshua's* original parable was optimistic, but the retelling in *Thomas* is pessimistic. The Sower of Thomas doesn't seem to scatter carefully, as the real sower of *Yeshua's* original parable would. The Coptic does not preserve Greek "a few…a few…but most others." Rather, it is only "a few others" who fall into good soil and grow—not very optimistic about humanity.

The *Thomas* Gnostics seem to have originated as a small group of proto-monastic Syrian male ascetics who believed that only a very few would achieve spiritual perfection— namely them. All others would fall short and continue to reincarnate. When we examine *davarim* of *Yeshua* such as "many are called, but few are chosen," this point of view has a certain justification, especially in the context of initiatic teachings like Logion 8. However, we have not only reliable examples of the original Parable of the Sower, but the entire deposit of *Yeshua's* teaching, that emphasize his optimism about humanity. The version in *Thomas* appears to have been redacted to promote a Gnostic view of redemption.

In the authentic *mashal,* "seeds" are the messianic proclamation, *halakah,* and divine energies for rebirth in the *Malkuth* received in hearing the *Basor.* The Sower scatters seed purposefully, not indiscriminately. As little seed as possible is wasted. *Yeshua* cautioned his Apostles not to cast their pearls to "swine," i.e. to preach to people unready or unwilling to understand, "lest they turn and rend you." Nor should they give the "children's food" or "holy things" to "dogs." He told them to go into a village, stay in a friendly home, and let people come to them—not to stand out in a public marketplace and evangelize whoever would listen.

Meaning for a disciple or Apostle: Do your best to proclaim the *Basor,* but be prepared to find that not all your efforts will be fruitful. Every person will receive the Divine Message differently, and even those who accept and become faithful to the *Basor* will manifest different results. Sow the spiritual seeds, but do not be attached to results.

Logion 10
I have cast a sacred flame onto the world and behold, I am tending it until the whole world is ablaze.

COMMENTARY

This saying does not appear in the New Testament, but seems to be authentic.

Aramaic *esh,* usually rendered with Greek *pur,* is elemental fire. When used in Hebrew and Aramaic to mean sacred fire as here, it refers to fire caused by lightning (fire from Heaven), which was used to ignite temple flames.[179]

The Greek word *kosmos* means the external or visible universe. However, it translates an Aramaic word spoken by *Yeshua.* There are two possibilities. One may have been *eretz,* which refers to the visible land or earth that is separated by an invisible foundation or "firmament" from the day and night heavens.[180] The other possibility is *'olam,* which has a meaning somewhat comparable to Greek *kosmos* and in kabbalistic theory would have been the World of *Asiah.*

However, since he "casts" fire onto the earth, and the image of sacred fire is that of lightning coming down from the heavens, I prefer the Aramaic *eretz.* As opposed to the Greek image of Prometheus giving mankind the gift of fire (meaning divine intellect or *nous*), *Yeshua* has called down upon the earth an agent of sanctification and transformation—an image that seems to be neither Greek nor Gnostic, but uniquely Hebrew. He nurtures the sacred flame until the entire world of mankind is ablaze with it.

The tending of the flame is a priestly form of spiritual protection for an entire community. *Yeshua* regarded himself as the protector of his disciples, praying that Heaven would not allow *Shaitan* to "sift" Simon Peter like wheat being separated from chaff.[181]

Are the elements of cosmic transformation in Logion 10 authentic initiatic teachings, or are they post-Pauline? At first glance a scholar would regard the "world" ablaze to be a later universalisation of Christianity indebted to Paul's theology of the redemption of mankind.

But this cannot be Gnostic. Already in John's Gospel, *Yeshua* is represented as "not praying for the world, but for those whom thou hast given me, for they are thine."[182] The *kosmos* and all fleshly people are excluded in Johannine theology, and even much moreso in the

---

[179] In the same way, only elemental water from the Heavens (rain, snow, or transported in underground streams and accessed through springs) was "living water" that could be used for *mikveh* or ritual purification ("baptism").

[180] cf. Gen. 1.1

[181] Luke 22.31, "sift" meaning to cause Peter to fail under the burden of his own spiritual shortcomings. The prayer for his disciples in John 17.6ff. is redactional, but it reflects *Yeshua's* reputation for protecting his disciples.

[182] John 17.9

Gnostic thought of *Thomas,* where "one out of a thousand and two out of ten thousand" are chosen.[183] By the second century, many churches of persecuted Christianity had developed very exclusive ideas of election and redemption.

The biblical quotations used to support modern evangelism, such as the longer ending added to Mark at 16.15, "Go ye into all the world, and preach the gospel to every creature,"[184] are clearly late and not original with *Yeshua.* However, they are rooted in his public proclamation of the *Basor* in the villages of the Galilee and Palestine, and in his sending out of disciples in pairs to spread the proclamation—not in the market place, but at private homes where they were hosted.

It is not unreasonable to assume that *Yeshua* foresaw his Apostles extending proclamation and teachings of the *Basor* into villages and synagogues of the Diaspora of Asia Minor, Egypt, and the rest of the Roman Empire. In fact, after his execution, that is exactly what they did.[185] If so, the sacred flame would grow into a "world ablaze." The prophetic vision of the Temple of God becoming a "house of prayer for all the gentiles" found in Trito-Isaiah[186] would be fulfilled.

In my opinion the logion represents an authentic inner-circle teaching of *Yeshua.* The implications of this *davar* seem to be as follows:
- The sacred fire represents the *Basor* and all of its halakic elements;
- *Yeshua* considered the *Basor* to have priestly dimensions.
- *Yeshua* regarded the *Basor* as serving all humanity, not just Israel, even though his prophetic mission was specifically directed to Israel;
- *Yeshua's* disciples would extend his mission into the wider world through the synagogues of the Diaspora;
- *Yeshua* intended to guide his disciples even after death as an arisen saint of the *Qimah.*[187]

Logion 11 [Kabbalistic Paradoxes]

This heaven and the one above it shall pass away. The spiritually dead are not alive, and the spiritually alive shall

---

[183] *Thomas* Logion #23
[184] Added a generation after Mark's composition in harmony with Matthew ending at 28.19-20:
[185] Luke-Acts is focused on the history of gentile Christianity, so focuses unduly on Paul and his missionary journeys. But the journeys of the original Apostles were to Jewish communities of the Diaspora outside of Palestine and the Galilee, which indicates that they were carrying out the vision of *Yeshua* for a "world ablaze."
[186] Isaiah 56.7
[187] cf. Matthew 28.20. "Lo, I am with you always;" also a saying of Hermes Trismegistos.

not die. In the days when you ate dead things, you made them alive. But when you enter into the Eternal Light, what will you do? On the day when you were one, you became two. But now that you are two, what will you do?

COMMENTARY

We find nothing like these sayings in any other literature claiming to present the teachings of *Yeshua,* whether canonical or Gnostic. They contain no identifiable Gnostic terminology other than the eating and duality references found only in other *logia* of *Thomas.* We have already identified the eating reference in Logion 7 (the Lion), as well as the implied eating reference in Logion 8 (the Fisherman), as authentic because of Aramaisms and other Jewish messianic content embedded in them. Is there any reason we shouldn't identify these paradoxical statements as authentic?

I ask a rhetorical question. The answer is implied by the question. This was semitic linguistic usage at the time of *Yeshua,* and it is still employed in rabbinic discourse today. Here we are twice asked "what will you do?" The answer lies in the initiatic teaching we will explore later in this commentary.

We have also seen earlier that *Yeshua* liked to employ paradox. Here we have "the dead are not alive, and the living shall not die," which I have paraphrased in my translation for clarity. Finally it is noteworthy that the concept of tiered heavens was basic to Jewish *Merkabah* cosmology, and here "this heaven and the one above it" point to a similar cosmology.

The answer to my rhetorical question is, "No." We have no reason to identify these five clustered sayings as Gnostic or otherwise inauthentic. But we do have good reason to identify them as linguistically rabbinic and Aramaic in expression, and they do employ the kind of paradox *Yeshua* used. Therefore I consider the sayings to be authentic.

They also show one more indication of authenticity. They are strung together not because of meaning, but simply because they are a series rhetorical one-liner questions and paradoxes. Each one reminds the Aramaic speaker of the next one because of form—not content. In other words, they are clustered together because they were remembered in sequence. The only thing that brings them together in sequence is the mnemonic process of dictation to a scribe.

Let us examine the elements of what seem to have originally been five separate *davarim* of *Yeshua*. First, the declaration that even the heavens are not imperishable.

In both his public and initiatic teachings, *Yeshua* emphasized what in Buddhist terminology are known as impermanence and non-attachment. Perhaps his most succinct *davar* about the latter concept is found in *Thomas* Logion 42, "Become passers-by." However the canonical Gospels also contain many teachings about non-attachment to worldly things and the impermanent of earthly treasure.

These teachings were misunderstood as endorsements of strict asceticism and, in fact, fueled the encratitic Christian and Gnostic movements that arose in the second century. But *Yeshua* was not an ascetic. He was accused of being a libertine because he did not require his disciples to wear hair shirts and fast, like those of John the Baptist, and because he associated and ate with "publicans and sinners."

A first-century Christian writer made an important distinction in the later Pseudo-Pauline epistle when he declared that it is not riches, but lust for tainted riches ("filthy lucre"), that is the root of all evil.[188]

Later Clement of Alexandria wrote his essay on "The Rich Man's Salvation" to counter the ascetic misapplication of the canonical story in which a wealthy young man seeking the *Malkuth* asks *Yeshua* what he must do. The Master advises him to keep all the Commandments, which he has done. The Marcan writer observes that *Yeshua* "loved him," that is, recognized great spiritual talent in the young man, and invited him to become a disciple, "but first, sell all that you own and give the proceeds to the poor." The young man was dismayed and left. *Yeshua* commented, "How difficult it is for a rich person to enter the *Malkuth*...yet with God, all things are possible."[189]

Yeshua taught non-attachment to worldly wealth. "You cannot serve both God and Mammon (the Babylonian deity of wealth)." But he did not teach that wealth was evil, nor that disciples should abandon wives, families, and parents to follow him. Instead, he taught what true wealth really is, and to maintain love and loyalty to God and one's spiritual family as a first priority.

"This heaven" (see chart on page 34) refers kabbalistically to the visible blue sky of the Day Heaven. "The one above it"[190] refers to the abode of the rebellious angels and rulers of

---

[188] I Timothy 6.10. "For the love of money is a root of all kinds of evil. Some people, eager for money, have wandered from the faith and pierced themselves with many griefs." New International Version translation.
[189] Mark 10.17ff. and parallels
[190] ⲧⲉⲉⲓⲡⲉ … ⲁⲩⲱ ⲧⲉⲧⲛ̄ⲧⲡⲉ ⲙ̄ⲙⲟⲥ Coptic "This sky...and the one beyond it."

certain stars—in other words, the Night Heaven. It is positioned directly below the Third Heaven, which contains the *Pardes* or Paradise as well as Purgatory—the place of temporary purification in Jewish thought compared by *Yeshua* to the burning garbage heap in the *Genom* valley outside of Jerusalem known as *Gehenna* or *Gehenom*.[191]

Why does impermanence stop with the Second Heaven in this *davar?* Because the Third and higher heavens are part of the eternal *'Olam* of God, also referenced in a following statement about the "Eternal Light." Thus what we can see with our eyes, and the invisible dark forces that obsess, possess, or otherwise enslave incarnate souls and humanity in particular, which constitute the traditional Hebrew Day and Night Heavens (the *Shamayim*), is impermanent.[192] Today we would describe that as the Earth, solar system, galaxy, and all we can see of the universe beyond, as well as invisible satanic forces. In other worlds, the entire physical, material universe is ultimately impermanent and will dissolve—an idea that agrees not only with modern science, but the science of the ancient Greeks.

In the teachings of *Yeshua,* the Aramaic word "life" with a definite article ("the Life") means the spiritual life of God, Heaven, and the awakened soul. His paradox that "the dead are not alive, but the living will never die," is reminiscent of the paradox of the Lion Logion 7. The first part is a statement anyone will agree with, but the second reveals the meaning. Here the "dead" refers to those who are spiritually unawakened, and the "living" to those who have become spiritually alive.

Yeshua said, "Let the dead bury their dead; but you, come. Follow my *halakah.*"[193] People who live in the exterior dreams and material illusions of incarnate life—which is most people—are spiritually unawakened. *Yeshua* taught his hearers not to be like those who obsess over food, clothing, and material treasure.[194] This *davar* of Logion 11 addresses the same issue as an initiatic paradox. Biological existence is not the Eternal Life of the *Malkuth*, but the souls of those who make themselves spiritually alive cannot be extinguished by physical death.

This is followed by another eating metaphor. "In the days when you ate dead things, you made them alive. But when you enter into the Eternal Light, what will you do?"

---

[191] Later Christian theology conflated this with the Orphic concept of Hades or Hell and confused *Yeshua's* description of the temporary purgatorial *'olam* or state with the Greek idea of eternity—"eternal damnation." Catholic theology retained *Yeshua's* kabbalistic version of Purgatory as the first step to Heaven, where time of "punishment" (not purification) can be shortened through church donations and other prescribed acts.
[192] ⲚⲀⲠⲠⲀⲢⲈ Future tense of Greek loan word from *paragein* indicates original Aramaic word *abar,* "to pass out of existence."
[193] Luke 9.59ff.
[194] Q material Matthew 6.25ff. and Luke 12.22ff.

This reflects the Hellenistic physiological view that by eating killed animal flesh and harvested plant fruits, they are made part of one's living self. The spirits of the plants and animals live on as part of the body of the eater. Thus eating the flesh, especially the hearts, of ferocious animals enhanced the spirit of courage in the eater. Consuming only plants established a spirit of serenity and passivity.

"But when you enter into the Eternal Light" refers back to Logion 8, where the Fisherman as a metaphor for the *Bar-Enash* eats or absorbs a big fish or great soul after death. That soul then becomes part of corporate messianic reality. The rabbinic device of throwing the question back to the student ("When you enter...what will you do?") is an idiomatical way of implying that what follows in this process, also allegorized as the Marriage of *Messiah* or the Mystery of the kabbalistic Bridal Chamber, cannot be easily understood or explained.

"On the day when you were one" was the *'olam* of *Adam Kadmon*, the archetypal heavenly First Humanity. "You became two" when androgynous Adam was divided into Adam and Eve and duality appeared.

"But now that you are dual, what will you do?" *Yeshua* challenges his spiritually reborn disciples to find their way out of this *'olam* and enter the Life of the *Malkuth*. How? By using the Gate of the Master. A Master of Israel entered into the mystical *Pardes* through his Gate—metaphorically his kabbalistic teaching and halakic practice. *Yeshua* said, "Strait ('strict') is the Gate and narrow is the Path that leads to Life."[195] His disciples were taught his Gate and his Path, which were embodied in private teachings and *halakah*.

So the answer to *Yeshua's* rhetorical question, "What will you do?" was reflected in the personal response of his disciples to the imperative *Halkeni*: "Follow me! Follow my *halakah*!"

---

[195] Q material paralleled in Matthew 7.14 and Luke 13.24

CHAPTER FIVE: Logia 12-23

The *talmidim*[196] said to *Yeshua,* "We know that you will disappear from our sight. Who is the one that will succeed you as our *Rav?"* *Yeshua* replied, "From whatever place you may be, you shall go to James the *Tzadik*, for whose sake Heaven and Earth came into being."

COMMENTARY

There are several Logia that are not seemingly isolated sayings but have a setting—in this case, a private dialogue with the disciples about succession. The Aramaisms in this logion suggest its authenticity.[197] The most interesting of these is the phrase "for whose sake Heaven and Earth came into being." This was a unique Hebrew-Aramaic expression of deep respect for a Jewish saint. We know from several other sources that James the Just/Righteous (*Tzadik*), was considered to be the greatest saint in Jerusalem after *Yeshua's* execution.

The Gospels of Matthew and Mark promote Peter as the greatest Apostle, while the later Johannine Gospel promotes John, just as the *Gospel of Thomas* promotes Thomas. But Luke-Acts preserves the fact that James *(Iakob)* "the brother of the Lord" was head of the Jerusalem church after the crucifixion, even though it promotes Peter as the greatest Apostle and Paul as the greatest missionary. The fact that the *Gospel of Thomas* also preserves this logion about James as the successor of *Yeshua,* in spite of its advocacy for Thomas as the greatest disciple and the twin brother of *Yeshua,* lends even more credence to the authenticity of the *logion.*

Early Christian legends from various sources tell us that *Iakob* or James was the younger brother of *Yeshua.* He was an unmarried Jewish saint greatly revered in Jerusalem, and like

---

[196] "Disciples." This indicates a private, inner-circle setting.
[197] "Go from eyesight" Aramaic idiom (Cf. Johannine "you will no longer see me"); Aramaic *Neddari* "be made great," term for installation of a *Rav* or "Great One" (Rabbi); "from whatever place you are" Aramaic expression; "go before the face of" Aramaic Idiom.

Yeshua he was a *cohen* or Priest with the right to serve at the Temple. After the death of *Yeshua*, he remained in Jerusalem praying daily outside the Temple until his knees were calloused like those of a camel. Prayer was normally done standing in *orant* posture with the arms raised, but saints prayed on their knees.

After the execution of *Yeshua*, the Roman-appointed High Priest of the Temple Ananas was so hated by the Jewish people that they demanded James be allowed to perform the sacred rites of *Yom Kippur* as High Priest. In this ritual of the Jewish New Year, the High Priest entered the Holy of Holies, intoned *Ha-Shem*[198] as a *Ba'al Shem Tov,*[199] and made intercession for the sins of Israel. Ananas later had James convicted in Roman court and murdered by being thrown off the Temple wall and beaten to death with a club.[200]

He is known in biblical accounts as James the Just (*Iakob Ha-Tzadik*), or James the Saint. He should not be confused with James the Apostle, who was the older brother of the youngest Apostle John—both of them sons of the man named Zebedee. James the Just, also known as James the brother of Jesus, is portrayed in the Book of Acts as the most revered of the three leaders of the Jerusalem Church. At the Council of Jerusalem in 49 C.E., he adjudicated the conditions for admittance of gentiles into the churches as envisioned by Peter (*Shimone Cephas*), the original advocate for the gentiles, and the newcomer Paul.

Was James the *Tzadik* an Apostle? That is, had he been an inner-circle disciple of his brother *Yeshua?* He does not appear in any of the canonical Gospel narratives as a disciple. Yet he was, in fact, greater than a disciple. He was a colleague of *Yeshua.* His spiritual training, though separate and independent, began with the same father and mother, which qualified him as a dynastic successor. [201]

The historical family that survived after *Yeshua's* execution were disciples. They consisted of brothers, sisters, aunts and uncles. According to well-attested legend, the mother of *Yeshua* later left her home in Nazareth to travel with the Apostles *Miriam Magdala* and John, son of Zebedee, to Asia Minor, where she died. The family lineage of *Yeshua* that survived into future generations was recorded by Church Fathers. Family members were

---

[198] The Holy Name of God given to Moses (יהוה), which was intoned like a magical incantation rather than simply pronounced. In the Galilee, people pronounced the Tetragrammaton as *Yahweh*, but this was forbidden in Judea, where only a substitute name like Adonai ("The LORD") was used. The knowledge of priestly intoning of the Tetragrammaton was passed down only in priestly families like that of *Yeshua* and his brother *Iakob* (James). In my fictional biography *Yeshua: The Unknown Jesus*, James follows his own spiritual path to sainthood, eventually becoming a disciple of John the Baptist, and finally successor to *Yeshua* in Jerusalem.
[199] "Lord of the Good Name" was the title given to medieval Jewish saints who preserved the proper priestly intoning of *Ha Shem*, the Teragrammaton. *kabbalistic* legend claimed that a *Ba'al Shem Tov* could save or destroy the world by using the power of the Name.
[200] I recommend a lengthy and accessible study on James available in English by the scholar Robert Eisenman entitled *James the Brother of Jesus.*
[201] For good research, go to http://www.biblicalstudies.org.uk/article_relatives_bauckham.html

known as the *desposynoi*, "those belonging to the Lord." There was absolutely no mention of a wife of *Yeshua* or a "holy bloodline." The *desposynoi* were considered to be normal human beings like all other disciples— not royal lineage-holders or sacred bloodline. The "holy blood, holy grail" idea was fabricated in mid-twentieth century by the esotericist and Nazi collaborator Pierre Plantard.[202]

The only "lineage" from *Yeshua* is that of the Apostles—what today is known as Apostolic Succession. The surviving records begin with Peter in Rome or Antioch of Syria because they were maintained in Roman Catholic and Eastern Orthodox churches. Other lines of succession, like those of Thomas, John, or Mary *Magdala*, were either not recorded or possibly suppressed by proto-orthodox and Byzantine Christianity.

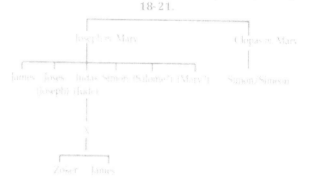

The first surviving generation of the family of Jesus. (Richard Bauckham, *Themelios* 21.2 (January 1996): 18-21.

Cleopas, the brother of *Yeshua's* Mother *Miriam* and therefore his Uncle, experienced one of the first Resurrection appearances on the road to Emmaus.[203] *Yeshua's* younger brothers other than James were travelling missionaries of the original Jewish churches, according to Paul (cf. I Corinthians 9.5).

Hegesippus records that two grandsons of *Yeshua's* brother Judas, Zoker and James, were brought before the Emperor Domitian on suspicion of fomenting revolt to establish a Jewish earthly kingdom. "They said that between the two of them they had only nine thousand denarii, half belonging to each of them; and this they asserted they had this not in money, but only in thirty-nine plethra of land, so valued, from which by their own labour they both paid the taxes and supported themselves." To prove that they were hard-working peasant farmers, they showed their tough bodies and the hardened skin of their hands. They also explained that the kingdom of Christ was not earthly (and so, Hegesippus implies, not a kingdom whose supporters would rebel against the empire) but coming at the end of history. Convinced they were harmless

---

[202] He fabricated false documents to support his claim to be a descendant of Jesus and inserted them into various esoteric and genealogical libraries in Europe to prepare for an attempt to be elected President of France. The bait was taken by several people including the authors of *Holy Blood, Holy Grail,* who were journalists, not critical scholars. The idea of a secret marriage and bloodline of *Yeshua* and *Miriam Magdala* (who was the age of *Yeshua's* mother!) has enriched many popular authors and has served as a weak antidote to patriarchal spirituality. But truth, when fully revealed, is a much more powerful antidote. See Robert Richardson, *The Unknown Treasure: The Priory of Sion Fraud and the Spiritual Treasure of Rennes-le-Château* (Houston, TX: NorthStar, 1998), available from Pratum Book Co., PO Box 985, Healdsburg, California 95448, USA, or go to http://www.alpheus.org/html/articles/esoteric_history/richardson1.html
[203] Luke 24.13ff.

and despising them as mere peasants, Domitian released them, and ordered the persecution against Christians to cease.[204]

It was probably James the Just who brought *Yeshua* into the inner circle of disciples around John the Baptist, where much of the messianic mysticism shared by the brothers coalesced. After that they seemed to have taken separate paths, perhaps by mutual agreement. *Yeshua* developed his prophetic messianic mission in the Galilee parallel to, but independent of, John. James developed his mission as priestly saint and Temple reformer in Judea at Jerusalem. After the execution of John, many of his disciples probably followed either *Yeshua* or James. The two must have reunited when *Yeshua* journeyed to Jerusalem to celebrate Passover.

Since the surviving early Christian writings, which were produced in the gentile churches, focused on late first-century issues, the only references that are made to John the Baptist and his disciples are designed to subordinate them to *Yeshua* and his disciples, and to marginalize their importance. Practically no reference is made to James. Paul tells us[205] that the risen Jesus was first seen by Peter,[206] then the traditional twelve Apostles, then by "five-hundred brethren all at once," then by James, and finally by all the rest of the Apostles.[207] This delayed sighting by James is described in a fragmentary legend from the lost Gospel of the Hebrews:

"And when the Lord had given the linen cloth to the servant of the priest, he went to James and appeared to him. For James had sworn that he would not eat bread from that hour in which he had drunk the cup of the Lord until he should see him risen from among them that sleep. And shortly thereafter the Lord said: Bring a table and bread! And immediately it added: he took the bread, blessed it and brake it and gave it to James the Just and said to him: My brother, eat thy bread, for the Son of man is risen from among them that sleep."[208]

All we can know of original Jewish messianic churches is what can be gleaned from fragments of the Gospels of the Hebrews, the Ebionites, and comments by early Church Fathers. We can also analyze traditions and rituals handed down orally in the few remaining communities of Mandeans, an ancient and origionally Jewish sect that regarded John the Baptist to have been the *Messiah Ben-Joseph*. But otherwise historical documents that might shed more light on Jewish saints like James the Just and John the Baptist are no longer extant.

---

[204] Quoted in Bauckham's article at http://www.biblicalstudies.org.uk/article_relatives_bauckham.html
[205] I Corinthians 15.5ff.
[206] *Cephas*, not Mary *Magdala*, although it is Peter who confirms that the stone has been rolled away from the tomb in the Marcan account derived from Peter. Was Paul the first one to marginalize *Miriam Magdala*?
[207] There were many more than twelve, according to Paul.
[208] Translation by Philipp Vielhauer and George Ogg in Wilhelm Schneemelcher, ed., translation by R. McL. Wilson, New Testament Apocrypha : Gospels and Related Writings (Louisville: John Knox Press, 1992), pp. 172-178.

Logion 13 [Inauthentic Gnostic *Logion*]

Jesus said to his disciples, "Compare me to someone; tell me whom I am like." Simon Peter said to him, "You are like a righteous angel." Matthew said to him, "You are like a great wise man and philosopher." [209] Thomas said to him, "Teacher,[210] my mouth is incapable of saying who you are like." Jesus replied, "I am not your teacher because you have drunk deeply from the bubbling fountainhead[211] which I have poured out, and you have become divinely intoxicated." And Jesus took him and withdrew into the wilderness. He spoke three words to him. When Thomas returned to his companions, they asked him, "What did Jesus tell you?" Thomas said to them, "If I tell you one of the words[212] that he said to me, you will stone me (for blasphemy), and then fire will come out from the stones and incinerate you!"

COMMENTARY

This logion is not authentic. It not only lacks Aramaisms, but uses jargon associated with Gnosticism and Greek philosophy in place of the language we would expect from Jewish mysticism (see footnotes). Its purpose it to glorify Thomas as the greatest of the disciples and promote the concept of Judas Thomas as the "Twin" of Jesus.[213]

It serves as Gnostic polemic recreating the "Who do men say that I am?" pericope of the Q Source (Mtt. 16.13f., Lk. 9.18f.), in which *Yeshua* self-identifies as the *Bar-Enash* ("Son of Man"). The Marcan parallel (Mk. 8.27f.) uses it to promote Peter as the greatest of the Apostles and the "rock upon which I will build my Church." The original logion in Q has *Yeshua* asking what people are saying about him—is he a reincarnation of Elijah, or Moses, or whom? Then he asks what the disciples think, and Peter identifies him as *Messiah Bar-Enash* ("Son of Man"). *Yeshua* then begins to instruct them that the "Son of Man" must suffer and die in Jerusalem. This would be the beginning of the "Birth Pangs of *Messiah*." Trial and suffering were necessary for all who would follow his *halakah.*

---

[209] Gr. Word *philosophos* "philosopher" not used in Aramaic and only once in NT. Used in a later period in Alexandria.

[210] Coptic "teacher" means "writer, book scholar;" not the Aramaic equivalent for *Rav.*

[211] A divine spring as "bubbling fountainhead" source of Muse-inspired prophecy, not Aramaic but purely Greek.

[212] "One of the words;" Coptic "words" means discursive speech, as opposed to Aramaic *dabar* = Gr. *Logos.* A "word" in Hebrew mysticism would be a discourse or entire science.

[213] I use the name Jesus when I translate clearly inauthentic *logia.*

Thomas Logion 13 is totally unrelated to the teaching about the suffering *Bar-Enash*, and I know of no scholars who find anything authentic in it.

Logion 14

14.a If you do a religious fast, you will beget sin for yourselves; if you pray, you will come under judgment; if you give alms to the poor, you will do evil things to your spirits.

14.b When you go into any region and enter into the district villages, if they welcome you, eat what they set before you and heal the sick among them.

14.c For what goes into your mouth will not defile you, but rather what comes out of your mouth—that is what will defile you.

COMMENTARY

Although this logion is not found in Q or other canonical sources, it is replete with Aramaisms and employs *Yeshua's* hyperbolic paradoxes to teach lessons. It is also joined with 14.c, a known authentic logion of *Yeshua.* It is most certainly a conflation of several separate authentic *davarim,* with the Gnostic redactor editorializing from canonical material by adding another authentic saying at 14.c.

Yeshua often employed uniquely semitic hyperbole such as, "You must hate your mother and your father," meaning that your natural, divinely mandated love of parents must pale in comparison to your devotion to God. By the same token, "If you do a religious fast, you will beget sin for yourselves" means that ritual *mitzvoth* like fasting promote pride rather than righteousness; wrong prayer for selfish or self-righteous motives engender karmic *mishpotim* or negative judgments, as does giving alms for public show.

This logion would have been given to *Yeshua's* close circle of disciples entrusted with going out into the villages in pairs to proclaim the *Basor,* exorcise, and heal. There is much evidence for healing among *Yeshua's* disciples in Acts (Peter heals, Ananias heals), but not in the canonical Gospels. This logion verifies that healing was part of their mission to demonstrate that God's *Malkuth* was indeed now appearing on Earth.

The Jewish disciples of *Yeshua,* both during his ministry and after his execution, followed practices not unlike those of peripatetic Buddhist monks, who were pledged to eat whatever was set before them. Like wandering Buddhist and Hindu saints, their devotion to God exceeded family loyalty. Healing and exorcism were practiced by both Christian and Eastern peripatetics. These disciplines and arts were also practiced by Apollonius of Tyana, who amplified his Pythagorean five-year vow of silence with a journey to the East for study of Brahmanic wisdom, according to legend.

Yeshua's teaching that ritual *kosher* purity was of lesser importance than hospitality and interior purity was probably the basis for Peter's declaration that all foods are permitted in the new era[214] as well as for relaxation of the Jewish kosher laws for gentiles in the 49 C.E. Council of Jerusalem headed by James, Peter, and John.[215] This was still at issue for many Jewish Christian at mid-century, when Paul wrote his opinions concerning "food offered to idols."

For *Yeshua,* purity and impurity arose from within the *yetzerim* or impulses of the heart. When the impure motivations of the *Yetzer Ha-Ra* were overcome by those of the *Yetzer Ha-Tov* or Image of God in thought, word, and deed, an act of internal sanctification had been achieved. Therefore, it was what came out of a person—not what went into a person, or what food was consumed—that sanctified or defiled him.

Logion 15 [Inauthentic Gnostic *Logion*]

> When you have a vision of Him Who was not born of a female, fall down on your face and adore Him, for He is your Progenitor.

COMMENTARY

This logion is clearly a production of a Syrian Gnostic redactor. It is based on a Hellenistic ascetic antifeminism quite alien to the Jewish kabbalistic traditions of *Yeshua.*

The mid-first century opponents of Paul in the Corinthian churches seem to have been Greek Gnostic Christians who represented themselves as having already achieved the spiritual perfection and Sovereignty of *Yeshua's* initiatic teachings.[216] They divided people into three spiritual classes: Sarkics (unbaptized, ignorant, and fleshly); Psychics (normal baptized Christians); and Pneumatics (elect and spiritually reborn initiates of God). The

---

[214] Acts 10.9ff.

[215] Acts 15.7ff.

[216] I Corinthians 4.8: "Now ye are full, now ye are rich, ye have reigned as **kings** without us: and I would to God ye did reign, that we also might reign with you!"

Pneumatics were thought to have been given spiritual birth by masculine deity ("Father"), which was rooted in the Pythagorean doctrine of the opposites:

- Male (Sun; divine and complete) vs. Female (Moon; earthly and mortal)

- Even (masculine) vs. odd (feminine) numbers

- Permanence (masculine) vs. impermanence (feminine), etc.

The Samaritan Gnostic Dositheus, who claimed to be a former disciple of John the Baptist, is said to have had 30 and ½ disciples because one was a woman,[217] and a woman was considered to be spiritually incomplete and constitute only half a soul. But the concept of woman, the female and the feminine being emblematic of mortality and corruption (i.e., waning of the moon) had no place in mystic and messianic Judaism, which venerated *Hochmah, Shekinah,* and the Motherhood of God.

This was the antifeministic world-view of the Syrian Gnostic Christians who possessed the secret sayings of *Yeshua* possibly through the Apostle Thomas. In the Logion 114 of *Thomas* it is clear that women can become Pneumatics only by being reborn spiritually as males.

But *Yeshua* was unique among the Masters of Israel in accepting female disciples. He did not advocate an antifeministic world-view. That makes it a bit easier to separate authentic from inauthentic sayings or parts of sayings in *Thomas.* Antifeministic comments are Gnostic. The marginalization of *Yeshua's* great female Apostles, especially Mary *Magdala,* occurred after the writing of Paul's epistles about mid-century and would not be reflected in authentic *logia* transmitted earlier than that.

We must conclude that this is not an authentic *davar* of *Yeshua.*

Logion 16

16.a People may think that the *Bar-Enash* will come to bring peace to the world, but they do not realize that the advent of the Son of Man will bring divisions on the Earth— fire, sword, warfare.

16.b [Redacted from Luke 12.53ff.]

---

[217] *Recognitions of Clement*

For there shall be five in one home; three shall be against two, and two against three; the father against the son, and the son against the father.

16.c [Inauthentic Gnostic Redaction]

But they [my brethren] will stand firm as monastics.

COMMENTARY

This seems to be an editorialized Gnostic version of an authentic *davar* that *Yeshua* gave about the Birth Pains of *Messiah*. The advent of the Son of Man was prophesied to initiate a period of suffering greater than mankind had ever experienced. *Yeshua* warned of these trials, which would include the total destruction of the Temple. As a result of his warnings, the Jewish Christians abandoned Jerusalem while escape was still possible before 67 C.E. Soon after the Roman general Vespasian besieged the city and starved it into submission.

The Birth Pains would be experienced on both societal and individual levels. Humanity would endure great catastrophes of nature, and human evil such as warfare would proliferate. It would get a lot worse before it got better! In the Epistle attributed to Peter, but probably composed by a disciple of Mark from Peter's memoires, the Apostle counsels, "Beloved, think it not strange concerning the fiery trial which is to test you, as though some strange thing happened unto you..."[218] By the time this epistle was composed, the gentile churches had accepted the Pauline understanding that suffering was a participation in the death of Jesus Christ. Originally, however, the coming trials were taught by *Yeshua* to be participation in the birth pangs of the New Humanity.

Yeshua's prophecies concerning the Birth Pains of *Messiah* were not about dissention within families divided by pro-messianic and con-messianic generations, as occurred in the first generation after the establishment of the Jerusalem church.[219] Nor were they about the internal conflict that broke up gentile families in the next generations as Christianity spread. The Lucan *logion* inserted by the Gnostic redactor of *Thomas* reflects these periods of dissention. Luke 12.53 was probably was a later interpretation or elaboration of the Birth Pain sayings adapted to the conditions of family conflict over the issue of Christian

---

[218] I Peter 4.12

[219] The messianic Jewish followers of the crucified *Yeshua* were ostracized and even arrested, as Saul (Paul) was on the road to Damascus to authorize when he was struck blind with a vision of the Risen Christ. Families were broken and divided. In Jerusalem after the Seige in 70 C.E., the messianic Jews were called *minim*, "heretics," and according to the Babylonian Talmud the following curse against them was added to the traditional 18 Benedictions recited in all synagogue: "For the renegades let there be no hope, and may their arrogant *Malkuth* soon be rooted out in our days, and the Nazarenes and the *minim* perish as in a moment and be blotted out from the book of life and with the righteous may they not be inscribed. Blessed art Thou, O Lord, who humblest the arrogant."

conversion. In *Thomas,* however, the dissention of the redactor's version probably reflects family opposition to converts abandoning their homes and becoming part of an ascetic Gnostic community. All these interpretations are anachronistic and inauthentic interpretations of an authentic *davar.*

Rather, the *davarim* that *Yeshua* gave concerning the Birth Pains of *Messiah* were about the human and cosmic consequences of the externalization of God's *Bar-Enash* within mankind and His *Malkuth* on Earth. No pain, no gain.

The final Gnostic amplification specifies that the true elect are the monastic members of their own gnostic cult.

Logion 17

The *Bar-Enash* shall give you that which no eye has ever seen, no ear has ever heard, no hand has ever touched, and which has never arisen in the human heart.

COMMENTARY

This clearly derives from the same source that Paul quotes as "scripture" in I Cor. 2.9: "But as it is written, Eye hath not seen, nor ear heard, neither have entered into the heart of man, the things which God hath prepared for them that love Him."

Paul quotes this unknown scripture when he talks about the hidden *mysteria* or *razim* of God. Scholars think Paul's scripture, which has only a slight resemblance to Isaiah 64.4, belongs to a lost version of Trito-Isaiah. It may have been quoted in the earliest kernel of the *Didache of the Twelve Apostles,* if scholar Alan Garrow's reconstruction of the missing parts and his thesis that a kernel *Didache* was used as a source by Matthew are correct. Harvard Professor Helmut Koester, in my opinion one of our most brilliant biblical scholars, praises Garrow and agrees.

Scholars have puzzled long and hard over this saying, which appears not only in *Thomas* but in many other sources, and is represented sometimes as a wisdom saying, sometimes as scripture, and other times as a saying of *Yeshua.*[220]

---

[220] Funk lists as parallels Isa 64:4, Luke 10:23-24, Matt 13:16-17, 1 Cor 2:9, 1 Clem 34:8, 2 Clem 11:7, Turfan Fragment M 789, Acts of Peter 39 (10), DialSav 57, The Prayer of the Apostle Paul 25-29.
Funk quotes Turfan Fragment M 789 as follows: "'I will give you what you have not seen with your eyes, nor heard with your ears, nor grasped with your hand.' (Hennecke 1:300)" (*New Gospel Parallels*, v. 2, p. 119).
Marvin Meyer writes: "This saying is also cited in 1 Corinthians 2:9, perhaps as a wisdom saying in use among the enthusiasts of Corinthians. Compare Isaiah 64:4. The saying occurs frequently in Jewish and Christian

We know that Trito-Isaiah was part of the Babylonian Son-of-Man tradition of *Yeshua*. This lost version of Trito-Isaiah was known to Paul, who had rabbinical training and attributed it to scripture ("as it is written"). Thus it was probably known to *Yeshua* as part of his Babylonian *Bar-Enash* tradition and connected to the revelation of the hidden *razim* of Heaven. Since this passage was so often quoted (see footnote #186), the version of Trito-Isaiah that was its source may eventually be discovered whole or in fragments, just as the version of *Enoch* known to *Yeshua* has recently been recovered (see my page 54).

It seems not unlikely, then, that this is an authentic *davar* quoted privately from scripture by *Yeshua* to his closest disciples as he revealed the *Razim* of the *Malkuth* to them. If true, this strongly argues my case for transmission of secret inner-circle teachings of *Yeshua* in the logia of the *Gospel of Thomas*—no matter how imperfectly.

We must distinguish between what *Yeshua* meant by quoting this scripture, and what it meant to the Thomas Gnostics.

Yeshua regarded this scripture from his version of what we know as Isaiah 64.4 to be a prophetic promise of spiritual life and the revelation of *razim* in the coming *Malkuth*. His version probably read something like what Paul quotes: "Eye hath not seen, nor ear heard, neither have entered into the heart of man, the things which God hath prepared for them that love Him." By quoting this, *Yeshua* emphasized the unknowable depth and beauty of the divine future for those who will remain faithful to God's way.

Did he say, "I shall give you" these *razim,* or did he simply quote scripture as what Heaven promised, or did he adapt the scripture to reflect what was promised through the Son of Man? I have opted for the latter based on the fact that the Gnostics and others such as the redactors of John's Gospel, who regarded Jesus to be Godhead, regularly spun *Yeshua's* teachings about the Son of Man into sayings about himself as Christ. So I recover the *davar* as "The *Bar-Enash* [Son of Man] shall give you..."

To the *Thomas* Gnostics, however, the man Jesus (Greek *Iesous*) was the Christ, cosmic Savior, and face of God incarnate. Any reference to the "Son of Man" in their understanding must refer to *Iesous* personally. Thus a Greek *logion* that began, "*Iesous* said, The Son of Man shall give you..." would have been reduced to, "I shall give you..." The Gnostic

---

literature, and sometimes it is said to come from the Apocalypse of Elijah or the Secrets (or, apocrypha) of Elijah. At other times it is said to be a saying of Jesus. A variant of the saying is also found in Plutarch, How the Young Person Should Study Poetry 17E: 'And let these (words) of Empedocles be at hand: "Thus these things are not to be seen by men, nor heard, nor comprehended with the mind." . . .' The parallels have been collected by Michael E. Stone and John Strugnell, *The Books of Elijah: Parts 1-2*, pp. 41-73." (*The Gospel of Thomas: The Hidden Sayings of Jesus*, p. 76). Quoted from online http://www.kunar.com/Gospel%20of%20Thomas/Collected%20Commentary%20on%20the%20Gospel%20of%20Thomas%2017.htm

understanding was that *Iesous* is the fountainhead of all cosmic mysteries, which he promised exclusively to the ascetic Syrian (later Egyptian) *monochoi* or "solitaries" of their sect.

Logion 18

The disciples besought *Yeshua,* "Tell us about our ultimate future." *Yeshua* replied, "Then have you uncovered the Begining *(Ha- Roshit)*[221] that you are now qualified to inquire about the End *(Ha-Acharit?)*[222] For where the *maqom*[223] of the Beginning exists, that will be the End. Blessed is he who is able to stand at the Beginning, for he shall know the End; and he shall never taste death."

COMMENTARY

This may derive from a private kabbalistic discussion between *Yeshua* and his close disciples, as it seems to be dependent upon kabbalistic terminology, which I have explained in footnotes. This appears to be based on a first-century interpretation of the *'Olam Ha-Ba* as the "World That Came and is to Come" from the school of *Yochanan ben Zakai*. [224]

Many Gnostic and Hellenistic Christian concepts are derived from Jewish kabbalistic counterparts, such as:

> *Roshit* of Genesis = Gr. *Arche;*
> *Acharit* speculated by Kabbalists = Gr. *Eschaton;*
> *Maqom* (like Hindu *Loka*) = Gr. *Topos;*
> *Hochmah* (Wisdom) = Gr. *Sophia.* This is evidenced by the fact that Gnostic systems like the Valentinian appropriated Hebrew kabbalistic terms directly. For example, Hebrew-Aramaic *Achamoth* is the Gnostic appropriation of Hebrew *Hochmah* (Wisdom = Sophia).

The rhetorical question, "Have you uncovered the Beginning that now you are qualified to inquire about the End?" is a rabbinic-kabbalistic device to throw the burden of thought

---

[221] Beginning of Divine Emanation in the *Ain Sof Aur* or Eternal Light of the *'Olam Ha-Ba,* which lies both at the primal beginning and transcendental eschatological end of all worlds.

[222] End of all worlds or *'olamim.*

[223] Divine aeon, *'olam,* or state of existence ("place").

[224] Cf. passage 160 of the *Bahir* in the Commentary on Logion #2.

over to the student, as when *Yeshua* declares in Lk. 12.49 (paraphrase) : "The *Bar-Enash* is coming to kindle [divine] fire upon the Earth, but what will He do if it is already kindled?"

Here, however, the disciples are asking about their own futures in the *Malkuth* as, for example, when James and John (sons of Zebedee) ask what their reward will be. In that case, *Yeshua* refused to speculate. But in this pericope *Yeshua* artfully turns the discussion into a teaching moment with his characteristic paradoxical saying about Begining being the same as the End.

Ha-Roshit refers to the first words of the Book of Genesis *Beroshit* "At the beginning/head of all creation..." Genesis was a major kabbalistic text. We know from the *Sepher Yetzirah,*[225] which first appeared in written form in the second century, that the derivation of the 32 Paths of Wisdom is done from the first chapter of Genesis. There are derived from the number of times that God's Name *Elohim*[226] appears. Of these, the expression "God said" appears ten times, which is associated with the ten *sephiroth,* and the other 22 with the letters of the Hebrew alphabet. "God made" appears three times. Those are associated with the three Mother letters *Aleph, Mem, Shin,* which form the firmament dividing Heaven from Earth and the corresponding aspects of the human microcosm. "God saw" appears seven times and is attributed to the seven double Hebrew letters, seven planets, and physiological corollaries. The remaining twelve *Elohim* expressions associate with the twelve single letters, the signs of the Zodiac, and human physiology.

When the disciples ask about the *Acharit,* or the end of time, which is known in the New Testament by the Greek word *Eschaton,* they are asked if they have understood the kabbalistic Work of *Ha-Roshit.* Unlike the *Ma'asei Merkabah* or Work of the Chariot, the kabbalistic practices associated with *Ha-Roshit* were magical rituals of creation using the Hebrew letters. They may have been employed to form a *Merkabah* as the mantic vehicle to make a divine ascent.

The rhetorical answer to *Yeshua's* question would be, No. He was a master of these arts, but the disciples were not. The point of the original periscope was somewhat like that made by another saying of *Yeshua:* "No one knows about that day or hour, not even the angels in Heaven,[227] nor the Son,[228] but only the *Abba.*"[229]

Even though no one knows these *razim,* contrary to apocalypticists who might claim to have decoded the prophecies, in this *davar Yeshua* says this much can be known: The End is in the same *maqom* as the Beginning. He reveals that the *Acharit* and the *Roshit* are one and

---

[225] Book of Formation
[226] This is a Hebrew masculine plural for *El,* God. The literal translation is "gods."
[227] The angels knew all the *razim* except this one.
[228] Meaning the Son of Mankind or *Bar-Enash.*
[229] Mark 13.32; Matthew 24.36

the same state of divine reality. That archetypal "place" might be compared to a Hebrew *'olam,* or to a Sanskrit *loka,* but without the existence of time.

In Hellenistic rabbinic discourse, the remedy for mankind's fall from Paradise was a return to the *Pardes.* This was both an individual mystical return and an apocatastatic final return of all things to the pre-fallen state known as *Tikkun.*[230] The disputation among early Church Fathers about whether Satan would be redeemed in the *Eschaton* originated in this rabbinic idea. Origin said yes, others (including the writer of the Book of Revelations[231]), said no. The Athanasian politicians of Constantine's councils rejected Origin's theology, thus burdening Christianity with a dualistic theodicy that never resolves.

The Gnostics took many of their ideas from Jewish *Kabbalah,* including their concept of the *Arche* or Beginning. However, they did not often speculate about the *Eschaton.* Rather, they took the realized eschatology of Johannine tradition to an extreme and immanentized the End Times into mystic experience. In contrast, *Yeshua* advocated the kabbalistic ideal of both immanent and future *Tikkun.* In this saying he implies a monistic kabbalistic theodicy that is echoed by Paul in many of his Epistles about so-called "predestination" from the foundation of the *Kosmos.*[232]

The *Thomas* Gnostics were Christian dualists in that they desired above all to redeem themselves from existence in the incarnate world through the instrumentality of strict asceticism. In that regard, they were more like the Stoics than other Gnostics. Valentinian and Marcosian Christian Gnostics regarded *Iesous* as a cosmic Savior who descended from Heaven and returned, leading the Elect Heavenward by mediating redemption as a Gnostic Revealer. Unlike the Thomasian ascetics, those systems did not develop a strong ethic of

---

[230] Modern Kabbalists understand the *Tikkun* as a future messianic reparation or healing of the world. In Christian Martinism, Jesus is known as the messianic Repairer or Restorer.

[231] Revelations was a late second-century pseudepigraphical production claiming authorship by the Apostle John while exiled on the Isle of Patmos. It is not written in the unique Greek style of the other Johannine literature (Gospel and Epistles of John), and many of the early churches rejected it as inauthentic. It was finally accepted as part of the Byzantine canon during the 4th century ecumenical councils required by Emperor Constantine, from which he demanded that one single official Bible be agreed upon. Previous to that different churches had New Testaments with variable content. At this time the heresy-hunting Athanasians declared Arius and Origin to be heretics. They promoted the idea of eternal damnation for all the enemies of Christendom, and supported works like Revelations that agreed with their political agenda. The ancient Jewish ideal of final *Tikkun* in which all, including the fallen angels, were reconciled to God as reflected in Origen's doctrine of Apocatastasis, was summarily rejected.

[232] Ephesians 1.4-5: God "chose us in Him [Christ] before the foundation of the world, that we should be holy and without blame before Him in love, having fore-ordained ("predestined") us to adoption as sons by Jesus Christ to Himself..." This is not the Calvinistic concept of double predestination to redemption or damnation, which posits dualistic theodicy, but *kabbalistic* monism probably not unlike Origen's *Apokatastasis* for final reconciliation of all with God, including *Shaitan.* He declares that the gentiles (i.e., all mankind) were predestined for inclusion in the Body of *Bar-Enash* at *Ha-Rosh.*

spiritual practice, but relied upon right *gnosis* or doctrine, much as the proto-orthodox Christians relied upon *pistis* or salvific belief.

Yeshua, on the other hand, taught his disciples that liberation from the evil of this world comes only through personal and social transformation. Faith cannot be separated from works. The practice of interior *halakah* was central to bringing about the sanctification of self and humanity, and this field of action was ultimately rooted in the heart of each person.

"Blessed is he who is able to stand at the Beginning" invokes the kabbalistic ideal of a Standing One or Jewish saint who lives on after death to guide Israel like an angel. The root meaning of Hebrew *Qimah* is "to stand." The ever-living *tzadikim* of the *'Olam* of God included such beings as the risen Moses, Elijah, and Abraham. "One who is worthy of the *Qimah*," said *Yeshua,* is no longer man or woman, but exists "as do the angels."[233] As we find in several other instances, a kabbalistic term crosses over into Gnosticism. In this case, Standing One became a Gnostic term for a fully realized monastic *asketes* or ascetic.

Here *Yeshua* says that only when a risen saint is able to stand—that is, to exist as a self-conscious being—at *Ha-Roshit,* the Head or Origin of all things, will he be able to know *Ha-Acharit.* Even though no one knows the End but God alone, when the blessed saint finally merges fully with Godhead he will know the greatest of all the *razim.* A parallel to this kabbalistic ideal may be found in the Roman-Hellenistic Mysteries of Hermes Trismegistos, which existed contemporary with *Yeshua*[234]

Was the undoubtedly authentic phrase "will never taste death" originally part of this *davar?* It is a semitic expression and was used by *Yeshua.* Perhaps it was a mnemonic phrase that recalled specific memorized *davarim* for the disciple who made the original dictation.

However, I think the phrase is independent, It was added by the Gnostic editor just as it was in other places like Logion 1. It seems to be ubiquitous in *Thomas.* Why? Probably because it points to the immanentized *Eschaton* of the Syrian Thomas Gnostics. The Gnostic saint would never taste death because he was already living in the divine *Eschaton.* Thus for the redactor, the "will never taste death" phrase is a logical conclusion of any *logion* about the virtue of *gnosis* and discovery of true Self.

---

[233] Q discourse concerning the women with seven husbands Mark 12.25; Matthew 22.30; Luke 20.35
[234] In Tractate 6 of Nag Hammadi Codex VI, the Hermetic Initiation discourse (paralleled in the *Corpus Hermeticum* 13), the initiand see a vision of ascended Hermetic saints guiding humanity telepathically from the *Ogdoas* or Eight Heaven of the Zodiac, then as they become more sanctified being drawn upward into the *Enneas* or Ninth Heaven beyond that, and finally upward into the Tenth Heaven, where they merge totally with Godhead. There are many other parallels to Jewish *kabbalistic* and early Christian mysticism in the literature of Trismegistos.

19.a Blessed is the one who existed before he was emanated into existence.[235]

19.b If you become my true disciples, and put my words into practice,

19.c these very stones will minister to you.

19.d There are five Trees in the *Pardes* which are unmoved in summer or winter and their leaves never fall. Whoever has knowledge[236] of them will not taste death.

COMMENTARY

Logion 19 seems to be a collage of four *davrim*. 19.a was previously unknown.

19.b is an exhortation of *Yeshua* known from several sources in the Gospel narrations. Here it is joined with 19.c, which possibly confuses a saying attributed to John the Baptist ("God can raise up children of Abraham from these stones")[237] with a version of the Temptation narrative where *Yeshua* is served not by ministering angels, but by the stones that *Shaitan* had challenged him to transform into loaves of bread.

However, the idea of stones becoming human servants in 19.c seems to have been a common Hebraic paradox of the sort that *Yeshua* liked to employ. Idols were carved from inanimate stone, but human beings were living stones. In the Genesis story, *Adam* was formed from the red earth that constituted the ubiquitous landscape of red stone in much of Palestine. But Eve was formed from a bone associated with his heart—the rib.[238] Bones and stones were understood as the matrix from which human beings came into being. A child, like Adam's wife, was "bone of my bone, flesh of my flesh."[239]

---

[235] Cf. Johannine "Before Abraham was, I Am." *Kabbalistic* and Pauline doctrine of pre-existent reality of a "Perfect Tree." This saying also appears in the Gnostic *Gospel of Philip* which, like *Thomas,* transmits Gnosticized *davarim* of *Yeshua* interspersed among longer Gnostic sermons—although their source may have been the *Gospel of Thomas.*

[236] Greek *gnosis* for Aramaic *manda.*

[237] Q material in Matthew 3.9 and Luke 3.8.

[238] Ezekiel had a vision of God breathing *ruach* into dry bones to make them live again. In Hellenistic alchemical thought, bones were earthen stone—that is, equivalent to stone. God could breath *ruach* into dry human bones or into earthen stone. Ezekiel 37.4.

[239] Genesis 3.23. Cf. Genesis 29.14 *et al.*

Logion 19.d refers to a five-tree form of kabbalistic *Pardes* that was a theme of rabbinic discourse at the time of *Yeshua* that we will examine later. This kabbalistic theme when taken with the Hebraic characteristics of the separate *davrim* of Logia 19.b,c,and d strongly argue for their authenticity. What about Logion 19.a?

Here we find usages that are both Aramaic and typical of *Yeshua.* The Coptic word ϣⲱⲡⲉ "become, exist" is used three times in a series of playful puns that could be translated, "Blessed is the one who *became* before he *became*. If you *become* my disciples..." This indicates two things. The same Greek and underlying Aramaic word was used for all three in the original *davar,* and it was stated in the usage that is typical of *Yeshua's* initiatic sayings—hyperbole, paradox, pun.

The Greek word that fits all three cases is *ginomai,* which was commonly used to translate Aramaic *hayah,* "to exist, be made, come to pass." In kabbalistic reference to so-called creation,[240] the best translation would be "to emanate" into existence from divine non-existence.

Thus for the kabbalistic view there are two states. The pre-existent (non-existent) state of unmanifested unity in Godhead, and the post-existent state of primordial emanated manifestation. This is the meaning of the paradoxical statement, "Blessed is the one who existed before he existed." I have rendered it for meaning and understanding by paraphrasing, "Blessed is the one who existed before he was emanated into existence."

The third use of *hayah* is in the *davar* of 19.b, "If you come into existence as my disciples," which I render, "If you become my true disciples." The initiatic meaning is that if you "come into existence" or are created (born) anew as true disciples, you will "hear" (Aramaic "obey, put into practice") the Master's words and teachings—in more accurate terms, follow his *halakah.*

This series of puns on Aramaic *hayah* provides the clue on why these *davrim* were remembered in this series by the disciple whose Aramaic dictation was recorded and rendered into Greek. Logion 19.a is the memory trigger for 19.b,c, which expands on the public teaching "be ye doers of the Word, and not hearers only." As an initiatic *davar,* it says that those who faithfully practice the *halakah* are emanated or born into existence. They are the "newly-born" of the other *Thomas logia.* As such, their faithful practice will elevate them to the status of *tzadikim* to whom all the elements of the Earth, animated by Divine *Ruach,* will make obesience and serve ("these very stones will minister to you").

---

[240] Platonic creation was the incarnation of spirit into irrational matter, which pre-existed creation. The Christian understanding is *creation ex nihilo,* creation out of nothing. In both cases the Creator (Demiurge) transcends and is distinct from the Creation. But in *kabbalistic* thought, Godhead emanated itself out of non-existence. All that manifests, whether in form or not, is a lower octave, harmonic, or vibration of Godhead. *Kabbalistic* creation is pantheistic. Nature is animistic. This was the view of *Yeshua.*

This *davar,* in turn, is linked mnemonically to the kabbalistic saying about the Five Trees of the *Pardes* in Logion 19.d. Let us remember that the *Pardes* or Paradise is the mystic primordial garden where enlightened Kabbalists meet in spirit to learn and share divine *manda* or knowledge. The Gate to the *Pardes* is allegorical for the halakic wisdom of an enlightened Master of Israel.

Philo of Alexandria,[241] recording kabbalistic *haggadah* about Noah, says that in Paradise he planted five trees: of Life, Immortality, Knowledge, Comprehension, and Knowledge of Good and Evil. In a commentary on Gen. 2:9, Philo writes that the leaves of the trees in Paradise are evergreen—they never lose their leaves. That specific reference locates the first-century chronological provenance of the *davar*—"unmoved in summer or winter and their leaves never fall."

The two trees planted by God in the *Pardes* were that of the immortal Life of the *Elohim,* and that of the "Knowledge" or Awareness of Good and Evil. Adam and Eve partook only of the latter before they were cast out of the Third Heaven into incarnation on Earth ("coats of skin"). All life was destroyed on Earth by the Flood because the hosts of *Shaitan* had corrupted humanity—all life except those of Noah, his family, and breeding pairs (or sevens) of the animals. In kabbalistic lore, Noah prefigured the *Bar Enash* or *Messiah.* He was the greatest of all *tazdikim* and the savior of humanity.

Here is my reconstruction of Philo's kabbalistic *haggadah* about the Trees of Noah.

When Noah died, he ascended into Paradise and was empowered to plant the kabbalistic Five Trees that would eventually redeem postdiluvian humanity. First and greatest was the Tree of the Life of the *Elohim,* which had been destroyed after the transgression of Adam and Eve, and whose fruits were reserved for only the greatest of the *tzadikim.* Second was the Tree of Human Immortality, whose fruits were reserved for those who were found worthy of the *Qimah.* Third was the Tree of *Manda, Gnosis,* or Divine Wisdom, whose fruits were reserved for those who sought *Hochmah* or Wisdom. Fourth was the Tree of Comprehension or Understanding, whose fruits were reserved for those who had purified and attuned their hearts to God's Way. Fifth, and the most accessible of the Trees, was that of the Knowledge (meaning Successful Discrimination) of Good and Evil—the two *yetzerim* of the heart, one being the true Image of God, the other the false and unreal shadow-image of the *qlippoth* that manifested by necessity in the world of duality.

When one achieved interior purity of motivation and "made the two one," he would begin to eat the fruit of the Fifth Tree. When his heart was attuned to heaven's guidance, he would eat the fruit of the Fourth Tree. And thus the disciple would advance until he or she was worthy to eat the fruit of the Tree of Life.

---

[241] A contemporary of *Yeshua.*

In this Logion *Yeshua* says, "Whoever has knowledge of them [the Five Trees] will not taste death." The Aramaic word *manda,* knowledge, is somewhat interchangeable with the Greek term gnosis—profound, non-discursive interior understanding that cannot be taught, but only learned through self-realization. However, *manda* developed from Hebrew *madda* in Chaldaean times,[242] meaning "mind" (like the Greek word *nous*) or divine intellect as opposed to human mental thoughts. *Manda* added the *"nd"* as a prophetic future verbal form made into a noun. It referred specifically to future or hidden transcendental knowledge as of the *razim.*

We find *manda* used in the context of Jewish messianic foreknowledge and prophecy as early as the second century before the Christian era. Indeed, surviving traditions of the ancient Mandeans (Keepers of the *Manda*)[243] extol the *Mandā d-Heyyi* or Knowledge-Mind of Divine Life as the true Name of Deity. Central to Mandaic tradition are Jewish *mikveh* rituals similar to those used by John the Baptist, who seems to have been honored as the *Messiah Ben-Joseph* in competition with early Christianity.

The *davar* spoken by *Yeshua* indicates that the *manda* of the Five Trees in Paradise was more than simple discursive familiarity with kabbalistic discourse or haggadic teaching. This *manda* referred to mastery of the spiritual attainment represented by all five of the Trees, beginning with victory in practice over the duality of heart and mind associated with the Tree of Knowledge or *Manda.* That is the initiatic meaning of *Yeshua's* teachings about making the two into a single one, empowering the *Yetzer Ha-Tov* to shine and overcome the *Yetzer Ha-Ra,* being not "double-souled" but pure of intention, without guile, and making your "yes" mean yes, and your "no" mean no.

The person who begins with this attainment and proceeds to the higher attainments represented by the other four Trees will never "taste death." Here death does not refer to physical death of the body, but spiritual death of the inner sentient being. One who gains *manda* of the Five Trees achieves communion with the Mind of God in this life, and the *Qimah* of God's *'Olam* after physical death—known in the New Testament as Eternal Life.

---

[242] As found in the Book of Daniel and other Babylonian wisdom literature.

[243] The Mandean communities may represent an older form of Jewish Gnostic community related to communities of married or moderate Essenes, as opposed to ascetic Essenes. They probably gave refuge to disciples of John the Baptist after his martyrdom. Diaspora communities survived in Iraq and Iran, where they were persecuted by Muslim extremists. By the 21st century, most of them had fled to Jordan, Syria, the U.S., and other nations.

Logion 20

The *Malkuth* can be compared to a mustard seed, which is smaller than all other seeds. But when it falls onto properly prepared soil, it produces a large branch and becomes shelter for the birds of Heaven.[244]

COMMENTARY

Mustard seeds

Before we discuss meaning, let us understand what the mustard "tree" was. In much of Palestine there were no true trees—merely shrubs and bushes. There were cedars to the north in Lebanon that were imported by the Romans for their building projects. But the only readily available building material was stone or bricks made from dried mud.[245]

Certain species of native mustard seeds were so tiny they were almost like grains of pollen. They were hard like nuts and could be ground into a fine paste. They were also extremely hardy, could remain viable for many years. and so full of vital force that they sent up shoots among rocks and any place there might be water. Their roots could crack open huge stones.

Their vitality was prodigious. Given good soil and a supply of spring or river water, some species of mustard bush were reputed to grow into gigantic tree-like bushes. However, botanists cannot agree upon what this special species of mustard shrub might have been, since modern species do not grow more than a few feet tall.

Below is a photograph of a native Palestinian mustard bush. It is a medium-sized shrub, but not a tree-like structure that can shelter birds. For centuries scholars have tried to identify the "mustard tree" of the parable, but no such thing grows today in Palestine or anywhere else in the world. Did mustard trees exist at the time of *Yeshua* that were

---

[244] In its canopy, the birds of Heaven (metaphorical for disciples of the *Malkuth*) can take shelter—somewhat comparable to the Buddhist concept of **taking refuge**.

[245] The Greek *tekton* used to describe *Yeshua's* trade as a builder is usually wrongly translated as "carpenter." But there was little or no wood available! The Greek word can mean builder or stone mason. The Hebrew-Aramaic word underlying it was *charas,* an engraver in stone. *Yeshua* and his father were stone masons—probably Master Masons and architects, as indicated by the Matthean lineage of Joseph through Zerubbabel (Matthew 1.12ff.), the founder of Jewish stone masonry for the rebuilding of the Temple after the Babylonian Captivity. Guild trades were passed on from father to first-born son. In the legend of Thomas in India, the Apostle is presented as the twin of Jesus and an architect (Master Mason), a detail that is probably rooted in the historical guild trade of *Yeshua*.

specially cultivated to become giants? There is no evidence of this, but we do find intriguing clues for a better explanation.

Palestinian mustard bush

The Babylonian Talmud (*Ktubot* 111b) tells us: "Rabbi *Yosef* told of an event in a place called *Shikhin*. A man inherited three branches of a mustard plant from his father. One of them split open revealing nine *kavim* of mustard [seeds], and with its wood [lumber] he built the roof of the potter's shed."

Nine *kavim* would equal almost 11 liters of seed, and enough wood to build a roof would be prodigious for a shrub. The Babylonian Talmud, like *Yeshua,* speaks of huge "mustard" trees that produce phenomenal yields. But these are fictional trees, haggadic trees, legendary trees, and probably kabbalistic trees.[246]

In the Marcan material of the New Testament,[247] which was redacted by the writers of Matthew and Luke, *Yeshua* spoke in prophetic *mashlim* ("parables") to the crowds. One of these *mashlim* was what we know as the Parable of the Mustard Seed. He ended his teachings with the kabbalistic admonition: "He who has ears to hear, let him hear."

When he retired with his disciples and the other patrons who accompanied them, they asked him privately to explain the *mashlim.* He told them, "The *razim* of the *Malkuth* of God have been given to you. But to those on the outside everything is said in *mashlim*...Don't you understand this *mashal?* How then will you understand any *mashal?*"[248]

In *Thomas* Logion 20, the Parable of the Mustard Seed did not refer to the common, everyday world of his hearers. Rather, it referred to a legendary tree of messianic *haggadah*—a tree such as those Five Trees that were planted in Paradise by Noah. It is no coincidence that this *davar* of the Mustard Seed immediately follows Logion 19 concerning the Five Trees of Paradise. The disciple or Apostle who originally dictated these sayings in Aramaic remembered Logion 20 in mnemonic series with Logion 19 because they were both *davarim* about kabbalistic trees.

---

[246] *Yeshua's* adherence to the Babylonian concept of the *Bar-Enash Messiah,* as opposed to the messianic theories of Palestine, and his reference to Babylonian *kabbalistic haggadah* about a prodigious mustard tree, point to the probability that his "lost years" were spent with the large Jewish community and its wisdom school in Babylon.

[247] Mark 4.1ff.

[248] Mark 4.11-13.

When *Yeshua* spoke in "parables" to the crowds, he delivered *davarim* and *mashlim* intended only for those who had "ears to hear." The Parable of the Mustard Seed, like the Parable of the Sower, could be interpreted only by those who had cultivated *manda* in their hearts. Only they would be capable of understanding the sayings, which would eventually lead them to seek discipleship with him. Seeking discipleship was simply a first step on the initiatic path to Divine *Malkuth*.

Yeshua's Application of the Mustard Seed Allegory: Public and Private

The mustand seed seems to have been referenced publically in at least two different ways by *Yeshua*. As a potent tiny seed, it served as a metaphor of faithfulness or fidelity ("faith"). The well known characteristics of hardy proliferation, prodigious growth into a large shrub that provided shelter and habitat, and ubiquitous presence of the mustard bush even in desert environments, its growth from tiny seed to largest of the shrubs allegorized the power of the coming *Malkuth* or Divine Sovereignty on Earth.

In the original Marcan tradition as remembered by Peter, the growth of the mustard seed is presented as a comparison to the coming of the *Malkuth*.

"What shall we say the kingdom of God is like, or what parable shall we use to describe it? It is like a mustard seed, which is the smallest of the seeds. Yet when planted, it grows and becomes the largest of all trees, with such big branches that the birds of the air can perch in its shade."[249]

In Mark the meaning is parallel to that of *Thomas*. The vitality of the tiny and seemingly insignificant mustard seed is like the power of the *Malkuth*. Over time it will persevere and grow into a great tree, like the legendary trees of the coming messianic age that rabbis describe in their haggadic speculation. For *Yeshua*, the tiny but powerful mustard seed possessed one powerful quality that made this possible—persistence, perseverance, fidelity to its purpose, or *emunah*. This Hebrew word from the trilateral root AMN was later translated with the Greek *pistis*, faith. But *Yeshua's* emphasis upon faith as faithfulness and fidelity to God's way was distorted in later generations to mean "belief" in Jesus as Christ (*Messiah*).

This distortion is illustrated by Matthew's redaction in 17.20. His Greek says, "If you have faith as small as a mustard seed, you can say to this mountain, 'Move from here to there' and it will move. Nothing will be impossible for you."

Here the idea of faith as blind, uncritical belief is established in Christian thought. Even though *Yeshua* said, "you cannot change a hair of your head merely by taking thought," the

---

[249] Mark 4.30ff.

early gentile Christians developed great dependence upon mental belief as a magical means to healing and power. Just believe it, and it will be so!

But what did *Yeshua* illustrate in his original public teaching about faith and the mustard seed? That by perseverant loyalty to the ways of God ("faith"), one can ultimately achieve Co-Sovereignty with God.[250] Ultimately, humanity is empowered by fidelity to truth, justice, wisdom, and all the other attributes of Godhead—not by guile, force, and violence.

However, in *Yeshua's* inner-circle teaching, the mustard "tree" was employed kabbalistically to reveal a *razim* of the *Malkuth* ("mystery of the Kingdom"). This is what we find in Logion 20, as in the Marcan-Petrine New Testament parable, but with one significant addition. He specified, "when it falls into properly prepared soil." The meaning is tilled soil that has been sifted for stones, fertilized, tilled, and watered. This is what allows a seed to grow into the fantastic tree of messianic legend. The same process in the spiritual preparation of the hearts of humanity is what will allow the *Malkuth* to grow into its full potential on Earth.

As a *mashal,* both public and private, the allegory of the mustard seed and tree emphasizes it's growing into a shelter or canopy. In Aramaic, this is a tent or movable dwelling *(shakan)* or possibly a tabernacle or portable temple *(ohel).*

Herein lies another part of the *razim.* Just as the ancient Aramaean ancestors of the Hebrews lived and worshipped in temporary tents and tabernacles, so the newly-borns of the *Malkuth* will dwell as passersby on Earth. This idea was beautifully expressed by a second-century Alexandrian Christian writer in his Epistle to Diognetus (probably Claudius Diogenes, procurator of Alexandria):

> They dwell in their own countries, but simply as sojourners. As citizens, they share in all things with others, and yet endure all things as if foreigners. Every foreign land is to them as their native country, and every land of their birth as a land of strangers. They marry, as do all [others]; they beget children; but they do not destroy their offspring. They have a common table, but not a common bed. They are in the flesh, but they do not live after the flesh. They pass their days on earth, but they are citizens of heaven.[251]

---

[250] In the language of semitic hyperbole, if you say to the mountain, "Be moved," it will move. In the 21st century, as humanity comes of age and begins to step into its role of co-sovereignty with God, we do move mountains. The day is not far off when we will mine asteroids and move their orbits away from potential collision with the Earth. One day we will cultivate and husband planets.

[251] *The Epistle of Mathetes to Diognetus*, Ch. 5.

Logion 21

21.a *Miriam* asked *Yeshua,* "What are your disciples like?" He said, "They are like small children who are dressing up and playing house with property they don't own. When the owners of the property come upon them, they will say, 'Give us back what we own.' They strip naked and give everything back to them.

21.b.1 "Therefore I say, if the head of the house knows that a thief is coming, he will remain awake until he comes and will not allow him to tunnel through [the walls] into his sovereign home to carry away his treasure.[252] You must keep vigil from the very foundations against the world and gird up your loins with great power, lest those who break into homes[253] find a way to penetrate into you, because they will always discover your weakness.

21.b.2 "May there be a perceptive person of understanding[254] among you: When the fruit splits open with ripeness, one comes quickly with sickle in hand to harvest it."

COMMENTARY

Logion 21 consists of a kabbalistic *mashal* (simile or parable) and two independent *davarim.* The Gnostic redactor has presented them in the same sequence they were originally dictated, except he has linked them with Greek *dia touto,* "therefore, for this reason," as though the *davarim* provided explanations or conclusions to the *mashal*—which they don't. The Nag Hammadi scholars who originally restored the Coptic text of *Thomas* left the three as one single *logion* in deference to the redactor. However, we will separate the *logion* back into the original three sayings in order to recover their meanings.

---

[252] lit. Greek *Skeuoi* = Aramaic *K'li,* "treasure vessels."
[253] Greek *Lestes* = Aramaic *Gedodim,* "those who cut or dig their way in."
[254] Greek *Epistemon* = Aramaic *Bin, kabbalistic Binah*

Logion 21.a

Miriam could be Mary, the mother of *Yeshua,* who was not a *talmid* or disciple of Jesus. In that case, she would be asking him about his disciples. But the answer is not coherent with the question if that were the case.

Most scholars have identified *Miriam* as Mary *Magdala.* In that case, she would be asking *Yeshua* to make a kabbalistic simile—the kind of formal question that a disciple would ask. In semitic usage of the period, as well as in the Talmudic literature, we often find the question "What is X like?" *Yeshua* is asked this question in set form by a disciple. To answer, he is expected to draw a parallel to some familiar sight, activity, or experience in order to illuminate the spiritual topic.

He tells Mary that she and all the disciples are like children who are imitating grown-ups by playing house and dressing in adult clothing. [255] When their mother finds what they are doing, she makes them take off the clothing and run back to their own homes.

This kabbalistic *mashal* means that the disciples have progressed from being spiritual newly-borns to young children—not fully developed immortal youths (Gr. *Kouroi*). They live as innocents in the world, which is possessed by *Shaitan* the "Prince of this world" and his elemental *elilim* (Greek *daimonia*). In this age, their physical bodies (clothing) are of this world and must be returned to the masters of this world upon death. But their souls are free, like the naked children of the *mashal,* to run away and return home.

The only connection between this *mashal* and the saying of Logion 21.b.1 is mnemonic. The disciple who dictated them remembered the saying about the thieves because in kabbalistic thought the dark forces—*qlippoth* and their *elililim*—are identical with the owners of the clothing in 21.a.

This is not so in Gnostic and other Hellenistic thought, where the owners of the field would be astrological-planetary rulers known as the "executioners" in Hermetic literature. Physical bodies were thought to dissolve back into their neutral elements at death. But in Jewish kabbalistic thought, flesh belonged to Satan. Satan even disputed the archangels over possession of the bones of saints like Moses.[256] The bones of the *tzadikim,* as opposed to their flesh, were considered to be sacred artifacts that did not corrupt. They were gathered and buried in special places like those of Joseph, which were carried home in the

---

[255] The *logion* has been misunderstood and mistranslated by scholars as "little children who have installed themselves in a field which is not theirs." That is because the Coptic word ϭελιτ has the general meaning "to dwell, visit," and the Coptic cⲱϣⲉ "property." But this has been translated as children playing in a "field" owned by others who strip naked when the owners of the field demand their field back (!), which makes no sense. The children are dressing up in adult clothing and playing house—probably in the home of one of their parents.

[256] Jude 9: But even the archangel Michael, when he was disputing with the devil about the body of Moses, did not dare to bring a slanderous accusation against him, but said, 'The Lord rebuke you!'

legendary Exodus from Egypt and buried by a later generation at Shechem, his father Jacob's ancient property.

Logion 21.b.1

Logion 21.b.1 and 21.b.2 linking spiritual thieves and the harvest of fruit are independent sayings, but would be associated in the memory of a disciple. Logion 21.b.1 is linked in Q to the advent of the Son of Man as prophesied by *Yeshua*—the Day of the LORD, of Judgment, of messianic woes, and the Birthpangs of *Messiah*. In *Thomas*, Logion 21.b.1 about thieves is linked to a *davar* about the harvester appearing as soon as the fruit is ready—a common semitic metaphor for the Day of Judgment. The mnemonic association with "thieves" is the Day of the LORD, which will come as a thief when one is least prepared. So we can understand how it is that an oral dictation of the sayings of *Yeshua* would result in linking them.

However, the two sayings 21.b.1 and 21.b.2 are independent. *Yeshua* did not deliver a teaching in which he linked 21.a, 21.b.1, and 21.b.2 in a series! It was only the process of memory and association in the mind of a disciple that linked them together. Therefore we must examine each of the sayings independently.

Logion 21.b.1 is an independent variation of the Q saying about a householder who would have kept watch if he had known what hour the thief would break in.[257] The Q saying, however, is connected somewhat paradoxically to the hour when the Son of Man will come.[258] I say paradoxically, because the *Bar-Enash* is never portrayed as a thief in the teachings of *Yeshua*. Rather, he portrays the wrath of Heaven in the Birthpangs of *Messiah* as coming suddenly upon humanity when least expected with the stealth of a thief. In some of his sayings the thief represents individual death rather than an eschatological event.

However, the phrase "thief in the night" is used by Paul to merge the prophetic doctrine of the Day of the *Yahweh*[259] with the Son-of-Man visions of Enoch: "This Son of Mankind *(Bar-Enash)* whom thou hast seen shall overturn the kings and the mighty from their seats, and the strong from their thrones, and shall loosen the reins of the strong, and break the teeth of the evil ones..." In I Thessalonians Paul first conflates the coming of the Son-of-Mankind *Messiah* in the *razim* or "clouds" of Heaven with the Day of *Yahweh* predicted by *Yeshua* and

---

[257] Matthew 24.43 and Luke 12.39.

[258] The two independent sayings as linked in Q: "But understand this: If the owner of the house had known at what time of night the thief was coming, he would have kept watch and would not have let his house be broken into. So you also must be ready, because the Son of Man will come at an hour when you do not expect him."

[259] Known as the Day of the LORD (*Adonai*, meaning Godhead) or the Day of Judgment, in messianic thought it was interpreted as the Birthpangs of *Messiah* and divine trials of the *tzadikim*.

many of the prophets.[260] Shortly after this he declares, "You know full well that the day of the Lord will come just like a thief in the night."[261]

For Paul, *Iesous* was *Christos Kyrios,* "the Sovereign Lord Christ." The prophetic Day of the LORD became merged in Paul's theology with a return in glory of *Iesous* as the coming sovereign Son of Mankind. He envisioned the Day of the LORD not as the ancient prophets had, but as an eschatological event in which Jesus the Lord Christ will come with all the Host of Heaven to redeem his elect from Satan's corrupt Earth.[262]

Paul's solution to the martyrdom of *Yeshua,* then, was to adapt the yet-unfulfilled messianic expectation of Israel to a second advent of *Iesous* in the victorious advent of the sovereign Son of Man. A coming victorious messianic advent was a convenient way to account for both the martyred *Messiah Ban-Joseph* and the conquering *Messiah Ben-David.* In the view of *Yeshua* and the Jewish rabbis, the advent of *Bar-Enash* would be an act of divine intervention to overthrew the evil that had enslaved mankind for ages. It would initiate the *Tikkun* or restoration of the Earth and humanity. But in Paul's proto-Gnostic view, it would be an act of redemption in which the elect were gathered into Heaven. The Earth and its Ruler Satan would be destroyed. Post-Pauline Christianity developed his theory into the doctrine of the Second Coming of Christ.[263]

Now we can see why the connection between the owners of Logion 21.a and the thieves of 21.b.1 is so important to understand. What we have is an independent *mashal* of *Yeshua* connected mnemonically to a saying about thieves, which in the mind of the disciple who dictated the sayings had an association with the owners in 21.a Both of these appear to be independent variants of pre-Pauline oral tradition.

Logion 21.b.1 is associated in the Q material with the Day of the LORD *Yahweh,* which is interpreted as the Birthpangs of *Messiah.* However, as we find the Q material redacted in both Matthew and Luke, the thief is interpreted as the Pauline Day of the Lord Christ, or Second Coming of the Davidic Messiah Jesus.

We do not find that association in Logion 21.b.1 of *Thomas.* This in itself is a strong indication that Logion 21.b.1 is pre-Pauline. When taken with the semitisms and kabbalistic simile and metaphor of 21.a and 21.b.2, it appears that all three independent

---

[260] I Thessalonians 4.16
[261] I Thessalonians 5.2
[262] The Pauline doctrine of Christ as a Heavenly Redeemer endeared him to second-century Gnostics like the Valentinian Marcion, who codified the first Christian New Testament by combining the long epistle Luke-Acts with selected epistles of Paul. It was in reaction to this that the proto-orthodox Christian churches began to codify what we know as the New Testament.
[263] Paul's words of comfort to those whose loved ones had died without ever seeing God's Sovereignty on Earth became rationale for the recent fundamentalist doctrine of the Rapture.

parts of this Logion are authentic. They have been linked together not by a Gnostic redactor, but through the mnemonic process of oral dictation.

What, then, does Logion 21.b.1 mean? "If the head of the house knows that a thief is coming, he will remain awake until he comes and will not allow him to tunnel through [the walls] into his sovereign home to carry away his treasure."

In *Yeshua's* teaching, death comes to all like a thief in the night—when they are unprepared for it. All too often they have filled their sovereign home or heart with love for material rather than spiritual treasure, and when this disappears at death they find themselves devastated and impoverished.

In life, the integrity of one's soul can be damaged by not keeping vigil against the evil impulses or *yezerim ha-ra* that defile and steal away spiritual treasure, which is the fruit of righteous *mitzvoth*. The heart is the spiritual temple of the *yetzer-ha-tov* or Image of God placed at the foundation of each human soul. Its divine light can be eclipsed when it is ignored or overshadowed by the evil impulses of the heart. The heart or sovereign home is also a treasure-house. Spiritual wealth is accumulated in the heart through the *mitzvoth* of good thoughts and deeds. Their benefit and merit—the spiritual treasure—can be diminished by the cultivation of evil thoughts and actions.

Therefore the heart must be guarded. How is this done? By constant vigilance of one's interior impulses and motivation so that all words and actions will be rooted in wisdom and true righteousness. This is the meaning of remaining "awake" until the thief comes.

But there is an even deeper level of vigilance that *Yeshua* required. He advised his disciples always to "watch," as translated in modern Bibles. The word "watch" is Aramaic *shaqad,* meaning a single-pointed meditation vigil or practice. The *shaqad* survived in Christian tradition as a "vigil."[264] Its most advanced form was the practice of the *Merkabah* night-vigil,[265] which was part of the *Razim* of the *Malkuth*. Daily *shaqad* was probably consisted of a morning prayer and communion with Heaven that was maintained during all activities of the day, then an evening contemplation to transform interior spiritual vices and vulnerabilities by reflection. This is probably the meaning of remaining "awake."

"You must keep vigil from the very foundations against the world and gird up your loins with great power, lest the *gedodim* find a way to penetrate into you, because they will always discover your weakness."

The *gedodim* were thieves who dug through the earthen and stone walls of a Palestinian home to gain entrance and loot whatever they found. They are compared to the *elilim* or

[264] In Western Christianity this survives mostly as the tradition of an all-night Easter Eve Vigil.
[265] Similar to the so-called Transfiguration event in the New Testament.

evil spirits that obsess and possess human beings or animals. According to kabbalistic thought, they are controlled by the dark forces of creation or *qlippoth* as servants of *Shaitan*. Only a skilled exorcist like *Yeshua* and some of his more advanced *talmidim* could dislodge possessing entities once they had gained control of the "sovereign home" by binding the victim's inner self or heart—the master of the house.

Their means of entrance was ignorance—lack of awareness or vigilance—and by exploiting any weaknesses or vulnerabilities of character, such as drunkenness or an uncontrolled temper. "They will always discover your weaknesses," therefore it is important to recognize them and develop ways to observe and strengthen character.

Logion 21.b.1 is a kabbalistic allegory that emphasizes the importance of constant spiritual vigilance and the practice of *shaqad*.

Logion 21.b.2

By pointedly observing that "when the fruit splits open with ripeness, one comes quickly with sickle in hand to harvest it," *Yeshua* stresses that all activity culminates in divine harvest or purpose. Existence is dense with meaning, if we can perceive it. But the *davar* is far more than a philosophical statement. It could be attached as a conclusion to many of the teachings of *Yeshua* because it transcends simple discursive language and leads into greater vision.

This *davar* about sickle and harvest is one of the most profound of the teachings. There is no simple way to interpret it, and translation yields only a very general sense of meaning. It may or may not have been spoken by *Yeshua* as a conclusion to the saying about thieves breaking into the sovereign home (21.b.1). If so, the connection might be that ripe fruit must be harvested and stored immediately or it will be eaten by birds and insects (thieves). Therefore, we must be constantly ripening and guarding our interior spiritual treasure for divine harvest so that it cannot be taken from us by negative forces that are constantly trying to steal its merit from us

A disciple of deep kabbalistic understanding (Aramaic *bin-*) can connect all the dots of *Yeshua's* teaching with the metaphor of ripening and harvest: No thoughts or deeds are hidden from God, and as one sows, so shall he reap; God allows weeds to grow among the grain stalks so that they can be separated at the harvest without damaging the wheat; when the time is fulfilled, the *Bar-Enash* will separate human souls like sheep from goats according to their deeds; the Wise Fisherman harvests only the large fish and throws the rest back into the sea.

In this kind of statement we hear echoes of the Jewish wisdom literature that underlies so much of *Yeshua's* teaching: "To everything there is a season, and a time to every purpose under the heaven: A time to be born, and a time to die; a time to plant, and a time to pluck up that which is planted; A time to kill, and a time to heal; a time to break down, and a time to build up..."[266]

It is not difficult to understand why the disciple who transmitted these oral *davarim* to a scribe mnemonically connected this saying about sickle and harvest to the one about thieves. At an early stage of transmission the parallel saying about thieves breaking into a house was linked to the inevitable but unknown Day of the LORD. In *Thomas,* the saying about the thieves is concluded by this one about harvest and sickle, which is a common biblical metaphor for the Day of the LORD.[267] The saying about sickle and harvest can serve as a logical conclusion to the one about thieves.

But it is also connected with *Yeshua's* teaching about the advent of the *Malkuth* on Earth. "This is what the kingdom of God is like. A man scatters seed on the ground. Night and day, whether he sleeps or gets up, the seed sprouts and grows, though he does not know how. All by itself the soil produces grain—first the stalk, then the head, then the full kernel in the head. As soon as the grain is ripe, he puts the sickle to it, because the harvest has come."[268]

Yeshua compares his disciples to fishers of men, and also to harvesters with sickles: "Do you not say, There are yet four months, and then cometh harvest? Behold, I say unto you, Lift up your eyes, and look upon the fields; for they are white already to harvest."[269] Here the white fields ready for harvest are human souls hungry for the *Basor.* The gathering of souls into the *Malkuth* communities itself is understood as the eschatological harvest.

It appears, then, that the most profound understanding of the *davar* of sickle and harvest merges messianic eschatology with mystic participation in the *Malkuth* that is "spread out upon the Earth and men do not see it."[270] This is not unlike the realized eschatology of Johannine tradition that is generally regarded by scholars to represent a late development. However, the evidence of *Thomas* suggests that the realized eschatology of John's Gospel, which reflects the historical preaching of the Apostles John and Mary *Magdala,* was rooted in the teachings of *Yeshua.*

---

[266] Ecclesiastes 3.1-3
[267] Logion 21.b.2 recalls the Day of Judgment in Joel 3.13: "Swing the **sickle**, for the harvest is ripe. Come, trample the grapes, for the winepress is full and the vats overflow— so great is their wickedness!"
[268] Mark 4.26-29
[269] John 4.35
[270] *Thomas* Logion #113, the probable original conclusion of the dictated oral sayings from Aramaic.

22.a *Yeshua* saw babies being suckled. He said, "Those who will attain the *Malkuth* are like these newly-begotten ones at a mother's breast."

22.b His disciples asked, "Then shall we, being spiritually newly-begotten ones, attain the Sovereignty [*Malkuth*]?" *Yeshua* replied, "When you make the inner as the outer, and the outer as the inner; and the above as the below; and when you make the male and the female into a single unity, so that the male will not be [merely] masculine, and the female [merely] feminine; and when you make [human] eyes to serve as [God's] Eye, and a [human] hand to serve as [God's] Hand, and a [human] foot to serve as [God's] Foot, [and] a human image to serve as [the Divine] Image; then you shall attain the Sovereignty.

COMMENTARY

Logion 22 is a mnemonic association of two separate *davarim*—one about "newly-born" disciples, and the other about internal unity and "putting on the Perfect Adam."

22.a Newly-Begotten Ones ("Small Children"), Newly-Borns

Aramaic word *yeled* "newly begotten" became Greek *paideion,,* then Coptic *kopyi,* "small children," which is used through the logia concerning disciples. But *Yeshua's* term meant "newly-begotten" in reference to the Johannine "birth that is from Above." This is an initiatic term.

In Greek chthonic mysteries, one who had descended into the Divine Underworld and communed with the King and Queen of the Night Heaven was designated a *kouros* or "youth." The term later was used to mean "servant" or "serving child." In the Gospels, *Yeshua's* references to children are also metaphorical for those "newly born" into the *Malkuth*—his disciples.

There are two uses of the Greek *paideion,* "child," in the Gospels. One refers to noisy children playing games who are compared to those who ignore his *Basor,* but the other to innocent children. The child he held on his lap and compared to one who entered the *Malkuth* was probably an obedient servant child *(Greek kouros).* The child whose angel always beheld the Face of God was probably metaphorical for a *yeled* or newly-begotten disciple.

In Jewish thought, male children were under the influence of evil spirits until *Bar Mitzva* at age twelve or thirteen. Commentators have often stated that *Yeshua* demonstrated as radical a view of children's innocence as he did of women's right to be his disciples. He healed women and children, but there are no accounts of his exorcising them. However, he equated "forgiveness" of sins (*shalach*—release from bondage) with physical healing. He did not consider children to be immune from sin, but rather from the adult consequences of sin. The sins of childhood were considered by *Yeshua* and all Jewish sages to be venial and not binding in adult life.

Later Paul and the writers of Hebrews and I Peter would contrasted *paideia* who could tolerate only the "milk" or neophyte teachings to spiritual adults who could digest the "solid food." While this usage was rooted in *Yeshua's* initiatic metaphor of the *yeled* or newly-born initiate, the Greek *paideion* had come to mean one who had been baptized. Christian baptism developed from the *mikveh* of John the Baptist, which was not initiatic, but gentile Christianity considered it to be so. The *galaktikon* or "milk-stone" was given the newly-baptized Christian to symbolize neophyte status (at the breast) as well as purity and the *psephos* or smooth stone used in Greek election to represent their "elect" or chosen status.

22.b Initiation and *Malkuth*

What does it mean to "enter into the Kingdom *(Malkuth)*?"[271] The *Malkuth* was not a place, but a community like Israel. Membership in Israel was by birth, circumcision, and rites of passage. For a proselyte, membership was more involved. Instead of right to membership by birth, it was by a form of adoption—the Pauline model for gentile membership in the New Israel that he compared to grafting a branch onto a tree.

Parallel to these, membership in *Yeshua's* community of the *Malkuth* was by divine rebirth and the halakic path of spiritual maturity. The *Malkuth* was not a place, and entrance into it was not physical, but initiatic. What do I mean by initiatic?

Logion 22.b clarifies the issue. The disciples ask, "Since we are newly-born initiates *(yeledim),* will we attain the Sovereignty?" It is clear that there are three stages: a *mikveh* purification (the Baptism of John) for hearers and practitioners of the *halakah* of *Yeshua*; invitation and initiation into inner-circle discipleship with *Yeshua*; and attainment of the Sovereignty or *Malkuth* of the *Bar-Enash.*

---

[271] For a detailed explanation of "entering into" the *Malkuth,* see the section on this topic in the Commentary for Logion 99

In John's Gospel, it is clearly stated that Jesus did not baptize anyone—only his inner-circle disciples (Apostles) baptized, and they were transmitting the Baptism of John on behalf of *Yeshua*. What constituted initiation as an Apostle or inner-circle *talmid* of *Yeshua*?

Again, the clues are to be found only in John's Gospel, *Thomas, Philip,* and Secret Mark. In the Gospel of John, Nicodemus is invited to receive the "birth from Above" by water (*mikveh* or water baptism) and *ruach,* spirit—not just by baptism. At this stage of development in Johannine tradition, the *mikveh* of John the Baptist (Christian baptism) is considered to be initiatic, but the initiatic aspect is *ruach.* The Johannine account of the *ruach* initiation, in which *Yeshua* breaths onto his Apostles to transmit the *Ruach Ha-Qodesh* (Holy Spirit), is perpetuated in the Christian Rite of Exsufflation, where a consecrating Bishop (Apostle) breaths onto the crown of the head of an Episcopal candidate and says, "Receive ye the Holy Spirit for the ministry of a Bishop," or words to that effect.

In *Thomas* the *talmidim* are always designated by the Greek term *mathetes,* "learner" of a *didaskolos* or teacher, which is used both for hearers practicing the *halakah* of *Yeshua* and the inner-circle disciples or Apostles of the New Testament. But the Aramaic probably distinguished between two kinds of *talmid,* as did Paul: the followers of Jesus, and the Apostles who were initiated, empowered, and sent forth to preach the *Basor.* The term for an initiated Apostle would probably have been *MeBasor,* one who proclaims the Gospel. Apostolic initiates would have been known as *MeBasrim.*

Secret Mark, which was written by Peter's closest disciple Mark, describes the initiation of a *kouros* or "youth" into the *Razim Ha-Malkuth.* He is clothed only in a white linen robe like a priestly levite, and after a week of preparatory instruction accompanies *Yeshua* to a secluded place on the top of a "mountain" or high hill. The initiation is done at night-time and seems to be an all-night session. The Gospel Transfiguration account and infernences that can be made from other references indicate instruction in *Merkabah* ascent. There is no mention of the Johannine transmission of *ruach.*

The Gnostic *Gospel of Philip,*[272] which seems to have been composed much later in mid-second to third century, brings together sermons, aphorisms, and teachings from several unidentifiable sources. Its theme of Gnostic initiation may preserve motifs from historical Apostolic initiation by *Yeshua.* Logion 11 of *Philip* implies that Gnostic initiates were given new names, as was done in early Christian baptism.[273]

---

[272] My paraphrastic translations of *logia* from *Philip* are based on the interlinear Coptic text provided online by Patterson Brown at www.earlychristianwritings.com.

[273] This is the basis of Christening at baptism, where the Christian name is given: "I baptize thee NAME, in the Name of the Father, Son, and Holy Spirit."

In addition to water baptism, the Gnostics of *Philip* used an anointing ritual called the Sacrament of the Bride Chamber.. The Bride Chamber was considered to an operation of chrism and fire: "There is water in a (baptism of) water; there is fire in a Chrism."[274]

They considered the Bride Chamber to be superior to baptism. "The chrism is made lord over baptism. It is because of the anointing we are called Christic[s,[275] but] not because of baptism."[276] Chrismation survives today in rituals of priestly ordination as well as in church rituals of Confirmation. In the New Testament, however, the only references to chrismation are for healing or anointing the dead. The one reference to ordaining or consecrating the Apostles is in John's Gospel where Jesus breathes *ruach* and they "receive" the Holy Spirit.

In Logion 73, *Philip* defines four sacramental rituals attributed to *Yeshua*: "The Lord [did] everything as sacrament: a Baptism, and a Chrism, and a Eucharist with Atonement, and a [Holy] Bride Chamber." Of these, the Sacrament of the Bride Chamber was the most Holy, according to Logion 82: "There were three places [in the Temple] for giving offering in Jerusalem— one open to the West called the Holy Place, another open to the South called the Holy of the Holy Place, and a third third open to the East called the Holy of Holies where the High Priest alone could enter. [By analogy,] Baptism is the Holy Place, [Eucharistic Atonement] is the Holy of the Holy Place, and the Holy of Holies is the Bridal Chamber. Baptism leads to resurrection, [but] Eucharistic Atonement leads into the Bridal Chamber. Thus the Bridal Chamber is more exalted than the others."

What was the Sacrament of the Bridal Chamber? It must be understood that in kabbalistic Judaism, sexuality in marriage was a metaphor for union with Godhead. On *Shabbat* Eve, *Adonai* made love to *Matronit*, the feminine aspect of deity comparable to the *Shekhina* and *Ruach Ha-Qodesh* or Christian Holy Spirit. Rabbi's were not allowed to study the canonical *Psalms of Solomon,* which was a collection of Hebrew wedding songs, until they had attained the age of fifty. That was because the high mysticism of divine union allegorized in the *Psalms* could be misunderstood and abused by those younger in understanding.[277]

The medieval Kabbalist Moses ben Nahman [1194-1270 AD], in his *Letter on Holiness*, said: "The sexual relationship is in reality a thing of great exaltation when it is appropriate and harmonious. This great secret is the same secret of those cherubim who copulate with each other in the image of male and female.... Keep this secret and do not reveal it to anyone unworthy, for here is where you glimpse the secret of the loftiness of an appropriate sexual

---

[274] *Philip* Logion 28.
[275] In Greek, the *Philip* Gnostics referred to themselves as *Christikoi* or Christics—followers of Christ. In Aramaic, the translated term would be messianics—followers of the *Messiah.*
[276] *Philip* Logion 101.
[277] Cf. Odes of St. Solomon 42:9-12— "Like the arm of the bride groom over the bride, so is my yoke over those who know me; and as the bed that is spread in the house of the bride groom and bride, so does my love cover those that keep faith with me."

relationship.... When the sexual relation points to the Name, there is nothing more righteous and more holy than it."

Philip Logion 89 states: "If it is appropriate to tell a mystery, the Father of the Macrocosm[278] mated with the Virgin who had come down— and a fire shone for him on that day. He revealed the power of the Bridal Chamber. Thus his body[279] came into being on that day. He came forth in the Bridal Chamber as one who has issued from the Bride Groom with the Bride. This is how *Yeshua* established the Macrocosm for himself in his heart. And thru these [operations], it is appropriate for each one of the disciples to enter into his repose."[280]

The Bridal Chamber was perhaps a kind of Tantric *Mahamudra yab-yum* union with an image of the Virgin *Ruach. Philip* Logia 64 states: "The Sacrament of Marriage is grand... [therefore] contemplate [the image of] sanctified sexual intercourse, for it has [great] power. Its imagery consists in a defiling [of bodies]...the aspect of strength [in union] with weakness. In eternity there are other [mysteries] in the likeness of sexual intercourse, yet we call them by other names."[281] Logion 85 says, "one shall be clothed with light in the Sacrament of Intercourse."

But did this involve physical sexual intercourse? Not at all. The Bridal Chamber was a *heiros gamos* sacrament of reuniting the masculine and feminine aspects of archetypal *Adam Kadmon* that had been divided into Adam and Eve in the *Pardes.* This division, which we find in the Hermetic creation story of *Poimandres* and many other Hellenistic sources, allegorized the duality that characterizes this world. Gnostic rebirth into the initiatic Sovereignty was an internal kabbalistic *Tikkun* or restoration to primordial unity. *Philip* may be quoting from *Thomas* when it follows up Logion 73 about the Bride Chamber with the familiar saying of *Yeshua* in Logion 74a: "I came to make [the inner] as the [outer (and) the] outer as the [inner]."

The Bride Chamber involved anointing with oil or chrism (understood as the creative fire), images of Mother God, and a holy kiss to transmit initiatic breath or *ruach.* "The perfect are conceived thru a kiss and they are born. Therefore we also are motivated to kiss one another— to receive conception from within our mutual grace."[282] We are also told, "the

---

[278] From Greek astrological term *to Pan,* The All, the Universe.
[279] Meaning his Son or Offspring, the *Kosmos.*
[280] From the Greek Gnostic term *anapausis,* the state beyond Sovereignty according to the Oxyrhynchus fragment of *Thomas* Logion 2.
[281] Probably in reference to Valentinian Gnostic dyads and syzygies.
[282] *Philip* Logion 35.

Companion[283] of the [Christ] is *Miriam Magdala*. The [Lord loved] *Miriam* more than [all the (other)] Disciples, [and he] kissed her often on her [mouth]."[284]

Those who have been reborn in the Gnostic Sacrament of the Bride Chamber were called "True Man and the Son of Mankind and the seed of the Son of Mankind."[285] In Aramaic terms that would be the undivided *Adam Kadmon*, the *Bar-Enash,* and the offspring of the *Bar-Enash.*

Was the Sacrament of the Bride Chamber comparable to Apostolic initiation by *Yeshua?* No. What we see described in *Philip* is a church ritual of highest initiation, not an ordination to Episcopate or Apostolic ministry. Other *logia* in *Philip* imply that Apostolic initiation could be given only by *Yeshua,* who received the anointing of the Bride Chamber internally, but that the Apostles carried this on as a church sacrament.[286]

What we have examined suggests that the historical initiation into the *Razim Ha-Malkuth* given by *Yeshua* was an all-night *Merkabah* experience. It was taught one-to-one after a week of instruction and preparation. Only some of the inner-circle disciples received this instruction, such as *Miriam Magdala.* Those who were chosen to travel in pairs and preach the *Basor,* whom we know as Apostles, were consecrated for their ministry by the *ruach* or breath of *Yeshua*—probably in the form of a *shalom* kiss that was used in the early churches, but may have included something like the Episcopal exsufflation on the crown of the head.

Hellenistic rabbinic wisdom traditions symbolized the divine union of a *hakim* and Godhead as the sexual union of bride and bride groom in their virgin bridal chamber, interpreting the *Songs of Solomon* in that way. The messianic mysticism of *Yeshua's* era extended that metaphor into *haggadah* concerning the marriage of *Messiah. Yeshua* infused his unique *Shabbat Seder* with the symbolism of the messianic Banquet, "our bread of the morrow."[287] Consequently, the allegory of mystic communion with Godhead in the

---

[283] Greek *koinonos,* Aramaic *haver,* meaning "peer, partner, close associate." This was never used of wives or lovers.

[284] *Philip* Logion 59. An initiatic kiss.

[285] *Philip* Logion 108.

[286] *Philip* Logion 101: The Chrism is made lord over the Baptism. For from the Chrism we are called Christic[s, and] not because of the Baptism. And [he] was called the Christ because of the Chrism. For **the Father** anointed the Son, yet the Son anointed the Apostles, yet the Apostles anointed us...The Father bestowed this upon him in the Bridal-Chamber [and] he received.

[287] Greek *epiousion* is a *hapax legomenon* or term that occurs only once in all the ancient Christian literature—in the Lord's Prayer, "give us today our *epiousion* bread." We do not know what the original Aramaic word might have been. It does not mean "daily bread!" Jerome translated the same words in his Latin Vulgate as *panis supersubstantialem,* "supersubstantial bread." It is transcendental heavenly bread of the future messianic Banquet—like the bread allegorized in John's Gospel for the Word of God—that was "eaten" in the presence of the Master while he gave private instruction during the *seder.* This meal—and not the traditional Last Supper or Passover Meal—is the origin of the Christian Eucharist. In John's Gospel, Jesus as divine

messianic Bride Chamber was probably used by *Yeshua.* However, it seems to have become a sacramental church rite only in second-century Gnosticism. The concept survived in Christian mysticism as the Marriage of the Lamb.[288]

22.b *Yeshua's* Initiatic *Halakah* for Divine Union

Making the inner as the outer, the Above and the below, and the male and female into a single unity was *Yeshua's* inner-circle teaching about the necessity to achieve divine internal union. It elaborated his public halakic teachings, which were a process of remedy for the moral and existential state of ambivalent duality characterized as double-minded or "double-souled" (Greek *dipsycheion*)—the ongoing conflict of good and evil impulses *(yetzet ha-tov, yetzer ha-ra)* in each heart.

The inner as the outer

Yeshua taught his disciples to make their "hearts single," to speak and act without guile, and to "let your yes mean yes, and your no mean no." In other words, be the same person on the outside that you are on the inside in order to strengthen the interior person with integrity, truth, and virtue.

His initiatic *halakah,* as illuminated by sayings about the Bride Chamber in the *Gospel of Philip,* probably interiorized this as a means of recognizing the Great Face of Godhead (*Macroprosopon,* the macrocosm) in the Small Face (*Microprosopon,* the interior microcosmic higher soul or *neshamah*). The soul was understood to be reflected in the *Tzelem* or Divine Image of God engraved in the heart when *Adam Kadmon* was emanated, generated, or begotten by Godhead. All this was understood to have occurred before the formation of the physical world or universe. It was done in the World or *'Olam* of *Yetzirah,* the invisible realm out of which the physical world manifested, comparable to Plato's world of archetypal and unmanifest form.

Paul wrote that God "chose us in him [the Christ or *Bar*-Enash] before the creation of the world to be holy and blameless in his sight."[289] *Yeshua* proclaims in *Thomas* Logion 18, "Blessed is he who is able to stand at the Beginning, for he shall know the End; and he shall never taste death." This is followed in Logion 19 with a saying that is also quoted in the *Gospel of Philip,* "Blessed is the one who existed before he was emanated into existence."[290]

---

teacher is the Bread of Heaven. The concept of the bread and wine of the Eucharist being the mystical flesh and blood of Christ became current in second-generation Christianity.

[288]Revelations 19.9: And he saith unto me, "Write, 'Blessed are they which are called unto the marriage supper of the Lamb.'"

[289]Ephesians 1.4

[290] *Philip* Logion 61: "The Lord says: 'Blest is he who is before he comes into Being!'"

When the disciple is able to "put on the Perfect Man," a phrase found in the *Gospel of Mary*[291] and other early Christian sources, he has returned to his true nature in the Image or *Yetzer* of God. Having done so, he must now externalize it—wear it in the world like outer clothing. This idea goes back to the shamanic wearing of totem animal skins and Egyptian priestly wearing of deity faces in the form of beautifully constructed masks for initiatic ritual. The priest puts on and assumes his divine or magical personality. However, in messianic mysticism the metaphor of putting on the Perfect Mankind or *Bar-Enash* meant to remember and identify with one's Higher Self[292] and project it into thought, word, and action accordingly.

To make the inner as the outer is to sanctify oneself by awakening and abiding in the consciousness of the true and non-dualistic divine nature that resides within the heart. The idea and the discipline is not unlike that of abiding in the Buddha Nature, which resides in every sentient being. The Christ Nature, however, was a theistic concept rooted in sanctified moral action and behavior, rather than in pure consciousness. Of all beings, only mankind with his microcosmic soul could attain the Christhood. The Epistle attributed to the brother of *Yeshua* strongly argues against the idea that the Life of the *'Olam* can be gained by pure *gnosis.* It must be grounded and incarnated in action: "For as the body without the spirit is dead, so *Emunah* [faithfulness] without works is dead!" he declared.[293]

The Above as the below

The Above refers to another aspect of sanctification—fully incarnating the spiritual high self within the personal self by means of consciousness and deeds. This was sometimes allegorized as adoption or regeneration as a child of God, sometimes as a marriage of Heaven and Earth.

The kabbalistic Divine Self or *neshamah* was equivalent to the Greek *Augoeides,* "shining or luminous image" in Pythagorean and Neo-Platonic thought contemporary with Hellenistic Christian Gnosticism, which developed an entire terminology concerning heavenly names and images. The *neshamah* was an "image" of the Divine Self lying at the foundation of every human heart and operating in the dualistic *'Olam* as the *Yetzer Ha-Tov.* The *neshamah* was known under many names: The Image, Guardian Angel, Genius, Higher Self. To establish conscious communion with one's personal *Imago Dei* could lead to the internal

---

[291] *Gospel of Mary* 9.6-9a, where Peter (who is often presented as an opponent of Mary *Magdala,* as in *Thomas* Logion 114—but this probably represents the opposition of proto-orthodoxy to Gnostic churches) is rebuked by Levi : "Levi answered and said to Peter, Peter you have always been hot tempered. Now I see you contending against the woman like the adversaries. But if the Savior made her worthy, who are you indeed to reject her? Surely the Savior knows her very well. That is why He loved her more than us. Rather let us be ashamed and put on the perfect Man..."
[292] Comparable to the Pythagorean and Neo-Platonic *Augoeides* or higher soul of radiant light.
[293] James 2.26

hieros gamos or marriage of Heaven and Earth that *Yeshua* taught. This was described in their own language by the Gnostics of the *Gospels of Thomas* and *Philip.* It was ritualized in the initiatic Sacrament of the Bride Chamber of *Philip,* but experienced phenomenologically in the *Merkabah* ascent of the *Gospel of Mary.* The *Merkabah* tradition under the name of Mary *Magdala,* which closely resembles the Hermetic transmission of divine rebirth,[294] was probably the way internal *heiros gamos* was historically awakened and transmitted by *Yeshua* under the kabbalistic name *Razim Ha-Malkuth,* the Mysteries of the Sovereignty ("Kingdom").

The Johannine *genesis* or spiritual begetting that is from *Ano,* the Above, is based on the Hebrew-Aramaic *yeled,* "to beget." The Coptic word for the Above is *Pe,* "sky or Heaven." This means to make the man of flesh into the Perfect Mankind or *Bar-Enash.* The process for this transformation is described in the Greek New Testament as *hagiosmos* for Aramaic *miqdash,* from the root *qadosh* (holiness, 'heaviness'), and means "sanctification, consecration." The earliest gentile Christians were called *hagioi,* "saints," which means those who were striving to sanctify themselves in thought, word, and deed.

Paul compared the discipline to a footrace (Greek *agon,* root of the English word agony), and the saint who strove to an athlete (Greek *askete,* root of the English word ascetic). He described the operative process as self-mastery through exercise like that of an athlete in training (*egkratatia,* literally "development of internal control").

Yeshua's halakah was centered on sanctification. *Thomas* Logion 98 compares the Sovereignty to a man who wants to kill a powerful enemy. Before he goes into battle with him, he practices driving his sword through the wall of his house until his hand is strong. Then he is able to defeat the enemy. This is an allegory of spiritual practice through constant introspection and self-awareness of motivation, intent, and the *yetzerim* or impulses of the heart. Through the practice and process of sanctification, the internal alchemy of spiritual *heiros gamos* was accomplished.

Making male and female into a single unity

In kabbalistic Judaism the sexual union of *Matronit* (Mother-God) and *Adonai* (Father-God) on *Shabbat* Eve sustained the life of this *'olam* or world, even though it was dominated by Prince *Shaitan.*

In Pythagorean and other Hellenistic philosophy, the male or masculine principle was divine and immortal, like the Sun, while the female or feminine principle was corruptible and mortal, like the waxing and waning Moon. Gnostics who subscribed to this view were male ascetics. In a fragment from the lost Gospel of the Egyptians, Jesus is made to declare, "I have come to destroy the works of woman," i.e., to make the mortal immortal.

---

[294] *Corpus Hermeticum* 13 and Nag Hammadi Tractate 6 of Codex VI.

In Logion 114 of the *Gospel of Thomas* when Peter (always portrayed as an adversary of Mary *Magdala* in later writings) declares that Mary should be expelled from the inner circle of disciples because "women are not worthy of the [Heavenly] Life," Jesus answers, "Behold, I shall guide her so that I will make her male/masculine [the Coptic word can mean either], in order that she, too, may become a living spirit, resembling you males. For every woman who makes herself male will enter the Kingdom of Heaven."

The antifeminism of this *logion* is consistent with Thomasian ascetic tradition as transmitted in the legends of Thomas in India, where Jesus appears to newly-weds in the bridal chamber and convinces a the intended bride and her prince to become ascetic and abstain from sexuality and other pleasures of the flesh.

"If ye abstain from this foul intercourse," says Jesus, "ye become holy temples, pure, being quit of impulses and pains, seen and unseen, and ye will acquire no cares of life or of children, whose end is destruction..."*Acts of Thomas* 12, quoted fully in Chapter Two.

Thomas Logion 114 is identified by its antifeminism as a composition of the Syrian Thomas Gnostics—not an authentic *davar* of *Yeshua.* However, *Yeshua's* injunction here in Logion 22.b to make male and female into a unity is not a Gnostic call to asceticism. Rather, it represents a return to the pre-dualistic world of *Adam Kadmon* and the angels. We can understand it best in the context of *Yeshua's* declaration that those who achieve the *Qimah* "no longer marry (male) or are given into marriage (female), but are like unto the angels (spiritually androgynous like Godhead)."[295]

In the Jewish kabbalistic thought of *Yeshua's* period, angels are androgynous—both male and female like Godhead—as are all heavenly beings. But in Valentinian and other Gnostic systems, the androgynous archangels of *'Olam Briah* are replaced by a *pleroma* of eternal *aeons.* These are male-female pairs or syzygies. They are not comparable to tantric *yab-yum* deities because they do not consist of a deity of one sex and its opposite-sexed consort. Rather, the *aeons* are father-mother pairs like the ancient emanations of Egyptian Atum, except understood as Gnostic powers or virtues. They are not "single ones" like angels, but dyads.

Yeshua taught that those who attain the Sovereignty make themselves *shalem* or whole and restored through sanctification, incarnating the *Qimah* in earthly life, no longer constrained by the illusions and limitations of earthly duality, and therefore "like unto the angels."

Incarnating the Image of the Perfect Mankind

Paul speaks of growing into "a perfect mankind, unto the measure of the stature of the fullness of Christ."[296] To replace the image of the First Adam with that of the Second Adam

---

[295] Mark 12.25 and redactions in Matthew 22.30, Luke 20.35
[296] Ephesians 4.13

was to "crucify" the old Adam and nurture the image of the *Bar-Enash.* These ideas are second-generation transformations of the original initiatic teachings of *Yeshua.*

In *Thomas* Logion 22.b *Yeshua* gives symbolic details about this process. To make one's hand (means of initiating action) serve for God's Hand, one's foot (walk through life or *halakah*) to imitate God's walk, and one's heart a field of activity only for the *Imago Dei* or *Yetzer Ha-Tov*, is to consecrate and sanctify all thought, word, and deed to God's Way.

Thus Logion 22b beginning with "When you make the inner as the outer..." outlines *Yeshua's* basic *tantra* for divine transformation—to become a Christ in flesh. It allegorizes the interior *halakah* that leads the "newly-begotten" *Bar-Enash* into full inheritance of the Sovereignty of Godhead.

Logion 23

The *Bar-Enash* shall select you, one out of a thousand, and two out of ten thousand; and you shall stand immortal as a Single Being.

COMMENTARY

This *logion* seems to preserve an authentic saying of *Yeshua,* based on its semitic construction and content consistent with other initiatic teachings of Jesus. To understand it, we must investigate the Hebrew concept of election or selection.

The Hebrews considered themselves to be the chosen people of God. This was not all fun and games. The Hebrew word for the chosen or elect people of God was *bahar,* meaning selected not for honors and rewards, but for testing and proving. That, indeed, was the painful essence of Jewish history up to the time of *Yeshua,* and it has continued to our present time.

In *Yeshua's* terms, "election" was a process of self-election and self-proving for those who would become the remnant upon which God would build a New Israel, and the seeds from which the *Malkuth* would manifest in Earth.

The operative concept was faithfulness, fidelity, *emunah.*[297] The faithful were newly-begotten members of the transcendent, corporate Body of the *Bar-Enash,* both in flesh and after death. But of these, only a very few souls would grow into "big fish" that the Son of Man would select out of his net to eat, meaning to accept and incorporate into his collective divine Sovereignty as full inheritors. These few in every generation would be those who

---

[297] Corrupted in gentile Christianity to Greek *pistis,* credal "belief."

had sanctified their lives, achieved the *Qimah,* and were found worthy to become Standing Ones who would no longer return to the sea of flesh.

The immortal Single Being in which they would "stand" is the archetypal Second Adam or *Bar-Enash* in his role as Sovereign of the Universe on behalf of God, and seated at the Right Hand of God. It is He who would select them. In Pauline Christianity, however, Jesus alone was understood to be the eternal Son of Mankind, and all baptized Christians to be members of his Body.[298] Christhood was not an aspiration of early Christianity, but redemption and salvation by Jesus Christ through his Church.

However, the *Thomas* Gnostics interpreted this *davar* to mean that their small minority of ascetic monks were the chosen people of God. They were the "one big fish" selected by the Wise Fisherman, whom they understood to be the Lord Jesus. All other people were unworthy to be selected.

---

[298] In gentile Christianity, Pauline election led to the concept of "the elect," who were chosen by God from the *Arche* or Beginning. The operative concept was "faith" meaning belief. Believers became parts of the Body of Jesus Christ, which was understood to be the corporate existence of the Church in flesh and after death. This was a radical departure from Hebrew election as understood by *Yeshua.* When Jewish and gentile Christianity became opponents, the Pauline concept of Christian election was enlisted in the campaign to characterize Jews as killers of their own *Messiah*, and to rationalize the concept of gentile Christianity as the true Israel and heir to God's Covenant.

CHAPTER SIX: Logia 24-35

24.a [Gnostic redaction] His disciples said, "Show us the *Aeon* where you dwell, for we are impelled by *Ananke*[299] to seek it." He said to them,

24.b Whoever has ears, let him hear. There is Divine Light within a Man of Light and he enlightens the whole *Kosmos*. When it does not shine, there is spiritual darkness.

COMMENTARY

Logion 24.a

The first part of this *logion* is a Gnostic redaction in order to link the authentic *davar* in the second part to their pleroma of the aeons. However, cosmological aeonology was originated by Valentinus (Valentinius) in second-century Rome. He had probably been a catechumen of the brilliant Christian philosopher Basilides in Alexandria and was familiar with the writings of the Jewish philosopher Philo. Valentinus claimed to have been a student of Theudas, one of Paul's close disciples, and therefore privy to the initiatic teachings of St. Paul.

Most of what we knew about Valentinus came from his detractors such as Tertullian,[300] who tells us that his system of aeons had been widely adopted and modified by many Gnostic sects, such as those of Bardasanes, Heracleon, Ptolemy, and Marcus, although they often denied their debt to Valentinus. With the discovery of the Nag Hammadi Coptic Gnostic library after World War Two, however, scholars recovered his *Gospel of Truth*, which the second-century Gallican heresiologist Ireneaus attributed to Valentinus. This gives us a look at his mystic ideas from his own hand. After losing a bid to be a bishop,[301] he

---

[299] Cosmological fate, astrological destiny.

[300] "Valentinus had expected to become a bishop, because he was an able man both in genius and eloquence. Being indignant, however, that another obtained the honor by reason of a claim which confessorship had given him [having been a "martyr" or witness under Roman persecution], he broke with the church of the true faith. Just like those (restless) spirits which, when roused by ambition, are usually inflamed with the desire of revenge, he applied himself with all his might to exterminate the truth; and finding the clue of a certain old opinion, he marked out a path for himself with the subtlety of a serpent." Tertullian in *Adversus Valentinianos*, iv.

[301] According to Epiphanius, Valentinus suffered shipwreck and became apostate from the "true faith" because he was driven insane by the trauma.

withdrew to Cyprus and established his own school. He died about mid-second-century, but his system was adopted by the influential Marcionites whose churches far outnumbered those of proto-orthodox and Gnostic Christians in the Roman Empire of the second century. Valentinian forms of Gnosticism were revived in medieval European esoteric tradition, and modern Gnostic churches still use the language of his Pleroma of Aeons.

Logion 24.a uses the term *aeon* in its Valentinian sense—not as a Hellenic usage of the kabbalistic Hebrew-Aramaic concept *'olam.* The text preserves a special use of the Gnostic term Coptic *ma,* for Greek *aeon,* and Greek *anagke,* for astrological *Heimarmene* or compelling necessity. Ananke or Heimarmene was the goddess of astrological destiny. As such, she was one of the "powers and principalities" that Paul said oppose, control, and strive against humanity. Gnostics and Hermetic adepts were able to read their influences in stars and planets in order to develop antidotes—just as a sailor reads tides, winds, weather, and currents in order to develop an itinerary for safe navigation over treacherous waters.

Here the disciples ask *Yeshua,* who is understood to be a Cosmic Gnostic Redeemer from the Pleroma, which of the great Aeons is his dwelling place. In the many versions of Valentinian Pleroma that were taught by different Gnostic sects, the Aeon of Christ was located differently. Here is the original Pleroma of Valentinus.[302] The Ogdoad is the Eighth Heaven of the Hermetics and the location of the fixed stars and Zodiac. The Decad and Dodecad with it comprise a total of 30 Aeons or Eternal Verities. Which of these is the dwelling place of the Christ?

---

[302] Public domain image at http://en.wikipedia.org/wiki/Aeon

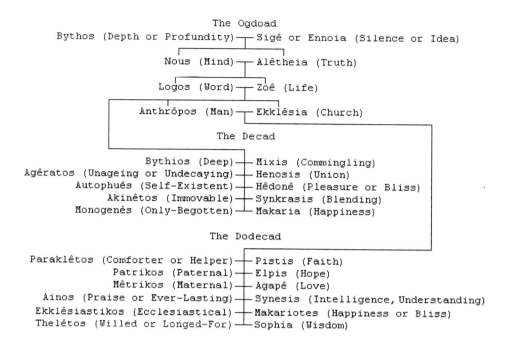

```
                          The Ogdoad
Bythos (Depth or Profundity)──┬─Sigê or Ennoia (Silence or Idea)
              Nous (Mind)──┬─Alêtheia (Truth)
             Logos (Word)──┬─Zoê (Life)
        Anthrôpos (Man)──┬─Ekklêsia (Church)
                          The Decad
           Bythios (Deep)──── Mixis (Commingling)
Agêratos (Unageing or Undecaying)──── Henosis (Union)
    Autophuês (Self-Existent)──── Hêdonê (Pleasure or Bliss)
        Akinêtos (Immovable)──── Synkrasis (Blending)
    Monogenês (Only-Begotten)──── Makaria (Happiness)
                          The Dodecad
Paraklêtos (Comforter or Helper)──── Pistis (Faith)
          Patrikos (Paternal)──── Elpis (Hope)
          Mêtrikos (Maternal)──── Agapê (Love)
  Ainos (Praise or Ever-Lasting)──── Synesis (Intelligence, Understanding)
Ekklêsiastikos (Ecclesiastical)──── Makariotes (Happiness or Bliss)
    Thelêtos (Willed or Longed-For)──── Sophia (Wisdom)
```

One might ask if these are the "many mansions" in the Father's House of John's Gospel. Absolutely not. The word in John is Greek *monoi,* meaning monastic cells or monadic dwelling places. The reference seems to be to the androgynous divine monads or kabbalistic *neshemoth* (souls) of the *'Olam* of God. But the Valentinian aeons are dyadic pairs that generate the ones below them, like ancient Egyptian or Greek cosmogenesis.[303]

Why do the disciples want to know which is the dwelling Aeon of the Savior? Possibly because Logion 24.a is an artifact of a dispute between Thomasians and other Gnostic sects about aeonic schemes. But the reason given here is that predestined astro-cosmological necessity *(Ananke)* compels them to return to the Aeon of the Christ. This kind of pre-destination is not what Paul describes in his epistles for the elect—predestination by divine intention from before creation. Rather, the Gnostic view expressed here is one of being impelled by *Heimarmene,* which, although an expression of the divine will, is post-creational and cosmological.

Logion 24.b

The question of Logion 24.a is answered with an authentic *davar* of *Yeshua* that has absolutely nothing to do with Gnostic aeonology, except in the mind of the redactor. First let us examine what it seems to mean for the redactor.

The light that exists in a Man of Light[304] emanates from Logos, as the opening Christian hymn of John's Gospel reads in scores of early Christian and Valentinian textual versions,

---

[303] In some later adaptations of the Valentinian Pleroma, Christ is paired with Church.
[304] This seems to be a special Coptic title for an enlightened Gnostic or "Pneumatic." The word is *Rmoyein,* "Man of Light," on the model of the traditional title for a wise man *Rmnhet,* meaning "Man of Heart." This term

"In the Beginning was the Logos, and the Logos abided in the presence of God, and the Logos was a divine being…All things were formed by him…Divine Life was generated through him, and Divine Life was the Light of Mankind."

In the original Valentinian Ogdoad of the Pleroma (see previous chart), *Logos* ("Word") is one of the unmanifested profundities comparable to the kabbalistic Hebrew Eternity or Greek *Chaos,* which is expressed as the static masculine-feminine syzygy *Bythos-Sige* or silent, infinite non-existence, and the fecund syzygy *Nous-Aletheia,* which is the pure self-consciousness of Godhead and the source of manifestation.

The masculine *Logos* of Valentinus springs from the pure self-consciousness of Godhead like Athena from the forehead of Zeus. In its feminine aspect, it is *Zoe,* (the Eternal or Divine Life of God's *'Olam*). *Zoe* is comparable to the Johannine concept: "And Divine Life was the Light of Man (*Anthropos,* Mankind, Adam, the syzygy generated by *Logos* and *Zoe*)." The feminine aspect of Mankind is *Ekklesia,* The Elect ("Church"). *Anthropos-Ekklesia* generates the Decad, which generates the Dodecad.[305]

Thomas Gnostics were influenced by the Christology reflected in the opening hymn and twenty-five instances of "light and cosmos" terminology of John's Gospel found in the Logos Hymn of chapter one.[306] That is because both Johannine and Thomasian traditions, though competitive, were rooted in the Christianity of Syria and Asia Minor. Thus the answer implied in Logion 24.b is that the Aeon where Christ dwells is the Logos. "Whoever has ears, let him hear. There is Divine Light within a Man of Light and he enlightens the whole *Kosmos.*" Here the Man of Light is primal *Adam Kadmon,* the *Anthropos* that is generated from Divine Life, in which is Light.

But Logion 24.b can be used to answer the Gnostic question about the dwelling of Christ in the Heavens only by forcing a connection through subtle Valentinian aeonology. Let us now examine the meaning of the *davar* in a kabbalistic framework without Gnostic spin.

We know that *Yeshua* used the terminology of light to represent spiritual life. For example, "You are the light of the world…Let your light so shine before men…" (Matthew 5.14;16). In Essene apocalyptic the Sons of Light will battle the Sons of Darkness. In a similar usage *Yeshua* concludes his parable about the Unjust Steward (Luke 16) by observing that "the children of this world are, in their generation, wiser than the children of light." In the *davar* about the eye being the light of the body (Q material used in Matthew 6 and Luke 11), he compares physical blindness to loss of spiritual light: "When thine eye is single, thy whole

---

indicates Coptic composition without translation from an earlier Greek manuscript. We have seen in another place where our Coptic *Thomas* shows independence from the Greek *Thomas* of the Oxyrhynchus Papyri.
[305] Many scholars have remarked on the resemblance of the Pleroma of Aeons to the 32 Paths of Wisdom in the emanation of Cosmos found in the pre-kabbalistic *Sepher Yetzirah* of the same Hellenistic period.
[306] The Logos Hymn was composed many decades after the time of *Yeshua.*

body also is full of light; but when thine eye is evil, thy body also is full of darkness (Luke 11.34)."[307] The phrase "light in/of the world *(kosmos)*" appears not only many times in Johannine tradition, but in the synoptic Gospels.

What was this light? In some sayings it appears to be enlightened or enlightening deeds *(mitzvoth),* as in "let your light so shine before men that they may see your good works and glorify your *Abba* in Heaven." In others it is a spiritual light that shines from within the heart—also an "eye," since *Yeshua* like all his contemporaries assumed that the operation of vision was based on emission of light from the eyes.[308]

What was the interior source of this spiritual light? In kabbalistic thought it was the *neshamah* or monadic high self—the ray or divine spark of God that could illuminate every soul that submitted to God in sincere prayer and communion. Those who were men of flesh emanated no divine light because they had disconnected themselves from the guidance of the *neshamah.* This state of spiritual ignorance is characterized in another authentic *davar* preserved in *Thomas* Logion 87, "Woe to the body that depends on a body, and woe to the soul that depends on these two." Those who lack spiritual life ("Let the dead bury their dead," Q material in Matthew 8.22 and Luke 9.60) do not shine forth their light. As in the Logos Hymn of John chapter one, the divine spark or light of *neshamah* shines forth from the Logos and the darkness cannot overcome it. But it can be "hidden under a bushel basket"[309] by human beings who do not keep faith with God's way.

Thus the *davar* of Logion 24.b concludes, "When it does not shine, there is spiritual darkness."

Logion 25

Honor your neighbor like your own heart, and protect him like the pupil of your eye.

COMMENTARY

---

[307] Here the "single eye" is not comparable to "making eyes in the place of an eye" of *Thomas* Logion 22.b. In Luke the single eye is metaphorical for making the *yetzer ha-tov* or image of God as *kabbalistic* Divine Spark sovereign over the *yetzer ha-ra* or evil impulse in the heart—being single-souled. But in *Thomas* the reference is to restoring the divine image of God in the body so that human hands, eyes, and feet serve divine will. St. Teresa of Avila said somewhere that saints must serve as the "hands and fingers of God" in the world.
[308] It was thought by Hellenistic philosophers and most people in the ancient world that the mechanism of sight was by means of light flowing as a kind of emitted fluid out of the eyes, where it made contact with sense objects. This Emission Theory was advocated by Plato, Ptolemy, and many others. The Muslim philosopher Ibn al-Haytham (Alhazen, 965-1039) did experiments proving that the ancient Emission Theory of vision was incorrect and that the Intromission Theory proposed originally by Euclid (light enters the eye from outside) was accepted and became the basis for a science of optics.
[309] Mark 4.21 cited in Matthew and Luke.

This is often translated "Love your brother like your soul, guard him as the apple/pupil of your eye." But that doesn't render the Aramaic parallelism between the heart and the eye that underlies this saying. Let's go word by word.

Coptic ⲘⲈⲢⲈ translates Greek *agapeiv*[310], which is used almost universally in the Greek New Testament when sayings of Jesus about "love" are transmitted. If we examine the concept of God's love for humanity and Israel's love for God in the Septuagint, we find that the Hebrew root used by *Yeshua* about the love humanity should have for God is *ahbah*, meaning devotion. This is the Hebrew word in his ruling about the weightiest commandments, "Thou shalt love YHWH thy God with all thy heart…"

But the love humanity should have for each other is the covenantal and kabbalistic word *hesed.* That was undoubedtly the Hebrew-Aramaic term used by *Yeshua* in all his teachings about love—whether love of neighbor or of fellow disciples. However, *Yeshua's* teachings on love were presented wholesale under the Greek word *agape,* and Christian love became something quite different than what *Yeshua* taught.

Hesed is one of the ten sephirotic Names of God found in *Sefer Yetzirah,* an important source for understanding the Hellenistic Kabbalism of *Yeshua's* time. It refers to the reciprocal responsibility between those in a covenantal relationship—God and humanity, husband and wife, parent and child, neighbor and neighbor. This two-way relationship depends upon mutual respect, honor, and good will. One must be as zealous about kindness, mercy, and justice for the other as he is for himself.

When *Yeshua* said to "love" one's neighbor, or enemy, or brother as oneself, that was an application of covenantal *hesed* as expressed in the well-known aphorism of Hillel, "Don't do unto others as you'd not have them do unto you." *Yeshua* took this well-known teaching to another level when he said, "Do unto others as you'd have them do unto you."

The Coptic word ⲤⲞⲚ translates Greek *adelphos,* "brother," from the Aramaic *ach,* meaning a relative, kinsman, ally, friend, or any other human being. In the New Testament, a "brother" was a fellow Christian as opposed to a "neighbor." But *Yeshua* made no such distinction— brother and neighbor were the same. That is why sayings of *Yeshua* about observing covenantal *hesed* are preserved in Greek as mandates to "love" *(agapein)* fellow Christians as well as both neighbors and enemies.

The Parable of the Good Samaritan was said to have been offered to answer the question, "Who is my neighbor?" The answer was all humanity. *Yeshua* taught essentially that each of

---

[310] An oversimplification repeated by many is that in Greek there are three kinds of love: *eros,* or erotic love, *philos* or brotherly love and friendship, and *agape* or divine love. But this doesn't hold true with the teachings of Jesus as they appear in Koine Greek. His word for neighborly and for brotherly love always appears in Greek as a form of *agape*—both in the Synoptic Gospels and in John.

us is in a covenantal and mutually dependent relationship with God and all other human beings. All other people, whether friends or enemies, should be given respect, honor, fairness, justice, and mercy.

This entire understanding was lost in gentile Christianity. The *hesed* teachings of *Yeshua* are now wrongly understood as commands to feel loving sentiment for your enemies. This is patently absurd. Idealists may try to feign such love, but it is not genuine, and *Yeshua* was strongly opposed to such guile. He didn't advise his disciples to "like" their enemies—only to treat them with the same honor, mercy, and justice as they would themselves or their friends. Not to hate them, and always to be ready to forgive them.

Logion 25 is an independent transmission of the teachings *Yeshua* gave about honoring all people, even as you do yourself. The Coptic uses the Greek loan-word *psyche*[311] for Hebrew-Aramaic *leb, labib* "heart, true self"). What he taught in Aramaic was to exercise covenantal love to all people, just as you would want yourself ("own heart"). This idea is then repeated in semitic parallelism in the phrase that follows.

The Coptic word ⲈⲀⲞⲨ translates the Greek *kores* "daughter," which was used in the Greek Septuagint to translated Zechariah 2.8, "the daughter of the eye," usually rendered "the apple of the eye."[312] This is a biblical Hebrew idiom that identifies Logion 25 as an authentic *davar* of *Yeshua*, as it cannot be found as a Greek idiom.

The word "daughter/pupil" appears as an object of the Greek verb *terein*, "to watch over, guard, protect," from the Aramaic root *shamar* meaning much the same, and qualified by the Coptic genitive of ⲂⲀⲖ ("eye"), scholars have rendered the phrase, "keep/guard him as the apple/pupil of your eye." You may recall what I said about the pupil of the eye, where light is emitted.[313]

Yeshua taught that we must "protect" our neighbor even as we would the pupil of an eye from dust, debris, or danger from projectiles. In John's Gospel we find this saying: "I give you a new commandment; love one another." In later church and monastic tradition, this came to be understood as the love of one Christian for another with absolute loyalty to the church.

---

[311] Another problem in the New Testament, who adopted the Pythagorean and Platonic three-fold terminology of body-soul-spirit *(sarx, psyche, pneuma)*. But the Hebrew-Aramaic of *Yeshua's* culture made several more *kabbalistic* distinctions, probably rooted in the ancient Egyptian constitution of man *(sadhu, ka, ba, etc.)*. Greek *psyche* and often Greek *pneuma* refer in the New Testament to both the pre-existent immortal soul of Plato, as well as to the *nephesh* ("self, personality"), *ruach* ("spirit'), and *neshamah* ("transcendent soul, higher self) or *yechid* ("vessel for the divine spark of God—Pythagorean monad") of the Jewish mystics.

[312] Biblical Hebrew does show three references to the pupil of the eye. Deuteronomy 32.10 and Proverbs 7.2 described the image of a person reflected in the pupil of the eye as "the little man" *ish*. Lamentations 2.18 calls it the "daughter," and Zechariah 2.8 designates the pupil of the eye as the "gate" (Greek *Kores* of the Septuagint).

[313] See Note 273 about the light that comes out of the eye.

However, in due course human nature triumphed. Epistolary and monastic injunctions were made against "eating the flesh" of your brother, meaning destroying his reputation with gossip and ill-willed statements behind his back. This is the origin of the vice known as "back-biting."

But *Yeshua's* original teaching, preserved in Logion 25, was that we should strive to treat all people with covenantal respect at all times.

Logion 26

You see the speck in your brother's eye, but you do not see the beam in your own eye. When you cast the beam out of your own eye, then you will see clearly to remove the speck from your brother's eye.

COMMENTARY

The reason this saying follows Logion 25 is the mnemonic connection "pupil of the eye...speck in your brother's eye." Here, however, we have an independent variation of a familiar *logion* found in the Q material of the Gospels.[314]

The meaning is quite clear. Before anyone is qualified to counsel another person about his character flaws and psychological blind spots, he must first rectify his own.

In Matthew's redaction, *Yeshua* calls the busybody disciple a "hypocrite," but there was no word for hypocrite in Aramaic. The word derived from the culture of Greek drama and it means "play actor, insincere pretender." But the Jews had no tradition of theater. Clearly Matthew has added the accusation of hypocrisy to the Q logion. It does not appear in the more authentic *davar* of *Thomas.*

Whenever we find the Greek word hypocrite used in the Gospel accounts of *Yeshua's* preaching, it translates an Aramaic idiom *nasa beaph,* "to take before the nose of, turn up the nose at." It meant to make a public show of spiritual superiority. The pious Pharisees of Jerusalem made a public show, having a servant blow a *shofar* to call attention to their almsgiving, glorify God, and educate the common people with their piety. But to *Yeshua* they were "takers" in public who exhibited only spiritual self-adulation, arrogance, and self-aggrandizement. They were "respecters of persons" who criticized *Yeshua* for eating with tax collectors and sinners.

---

[314] Matthew 7.3f; Luke 6.41f.

Logion 27 [Inauthentic Gnostic *Logion*]

If you do not fast from the world, you will not find the Kingdom. If you do not observe the Sabbath as true Sabbath, you will not see the Father.

COMMENTARY

Logia #27-30 are loaded with Gnostic ideas but probably do not constitute a Gnostic sermon as such, since there is no coherent linkage of ideas. In Logion 27 the Greek loan-word for fasting is *nesteuein,* and for world is *kosmos.* Fasting from the *kosmos* is an ideal of monastic withdrawal from society into private cells or communities of ascetics. The Gnostic idea of finding the Kingdom takes Greek *Basileion* even another step removed from Aramaic *Malkuth.* Instead of entering the (Greek) Kingdom, they must find or discover it, just as the Gnostic seeker is told that whoever discovers the meaning of the *logia* in *Thomas* will never taste death (Logion 1). Just as *Yeshua* did not teach faith as "belief," but as fidelity, neither did he teach the *Malkuth* as the object of a Gnostic hide-and-seek. In Logion 2, the persistent seeking after Wisdom leads not to finding the *Malkuth,* but to the "fear" or divine awe of God.

The second phrase applies a Gnostic understanding of the true *shabbat* as *anapausis* or abiding in the Ogdoad. It has nothing to do with observance of a Jewish *seder* and, in fact, is very far removed from any Jewish or kabbalistic meaning. It says that if the monk does not observe a form of contemplation or meditation that elevates his consciousness into the *anapausis,* he will not be able to have a vision of the *Autogenes* or Self-Born Progenitor of the All.

Logion 28 [Inauthentic Gnostic *Logion*]

I took my place in the midst of the world, and I appeared to them in flesh. I found all of them intoxicated; I found none of them thirsty. And my soul became afflicted for the sons of men, because they are blind in their hearts and do not have sight; for empty they came into the world, and empty too they seek to leave the world. But for the moment they are intoxicated. When they shake off their wine, then they will repent.

COMMENTARY

Like Logion 27, this is replete with Gnostic Greek terminology and themes. We have most of it in the original Greek version of the Oxyrhynchus papyrus. The themes of human spiritual blindness and intoxication derive from Greek philosophy, the final motif of repentance *(metanoia)* is rooted in gentile Christianity, but the image of the Heavenly Redeemer manifested in flesh is purely Gnostic.

John's Gospel is a second-century composition from Asia Minor based on sermons of the long-lived Apostle John. In Johannine tradition, *Yeshua* is represented as speaking like a megalomaniac : "I am the True Vine...I am the Bread of Heaven...I am the Light of the *Kosmos*..." But if *Yeshua* gave teachings about the True Vine, etc., they would have been in the form, "The Son of Man *(Bar-Enash)* is the True Vine," and not intended to be sermons about himself.

The earliest Christian creed, encapsulated in the title "Jesus Christ" promoted by Paul to the gentile churches, identified *Iesous,* and him alone, as the incarnate Son of Man *(Bar-Enash),* *Messiah Ben-Joseph*, or Christ. Jewish messianic understanding of the *Bar-Enash* as a corporate new humanity was replaced by the gentile Greek ideal of Jesus as Son of God.[315] Therefore the teachings given by *Yeshua* about the Son of Man were applied directly to the gentile version of the deity *Iesous.* Thus in Johannine and Thomasian tradition, *Yeshua's* sermons about the Son of Man were not only applied directly to the person of Jesus, but represented as actually spoken by Jesus about himself![316]

This was also brought about by early Christian pneumatic practices in which a *prophetes* (or female *prophetis*) channeled advice and teachings of the Holy Spirit for the churches. Visions of the Risen Christ, which occurred for six weeks after the crucifixion of *Yeshua,* and then was claimed by Paul on the road to Damascus many years later, began to multiply in second-century Christianity. The forms of Gnosticism represented by many of the second- and third-century gospels and apocalypses recovered at Nag Hammadi are in the form of long sermons by the Gnostic Revealer *Iesous.*

Logion 27, like others in *Thomas,* probably represent sermons or revelations about Jesus given by founders of the Syrian Gnostic community.

---

[315] The Hebrew-Aramaic term "son of God" was applied to any *tzadik* or Jewish saint whose works exemplified the ways of God. The gentile misunderstanding of this phrase, which simply identified *Yeshua* as a saint, led to early Christian legends about divine conception and virgin birth ala Mithra and other Hellenistic deities.

[316] A variation of the Hellenistic conventions of pseudepigraphy—putting one's own words into the mouth of a deity or saint. Thus was allowable for those who were in a lineage of discipleship. Thus several of the Epistles of Paul in the New Testament, most notably the late Pastoral Epistles in which he is made to say "I do not allow a woman to speak in church," were not written by Paul, but by one of his disciples after Paul's death. (According to Paul's authentic Epistles, as much as 40% of early Church leadership was female.)

Logion 29 [Inauthentic Gnostic *Logion*]

If the flesh came into being because of spirit, it is a wonder. But if spirit came into being because of the body, it is a wonder of wonders. Indeed, I am amazed at how this great wealth has made its home in this poverty.

COMMENTARY

This seems to be a Gnostic clarification of Logion 112, which appears to be authentic and translates, "Woe to the flesh that *[because it]* depends upon the soul; woe to the soul that *[if it]* depends upon the flesh." That is the kind of paradox that we find in many authentic teachings of *Yeshua* such as Logion 7, and the semitic parallel construction is preserved here in Logion 29 with the "wonder...wonder of wonders."

Yeshua and contemporary kabbalistic mystics taught that the physical world manifests from the invisible world of *Yetzirah* or spiritual formation—not unlike Plato's Pythagorean world of ideation. In kabbalistic terms, flesh came into being because of spirit. This is mysterious and wonderful. But if the reverse were to happen—spirit coming forth out of flesh—that would be a wonder of wonders, like time reversing and running backwards. In other words, ridiculous. "This great wealth" that has made its home in flesh is, for the Gnostic, the immortal human *psyche* or soul.

As the saying stands, it is classic Greek mind-body dualism. But interestingly, it does not use Gnostic terms like *psyche.* "This great wealth" could very well have been a phrase originally used by *Yeshua* to designate the *yetzer ha-tov,* image of God, or "divine spark" that animates human flesh through the *nephesh* and its *neshamah.* However, as the Logion stands, it is probably a continuation of the Gnostic teachings of Logion 28.

Logion 30 [Inauthentic Gnostic *Logion*]

Coptic *Thomas:* Where there are three gods, they are gods. Where there are two or one, I am with him.

Oxyrhynchus Greek *Thomas*: Where there are [three, or gods *theoi*] they are atheists/lacking God. Where there is one God, I am with him. Split a piece of wood, and I am there. Lift up the stone, and you will find me there.[317]

COMMENTARY

---

[317] This is an extension of the Gnostic sayings from the source used for the previous *logia.* They are preserved in the earlier Greek Oxyrhynchus papyrus, to which *Thomas* Logion #77 is attached.

The original Gnostic saying, which is extant in the Oxyrhynchus Papyrus, makes the meaning more clear than we find in Coptic. This is a Syrian teacher responding to Johannine proto-trinitarian theology by putting Thomas community doctrine into the mouth of the Gnostic Revealer *Iesous*.

Messianic Jews were not the only ones who found gentile Christian Trinitarian views objectionable. John's Gospel laid the foundations for Trinitarian theology which, to its critics, was a corruption of monotheism and philosophical monism. The later Coptic "where there are three gods" appears as "where there are three" or "where there are gods [plural]" in the Greek. The Coptic reads "they are gods," meaning "they are divine." The Egyptian Thomas Gnostics accepted Trinitarian theology.

Not so with the earlier Syrians, who wrote "where there are three [gods], they are atheists *(atheio)*." This was probably directed against the Johannites of Asia Minor who (as the Gospel of John makes clear)[318] not only took issue with, but demeaned the Thomasians. One issue was the Resurrection. Johannites advocated a Resurrection of the body and flesh; Thomasians taught a docetic doctrine that the soul that was raised, not the body. In John's Gospel, Thomas is humiliated by being forced to touch and feel the bloody wounds of Jesus in his resurrected body, thus proving the Thomasians wrong.

In Thomasian tradition, there was one God and his vice-regent Jesus, to whom all sovereignty had been given, as to the Jewish *Bar-Enash*. Johanine tradition advocated three divine faces—the Father, the Son, and the Holy Spirit, three gods. Here in the Greek version of *Thomas,* the Trinitarians are labeled as outright atheists.

"Where there is one God, I am with him," says the *Iesous* of the Greek version. In Coptic *Thomas* this is rendered, "where there are two or one, I am with him."

Why does Coptic *Thomas* accept Trinitarian doctrine ("where there are three gods, they are divine")? Because the later Thomas Gnostics of Egypt were probably forced by the same proto-orthodox Christian persecution that eventually drove them out of the regions of Alexandria to acknowledge the Athanasian Doctrine of the Trinity. Why does the Coptic *logion* specify that "where there are two or one [gods], I am with him?" Because there were also Jewish messianic churches (one God) and Arian Christian churches (two gods) operating in Alexandria and Egypt. It was only a few generations later that they would be condemned by Nicene theology. Apparently the Thomasians of Egypt found it wise to minimize conflict with other Christian churches.

---

[318] Thomas is not present when the risen Jesus appears to the disciples the first time (John 20.24), and "doubting Thomas" doesn't believe until he sticks his hand into Jesus' wounds (John 20.26f.).

It is significant that we find Logion 77b about splitting the wood attached to our Logion 30 in Greek *Thomas.* The Gnostic identification of Jesus as the divine spark resident in all life is proto-Manichaean. More about that later.

Some scholars connect this to the saying given only in the special M material[319] of Matthew 18:20, "Where two or three are gathered in my name, I am there with/among them."

Since there is evidence that *Thomas* had access to the M material, either through the Gospel of Matthew or one of its sources, it is possible that Logion 30 represents a radical revision of that saying to support Gnostic theological views. But as the *logion* appears in the two irreconcilable versions found separately in Greek and Coptic *Thomas,* it cannot be identified as an independent variation of Matthew 18.20. It simply has no connection in meaning, and only a superficial one in form.

Logion 31
No prophet is accepted in his own village; no resident physician practices healing upon those who know him.

COMMENTARY

This is an independent version of the saying found in Mark 6:4, Luke 4:23-24, and John 4:44. It does not seem to have been part of the Q material, yet it is early and authentic, reflecting the initial rejection of Jesus *in patris* by the synagogue at Nazareth. It also appears in Greek *Thomas.*

In the Gospels this is a saying about prophets being honored[320] everywhere except in their own homes and villages. This, when taken with the early Marcan representation of Jesus' mother and brothers standing outside the home of Peter seeking Jesus because they think he is insane,[321] indicate that *Yeshua* was initially not accepted as a prophet by either his home synagogue or his own family. We know that later his mother, brothers, and sisters came to acknowledge him. His family descendants (the *desposynoi*)[322] were honored in Christian tradition for several centuries as followers of Jesus.

This saying also clarifies the issue of *Yeshua's* self-consciousness. He saw himself as a prophet of *Messiah*—not as the *Messiah.*

But *Thomas* adds "no resident physician practices upon those who know him," which is not present in New Testament versions of the saying. This does not indicate self-consciousness

---

[319] See discussion in section of Logion #32-33.
[320] **Greek δεκτὸς (Coptic ϣΗΠ)** usually translated Aramaic ***Razon*** "to accept, appreciate"
[321] Historically, the probable concern of mother and brothers was that *Yeshua* would make himself a target for the Herodians.
[322] See pp. 79-80

as a physician. Rather it is a semitic parallelism that draws comparison to the fact that physicians were often unsuccessful in treating their own friends and family and instead brought in another physician to treat them. Indeed, even today most medical doctors prefer to refer close relatives to others, even though that is not part of the Hippocratic Oath.

We know that *Yeshua* compared himself to a physician in an authentic Marcan saying repeated in Matthew and Luke. He was also known publically as a healer, being mocked on the cross by those who said, "Physician, heal thyself."[323] It is not unreasonable to speculate that some of the lost years of *Yeshua* might have been spent as a member of the Jewish community of healers known as the Theapeutai who lived by Lake Meriotis near Alexandria in Egypt.[324]

By comparing the words of the earlier Greek version of *Thomas* to those in the New Testament and the Greek loan-words in Coptic *Thomas,* we can find insights into the original Aramaic term for physician used by *Yeshua,* which is crucial to understanding the comparison. The Greek word for physician we find is ἰατρὸς (Coptic ⲙⲁⲣⲉⲥⲟⲉⲓⲛ), which translates Aramaic *rofe,* "healer; one who sews wounds together, binds up wounds." For verb following it, the Greek loan-word in Coptic *Thomas* is *therapeuein* "to serve, treat, heal," but the Greek word used in the earlier Greek *Thomas* is *poieitherapeia* "practitioner of healing arts" that never appears in the physician statements of the New Testament Gospels.[325]

The Hebrew-Aramaic word that was translated into the Greek of the Septuagint (Jewish Bible contemporary with *Yeshua*) for *therapeuien* was from the root *yashav,* meaning one who resided or was in resident healing service. The original Aramaic phrase would create the parallelism that we know was favored by *Yeshua* if that is what underlies the words of Greek *Thomas.* When we translate it from Aramaic, a clear parallelism becomes evident: "No prophet is accepted in his <u>own village;</u> no <u>resident</u> physician practices upon those who know him."

The Aramaic parallelism we have uncovered in this saying indicates that the two-part *davar* as recorded in *Thomas* is probably authentic. For *Yeshua,* it meant that the familiarity of his villagers with him and his childhood actually inhibited their ability to respond to his preaching as an adult. Then we must ask, how would he have used this *davar* in his teaching?

---

[323] Luke 4.23; 23.35; Matthew 27.42
[324] Cf. my fictional biography *Yeshua: The Unknown Jesus.*
[325] Mark 2.17: "Those who are whole have no need of the physician, but those who are sick: I came not to call the righteous, but sinners, to submit to Heaven." Cf. Matthew 9.12; Luke 5.31 *et al.*

He probably used it when he sent his disciples into the villages of Judea and the Galilee to preach the *Basor*.[326] His purpose was to remind them to learn from his own negative experience at Nazareth. None of them should try to preach the *Basor* to his own family and villagers. Rather, each should go to villages where he is not known. If rejected in strange villages, he told them to "shake the dust off your sandals as a testimony against them."[327]

All the instructions given by *Yeshua* recorded in Mark and repeated with some elaboration in Matthew and Luke are based on purity laws for entering the Temple.[328] Theirs was a sacred journey, as for a Temple pilgrimage. [329]

> "It has been taught . . . a man must not go up to the hill of the Temple neither with shoes, nor with dust on his feet, nor with money wrapped in a cloth, nor with a girdle on. . . . Nor may a man make use of it as a shortcut, and less still may he spit there."[330]

> "As it has been taught: 'A man should not enter the Temple Mount either with his staff in his hand, or his shoe on his foot, or with his money tied up in his cloth, or with his money bag slung over his shoulder, and he should not make it a short cut, and spitting [there is forbidden]."[331]

Removing sandals and washing the feet was one way of keeping profane energy out of a sacred place; another was dusting off the sandals. When *Yeshua's* messianic preachers resumed their sacred journey through Israel to proclaim the *Basor* after having been rejected in a village, they re-consecrated themselves by shaking off the dust of the village streets. That act did not curse the people of the village, but purified the disciple from the *qlippoth*[332] and *elilim*[333] of rejection. Their influence was transmitted through contagion. Therefore the dust of a place where evil forces ruled must be removed for purification.

---

[326] *Yeshua* compared the work of his preachers to the practice of a physician, just as many writings of Jewish scripture refer to God's healing or binding up sin and all the spiritual wounds of Israel. Gautama Buddha also compared his teachings to the medicine of a physician used to treat the human condition.

[328] Mark 6.8-13: "These were his instructions: 'Take nothing for the journey except a staff—no bread, no bag, no money in your belts. Wear sandals but not an extra tunic. Whenever you enter a house, stay there until you leave that town. And if any place will not welcome you or listen to you, shake the dust off your feet when you leave, as a testimony against them. They went out and preached that people should submit to the *Malkuth*. They drove out many demons and anointed many sick people with oil and healed them." Cf. Matthew 10.9f., Luke 9.3f.

[329] From http://www.echoofeden.com/digest/slaveofone/2008/07/30/shake-the-dust-from-your-feet-p1/

[330] *Palestinian Gemara, Tractate Berakot 9:5 (8)*

[331] *Babylonian Gemara, Tractate Berakot 62:b*

[332] Fragments of the sephirotic vessel necessary to be broken to activate creation and manifestation—"necessary evil."

The ceremonial act of shaking the dust off the sandals as they left stood as a sign or testimony that the village was under the control of evil forces and would eventually suffer the consequences. It also was a sign that the *shalom* or blessing of peace that the disciples brought with them could not rest in such a spiritually polluted place.

Logion 32-33

32. A city built on a high mountain and fortified cannot fall, nor can it be hidden.

33. Proclaim from your housetops what you will hear in your ear. For no one lights a lamp and puts it under a bushel, nor does he put it in a hiding place, but rather he sets it on a lampstand so that everyone who enters and leaves can see by its light.

COMMENTARY

I am taking *logia* 32 and 33 together, as they probably represent one original saying of *Yeshua,* and not two separate *davarim.* Let me explain why.

The City on a Hill saying appears in Matthew's special material[334] connected with the longer Light of the World metaphor, "You are the light of the world. A city built on a hill cannot be hid. Neither do men light a candle and put it under a basket, but on a candlestick, and it gives light uto all who are in the house. Let your light so shine before men that they may see your good works and glorify your *Abba* in Heaven."[335]

Many scholars consider these and many other special teachings of *Yeshua* found only in Matthew's Gospel to represent a lost source comparable to Q and Thomas, which they designate M. Here is a chart of hypothetical M as given by Van Voorst:[336]

---

333 Jewish "little gods" or demons animated by the *qlippoth.*
334 The hypothetical M source.
335 Matthew 5:14-16.
336 This has been tabulated by Robert E. Van Voorst in his *Jesus Outside the New Testament* based on the work of G. D. Kilpatrick in *The Origins of the Gospel According to St. Matthew* and subsequent studies.

The Contents of M in Matthew

	I. Discourse
5:21-24, 27-28, 31-37, 38-41, 19-20, 6:1-8, 16-18	Teachings on murder, adultery, swearing, nonretaliation, true righteousness
from other contexts: 5:23-24, 36	Be reconciled to other believers
from other contexts: 6:7-8	Pray briefly and expectantly
	II. Missionary Charge
10:5-6, 8b, 16b, 23, 24, 25a, 25b, 41(?)	Instructions for mission: go only to Jews, give freely; be wise yet innocent; flee from persecution until Son of Man comes; be like your master
	III. Collection of Parables
13:24-30	The weeds in the wheat
13:36-52	The parable of weeds explained. Hidden treasure, pearl of great value, dragnet of fish, the scribe trained for the kingdom of heaven
18:23-34	The unforgiving servant
20:1-15	The laborers in the vineyard
22:2, 11-14	Guest without a wedding robe
25:1-10	Wise and foolish bridesmaids
other: 21:28-32	John the Baptizer rejected
other: 25:31-45	The last judgment
	IV. Against [Jewish] Religious Leaders
23:2-3, 5, 7b-10, 15-22, 24, 26(?), 27	Do as they say, not as they do; hypocritical practices, false missionary zeal; false swearing; straining gnats and swallowing camels; whitewashed tombs
	V. Fragments
5:7-9, possibly 4 and 10	Beatitudes
5:14, 16-17	You are the light of the world
6:34	Do not worry about tomorrow
7:6, 13, 14, 15	No pearls to swine; the narrow gate; false prophets
11:28-30	Take my easy yoke
12:5-6, 7, 36-37	Something greater than Sabbath, judged by your words
15:12-13	Opposing Pharisees to be uprooted
18:10, 18-20	Do not despise "little ones"; binding and loosing
19:10-12	Eunuchs for the kingdom

There is nothing mnemonic that connects the City on the Hill with the Light of the World sayings. Thus the significance of the appearance of these two *logia* in Matthean order, when taken with the evidence of all the other instances of M in *Thomas*,[337] may indicate independent use of a written source M.[338]

Logion 32

Ancient Hebrew cities were always built on a *tel* or hill in the flat plains of Palestine so that watchtowers could be built to detect invading forces. The watchtowers were carefully manned, and when an alarm was given, the city quickly formed its defenses within its walls. This form of defense was not always successful, and a strong army could break down the earthen or rock walls and sack the city, leaving it a pile of rubble.[339] The city was rebuilt and strengthened using the same rubble as a foundation, raising the level of the *tel*. Over

[337] We find special M material in *Thomas* in Logia 8 (Fisherman), possibly 30 (Where Two or Three Gathered), 39b (Wise as Serpents, Innocent as Doves), 57 (Enemy Plants Weeds in Field), 62.b (Not Let Left Hand Know What Right Hand is Doing), 69 (Bless Are Pure in Heart), 90 (My Yoke is Light), 93 (Holy Things to Dogs), and 109 (Kingdom Like Treasure Hidden in Field). However this seems to be the only instance where two M *logia* are given in Matthean sequence.

[338] As an argument *e silencio*, it can be noted that none of the occurrences of M material in *Thomas* exist in extant Greek Oxyrhynchus fragments of the text. If that is significant, it would mean that the Syrian Gnostics who originally produced *Thomas* did not have access to M, but those in Egypt who translated Greek *Thomas* into Coptic may have added the Matthean *logia* either from a recension of Coptic Matthew or an hypothetical written M source.

[339] Breached city walls always fell inward. However, in the story of another *Yeshua* (Joshua), the walls of the Canaanite city Jericho fell outward due to divine intervention and the cooperation of internal spies when the Hebrews invaded.

many centuries, scores of new cities were erected on the same hill.[340] Scientists can identify the conquering and defeated civilizations by the artifacts found in various strata of an archaeological dig.

There were no "mountains" upon which to build cities, but in addition to man-made *tels* there were also hills overlooking plains that were used as building locations. All cities were walled and with tall watchtowers. Water was not often available within city walls, so cisterns, wells, and structures to hold rainwater were built in addition to roads leading to nearby natural springs.

Walled cities built on hilltops were visible from long distances across the plains. A large, wealthy city attracted caravan trade and admiration. Travelers were able to see great city from distances of two to three days away. Thus a city built on a hill "cannot be hidden."

What is the connection with a lamp on a lampstand? Large caravan cities remained lamp-lit at night so that caravans and travelers could find their way to the gates, where they would set up camp. The city lamps could be seen at night flickering on a hilltop. Thus the hilltop cities were like lamps set on a lampstand.

The injunction to "proclaim from your housetops" is a semitic idiom referring in this case to public proclamation. The *Basor,* unlike normal rabbinic teaching, was a public proclamation by a messenger from the Throne of the *Melek* or King.[341] That is why *Yeshua* began his ministry with a public proclamation of the advent of *Bar-Enash,* heir to the divine *Malkuth* or Sovereignty. Here he enjoins his disciples to not only to proclaim the *Basor,* but offer the teachings about it given to them privately (literally, "what you will hear [whispered] in your ear"—an idiom for receiving kabbalistic teachings). They were to do as he had done.

In the *davarim* of *Yeshua* all true disciples, holy teachings, and true good *mitzvoth* or works inspired by the *yetzer ha-tov* were symbolized by light. As I previously described,[342] Jewish mystics and Hellenistic philosophers understood light as originating in the heart and emitted through the eyes. For *Yeshua,* all the things that originated in the heart had either the nature of of light *(yetzer ha-tov)* or darkness *(yetzer ha-ra).* Thus all sight, speech, and acts were emissions of light or darkness from the heart. Ordinary people were dual in their hearts and influenced by both good and evil impulses. Only those whose hearts who had become unitative and wholly sanctified to the *yetzer ha-tov* would be able to see a vision of Godhead. They would be full of light and thus *shalem*—whole or "perfect."

---

[340] Modern archaeologists dig down through layers of cities and levels of civilization on the same raised *tel* whose rubble and pottery provide reliable means of dating the civilizations that inhabited each stratum.
[341] Cf. p. 41, Chapter Three, section on the Gospel Proclaimed by *Yeshua.*
[342] See footnote 273.

What light is to be "set on a lampstand?" Not just the Gospel *(Basor)* or the teachings, but the lives, works, and examples of true *tzadikim.* Thus Matthew connects this *logion* with the beautiful and oft quoted injunction, "Let your light so shine before men that they may see your good works and glorify your *Abba* in Heaven."[343] Was this also a *davar* of *Yeshua?* Possibly. But we don't find it anywhere else in early Christian literature, and it seems to reflect early church teaching about living above reproach in a hostile society. It was added by the Matthean redactor(s) as a conclusion to this *davar.*

If we compare Matthew's Sermon on the Mount to Luke's Sermon on the Plain—both of them baased on similar Q material—we can appreciate the genius of the Matthean editor(s). The Sermon on the Mount is a classic of spiritual literature, while Luke's version of the same teachings is bare and simple. Matthew's addition of the "let your light so shine" conclusion epitomizes the finest of early Christian interpretation.[344]

Logion 34

If a blind man leads a blind man, they will both fall into a pit.

COMMENTARY

This is an authentic semitic proverb and an independent version of a Q saying.[345] The "blind" were the Pharisaic synagogue and Sanhedrin Temple leaders who opposed John the Baptist and the *Basor.* Their blindness was rooted in a lack of light in the heart—a condition they had brought upon themselves by choosing to be "stiff necked," obstinately refusing to recognize the validity of contemporary messianic prophecy. They rejected the preaching of John the Baptist, refusing to submit[346] and keep faith with[347] the *Basor.* They had "hardened their hearts," blocking out perception of the new prophetic works of spirit with the "evil eye," or projection of the darkness in their hearts, not the light. They had

---

[343] Matthew 5.16
[344] Readers should familiarize themselves with the Apostolic Fathers and other literature originally included in early canons of the New Testament such as the Epistles of Bishop Ignatius of Antioch, the *Didache* (which includes many *logia* attributed to the teachings of the Apostles), the *Shepherd of Hermas,* as well as the *Letter of Aristeas* and the *Odes of Solomon,* to name a few classics.
[345] Matthew 15.14; Luke 6.39
[346] Aramaic *nacham,* later twisted into gentile Greek New Testament *metanoiein,* "to repent."
[347] Aramaic *emunah,* "faithfulness, fidelity," later understood in gentile Greek New Testament as *pistis* meaning "belief." Most of the teachings of *Yeshua* about "faith" in the New Testament mean faithfulness, fidelity, not belief. *Yeshua* did not teach creed or belief, but *halakah* or practice. That is why the traditions from his brother James flatly state that "faith *(emunah)* without works *mitzvoth)* is dead (James 2.20)." Faith is not merely belief, i.e. opinion or theological dogma and creed. It is thought, word, and deed in life.

allowed the darkness of the *yetzer ha-ra* to dominate the divine light of the *yetzer ha-tov* in their hearts, thus their "eye" or perception had become blind.

There were many blind beggars on the streets of cities and villages. They occupied specified areas near the market place by day begging for alms. Sighted relatives led them out to their places in the morning and back to their beds in the evening, but sometimes two blind people held hands and tried to find their way over to the market to purchase food. The folly of one blind person leading another, then both falling into a ditch, was proverbial.

The blindness of those being guided by religious leaders in the synagogue or rabbis making rules of life for their followers was perhaps a different form of darkness in the heart. We would call it ignorance or misplaced trust. It, too, was rooted in the *yetzer ha-ra,* but not willfully. Rather, it was illusion and delusion—blind "faith" in the religious establishment rather than self-examination in the light of good-willed reason. The followers of these blind leaders were also blinded by the domination of darkness in the heart. However, they were less to blame. In the teachings of *Yeshua* they were like sheep whose shepherds were carnivorous wolves "in sheep's clothing." The main blame, in his view, fell squarely on the religious leadership.

The implication of *Yeshua's* application of this proverb is that true shepherds should lead and protect the flock of the faithful. The earliest Christian name for an Apostle and the appointed or elected successors of the Apostles was Greek *Episkopos,* "Shepherd, Overseer," taken from the several parables of *Yeshua* that allegorize religious leadership as a form of shepherding.

It was the *Episkopos* who was trusted to appoint and ordain deacons and priests as the threefold ministry developed in first and second centuries. The ministry of priest and deacon was a delegation of Episcopal authority that could be revoked by the *Episkopos.* It was the *Episkopos* who had authority to consecrate another *Episkopos,* who met in synod with other *Episkopoi* to decide issues of church order and doctrine, and whose line of Apostolic Succession was transmitted down through history.

For a thousand years before the Protestant reformation, the basis for church authority was the traditions and deliberations in synod of the bishops or successors of the Apostles. The Bible was consulted as part of Apostolic authority, but its main use was for scholarly research, homiletics, liturgical readings, and scripting mystery plays. It was only when Protestantism, which was founded by priests who lacked the Episcopal authority to ordain ministry, needed something to replace Apostolic authority for their reform churches that the Bible became central and ministry became congregational rather than priestly.

Today Christian Apostolic Succession is the oldest continuous lineage that exists.[348] There are about twenty-two lines of succession, many of which have been incorporated into Roman Catholicism through its conquest of third-world churches over the ages in uniate pacts. All of them have been incorporated into the lineages of many contemporary independent bishops or *Episcopi Vagantes*.[349]

Logion 35

It is not possible for anyone to enter the house of a strong man and take it by force unless he first binds his hands; then he will ransack his house.

COMMENTARY

Yeshua was an exorcist and in the Synoptic or Marcan-based Gospels his ministry begins with exorcism and healing, which were considered to be related phenomena. This is an independent variation of the *logion* found in Mark 3.27 and repeated in Matthew12:29 and Luke 11:21-22. As such, it is a *davar* about invasion by evil spirits or *elilim* similar to what is found in Logion 21.b.1 about thieves breaking in.

There are two ways it can be understood. The first is as an isolated *davar*, in which case it is about the means by which a demon binds and possesses a human. The second is in the context of the pericope given in Mark and elaborated in Matthew and Luke, in which case it is about the means by which *Yeshua* bound and exorcized a demon. I shall refer to these as Case 1 and Case 2.

Case 1

The "strong man" of Logion 35 is the master of his "sovereign home" (Logion 21.b.1) or *nephesh,* wrongly carried over into Greek as *psyche* or soul.[350] In addition to the

---

[348] Each bishop consecrated successor bishops. Ecclesiastical records were kept and maintained from the beginning for some 2000 years, so that today we can trace each line of succession, bishop to bishop from the founding Apostles. There are older lineages in Judaism and Buddhism, for example, but they are not continuous. That is because records were not kept or they were destroyed in persecutions so that there are gaps of many centuries in extant records with no certainty of continuous lineage. The second oldest continuous surviving lineages are those of Islam from Mohammad, and Tibetan Buddhism from Padmasambhava, which are both about 1300 years old.

[349] Cf. my *Wandering Bishops,* available online as a free download at www.hometemple.org.

[350] The *nephesh* was subject to invasion and corruption through the heart, but it was not the immortal soul. That would be the *neshamah,* which was defiled or purified through the *mitzvoth* of the *nephesh.* The *nephesh* was the incarnate personality that would survive death for six weeks then, in a healthy death, dissolve back into its elements while the *neshamah* withdrew from it and ascended to the Third Heaven for purification, sleep, and reincarnation. The *nephesh* of the *tzadikim,* however, had purified the immortal *neshamah* and

vulnerability of the heart to corruption through either choosing to follow the impulses of the evil *yetzer* or not applying self-examination to motives that allowed the night-thieves to invade, there was also vulnerability to possession by the *elilim.* These were entities controlled by the *qlippoth* who lived in a meta-world between flesh and spirit.

An *elil* might be a corrupt human personality whose *nephesh* had refused to fall asleep after death (dissolve in the second death) by living parasitically on human or animal vital force. It gained access to this infernal sustenance through obsession or possession. Obsession was a lesser stage of possession in which the victim was subject to constant suggestion that influenced decisions and corrupted behavior. It was described as the "bondage of *Shaitan*" by *Yeshua.* But the invading spirit might also be a nature spirit local to the geographical area, the spirit of a crazed wild animal, or other kind of spirit trying to prolong its life through parasitic human sacrifice. The nutrition that sustained it was the etheric vital spirit in blood—human or animal.

One special type of obsessing spirit in Greek folklore was the *lamia* or vampire, which the divine Apollonius of Tyana exposed at a banquet in Corinth. We are told in Philostratus' *Life of Apollonius of Tyana:* "But Apollonius insisted and would not let her off, and then she admitted that she was a vampire, and was fattening up Menippus with pleasures before devouring his body, for it was her habit to feed upon young and beautiful bodies, because their blood is pure and strong."

Obsession resulted in moral defects for those of weaker character, or physical illness for those whose energies were drained by internal stress and struggle against obsession. Obsessive dark forces could be removed, and illness relieved, by the spiritual power of a great *tzadik* trained in the Solomonic art of exorcism.[351] However *Yeshua* did not employ amulets, magical incantations, or Solomonic magic, using instead the power of his voice as a prophet and *tzadik* to command the *elilim,* since as a *Bar-Enash* he held rank and sovereignty over all angelic and infernal beings. As a *Merkabah* adept, Godhead had put the prophetic words he spoke into his mouth and would cause them to be fulfilled.

---

their "souls" would experience continuity of consciousness after the dissolution of the human personality. They would enter the *Qimah* and live as awakened beings in the *Pardes* of the Third Heaven.

[351] There were many methods of Jewish exorcism.. Josephus, a first-century Jewish writer, describes Solomonic ritual exorcism in *Antiquities of the Jews* viii.2: "I have seen a certain man of my own country, whose name was Eleazar, releasing people that were demoniacal, in the presence of Vespasian and his sons and his captains and the whole multitude of his soldiers. The manner of the cure was this: He put a ring that had a root of one of those sorts mentioned by Solomon to the nostrils of the demoniac, after which he drew out the demon through his nostrils; and when the man fell down, immediately he abjured him to return into him no more, still making mention of Solomon, and reciting the incantations which he composed. And when Eleazar would persuade and demonstrate to the spectators that he had such a power, he set a little way off a cup or basin full of water, and commanded the demon, as he went out of the man, to overturn it, and thereby let the spectators know that he had left the man; and when this was done the skill and wisdom of Solomon were shown very manifestly."

Full-blown possession occurred in those of weaker character. The invading "demon" had completely subverted the internal master of the human *nephesh* by binding his "hands" or internal sovereign powers over himself. The possessing spirit was considered to "ride" the victim as a horseman rode a horse, or a charioteer controlled a chariot. It now took control of the victim's speech and actions. It could do the same with animals, especially wild beasts, whom it would incite to attack humans.

Case 2

This *davar* of *Yeshua* is connected with the original pericope in Mark 3.22-30 about the Pharisees who accused him of casting out *elilim* by a pact with *Beezeboul,* the Prince of this kind of demon.[352] *Yeshua* argues, "How can *Shaitan* cast out *Shaitan?*" In this pericope, *Thomas* Logion 35 refers not to the possession of a human by an *elil,* but to *Yeshua's* means of freeing the possessed person from a demon. This method would be magical and Solomonic—by "binding" the demons "hands."

First he demands to know the demon's name,[353] which the spirit is compelled to reveal through the mouth of his victim. That knowledge allows *Yeshua* to bind the demon and command him to depart from his human host. This kind of exorcism is successful because it is done by the authoritative *davar* or divine word of a *tzadik* and prophet of God. Lesser saints like the disciples, who themselves were given the power of exorcism by *Yeshua,*[354] might find themselves lacking in power against certain kinds of demons.[355]

The Marcan pericope as recounted in both Matthew[356] and Luke [357] becomes a literary device for presenting all the *logia* of *Yeshua* concerning or relating to demon possession and the corrupting of the human heart, including *Thomas* Logion 35. The Pharisees, who accuse *Yeshua* of casting out demons through a pact with *Beelzboul,* become foils for a string of anti-Pharisaic sayings including the apocalyptic prediction associated with the tale of Jonah and Ninevah.[358]

---

[352] Talmudic Aramaic *Zebul,* the Ba'al or Lord of Dung—corrupted from a Babylonian deity.

[353] As any public school teacher knows, you gain control over a classroom by knowing each child's name. New teachers are taught the first rule for class management in the unmanageably large classrooms of 35-40 students that characterize American public education—*learn each child's name.* With knowledge of his name, you have a means of addressing and controlling an unruly child. Interestingly, this works for demons, too! (Draw your own conclusions.)

[354] Cf. Mark 6.13.

[355] Cf. Mark 9.28-29.

[356] 12.22ff.

[357] 11.21ff.

[358] Since the Marcan source for the pericope does not include this extra material, which appears in the same order in Matthew and Luke, and their common Q source consisted of simple *logia* without context like *Thomas,* some scholars have argued that (A.) Matthew used the less elaborated text of Luke as a source, (B.) others that Luke used Matthew as a source and simplified the text. Still others (C.) dispute the priority of Mark citing minor agreements of Matthew and Luke against Mark—which, however, could also be explained by A or B. Other possibilities have been argued as well. These kinds of issues constitute what is known as the

But the evidence of *Thomas* Logion 35 transmitted independent of its context in Mark suggests that it originally stood as a simple, isolated *davar*. If so, then my explanation for Case 1 would seem to be correct. It describes the means by which the *elilim* obsess and eventually possess their victims and is consistent with *Yeshua's* language about those who are possessed or sick being "bound by *Shaitan*."[359]

Synoptic Problem. My view is that Mark is prior to the original redactions of Matthew and Luke, which also incorporated Q with special M and L sources or traditions known in their churches, and that minor exceptions such as the problem noted above stem from the fact that we do not have autograph copies from the first century, but only later versions with Luke available to Matthean copyists and vice-versa. Luke was expanded and modified more radically than the other Synoptic Gospels over the next centuries, which may indicate a recursive process in ensuing recensions—i.e., Luke was adapted to reflect Matthean material, thus creating an illusion that "Luke copied from Matthew." In fact, many of Luke's presentations of the *davarim* appear to be less modified than those in Matthew when we examine the early or short versions of Luke.

[359] As in Luke 13.16, "And ought not this woman, being a daughter of Abraham, whom Satan hath bound, lo, these eighteen years, be loosed from this bond on the Sabbath Day?

CHAPTER SEVEN: Logia 36-49

Logion 36

Do not worry from morning until evening and from evening until morning about what you will wear.

COMMENTARY

This is not a *davar*, but part of a short but memorable homily given by *Yeshua*. The phrase "from morning until evening, and from evening until morning" is idiomatic Aramaic. In Coptic *Thomas*, it is given out of context of the original sermon.

Greek *Thomas*, however, preserves an independent version of the Q homily elaborated in Matthew's Sermon on the Mount and Luke's long section of parables following the pericope about exorcising the demoniac where *Thomas* Logion 35 appears.[360] It reads:

> **Jesus said, "Do not worry from dawn to dusk and from dusk to dawn about [what food] you [will] eat, [or] what [clothing] you will wear.** [You are much] better than the [lilies], which [neither] card nor spin. And for your part, what [will you wear] when you have no clothing? Who would add to your stature? It is he who will give you your clothing.

Significantly, Greek *Thomas* adds the Gnostic question, "what will you wear when you have no clothing...?" The authentic part of the *davar* are the first two lines only, the first of which is given as Logion 36 in Coptic *Thomas*.

This is not the first time we have seen material in Coptic *Thomas* that may have been translated from an earlier and less elaborated Greek version than the extant Oxyrhynchus recension. Since the Oxyrhynchus version seems to date from about 200 C.E., it seems that Coptic *Thomas* might have been translated from an earlier second-century Greek recension that had not been expanded as much with Gnostic theological concepts.[361] The other possibility is that the redactor of Coptic *Thomas* deliberately abbreviated the material in his

---

[360] At this point *Thomas* could be said to follow the Lucan order, which may have been that of Q.

[361] The quotations from *Thomas* found in various church fathers are, unfortunately, third- to fifth-century, so do not give us a look back at a second-century proto-Greek *Thomas*. However, the quotations from later versions do demonstrate significant variations from both extant Greek and Coptic versions. This indicates that *Thomas*, like Luke, was a work in progress over several centuries, and that the earliest recensions were probably sparse and less elaborated.

Greek version when he made the translation in order to skip to the next "clothing" themed *logion.* However, this is unlikely, as we will see when we examine the Gnostic Robe of the Soul just ahead.

The thread that links Logion 36 to #37 is the theme of clothing. But in *Thomas,* clothing is a metaphor for fleshly incarnation—not a literal concern about mundane clothing. While Matthew and Luke presented the *logion* as it was probably embedded in *Yeshua's* Lilies of the Valley sermon concerning anxiety about food and clothing, the redactor of *Thomas* had no such issues. The Thomasians were ascetics, not concerned with mundane food and clothing. Since Luke and Matthew each present the full Lilies of the Valley sermon, we can assume *Thomas* Logion 36 was originally part of a longer sermon in Q resolving the anxieties of mundane life.

Why is it given in Coptic *Thomas* in isolation? Even Greek *Thomas* preserves the references to Lilies of the Valley. I propose two possibilities.

First, it might have been an editorial decision to remove any reference to irrelevant mundane concerns of ordinary non-ascetics. The Thomasian monks had no anxieties about food and clothing as they were provided by the community.

But the reason Greek *Thomas* preserves the Lilies of the Valley theme was that Syrian Gnostics regarded one's true raiment to be the glorious divine Robe of the Soul extolled in the beautiful and eloquent Thomasian *Hymn of the Pearl.* This idea originated in Jewish mysticism, but was later adapted to Gnostic theology.

When *Yeshua* said, "If God so cloth the grass (lilies of the valley)...how much more will he cloth you?" he referred to the kabbalistic Robe of Righteousness—multifaceted and multicolored, of which Joseph's coat of many colors was an allegory. The concept first appeared in the Babylonian Trito-Isaiah.[362] In messianic interpretation, this would become the raiment worn by the *tzadikim* of the *Qimah.* Paul's spiritual body *(soma pneumatikon)* probably represents an early Christian adaptation.

These were kabbalistic antecedents to the Gnostic multifaceted royal robe of the purified soul that returns to his aeonic home in Heaven after laying aside his outer garments of flesh (dying). The *Hymn of the Pearl* is found in the *Acts of Thomas.* It describes the perfected soul's return to Heaven after successfully completing its mission to recover the Pearl, or original divine identity that has been lost in the bondage of fleshly incarnation:[363]

---

[362] Isaiah 61.10: "I will greatly rejoice in the LORD, my soul shall be joyful in my God; for he hath clothed me with the garments of salvation, he hath covered me with the robe of righteousness, as a bride groom decketh himself with a garland, and as a bride adorneth herself with her jewels."
[363] Translation by G.R.S. Mead from the Old Syriac text, in his book, *The Hymn of the Robe of Glory,* available online at http://www.gnosis.org/library/grs-mead/grsm_robeofglory.htm

XVII.

The Glorious Robe all-bespangled
With sparkling splendour of colours:

With Gold and also with Beryls,
Chalcedonies, iris-hued [Opals?],

With Sards of varying colours.
To match its grandeur [?], moreover, it had been completed:

With adamantine jewels
All of its seams were off-fastened.

[Moreover] the King of Kings' Image
Was depicted entirely all o'er it;

And as with Sapphires above
Was it wrought in a motley of colour.

XVIII.

I saw that moreover all o'er it
The motions of Gnosis abounding;

I saw it further was making
Ready as though for to speak.

I heard the sound of its Music
Which it whispered as it descended [?]:

"Behold him the active in deeds!
For whom I was reared with my Father;

"I too have felt in myself
How that with his works waxed my stature."

XIX.

And [now] with its Kingly motions
Was it pouring itself out towards me,

And made haste in the hands of its Givers,
That I might [take and] receive it.

And me, too, my love urged forward
To run for to meet it, to take it.

And I stretched myself forth to receive it;
With its beauty of colour I decked me,

And my Mantle of sparkling colours
I wrapped entirely all o'er me.

XX.

I clothed me therewith, and ascended
To the Gate of Greeting and Homage.

I bowed my head and did homage
To the Glory of Him who had sent it,

Whose commands I [now] had accomplished,
And who had, too, done what He'd promised.

[And there] at the Gate of His House-sons
I mingled myself with His Princes;

For He had received me with gladness,
And I was with Him in His Kingdom;

Why would the redactor of Coptic *Thomas* omit the parts of the sermon about the lilies of the valley and raiment of the soul? I don't think he would have. My conclusion is that the Greek manuscript he translated also lacked the rest of the sermon. Most probably, it was earlier and less elaborated than the Greek Oxyrhynchus document and therefore more faithful to the original dictation from Aramaic. The mnemonic connection of "clothing" to the next *logion* that follows in sequence also argues for this conclusion.

Logion 37

His disciples asked, "When will the *Bar-Enash* be revealed to us, and when shall we see him?" Jesus answered, "When you disrobe without being ashamed and take up your garments and place them under your feet like little children and tread on them, then will you see the son of the living one, and you will not be afraid."

COMMENTARY

Like the sayings and sermons of Jesus in John's Gospel in which the Son of Man is always referred to himself,[364] the disciples' question about when they will see the *Bar-Enash* face-to-face (i.e., not merely in a vision) is referred in *Thomas*—and possibly in the originally dictated Aramaic—to Jesus. I have restored it to what *Yeshua* would have said if the *davar* were authentic—and I think it is. The first line uses the semitic *vav* consecutive to restate the question in typical semitic form "when...and when..." This suggests that it was probably not composed in Greek or Coptic, but stood as part of the original Aramaic setting.

Yeshua's answer constitutes the *davar,* since this (like a few other *logia* in *Thomas*) actually contains an introductory setting required to understand the *davar.* Whenever a saying begins with specified questioner(s) such as Peter, Salome, Mary, or the disciple, this identifies it as an initiatic teaching. Others may or may not have been public teachings, although we can say with some assurance that most of the authentic sayings in *Thomas,* including independent versions of sayings known from the Q material, are probably inner-circle teachings or initiatic versions of public teachings.

The motifs of clothing, garments, and disrobing are used in other *davarim* as kabbalistic metaphors for incarnate *basar* (flesh) and *nephesh* (outer self, personality). To "disrobe" was to die consciously, a practice that was taught in Rosicrucian and other medieval mystic traditions, and is still taught today in Tibetan Buddhism and other meditation traditions.

This occurred in two stages. The first was physical death, in which *ruach* or spirit withdrew from flesh and the human body died. The second occurred about six weeks later when *ruach* withdrew from the *nephesh* or invisible personality that survived death.[365] *Yeshua's* Resurrection appearances for six weeks after his execution were in his purified *nephesh* body that could appear, transmit speech, disappear, and walk through walls, according to witnesses.[366]

With normal human beings, the roughly forty-day period after death is when those close to the deceased might hear their voices, catch glimpses of them out of the corner of their eyes,

---

[364] See the earlier discussion under inauthentic Logion #28

[365] Known in medieval Paracelsian language as the *astrum* or "astral body" because it was the result of astrological influence, date, time, and place of birth.

[366] The Resurrection phemonena gave rise to the Docetic idea that *Yeshua* had always been a spirit who never left footprints. It was not he, but another who suffered crucifixion in his place. The emphasis upon not only the reality of *Yeshua* as an incarnate flesh-and-blood human being, but in Johannine tradition of his bodily nature even as the Resurrected Christ in the anti-Thomasian "doubting Thomas" story, is evidence of how early the Resurrection appearances were understood as spirit phenomena and visions. The Syrian Thomasians promoted Docetic ideas, as a casual reading of the *Gospel of Thomas* reveals. Their Gnostic view of Jesus as Docetic Revealer is always a red flag when separating authentic from inauthentic layers in *Thomas.*

and mediums have their best luck in contacting the dead. The astral shell[367] or *nephesh* of the deceased seems to dissolve and the pall lift after a normal mourning period except in certain cases that can produce ghost and even possession phenomena.[368] As a saint of the *Qimah,* however, *Yeshua* was able to move and operate consciously in his *nephesh*-body, which he manipulated at will until the time came for his fully conscious second death, or dissolution of the *nephesh,* followed by his *aliyah* or "ascension" as *ruach* into the *'Olam* of Heaven. The Christian stories of his Resurrection and Ascension reflect a misunderstanding of the same kabbalistic process for a saint in death.

The *davar* preserved in Logion 37 seems to reveal the following: When the disciples are able to die consciously and without fear ("without being ashamed"), and when they are able to retain telepathic communication in service to those who are living in flesh ("tread on your garments and place them under your feet"),[369] then they will be able to see the Son of the Living One *(Bar-Enash)* face-to-face, and they will be able to stand in that presence ("not be afraid").[370]

Could this be accomplished apart from physical death? Apparently so. The legendary Enoch and others had successfully made the *Merkabah* ascent and returned. *Yeshua* had done so, as we can infer from his proclamation of the *Basor* as a messenger sent from the Throne of God. There is evidence that *Yeshua* taught the *Merkabah* ascent to his most advanced disciples, as I discussed earlier.

---

[367] Or sidereal body, so-called because it was thought to be formed by a soul's descent through the planetary spheres of Heimarmene. The incarnate personality derived from the planetary, zodiacal, and house aspects obtaining in the moment of taking the first breath at birth.

[368] Ancient Egyptian mortuary priests nourished the Ka of a Pharaoh so that the Ba would have a means of physical communication and his earthly personality could be psychically consulted through the Ka in serious matters of state when the young heir had to be closely advised. Medieval Rosicrucians used other techniques to remain in contact with the "astral shells" of their wise ones. These practices were rooted in the most ancient forms of ancestor worship in which blood and other sacrifices were offered to vivify the *nephesh* and maintain contact. However, when the deceased has so degraded his *nephesh* with vice, he struggles to stave off the "second death" and remain an invisible entity that must nourish itself on the vital force associated with blood. This was considered to be one of the several types of entities that possessed people and animals. They had to be killed or put to sleep so they could complete the process of death. Exorcism deprived them of vital force, and salt water could destroy them. That is why *Yeshua* sent "Legion" into a herd of dangerous wild boar who stampeded themselves into the salt water of the Sea of Galilee. Cf. Mark 5.9f; Luke 8.30f.

[369] The concept of deceased or martyred Christian saints who telepathically assisted those in flesh who sought their aid was rooted in the Hellenistic Jewish saint-and-martyr traditions. Similar ideas are found in the Greek worship of "heroes" or ascended saints, and in the contemporary Hellenistic Hermetic saints of the Ogdoad, concerning whom the Hermetic teacher says, "My son, they are spiritual ones. For they exist as forces that grow other souls. Therefore I say that they are immortal."*Discourse on the Eighth and the Ninth.*

[370] The idea of being able to stand in the presence of the Divine Face or Throne without fear does not refer to the "fear or awe of God" experienced in the first stages of entering the initiatic path, as in Logion #2. It refers to the ability of great revealers like Enoch to see Godhead face-to-face without danger of death because they had achieved human "perfection" or absolute purity of heart.

This, then, seems to be an initiatic *davar* about *Merkabah* ascent as a goal of Apostolic discipleship. If not accomplished in life, it will be attained after death.

In Greek *Thomas,* Logion 37.a the disciples ask a slightly different question, "When will you become visible to us?" They are asking about Post-Resurrection visions or appearances of Christ. The Gnostic answer is different than the kabbalistic answer. The Thomasians seem to have taught that they will not see the Christ until after they die, and only if their death has been sanctified with a life of ascetic *gnosis* that makes them worthy to see Christ.

Logion 38 [Two Separate Sayings, the First is Authentic]

38.a Many times you have desired to hear these *davarim* that I am revealing to you, and you have no one else to hear them from.

38.b There will be days when you will look for me and will not find me.

COMMENTARY

These reflect the question of Simon Peter in John 6.68, "Lord, to whom shall we go? Thou hast the words of eternal life," and Jesus' sermon in John 7.34, "Ye shall seek me, and shall not find me: and where I am, thither ye cannot come." Are they authentic *davarim?* Or do they represent familiarity with the sources of Johannine tradition, or with John's Gospel itself?

The first thing to notice is that Logion 38, which I have separated into what seem to be two possible *davarim,* immediately follows Logion 37, which represents initiatic teaching. The first part seems to refer back to that when Jesus says, "Many times you have desired to hear these *davarim...*" We don't have a Greek fragment to show us whether these were consecutive in an earlier version, but this seems to represent a redactional link rather than a mnemonic connection.

The second thing is that similar sayings are known only in the Gospel of John, and they come in succeeding chapters (6 and 7) that seem to have been adapted from the preaching of the Apostle John about Jesus as the Christ. The Thomasians originated in Asia Minor like the Johannites, and while they strongly disagreed with each other, they probably both had access to similar kerygmatic resources.[371]

---

[371] The special Greek word for preaching and proclamation of the Gospel was *kerygma.* What I refer to as kerygmatic resources would be sermons or other oral preaching that had been heard or memorized by Syrian monks, much of which would have derived from Johannine Apostolic teaching in Asia Minor.

I would agree with Prof. April De Conick, who places 38.a (her 38.1) as part of the original dictation, but 38.b (her 38.2) in a period of later accretions.[372] However, she thinks 38.b was added between 60 and 100 C.E., while I would point out that the familiarity with John chapters 6 and 7 would indicate a later period after the circulation of John's Gospel—perhaps 100-150 C.E.

The use of what must have been an Aramaic *vav* to connect the phrase beginning "many times..." with "and you have no one else..." was translated by Greek *kai* (usually meaning "and"). We can infer *kai* because in Coptic the conjunction used is ⲁⲩⲱ, which always translates Greek *kai*.

However, the inherent meaning within the saying is adversative, not conjunctive. In Greek composition, an adversative would have been translated with *alla,* but in translation from Aramaic dictation the *vav* would have been rendered with Greek *kai.* The evidence that the Greek recension from which the Coptic of *Thomas* was translated used *kai* points to an original dictation from Aramaic expressed with the adversative *vav.* This is often found in semitic construction. It is one indication that Logion 38.a is authentic.

This authentic *davar* of *Yeshua* implies several things. First, no one else was offering the teachings that he gave. They were unique. That means his proclamation of the *Basor* and related halakic instruction were not the same as what John the Baptist or his disciples proclaimed. His understanding of the *Messiah* was not that of other Palestinian rabbis. His kabbalistic interpretations of scripture were not given by any of his contemporaries. As Simon Peter says in the Gospel of John, "To whom else can we go? You have the revelations[373] of eternal life."

Those who classify *Yeshua* as an apocalypticist whose eschatological views mimicked those of his contemporaries are wrong. While we can try to understand him in terms of what scholars can discover about his contemporaries and their messianic ideas, *Yeshua* was ultimately unique. His teachings and practices were not only different than those of his contemporaries, but often repugnant to them.

Logion 38.a also implies that *Yeshua,* as well as his disciples, regarded himself as not only a prophet, but a revealer. His words were divine *davarim* from God given to the public in parables and sayings, but to his inner circle with interpretation and clarification.

Logion 38.b is a redactor's conscious reference to the Johannine saying that in future days *Yeshua* would be absent from them and "from your sight," like the lord of his parables who

---

[372] See her chronological chart in Chapter Two under my section entitled Recovering the Original Kernel of *Thomas* and the Historical Teachings of *Yeshua*

[373] *Davarim* or Divine Words are revelations.

went on a long journey. This and the Johannine emphasis on the absence of Jesus imply that disciples would not be able to contact him through visions.[374] Instead, they would be taught by the form of the *Ruach Ha-Qodesh* known to the Hellenistic Jews as the *Parakletos,* Paraclete—in Hebrew a legal counsel or advocate.[375]

Logion 39

39.a The Pharisees and the scribes have taken the keys of spiritual knowledge [*manda*] and hidden them. They themselves have not entered, nor have they allowed those who wish to enter.

39.b You, however, Be as wise as serpents and as pure as doves.

COMMENTARY

These are independent versions of two authentic but unrelated *davarim.* The first is spoken against the scribes or Pharisaic rabbis who ruled on interpretation of Jewish Torah. It appears in the special or L material of Luke 11.52. The second saying appears in the special M material of Matthew 10.16.

The "keys" of spiritual knowledge were the kabbalistic interpretations of scripture known to the Pharisaic proto-rabbis,[376] but rejected in favor of ritual piety. They did not offer deep

---

[374] The first recorded claim to a vision of the Risen Christ after the Resurrection period of forty days was a generation later, when Paul saw him in a vision on the road to Damascus. Before that, communication with Heaven was done by Christian prophets and prophetesses who channeled or were otherwise taught by the *Ruach Ha-Qodesh.* In Johannine tradition, Jesus was gone but sent them the *Parakletos* (a Jewish Name of the *Ruach Ha-Qodesh*) to teach them. Those who channeled the *Parakletos* either in tongues or through dreams and visions delivered their messages to the early Christian churches. That was the origin of church preaching. But they did not see Jesus or the Risen Christ. It was probably Paul's vision "out of due season" that inspired the entire second-century Gnostic Christian penchant for visions of the Revealer Christ, whose philosophical revelations became the basis for many Gnostic writings.

[375] The Greek term appears in earlier intertestamental literature like the *Testaments of the Twelve Patriarchs.* In Jewish *haggadah* the Divine *Ruach* apparently played the role of defending attorney in the court of God versus the prosecuting attorney *Shaitan.* A rabbinic term found in second-century Talmudic literature is Hebrew פרקליטא "friend of the accused." In the parable of the Unjust Steward, the good deeds of the accused acted as defending attorney or advocate in the judgment that occurred in the interim after death. This determined the length and type of purification required in the Purgatory of the Third Heaven before admittance of the *neshamah* into Paradise and rest.

[376] The term *rav* meant "great one, great soul," and *ravvi* or rabbi was a title of respect for a Torah scholar meaning "my great one." But this was before the days of rabbinic Judaism. A *rav* had trained for many years as a *talmid* or disciple in the school of an acknowledged Torah scholar. Paul, for example, was a *talmid* of Gamaliel. So there was rabbinic lineage in various schools at the time of *Yeshua,* such as that of the

spiritual teachings of scripture to the synagogues that were derived by allegory and gematria, such as found written in the later Talmudic literature. Instead they imposed interpretations of Jewish Law that set aside justice in order to favor the wealthy Temple priesthood or the ascetic rules of Chasidic piety. For example, even though the Pentateuch stresses the honor and obligation that must be rendered to parents, rabbinic interpreters had provided a *qorban* (Temple altar offering) exception that allowed people to dedicate wealth to the Temple and neglect support of their aged parents.[377] In so doing they were able to keep their wealth and give the Temple a small tithe in exchange for the much larger sum they would otherwise have been obligated to dedicate for the support of their parents.

One of *Yeshua's* ongoing criticisms of the small number of Pharisaic leaders who dominated the synagogues and the Temple at Jerusalem was that they took advantage of their position and looked down upon the masses of Jewish people. They maintained a self-righteous attitude based on neurotic observance of complex ritual. This was developed from a myopic form of rabbinic interpretation that focused on religious externals rather than spiritual essentials. For example, they wore phylacteries on their forehead inscribed with the Ten Commandments to fulfill the injunction to be ever mindful of God's Laws. They strained gnats from their soup so they wouldn't transgress the rules of *kosher* food. They hired servants to walk with them and blow the *shofar* each time they gave alms to a beggar.

The many criticisms leveled by *Yeshua* publicly against the Pharisaic proto-rabbis is found organized into lists of prophetic "woes" in the Gospels. But the Gospel writers have spun them and other sayings into anti-semitic indictment of all Jews—not just the small party of Pharisees and Sadducees who controlled the Jerusalem Sanhedrin and constituted what I have called the Temple establishment.

In Logion 39.a the word translated as "spiritual knowledge" is Greek *gnosis.* However, this is not a Gnostic concept, but one of mystic Judaism. The Aramaic word was *manda.* For *Yeshua,* the scribes or rabbis of the Pharisees had hidden the true keys or interpretations of scripture from both themselves and the people of Israel. Therefore the *manda* or spiritual knowledge that led to the *Pardes* was not understood. The keys to the Gate of the *Pardes*

---

conservative Shammai and the liberal Hillel. *Yeshua* knew the teachings of Hillel. His Golden Rule is the positive restatement of one of Hillel's most famous *davarim.* He also knew the teaching of Shammai, which he echoed in his ruling on divorce as adultery. When *Yeshua* was asked by what authority he taught and ruled on Torah, the question was about rabbinic lineage. He answered by asking, "By what authority did John the Baptist teach?" This probably originally indicated that *Yeshua* acknowledged John as his teacher, but in the Greek Gospels John is deliberately minimized. Mark spun it the way it now appears as repeated in Matthew and Luke such that *Yeshua* silenced the Pharisees by asking them to tell him the basis for John's authority, knowing that they refused to acknowledge the prophethood of John, but dared not publically renounce him. Whatever the case, *Yeshua* is addressed by Mary *Magdala* as *Rabboni* in John's Gospel, which means "Our Great One, Our Master."

[377] "But you declare it lawful for people to say to their parents, 'Any financial help you might have received from us is dedicated to the Temple instead *(qorban)*,' thus allowing them to abandon their parents." Mark 7.11-12

had themselves been locked away by those whose responsibility it was to unlock the Gate for themselves and others.

"Nor have they allowed those who wished to enter" refers specifically to Pharisaic bans against teachings of mystics and the wisdom schools that were not in accord with their tradition. Such teachers were shunned as impious or even blasphemous. The ritual for a legal accusation of blasphemy was for the High Priest to publicly rend his robe. Thus the Sanhedrin could function like the Vatican Congregation for the Doctrine of the Faith,[378] and the High Priest like its Prefect.

The *davar* of 39.b is also authentic. Its reference to the prudence (Greek *phronimos*, Hebrew *chakam*) of serpents is not a reference to the serpent in the Garden of Eden, who is said to be the craftiest *(arum)* of all the beasts. *Yeshua* opposed craftiness and guile. Satan is characterized as a serpent in the intertestamental literature, and later in Matthew *Yeshua* repeats the phrase attributed to John the Baptist when he refers to the Pharisees as a "nest of snakes."[379]

The Hebrew word *nachash* is the same for each usage—the many negative usage, and the one positive usage we have in this *davar.* The word can be translated snake, serpent, viper—all negative symbols. What positive thing can the serpent symbolize in Hebrew tradition? We know that in Greek religion where snakes were kept like pets in burrows near the hearth and caught rats and mice, the serpent was a sacred symbol. But what is the positive symbology for Judaism, and what is the "prudent wisdom" of serpents?

We find the answer to *Yeshua's* serpent reference in the most ancient Hebrew Temple iconography, which included heavenly serpents, and in the *Merkabah* vision of Isaiah, where the Throne of God was protected by the *Seraphim* or Fire-Serpents. Isaiah 6:1–3 records the prophet's vision of the *Seraphim*, or Divine Serpents of God's Throne:

> I saw the Lord sitting upon a throne, high and lifted up; and His train filled the *Hekhal*(sanctuary). Above Him stood the *Seraphim*; each had six wings: with two he covered his face, and with two he covered his feet, and with two he flew.

They continually cried the *Kadosh*, "Holy, holy, holy, is the Lord of hosts: the whole earth is full of His glory." The foundations of the thresholds of the Temple were moved by the sound of their voices.

In the later *Merkabah* ascents of Enoch, we find the *Seraphim* inhabiting the Seventh Heaven associated with *Shemesh,* the Sun. At the time of *Yeshua* the *Seraphim* were

---

[378] Originally founded in the sixteenth century as the Sacred Congregation of the Universal Inquisition. The committee was given the new sanitized title in 1988 by Pope John Paul II and the current Pope Benedict XVI served as its Prefect for many years.
[379] "Generation of vipers." Matthew 23.33

understood to be divine Fire-Serpents who protected the Throne or *Merkabah* of God. Talmudic kabbalistic interpretation associated the *Seraphim* with the transformation of Aaron's staff into a great serpent that ate all the little serpents the priests of Pharaoh magically produced by casting down their *wuz* wands.[380]

Here in Logion 39.b we find a unique kabbalistic *davar* given by *Yeshua* privately to his disciples. He advises them not to be crafty as snakes, but wise as the *Seraphim.*

The King James Bible translated Greek *akeraios,* meaning pure, unmixed, with a secondary metaphorical usage, "innocent, harmless" as doves. That is because the translator thought the characteristics of doves were being contrasted with those of snakes. But "and pure as doves" is not the adversative phrase as usually translated ("wise as serpents, but innocent as doves"). It is an Aramaic *vav* consecutive implying parallelism. Wisdom and purity are not opposites, but parallel virtues. They are, in fact, divine virtues ascribed to Godhead.

In Hebrew literature the dove symbolizes the *Ruach* of God, as it does in the Gospel story of John's baptism of Jesus in the Jordan. In fact, the dove was sacred to Astarte,[381] the ancient Phoenecian, Babylonian *(Astoreth),* and Canaanite Goddess whose terebinth-tree Ashera stood on the hills from Neolithic through Bronze ages. She was the original feminine aspect or wife of Yahweh worshipped by Solomon and, in the Jewish wisdom tradition, she represented *Hochmah,* the wisdom and purity of the virgin (young woman) instructress and disciplinarian Mother God. She was known to *Yeshua* and the messianic mystics as the *Ruach Ha-Qodesh* or Spirit of Holiness, which became the neuter Holy Spirit of New Testament Greek *Pneuma Hagion,* and with the Latin Vulgate translation of St. Jerome the masculine *Spiritus Sanctus.* I have quoted from James Still's excellent summary in the footnote below.[382]

---

[380] Exodus 7.9-13

[381] Just as the owl was sacred to Athena. The presence of dove was taken as a sign of the blessing and protection of Astarte. In more ancient iconography, Astarte is also seen with owls, the messengers of wisdom later associated with Greek Athena

[382] Long before the *Yahweh* cult emerged among the Hebrews in the Ancient Near East the Goddess Astarte was worshipped by them. Her oldest temple at Byblos dates back to the Neolithic and she flourished in the Bronze Age where she was also known as Demeter in Greece and Ishtar in Babylonia. King Solomon worshipped Astarte when the Israelites had not yet fully committed to monotheism with a *Yahweh* cult (1 Kings 11:5). During the Bronze Age some Israelites perceived her as the female consort to *Yahweh.* Her symbol was the dove and coinage portrayed Astarte as the heavenly dove of Wisdom (Walker, 1983, p. 253-54). At the height of her powers there were many gods and goddesses one of which was *Yahweh*; the Psalmist refers to a "Divine Council" of these gods which *Yahweh* addresses: God has taken his place in the divine council; in the midst of the gods he holds judgment: "How long will you judge unjustly and show partiality to the wicked? *Selah.* Give justice to the weak and the fatherless; maintain the right of the afflicted and the destitute. Rescue the weak and the needy; deliver them from the hand of the wicked." They have neither knowledge nor understanding, they walk about in darkness; all the foundations of the earth are shaken. I say,

Yeshua is portrayed in Mark and Luke as a devotee of the *Ruach Ha-Qodesh* and warns that blasphemy against Her was the most serious spiritual offense.[383]

In the *logion* of Matthew 10.16, the preamble to the *davar* is, "Behold, I send you forth as sheep among wolves; therefore..." The wolves (in sheep's clothing) are the rabbis of the Pharisees. In Logion 39, the preamble is another saying about the hostile rabbis. It is clear that whatever the context of the original advice given by *Yeshua* to his disciples, the *davar* of Logion 39.b is meant to prepare them for survival in a hostile religious environment.

In Matthew, the Greek version that the redactor of *Thomas* translated, and in the Greek Oxyrhynchus fragments, the word used is *phronimos,* "prudence and practical wisdom." In the Jewish tradition we cannot find evidence of snakes symbolizing prudence. The original Aramaic word was more likely from the root *hakam*—divine wisdom of the magical *Seraphim.* My reconstruction of the original *davar* uses the English word "wise" in the sense of *Hochmah,* Divine Wisdom, and this is parallel in meaning to the divine purity of doves as symbols of Spirit. In fact, the Hebrew-Aramaic word for dove was the feminine *yonah,* which complements the masculine *nachash* snake. The *davar* may represent a kabbalistic reference to the masculine-feminine nature of Godhead that each disciple must emulate through the divine attributes of Wisdom and Purity.

"You are gods, sons of the Most High, all of you; nevertheless, you shall die like men, and fall like any prince" (Psalms 82:1-7). *Yahweh* is upset with his fellow gods and accuses them of not looking after the needs of the weak and destitute. If they do not help, *Yahweh* predicts that they will be overthrown--a prediction which unfolds within the Hebrew scriptures as the gods (to include Astarte) are eventually cast off for a monotheism under *Yahweh.* Astarte will return during Hellenistic Judaism in the apocalyptic and wisdom literature. Wisdom (*Sophia*) becomes personified in 3d-century BCE Judaism as a strong female principle of *Yahweh.* We learn from Proverbs that she calls to "the sons of men" crying aloud at the portals of towns (Prov. 8:1-4). She signals her approval of the Christ by appearing to Jesus as an epiphany in dove form at Jesus's baptism (Mk. 1:9-11; Mt. 3:13-17; Lk. 3:21-22). But with the destruction of Jerusalem (and so the normative Judaism of the Second Temple Period) this feminine principle of *Yahweh* will disappear forever from Judaism...Astarte's decline resulted from a radical shift toward masculinity in [late Hellenistic] religion. http://www.infidels.org/library/modern/james_still/astarte.html

[383] The Sin Against the Holy Spirit saying as it was redacted in Mark 3.29 and Luke 12.10 reflects the earliest form of Christian Trinitarianism (Father, Son, and Holy Spirit, where the Son is the *Bar-Enash,* not Jesus *per se*). It can be argued that the saying emerged from the pneumatic churches and was not original with *Yeshua,* since the Holy Spirit is mentioned in only one other authentic *davar* of *Yeshua,* but appears everywhere in Gospel-Acts narratives. But the centrality of early Christian pneumatic phenomena may point to origins in authentic inner-circle teachings about the *Ruach Ha-Qodesh.*

A grapevine has been planted without the *Abba*, but because it is corrupt, it will be pulled up by its roots and destroyed.

COMMENTARY

This is an independent version of one of *Yeshua's* prophecies against the Jerusalem Temple establishment. One quite similar to it is found in the special Matthean material.[384] He declares that the wealthy Pharisaic and Sadducean rulers who control the Sanhedrin and have made corrupting accommodations with the Roman occupiers will fall. Many of the accusations he made about the corruption of religious authorities along with his prophecies about the coming destruction of the Second Temple appear in the New Testament Gospels as prophecies against all Jews.

Why? Because by mid-century the conflict between messianic Jewish and gentile Christian communities had come to a head, and the Gospels were written in that context. The so-called Judaizers that Paul railed against in his Epistles argued that gentile Christians should become Jewish proselytes, be circumcised, and follow Jewish *kosher* food rules. What is more, they proclaimed a different gospel than Paul,[385] which however was probably truer to *Yeshua's Basor* than was the gospel of Paul.

Jewish Christianity was rejected by synagogue Judaism. The so-called *minim* or heretics were cursed daily in the new prayer that was added to the *Amida*, as I earlier explained. Gentile Christianity was Pauline and rejected the Judaizers. After this the gentile Greek Gospels and Acts were written and circulated in the churches. They included apologetic spin to show that God had made a "new testament" or covenant with the gentile believers, who were now the true Israel. The Jews had rejected and killed their own *Messiah*. This anti-semitic polemic permeates all four of the Christian Gospels.

Mark and the Synoptics absolve the Romans for the crucifixion of Jesus by portraying Pilate as an unwilling judge. Matthew goes farther and describes Pilate doing a purification *mikveh* to absolve him of Jesus' blood using Jewish ritual (washes his hands) and has the Jewish people accept corporate guilt: "Then answered all the people, and said, His blood be

---

[384] Mt 15:13. "Every plant that my heavenly Father has not planted will be uprooted."

[385] Romans 11.28: "As concerning the gospel, they [the Jews] are enemies for your sakes: but as touching the election, they are beloved for the father's sakes. II Corinthians 11.4-5: "If someone comes and proclaims another Jesus than the one we proclaimed, or if you receive a different spirit from the one you received, or if you accept a different gospel from the one you accepted, you put up with it readily enough. [5]Indeed, I consider that I am not in the least inferior to these super-Apostles..." Galatians 1.9: "...if any man preach any other gospel unto you than that ye have received [from me], let him be accursed."

on us, and on our children."[386] While all the Gospels blame the Jewish Temple establishment for *Yeshua's* crucifixion, they don't go as far as Matthew in their Christ-killer implications. But they all spin *Yeshua's* prophecies against the Jerusalem Temple establishment into blatant condemnations of Judaism and all Jews.

The facts, however, are that Herod executed John the Baptist because he was inciting popular messianic expectation that could result in Jewish revolt against Roman occupiers, and Herod planned to do the same with *Yeshua.* The Herodians of the Gospels, who are correctly portrayed as the enemies of *Yeshua,* were both Roman spies and Jewish collaborators.[387]

Pilate was under orders to seize and execute *Yeshua* because he was dangerously popular with the Jewish people. His presence in Jerusalem at the *Pesach* with tens of thousands of pilgrims seeking a *Messiah* could not be tolerated. The Romans had already executed and crucified scores of messianic pretenders. *Yeshua* posed a serious threat that could spark messianic rebellion in Jerusalem. His decision to enter the city riding up the prophesied messianic "foal of an ass" was probably calculated to publicly promote the *Basor.* Whether it was a "passover plot" is another question.[388] But that was certainly the act that precipitated his arrest by the Romans.

The anti-Jewish polemic in the Christian Gospels presents a distorted picture of the prophesies and crucifixion of *Yeshua.* When we understand that the early churches were confronted with the preaching of travelling Jewish Apostles and disciples of *Yeshua,* that these teachings were opposed to the gospel of their founder Paul especially on the issues of circumcision and *kosher* rules, we can understand why the "party of the circumcision" came to be rejected by the gentile churches.

But the early Greek Christians understood that these so-called Judaizers, unlike Paul, had walked with *Yeshua* and received his teachings. That was why they were a threat to Pauline Christianity, why the Lucan account in Acts is careful to attribute a revelation reversing the rules of *kosher* food and opening the messianic door to gentiles to the Apostle Peter (not Paul), and John's Gospel tells of Jesus being approached through Philip by gentile

---

[386] Matthew 27.25

[387] Mark 3.6; 12.13; Matthew 22.16

[388] Proposed by Hugh Schonfeld in his 1965 *Passover Plot*, as summarized in Wikipedia: "His reading of that Gospel convinced him that John's account, though probably filtered through an assistant and transcription in John's old age, suggests that Jesus had planned everything. Among other things, so that he would not be on the cross for more than a few hours before the Sabbath arrived when it was required by law that Jews be taken down, so that one of his supporters, who was on hand, would give him water (to quench his thirst) that was actually laced with a drug to make him unconscious, and so that Joseph of Arimathea, a well-connected supporter, would collect him off the cross while still alive (but appearing dead) so that he could be secretly nursed back to health. Schonfeld suggests that the plan went awry because of a soldier's actions with a spear." http://en.wikipedia.org/wiki/The_Passover_Plot

emissaries wanting to be initiated into the *Malkuth.* Even though his mission was only to the Jews, it was reasoned, Jesus planned for it to eventually go out to the gentile world, as Paul had envisioned.[389]

The Gospel writers read evidence for this view into messianic prophecies from the Old Testament and used proof-texts to construct narratives. In their view, the historical teachings as remembered and represented in Jewish Christianity had grown obsolete in comparison to what gentile Christian prophets were receiving directly from the Holy Spirit and had been written by the Greek-speaking Paul, who had seen a vision of the Risen Christ.[390]

Logion 40 transmits one of *Yeshua's* prophecies about the coming destruction of the Jerusalem Temple establishment, but without the later anti-semitic spin of the New Testament. There are several things to note in this early independent *davar.*

First, he compares the institution of the Second Temple to the planting of a grapevine outside of the *Abba's* vineyard. The vineyard is a kabbalistic symbol of the *Pardes,* a spiritual sanctuary where the *Tikkun* can be experienced by *tzadikim* and mystics temporarily on Earth. In Talmudic literature it is usually no more than a private room or even an outdoor setting like and oasis or resting place. But in the period of the Second Temple, its sacred precincts were supposed to be the sanctuary of God on Earth where scripture was studied and inspiration was received.

But the Temple had been corrupted. Collaborators had allowed the Herodian to glorify the Temple by erecting Roman splendors and trimming it with gold and precious stones. It had become one of the wonders of the ancient world to satisfy Herod's pride. The High Priest, a Sadducean politician and plutocrat, was appointed and controlled by Herod. He was beholden to the Romans, not the Jewish people. In *Yeshua's* day it was the vain Caiaphas who served as Herod's puppet. This Roman-appointed High Priest was so hated, according to some accounts, that *Iakob* (James) the brother of *Yeshua*—a recognized saint in Jerusalem—was acclaimed High Priest by popular demand and carried out the *Yom Kippur* rituals in the Holy of Holies.[391]

Thus the vine of Logion 40 had been planted not by God, but by self-serving men—outside of the divine vineyard. "It is diseased" translates the negative of the Coptic word from ⲧⲁⲭⲡⲟ, meaning "firm, established, well-founded." Thus *Yeshua* compares the Temple

---

[389] Indeed, unlike Palestinian messianic expectation, *Yeshua's Basor* was about the sanctification of all humanity—not merely Israel. He undoubtedly intended it to eventually be preached worldwide.

[390] This explains the need for careful scholarly investigation if we are concerned with recovering the historical teachings of *Yeshua.* They can't be taken literally from the Greek Christian Gospels because their redaction represents as much manipulation of authentic material as we find in Gnostic *Thomas.* We can't get behind the external façade unless we understand the principles upon which it was erected.

[391] Cf. Robert Eisenman *James the Brother of Jesus,* Chapter 13, "James as Opposition High Priest and *Oblias.*"

establishment to an infirm, corrupt, or diseased grapevine that does not produce fruit. Therefore, as every Hebrew prophet and vine-dresser knew, it must be torn up by the roots, destroyed, and replaced. God will not do the uprooting--that will be accomplished by *qlippotic* forces as the natural and necessary consequence of sin.[392]

Yeshua prophesied in Logion 40 that because the Temple establishment and the Second Temple of Solomon had no fidelity to God, they will be destroyed. He also prophesied the coming inevitable suffering of Jerusalem itself in sayings about the Birth-Pangs of *Messiah* that were later interpreted in the gentile churches as eschatological revelations about the imminent end of the world.

Yeshua's prophecies came to pass a generation later (66-70 C.E.) when Zealot and *sicarii* revolutionaries took over Jerusalem and, in response, it was besieged by Roman forces According to Josephus, the four years of suffering was so great that people survived only by eating the flesh of their dead. After Emperor Vespasian's son Titus finally breached the walls and recaptured Jerusalem for Rome, his troops utterly destroyed the Temple of Solomon. As *Yeshua* had prophesied, not one stone remained standing.

The Pharisees regrouped in Jamnia *(Javne)* under the leadership of the Pharisaic *Rav Jochanan ben-Zakkai,* R. Hillel's greatest student. He had advocated pacifism during the Seige of Jerusalem and finally employed his disciples to take him through Roman soldiers pretending to be dead and taken for burial in a coffin.[393] Instead they took him to Vespasian's tent, where he prophecied that General Vespasian would soon become Emperor and requested to be allowed to settle in *Javne* or Jamnia with his disciples and found a peaceful rabbinic school to preserve the venerable traditions of Judaism. Vespasian, who later did become Emperor, agreed to this, and Pharisaic Judaism survived as Rabbinic Judaism. After this time, however, the Sadducean sect and Temple Priesthood disappear from history. The Second Temple and its religious rulership had been completely destroyed, as *Yeshua* foretold.

---

[392] *Yeshua* taught that God is good. There is no such thing as a so-called catastrophic "act of God," as *Yeshua* makes clear in his comments about the tower that fell in Siloam killing eighteen people, "Think ye that they were sinners above all men that dwelt in Jerusalem?" [The rabbinic question implies a negative answer—No it was not as a consequence of their sins that they were killed, any more than the man was born blind because of his or his parents' sins in John 9.2f.] All evil events are under the provenance of *Shaitan* and the *qlippoth*. They are the rulers of injustice and random acts of natural and human violence. In the teachings of *Yeshua* as transmitted through the traditions of his brother James, God does not destroy or do evil. Rather, it is the evil *yetzer* or "desire, lust" that, when fully developed, leads to death and destruction. James 1.13-17: "Let no one say when he endures trials, I am tested by God: for God cannot be tested with evil, neither does He test anyone. But everyone is tested when he is drawn away by his own *yetzer ha-ra* and submits to it. Then when the evil impulse has conceived, it brings forth sin: and sin, when it is finished, brings forth death. Do not err, my beloved brethren. Every good gift and every perfect gift is from above, and cometh down from the Father of lights, with whom is no variableness, neither shadow of turning."

[393] According to legend, a Roman soldier pierced the coffin with his sword to ensure the rabbi was dead. This inflicted a wound, but in spite of that the elderly *ben-Zakkai* kept silent and they were allowed to pass.

Because of his prophesies, the messianic Jewish followers of *Yeshua* recognized the signs of coming disaster and left Jerusalem before the siege in the year 67 C.E. Scholars speculate they may have been one of the groups who concealed their scriptures in the caves of Qumran, hoping to eventually return. They survived in desert communities that centuries later would influence the prophet Mohammad. But Jewish Christianity had been totally marginalized in the Roman Empire by the end of the first century, leaving only small Ebionite and Gnostic *(manda)* sects to carry on outside of Judaism. Gentile versions of Christianity defined the new religion to the world.

Logion 41

Whoever has will receive more; but whoever lacks will be deprived of even what little he has.

COMMENTARY

This is an independent version of the Q *logion* that says "To one who has, more will be given; to one who lacks, even what he has will be taken away."[394]

Many of *Yeshua's* inner-circle *davarim* are expressed as paradoxes that cannot be literally understood. They are probably intended to summarize a long discourse in one memorable phrase.

In this case, the hearers would have understood that Godhead has no need or lack, but is perfect and *shalem* or whole. God needs no sacrifices or prayers, but desires them from us only so that we ourselves may be filled with divine gifts. God is a giver, not a taker. The disciple must try to imitate God, and therefore "it is better to give than to receive."[395]

Spiritual perfection is a matter of expressing, and thereby accumulating, the fruits of the divine image or *yetzer ha-tov* within one's heart. A person who "has," or in Gnostic terms "possesses," is one who has become single-hearted and restructured himself in the *imago dei*. It is by his/her fruits or works *(mitzvoth)* that the *tzadik* can be recognized as a Son (Offspring) of God—not by his words. Yet words are also important in that his yes will mean yes, and his no mean no. That is to say, he does not disguise his intentions to himself or others with guile or double-minded equivocation.

Like God, who causes his rain to fall equally upon the just and the unjust, the *tzadik* is not a "respecter of persons." He treats both friends and enemies with equal *hesed,* or respect and fairness. He does not return evil for evil, but treats others as he would want to be treated.

---

[394] Matthew 25:29; Luke 19:26
[395] One of the few *davarim* of *Yeshua* that is quoted in the Pauline Epistles rather than the Gospels.

He has replaced his personal self with a divine self—as Paul said, the First Adam with the Second Adam, the Mind of Christ.

This is the one who "has." What does he have? Spiritual riches. To him will be given royal spiritual sovereignty and the *Abba* will grant all that he/she asks on behalf of the needs of others.[396]

The one who lacks spiritual development has allowed the evil *yetzer,* which is merely a shadow of reality, to dominate his heart and rule his works. He may think he possesses riches because he has gained material wealth or power. But in this world ruled by dark forces, all too often he has gained them by compromising his conscience, abusing trust, or using guile. He may not think so, but his victims will know. If he has simply inherited material wealth that has been squandered on selfish pursuits, or been born with talent or beauty and not shared for the benefit of others, his life is still ruled by the *yetzer ha-ra.* "By their works shall ye know them."

Such a person is one who lacks spiritual substance. Eventually all he trusts in for security and happiness will be taken away by misfortune, illness, or death. Then even that which he has will be taken away.

In the world of unchanging reality, as opposed to the fleeting world of flesh, "Them as has, gets; them as lacks, loses."

Logion 42

Become passers-by.

COMMENTARY

This is one of my favorite sayings. It is certainly the shortest of the *davarim.* There is little doubt about its authenticity because it restates *Yeshua's logion* from Q transmitted by Matthew and Luke, and also in *Thomas* Logion 86: "Foxes have holes, and birds of the air have nests; but the Son of Man *(Bar-Enash)* has nowhere to lay his head."[397]

Christians understand the Son of Man to be Jesus the Christ. But *Yeshua* understood himself to be a prophet of the New Adam. His disciples sought regenerative transformation to become worthy of the *Bar-Enash* and his *Malkuth.* To become like *Yeshua*—to become a

---

[396] *Yeshua's* teachings on correct prayer (*tiphlah,* intercessory prayer) stipulated several things: It should be done on behalf of others, not self; it should be done in third person plural (we, us), not first person singular (I, me); it should be done privately, with a clear conscience, and in a attitude of sincerety and of deep humility.
[397] Matthew 8:20; Luke 9:58

member of the corporate New Humanity—they must free themselves from attachment to the ways of the world, the flesh, and bondage to *Shaitan,* the Prince of this world.

As Paul explained, it is not money that is spiritually corrupting, but greed for it. By the same token, *Yeshua* taught not that food and clothing were corrupting, but that constant anxiety about them was. He said that one cannot serve both God and Mammon—the Babylonian deity of wealth and riches. "How difficult it is for the rich to enter the *Malkuth,*" he declared.

The essence of Logion 42 is what is known in Buddhism as non-attachment. It was a form of wisdom learned from harsh experience by Jews of the Diaspora, whose lives could at any time be turned upside down by vagaries of their host kingdom. Like the ancient Hebrew nomads, no matter how secure, welcome, and settled they might feel, a time would come when they would need to be travelers once again in search of a homeland. *Yeshua* tells his disciples that this is the existential condition of his *halakah.* The only remedy for impermanence is non-attachment.

Christian philosophers integrated *Yeshua's* teaching of non-attachment into their views of world citizenship. Review the quotation from the Epistle of Diognetus at the end of my commentary on Logion 20 ("They dwell in their own countries, but simply as sojourners..."). See also the commentary on Logion 86.

Logion 43 [Inauthentic Logion with Authentic Conclusion]

> 43.a His disciples said to him, "Who are you, that you should say these things to us?"
> <Jesus said to them,> "You do not realize who I am from what I say to you, but you have become like the Jews, for

43.b They love the tree and hate its fruit, or love the fruit and hate the tree."

COMMENTARY

Can you spot the clues in 43.a? Discussion about "who" or what heavenly being Jesus might be. Anti-semitic declarations about all Jews. Clearly Logion 43.a is late Gnostic elaboration attached to a fragment or phrase of authentic dominical teaching, as the redactor of *Thomas* often does.

But 43.b has all the earmarks of authenticity. It is a semitic phrase. It uses Coptic ⲁⲩⲱ to translate Greek *kai* for Aramaic *vav* meaning "or," not "and." If it had been composed in Greek, we would expect *alla.*

It is also in the form of chiastic[398] semitic construction we often see employed by *Yeshua* to summarize or epitomize longer discourses. The fickle "they" he characterizes are not the Jews, but his Pharisaic and Sadducean opponents, who represented only a small fraction of the Jews of his time. At this late stage in the development of *Thomas,* however, the Jewish Christian have become villains. All of them are portrayed as opponents of Jesus.

In the first phrase, *Yeshua* summarizes his critique of the Sadducees, who "love the tree but hate the fruit." The tree is the Pentateuch. The Sadducees accepted only the first five books of the Old Testament. They rejected the rest of what is known today as the Jewish and Christian Bible—the Prophets and the Writings, as they were called. The fruits were not only these other scriptures, but the kabbalistic interpretation of them that was developed in Pharisaic tradition. These interpretations were used to develop kabbalistic concepts of death, *Qimah,* sainthood, all the messianic *haggadah,* and basically the entire wisdom tradition that *Yeshua* incorporated into his teachings. But the Sadducees rejected all these fruits of the original tree.

The Sadducean denial of Resurrection *(Qimah),* which does not appear in the Pentateuch, was epitomized in the hypothetical case they presented to *Yeshua* about the woman who was legally married in sequence to each of seven brother after the previous had died, in keeping with Pharisaic tradition. Then whose husband could she be in the *Qimah? Yeshua's* answer was that those who are worthy of the *Qimah* are no longer male or female, but like the angels, and do not marry. The writer of Acts tells how Paul capitalized on the acrimonious disagreement between Pharisees and Sadducess about the issue of Resurrection to side-track the entire Sanhedrin when he was on trial, and thus was able to escape a unanimous ruling against him.

The second phrase "love the fruit and hate the tree" criticizes the Pharisees. The fruit is the heavy burden of nit-picking laws, rules, purifications, tithes, rituals, and minor *mitzvoth* they have added to the Torah and all the other scriptures through rabbinic interpretation— what Paul referred to as the "letter" that kills, whereas the spirit gives life. Here the tree is again the Torah, but including all scripture and especially the Prophets, whose spirit of justice the Pharisees have hated by dishonoring it in their traditions.

Yeshua accuses the Pharisees of persecuting prophets and saints while they lived, but honoring their tombs after they had died. Thus he says that they love the fruits of their own interpretation, but hate the spirit and true meaning of scripture.

---

[398] So designated because the construction resembles a Greek chi (χ). Here the forms is "Either AB, or BA." John's Gospel, though late, contains many chiasms and semitic constructions that has led some scholars to speculate that the prototype to it was composed much earlier. In my view, the semitic construction is rooted in the speech patterns of the Apostle John, whose sermons were committed to paper in Greek by his disciples. But the redaction we know as John's Gospel doesn't appear in manuscript history until the end of the first century—much later than the Synoptics.

Logion 44

Whoever blasphemes against the *Abba* will find release, and whoever blasphemes against the *Bar-Enash* will find release; but whoever blasphemes against the *Ruach Ha-Qodesh* will not find release in this *'olam.*

COMMENTARY

As it appears in *Thomas,* this authentic *davar* has been redacted with an ecclesiastical interpretation. I say ecclesiastical rather than Gnostic, because it represents the Trinitarian view of Coptic *Thomas,* as opposed to the earlier view of Greek *Thomas.* Refer back to my comments on Logion 30, "Where there are three gods..."

Logion 44 translates, "Whoever blasphemes against the *Abba* will be forgiven, and whoever blasphemes against the Son will be forgiven; but whoever blasphemes against the Holy Spirit will not be forgiven, in this world or in Heaven." It is very similar to Mark's version, which is copied in Matthew and Luke, but differs from Logion 44 by saying, "but whoever blasphemes against the Holy Spirit can never have forgiveness, but is guilty of an eternal sin."

The sin against the Holy Spirit has given children nightmares for centuries. In the Gospels, the offender has committed an eternal sin. In *Thomas* he will never be forgiven on Earth or in Heaven. But what did the *davar* mean in the original Aramaic?

First let's clear up the "eternal" concept. The kabbalistic concept of the *'olamim,* which the Gnostic Valentinus apparently altered to create his Pleroma of the Aeons (eternities), was probably the basis for development of the medieval kabbalistic concept of the Four Worlds. An *'olam* was a state of being, a modality of existence not unlike the Hindu concept of the *lokas* or divine worlds. This fallen, phenomenal world that is currently ruled by *Shaitan,* designated in the Greek of John's Gospel as the *Kosmos,* was designated by *Yeshua* and kabbalistic mystics as "this *'olam.*" It was also known as this age. It was not eternal, but as time passed would pass into other *'olamim.*

The divine world of God or Heaven, which is invisible to mankind but lies spread out upon this *'olam* as the universal *Malkuth* or Sovereignty of God, was known to *Yeshua* as The *'Olam.* It was the state of "eternal life" or the Life of the *'Olam* that those worthy of the *Qimah* would inherit. It contained all the other *'olamim,* each of which had its season. The only eternal permanent, unchanging, and eternal *'Olam* was that of God. All the others were temporal. However, Hebrew had a way of indicating eternal time with the expression "an

'Olam of *'olamim,"* meaning the never-ending or Eternal World of God. The concept of never-ending time was indicated in prayer with the phrase, *ad 'Olam ed*.

The Greek writers of the New Testament did not understand these distinctions, nor did the European translators of the Bible. The Greek word for *'olam* is *aeon*. Whether the Greek said "unto an aeon," which means for the duration or state of existence in this world, or "aeonic life," which means the Life of God's Aeon, the term was always wrongly translated as "forever, eternal." That's how inauthentic doctrines like eternal damnation and eternal sin were attributed to Jesus.

But *Yeshua* never spoke of anything as lasting until the end of time. His so-called eternal punishment in Hell *(Gehenom)* was an after-death form of short-term purification that can be found in Hellenistic Jewish Talmudic references. It is probably the basis of the Catholic doctrine of Purgatory. Both Heaven *(Pardes)* and the place of after-life purification *(Gehenom)* were located in the Third Heaven. The Jewish "soul" or *neshamah* of a sinful person needed purification before it could sleep in Paradise. But this was not eternal. Rabbinic doctrines specified periods of days or weeks for purgatorial suffering, but never an eternity.[399] That came later in Christian doctrine.[400]

When Mark represented Jesus as teaching that one who blasphemes against the Holy Spirit "can never have forgiveness, but is guilty of an eternal sin," what did that really mean in Aramaic?

First, let us look at the concept of forgiveness. The Aramaic word was *shalach,* release from debt or bandage. Sin was *hub,* debt. When the Pharisaic critics saw *Yeshua* casting out demons, they perceived it through the evil eye of the *yetzer ha-ra.* A patently good act became evil in their sight. Good acts come out of the *yetzer ha-tov* in the heart. They are an inspiration of the Spirit of God—not *Shaitan.* But those who are bound by *Shaitan* perceive only with the evil eye. In their bondage to evil, they sin against the Holy Spirit. As long as their eye remains evil, they compound sin in this *'olam.*

---

[399] The first-century leader of Judaism, Rabbi Akiba, taught: "The punishment of the wicked in Gehinnom last twelve months; for it is written [Isaiah 66.23, the verse quoted by *Yeshua* in his pronouncements about Gehinnom or Purgatory], 'It will be from month to (the same) month." This doctrine was accepted in the later Mishnaic and Talmudic writings.

[400] Even in the *Apocalypse of John,* a late and highly disputed book that was only accepted as part of the New Testament canon in the fourth century, *Shaitan* is bound and thrown into the bottomless abyss for a the specified term of a thousand years—which may reflect the original Jewish purgatorial concept. But finally he is released, defeated, and thrown into a lake of fire and brimstone where he will be tortured day and night "unto aeons of aeons (Revelations 20.10)," meaning forever and ever. The fourth century *Gospel of Nicodemus,* which describes the descent of Jesus into Hell to release all the saints of the Old Adam, is the oldest Christian document about the harrowing of Hell. It contains this interesting line spoken by Jesus as the *Messiah*: "And the Lord stretching forth his hand, said: 'Come unto me, all ye my saints which bear mine image and my likeness (VIII).'" Here the image of Christ has been conflated with the Hebrew Image of God.

It is like a man who has chosen to look away from the light and see everything in his own shadow.[401] He can never see the light until he makes the decision to turn and seek the light. The state of seeing with the evil eye is part of this 'olam—the world of human sin ruled by *Shaitan.* As long as the Pharisaic critics choose to remain in this state of existence or negative consciousness, they can never find release from their bondage.

What *Yeshua* taught is that those who choose to be complicit with sin will remain in the bondage of sin in this world or 'olam. The Marcan version of the saying simply says that those who sin against the Holy Spirit have an aeonic or 'olamic sin. But Coptic *Thomas* redacts it to say, "whoever blasphemes against the Holy Spirit will not be forgiven, in this world or in Heaven." In other words, he will not (instead of cannot) be released either in this 'olam or in The 'Olam. He is toast! This was also the Christian interpretation.

That is simply inauthentic. I have rendered Logion 44 correctly as the original Aramaic would suggest.

Logion 45

Grapes are not harvested from thorns, nor are figs gathered from thistles, for they do not produce fruit. A good man brings forth a good thing from his storehouse; an evil man brings forth evil things from his evil storehouse, which is in his heart, and says evil things. For out of the impulses of the heart he brings forth evil.

COMMENTARY

This represents an independent transmission of the Q *logion* found in Matthew 7.16-20 and Luke 6.43-46. Of the two, Luke[402] preserves the *logion* almost exactly as we find it in Coptic *Thomas.* Matthew[403] tends to create more elaborate redactions of the Q material, so here Luke and *Thomas* offer the most authentic versions.

---

[401] Like the prisoners in Plato's Allegory of the Cave, they turn against the messenger of light.

[402] "No good tree bears bad fruit, nor does a bad tree bear good fruit. Each tree is recognized by its own fruit. People do not pick figs from thorn bushes, or grapes from briers. The good man brings good things out of the good stored up in his heart, and the evil man brings evil things out of the evil stored up in his heart. For out of the impulses of his heart his mouth speaks."

[403] In my opinion, the few scholars who advocate that Luke copied from Matthew have a poor basis for this idea. If anything, they should advocate the opposite when comparing the earliest recensions of Luke to those of Matthew. But the best evidence is that they both used the Q *logia* in their own ways. However, it is also possible that they each had different variations of Q, since unlike the dictated source of *Thomas* it was a

Review the Hebrew concept of the heart in the commentary on Logion 3. It is not only the abiding place of good and evil *yezterim*, but the storage vessel (Aramaic *atzad*) of the precious treasure generated by good *mitzvoth*, and the foul husks of evil intention, deeds, and their fruits. The heart was considered to be a storehouse that essentially recorded one's good and evil deeds in life. The good works or *mitzvoth* testified like a defense attorney for the soul in the afterlife court of God, according to *Yeshua's* Parable of the Unjust Steward.[404]

Here the things that one brings forth from the heart are not defined, as the underlying Greek loan words use the constructions *agathon* "a good" and *hen-ponereron* "some evil." But they represent Hebrew-Aramaic *tov* and *ra*, the designations of the two impulses or images within the heart—*yezter ha-tov* (good, divine) and *yetzer ha-ra* (evil, infernal). Each *yetzer* has its own *atzad* or storehouse.

Matthew quite correctly prefaces and concludes his redaction of this *logion* with a related authentic *davar* that does not appear in Luke or *Thomas*, but was transmitted though his own special or M material: "You shall know them by their fruits." This means that the disciples are advised to examine their own deeds and those of others—not just their words—in order to understand whether they operate from a good or evil heart. *Yeshua's* characterization of religious leadership as wolves disguised as sheep is another related saying. One must judge by the purity of a heart, not by externals like words and things done for show. The results of a bad tree will be bad fruit—another related saying.

Logion 46

Among those born of women, from Adam until John the Baptist, there is no one so superior to John the Baptist that his eyes should not be lowered (in his presence). Yet I have said, whichever one of you comes into being as a newly-born will know the *Malkuth* and will become superior to John.

COMMENTARY

---

written source—possible from actual notes taken by the Apostle *Shimone Cephas* ("Peter") and transmitted by his disciple Mark.
[404] Luke 16.1-12. The parable appears only in the special Lucan material or L.

This is an independent variation of the authentic Q *logion* that appears in Matthew and Luke: "I tell you, among those born of women there is no one greater than John; yet the one who is least in the kingdom of God is greater than he."[405]

The version of this saying in *Thomas* preserves a more authentic Aramaic way of speaking in the phrase "there is no one so superior to John the Baptist that his eyes should not be lowered (in his presence)." The ancient Egyptian wisdom tradition, whose proverbs along with many others from Edomite wisdom have come down to us in the Hebrew Book of Proverbs, is a starting place to understand this phrase.

In the Instruction of the Vizier Ptah-Hotep, the bright children who have been selected from the villages to be educated as priests and officials are told: "If thou art one of those sitting at the table of one greater than thyself...do not pierce him with many stares, (for such) an aggression against him is an abomination to the *ka*. Let thy face be cast down until he addresses thee..."[406]

In all near eastern cultures, social deference was given according to a strict pecking order, especially at a meal table or in a rabbinic school. One always "broke" or lowered his eyes in the presence of a great one or *rav*. John the Baptist was considered in his time by most Jews[407] to be the greatest of all prophets. Many considered him to be the *Messiah*—a dangerous reputation to hold. His decision to publicly criticize Herod for breaking Jewish marriage law, in view of his influential reputation, was the reason Herod privately executed him. *Yeshua's* decision to do a triumphal entry into Jerusalem during the Passover week and drive the sellers of sacrificial animals out of the Temple precincts, when taken with his influential reputation as the messianic successor to John, convinced the Herodian spies[408] they finally had a legal case to recommend arrest and execution.[409]

It would have been conventional in Jewish culture for a disciple or any hearer to lower his eyes in the presence of John the Baptist. "There is no one so superior to John the Baptist" is

---

[405] Matthew 11.11; Luke 7.28

[406] Translated by John Wilson in *Ancient Near Eastern Texts Relating to the Old Testament*, ed, James C. Pritchard, p. 412 (Princeton University Press, 1955)

[407] The small Pharisaic and Sadducean sects who opposed John were in the minority. Both John and Jesus were extremely popular with the Jewish public.

[408] The Herodians tried to catch *Yeshua* advocating non-payment of taxes, to which he made his classic rabbinic ruling that one should "render unto Caesar what is Caesar's, and to God what is God's." That could be not used against him as evidence of treason in either a court of Jewish or Roman law. *Yeshua* was finally convicted on making terrorist threats against Herod's Temple in Jerusalem because he publicly prophesied its destruction..

[409] Was this *Yeshua's* goal? Did he purposely invite crucifixion? I doubt it. Friends had been hiding him in Galilean and Judean safe-houses for a long time, as the Herodians had been spying and seeking a legal excuse to justify arrest for treason. According to the Judas legend (which doesn't appear in Christian tradition until a generation after Paul and is probably an anti-Semitic addition), someone betrayed *Yeshua's* whereabouts to the Romans. If so, he was trying to avoid capture.

an idiomatic way of saying that no one born of woman (i.e. no human being), from Adam until John the Baptist (including all the patriarchs and prophets) is of higher spiritual status. All of them should defer to him and avert their eyes in his presence.

This saying, like the one about James the Just in Logion 12, reveals the great esteem in which *Yeshua* held John. The Baptist was so important to *Yeshua* that even though he competed in the heart of Judaism for the title of the suffering *Messiah Bar-Joseph*, the writers of the New Testament Gospels could not merely ignore him. So they portrayed him as a forerunner prophesying the coming of Jesus and as the authority who endorsed Jesus as the *Messiah*. They minimized his importance with this *logion*.

There is no doubt that *Yeshua* said the least of the newly-borns of the *Malkuth* were greater than John, but that was *Yeshua's* characteristic use of semitic hyperbole. The fact that he used it as hyperbole is evidence of his high esteem for the Baptist, whom he implied was greater than Moses and Elijah.

The *davar* is intended to emphasize the superiority of the *Bar-Enash* or New Adam and its spiritual offspring to the Old Adam, whose offspring were "born of women." But the children of the New Humanity are born, as the Prologue to John's Gospel says, not of blood, nor of the will of the flesh, nor of the will of man, but of God.[410]

My previous commentary on newly-borns and *Malkuth* are found in the sections on Logion 2 *(Malkuth in Stage Four)*, and #21.b *(yeledim)*.

Logion 47

47.a It is impossible for a man to mount two horses or to stretch two bows. And it is impossible for a servant to serve two masters; otherwise, he will honor the one and treat the other contemptuously.

47.b No man drinks old wine and immediately desires to drink new wine.

47.c New wine is not put into old wineskins, lest they burst; nor is old wine put into a new wineskin, lest it spoil it. An old patch is not sewn onto a new garment, because it will split apart.

---

[410] John 1.13

COMMENTARY

These sayings appear as two separate *logia* in the Gospels. 47.a is a Q saying that appears only in Matthew and Luke,[411] and 47.b is a Marcan saying[412] repeated in Matthew and Luke. In other words, they are not connected either in Q or the Marcan sources. We must view them as unrelated *davarim.*

Logion 47.a is concluded in Q with, "You cannot serve both God and Mammon."[413] But that saying is left out here and instead another *logion* follows. Why?

It seems that the Aramaic dictation behind *Thomas* jumped to the mnemonic connection provided by the Aramaic negative *ayn* sequence "not possible, not possible, not drink, not put, not put." That is the only logic I can find for the appearance of these unrelated *logia* as one *logion* in *Thomas.* There certainly is no clear Gnostic redactional purpose for the sequence. This further points to my theory that the order of the sayings in *Thomas* derived from an original Aramaic dictation that was translated into Koine Greek by a bilingual scribe as he committed it to writing.

In any case, *Yeshua* taught that one cannot successfully serve two different masters, such as the good and evil *yetzerim,* any more than he can bend two bows simultaneously or ride two horses at the same time.[414] This is consistent with his teachings about singleness of heart and similar to the ancient Hebrew Two Ways doctrine, and the common idiom of looking neither to the left or right, but proceeding directly ahead.

It is interesting that a misunderstanding of Hebrew construction in a messianic prophecy on the part of the redactor(s) of Matthew led to a portrayal of Jesus entering Jerusalem mounted on two animals—an ass, and the foal of an ass. That ontradicts the very saying under consideration in this *logion* that one cannot ride two horses simultaneously![415]

The proper translation of the Hebrew phrase "ass, and the foal of an ass" indicates one animal only. The restatement of the first clause in the following *vav* "and" clause simply intensifies or clarifies the first clause. If the redactor(s) of Matthew had been Jews or fluent in Hebrew, they would have recognized that the messianic passage from Zechariah read, "upon an ass, namely a colt, the foal of an ass." Then they would have followed Mark and

---

[411] Matthew 6.24; Luke 16.13
[412] Mark 2.21-22; Matthew 9.16-17; Luke 5.36-39
[413] *Mammon* was the Babylonian deity of wealth—another Babylonian connection with *Yeshua's* teaching.

[415] Zechariah 9.9 was interpreted as messianic prophecy. It reads, "⁹Rejoice greatly, O daughter of Zion; shout, O daughter of Jerusalem: behold, thy King cometh unto thee: he is just, and having salvation; lowly, and riding upon an ass, and upon a colt the foal of an ass."

Luke in portraying Jesus as sitting upon only the young colt or foal of an ass—one animal, not two.[416]

In Logion 47.a, the two masters that cannot be served simultaneously are not identified in *Thomas,* but clearly so in Q through the statement that one cannot serve God and Mammon. If this seems to contradict the saying about rendering unto Caesar what is Caesar's, and God what is God's, it does! That is because former about God and Mammon is a true *davar* of *Yeshua,* but the latter about Caesar was merely a clever answer to a dangerous political test engineered by the Herodians who wanted to legally entrap *Yeshua.* (See previous footnote at the end of the commentary on Logion 46.) That was not a prophetic *davar,* but a clever way to avoid being tricked into making a rabbinical ruling that would have either provided justification for an arrest warrant (refuse to pay Roman taxes), or caused loss of face among the Jews (cooperate with the Romans). Jewish collaborators who collected taxes for the Romans—the publicans of the King James Bible—were despised even more than the Roman occupiers.

The saying in 47.b is not present in the Marcan source or Matthew's version of it. However, it is added as a conclusion at the end of Luke's version, so has been known as part of the special Lucan material L. But we find it here in *Thomas* as an introduction—not a conclusion—to the wine sayings. This again indicates oral dictation and memory as the main organizational principals.

Wine that has been aged ("old wine") has much better flavor than raw new wine. As in John's story of the Wedding in Cana, the good, aged wine was served first to guests. When that ran out, the new wine was served—after all, by then who cares! In John's story, when all the wine ran out, Jesus magically turned pots of water into aged wine.[417]

The allegory in this *davar* is that it is human nature to prefer and trust the old ways of religion over the new things that Spirit introduces. *Yeshua* was opposed by those who objected that what he taught was not in line with Pharisaic tradition. But *Yeshua's* response was that the ways of God should be preferred to the "traditions of men."

Pharisaic religion was ultra-conservative. In the first-century School of Jamnia, the rabbis ruled that after the Book of Daniel, the Spirit of Prophecy (*Ruach Ha-Qodesh* of the pneumatic Christians) had left Israel, and all the later scripture was not inspired or to be included in the Hebrew canon. Why? Probably because the so-called intertestamental scriptures (Old Testament Apocrypha and Pseudepigrapha) were used extensively by messianic Jews and Christians. Yet a few centuries later the Christians removed the same literature from their regular canon because the same scriptures now seemed too Jewish. In

---

[416] Cf. The Triumphal Entry in Mark 11.1-10; Luke 19.28-40; Matthew 21.1-9

[417] A miracle attributed to several Greek gods and considered to be evidence of divinity. It was also a trick used by the Gnostic *Markos* at his Eucharistic liturgies, according to Ireneus.

fact, however, many keys to understanding the teachings of *Yeshua* can be found only in the intertestamental scripture, as it comprised much of the scripture used by *Yeshua* and his disciples.

The sayings about wineskeins and patching old garments in Logion 47.c refer symbolically to attempts to reform Pharisaic Judaism by editing and tweaking. New wine expands as it ferments, and will burst old wineskeins that have already reached their limit of expansion. Also, if aged wine is poured into a new wineskein in which it has not aged, the taste and fragrance will be spoiled. New cloth that is patched onto old garments will shrink when washed and tear the places they patch.

By the same token, Pharisaic Judaism, which ruled most of the synagogues in Judea and the Galilee, was beyond reform by patching. It simply couldn't accommodate the radical regeneration that the appearance of God's *Malkuth* on Earth and among humanity required. God was pouring new wine upon humanity. It could not be contained in the old vessels, nor could the old wine of tradition be perpetuated through the new vessels that will arise.

Yeshua was not merely a reformer of synagogue Judaism. He was a prophet of the New Humanity and the messianic Age. The *davar* about new wine and new cloth is an answer to those who wanted to "work within the system." The religious system couldn't handle it. Therefore, he sent his disciples directly to the people.

Logion 48

If two were to make peace with each other in this one house, they will say to the mountain, 'Move away from here,' and it will move away.

COMMENTARY

This is probably the original *davar* that we find severely redacted in Mark, and wholly reinterpreted in Matthew. Let us look first at the Marcan and Matthean counterparts.

Marks' version is spun to support the gentile Christian doctrine of magical belief, which developed from the Pauline idea of salvific belief that Jesus is the Christ. Believing became the basis for Christian creed and dogma.

Mark 11:23 reads, "Truly I tell you, if you say to this mountain, 'Be taken up and thrown into the sea,' and if you do not doubt in your heart, but believe that what you say will come to pass, it will be done for you. So I tell you, whatever you ask for in prayer, believe that you have received it, and it will be yours."

But did *Yeshua,* who taught that you cannot add one cubit to your stature by "taking thought,"[418] really teach that intellectual opinion or belief was the basic requirement of religion and could be used magically? We already have seen that the Aramaic word translated as "faith," which *Yeshua* strongly emphasized, meant faithfulness, fidelity—not belief. Is there some other Aramaic word he might have used to advocate the magical power of belief? Absolutely not. There is no such concept in Hebrew-Aramaic language and thought. Rather, this is a gentile Christian misunderstanding of Jewish messianic religion that developed into doctrine as Koine Greek became the language of the early churches.[419]

Neither Luke nor Matthew repeat this bizarre Marcan saying, but Matthew may have reinterpreted it in this saying that appears only in his Gospel: "Truly I tell you, if two of you agree on earth about anything you ask [in prayer], it will be done for you by your *Abba* in heaven."[420]

Then, what is Logion 48 about? It is a *davar* about the Sovereignty *(Malkuth)* of the perfected messianic saint. "If two were to make peace with each other in this one house" means that if one achieved the internal unity of the heart, known in other *logia* as "single, single-minded, single-souls, like unto the angels"—that is, if one became *shalem* or spiritually whole, the goal of advanced discipleship, as in Logion 22.b "when you make the two one"—then he could exercise the Sovereignty of the *Bar-Enash* while yet in flesh. The idea of commanding a mountain to move was a Jewish and Greek expression for the divine power expressed through a prophet or *Theos Aner,* God-Man.[421]

In rabbinic literature the metaphor of uprooting a mountain is used to emphasize determination, and once to make his point, R. Eliezer is said to have cried, "If the *halachah* agrees with me, let this carob tree prove it!" Then the tree was uprooted and moved 100 cubits away.[422] In this case, the uprooting is proof of fidelity to God's teachings—not as a result of commanding the tree to move by the strength of one's belief that it will move!

---

[418] Q material: Matthew 6.27; Luke 12.25

[419] Paul refers derisively to "faith" that can move mountains in I Corinthians 13.2, which he lists as part of several pneumatic charisms developed in the early Christian churches such as glossolalia or speaking in tongues—which he also disdains—that are inferior to *agape* or divine love.

[420] Matthew 18.19

[421] In her book *Faith in Jesus and Paul,* Maureen Yeung tries to argue for continuity between the historical teachings of *Yeshua* and those of Paul. In her long section entitled "Faith That Can Remove Mountains" she looks everywhere in ancient literature for a connection between belief and moving mountains. She finds that from Homer's description of the Cyclops hurling a mountain into the sea to all the Old Testament references to God's making mountains move and tremble, there are no real connections between belief and mountain moving. It is always a metaphor for divine omnipotence. Her only evidence for connection between Jesus and Paul in respect to belief as a cause for miraculous events is the one highly redacted saying in Mark I have already discussed.

[422] B. B. Mes. 59b

It was said that the powers of Godhead could be expressed through a Jewish prophet and, in later tradition, through a great *tzadik* or *Merkabah* adept. Whatever they spoke, God would make good. Eliezar commanded the carob tree to move, and it did so. In the even later traditions of the Desert Fathers, the story is told of a grieving father who laid his son's corpse at the entrance to the cave of a great hermit hoping that the saint would bring the boy back to life. When the old man saw the boy laying there, he was irritated and said, "Get up and leave my cave!" Life immediately returned to the corpse, and the little boy ran home.

In other words, "making the two into a single unity" is another way *Yeshua* described the *emunah* or faithfulness of a messianic saint. By filling his heart with the light of the good *yetzer,* he sanctifies himself and eventually becomes *shalem* or perfect. That is represented in the metaphor of two making *shalom* with each other. It is also what is represented by the metaphor of Logion 22.b: "...and when you make [human] eyes to serve as [God's] Eye, and a [human] hand to serve as [God's] Hand, and a [human] foot to serve as [God's] Foot, [and] a human image to serve as [the Divine] Image; then you shall attain the Sovereignty."

Then, being a saint, whatever he was inspired to speak would be made good by Heaven. The rabbinic expression for this was, "If he tells the mountain to move, it will move."

In the teaching of *Yeshua,* this was not the result of belief or opinion, but of the faithful pursuit and practice of spiritual *halachah.*

CHAPTER EIGHT: Logia 49-62

Logia #49-53 [Inauthentic Gnostic Sayings]

49 Blessed are the solitary and elect, for you will find the Kingdom. For you are from it, and to it you will return.

50 Jesus said, "If they say to you, 'Where did you come from?', say to them, 'We came from the light, the place where the light came into being on its own accord and established itself and became manifest through their image.' If they say to you, 'Is it you?' say, 'We are its children, we are the elect of the living father.' If they ask you, 'What is the sign of your father in you?' say to them, 'It is movement and repose.'"

51 His disciples said to him, "When will the repose of the dead come about, and when will the new world come?" He said to them, "What you look forward to has already come, but you do not recognize it."

52 His disciples said to him, "Twenty-four prophets spoke in Israel, and all of them spoke in you." He said to them, "You have omitted the one living in your presence and have spoken (only) of the dead."

53 His disciples said to him, "Is circumcision beneficial or not?" He said to them, "If it were beneficial, their father would beget them already circumcised from their mother. Rather, the true circumcision in spirit has become completely profitable.

COMMENTARY

This entire section of five *logia* represents Thomasian Gnostic ideas that are not redacted from authentic *davarim* of *Yeshua*. Interestingly, the last three begin with "His disciples said to him," a claim that these are inner-circle teachings.

Logion 49 adds a new beatitude extolling the "solitary and elect," that is, the Thomasian monastic way of life in separation from society.

Logion 50 elaborates on the elite status of the Thomasians by applying Valentinian theodicy and Gnostic terminology like *anapausis.*

Logion 51 uses more Gnostic terminology as well as the radical Gnostic eschatology used by Paul's opponents in the Corinthian epistles, that initiate Pneumatics are already living as Sovereigns. This Logion seems to have been a Gnostic interpretation of an authentic *davar* such as is preserved in Logion 113 about the *Malkuth* being spread out upon the Earth but men cannot see it.

Logion 52 refers to the Jewish prophets as dead, rather than as saints living in the divine aeon, in direct contradiction to the kabbalistic teachings of *Yeshua.* It represents a form of Gnostic Christian anti-Semitism.

Logion 53 applies gentile Christian anti-circumcision critique to its anti-Semitic discourse. *Yeshua* never spoke against circumcision. That was a later gentile Christian issue.

All the Logia from 49 to 53 are inauthentic.

Logion 54
Blessed are the poor, for theirs is the Sovereignty of Heaven.

COMMENTARY

This is the first of the Beatitudes from the Q material. In both Matthew and Luke they are spoken to the disciples as their first instruction after he has chosen them, not to the public. In Matthew the setting is a high hilltop (Sermon on the Mount), but in Luke a low plain (Sermon on the Plain). In both settings *Yeshua* and his disciples have attracted a large crowd of people—many of them poor villagers and beggars.

The Coptic word for "poor" in *Thomas* is *heke,* which is also used in Logia #3 and #29 to denote spiritual destitution and poverty. In Q the Greek word is *ptochoi,* which refers to the lowly in society who crouch or cower in the presence of others, i.e. beggars and outcasts. There are several possible original Hebrew-Aramaic words translated *ptochos* in the Septuagint: *ani,* "afflicted, wretched, poor;" *dalal,* "weak, powerless;" *rosh,* "poor, needy, in want." But in the Septuagint we find the root *ani* for Greek *ptocheia,* meaning beggary, destitution, in contrast to *plousios* "rich, wealthy." That, in fact, was the social contrast in the Palestine of *Yeshua's* day—the wealthy and the beggars, who were known as the "poor." So the best candidate for *Yeshua's* Aramaic word is *ani.*

Matthew redacts the Q saying to read, "Blessed are the poor in spirit." That was a Greek idiom meaning those who are humble. Humility (not humiliation)[423] was a virtue taught by *Yeshua.* But that is not what the *davar* was intended to say. Coptic *Thomas* and Luke transmit the more authentic version.

Significantly, in *Thomas* the Greek loan-word *ptochos* from Q and the Gospels is not used. This is another indication of independent transmission, especially when we consider the fact that normal Thomasian usage of *heke* means those who are in spiritual poverty—i.e., those who are very far away from the Sovereignty and, in Logion 3, in spiritual poverty. Yet here, *heke* preserves the original Aramaic meaning of material poverty. Why does *Thomas* include it following his Gnostic Beatitude in the preceding Logion 49? Probably because the Thomasian Gnostics, like the Jewish Ebionites, took vows of poverty when they joined the community of monks. Therefore the Beatitude about the "poor" was understood as applying to Gnostic renunciates.

Let us examine the original meaning of *Yeshua's davar* about the poor. According to both Matthew and Luke, it was given to his chosen *talmidim* at the beginning of their discipleship. It was given in the context of a large crowd that had gathered, most of whom were poor villagers and beggars. *Yeshua* wanted his disciples to understand from the very beginning that these *amme ha-aretz* or "people of the land," the lowly non-synagogue attending Jews whom the Pharisees looked down upon, could attain the *Malkuth.*

Yeshua elaborated on this theme in his parable of the Marriage Feast. The wealthy city leaders and merchants had been invited, but each had excused himself from attendance. It was Jewish custom to invite all the poor to come after the celebration was over and eat what remained of the banquet, but in this case all those invited had refused. Therefore the master told his servants to go out and invite whoever they found to the feast in place of the merchants.

The meaning was clear to *Yeshua's* hearers. The Jewish religious leaders of synagogues and Temple had refused to accept their invitation to the Messianic Banquet. They had spurned John's messianic baptism and preaching. Therefore *Yeshua* and his disciples had been sent forth to proclaim the *Basor* to all regardless of social status. That included all those considered by the pious to be sinners. (Cf. Logion 64.)

Poverty was a sign of great sin, according to the Deuteronomic theology espoused by the Sadducees. It stated that God rewarded the righteous and punished sinners in this life.

---

[423] Humility is to place oneself level with all others—not below them. Taking the lowest seat at a banquet where seating order was not established was not to lower oneself beneath all others, but to offer the choice of "pecking order" to the master of the table, rather than acting presumptuously. *Yeshua* taught his disciples not to be "respecters of persons," meaning having an attitude of superiority to others, respecting some people but not others, or otherwise discriminating against people.

Therefore, if someone was rich and powerful, that was evidence that God loved him. But if he were poor and lowly, that was due to his sinfulness.

In contrast to that philosophy were the Hasidic wisdom schools who composed the Book of Job and expanded it over several centuries, producing a great deposit of other scripture after the Babylonian Captivity. They taught that reward and punishment came after death—not in life. One's material and social status in life did not necessarily reflect his righteousness. Although Pharisaic tradition was rooted in this Hasidic stream, however, it had developed a separate rabbinic interpretation of Torah. *Yeshua* contrasted these "traditions of men" with the traditions of God—i.e., the basic justice and mercy advocated by the prophets.

The result was the paradox that God's messianic Sovereignty was far away from the rich and self-righteous rulers of the synagogues and Temple, but near and accessible for the despised masses. Why? Because they recognized themselves as alienated from Heaven. They had the humility required for making a sincere approach to Godhead and *Malkuth*.

Matthew adds, "Blessed are the lowly, for they shall inherit the Earth."[424] Here the Greek word *praus* is derived from Aramaic *ani* and means the poor who are lowly in station. The redactor(s) already altered the Beatitude about the poor to "poor in spirit," meaning those who are humble, so this may be a redaction restating the original Q *logion* or it may transmit another version of the same *logion* from Matthew's special M source. In any case, it has the earmarks of an authentic *davar*. It meant that the *amme ha-aretz* would inherit the Sovereignty of heaven on Earth, as the *Basor* of both John the Baptist and *Yeshua* proclaimed.

John the Baptist had attracted hearers and disciples from among the poor and religiously disenfranchised of the villages. It was they who journeyed into the wilderness of the Jordan to hear him preach, and it was they whom he baptized. When some of the rich and powerful Pharisees came out to spy or oppose him, he is reported to have employed the same phrase of condemnation ascribed to *Yeshua* in his condemnation of the Pharisees: "You nest of snakes!"[425]

Yeshua had tried to preach to his own synagogue in Nazareth, but was rejected. He rarely spoke in synagogues after that, but in private homes or public gatherings. Both John and Jesus were convinced that true messianic religious regeneration could not emerge from the religious or Temple establishment. It had to arise directly from the people. It was to the villagers that they preached the *Basor*.

---

[424] Matthew 5.5. King James translates "lowly" as "meek."
[425] King James translates "generation of vipers." JOHN THE BAPTIST: Matthew 3.7; Luke 3.7. JESUS: Matthew 12.34; 23.33

Logion 55 [Authentic Logion with Christian Expansion; see parallel in Logion 101]

55.a Whoever does not hate his father and his mother cannot become a disciple to me.

55.b And whoever does not hate his brothers and sisters and take up his cross in my way will not be worthy of me.

COMMENTARY

Logion 55.a is probably the original form of *Yeshua's davar,* and possibly the original form underlying the parallel Q material of Matthew and Luke. The construction "a disciple to me" is literal oral Aramaic as opposed to the phrase "my disciple" of Q, which seems to have been a Greek written source.

The *davar* is typical of *Yeshua's* semitic hyperbole—a form of shocking exaggeration in order to make a point. *Yeshua* did not advocate hatred of parents. Quite the opposite, honoring of parents was a root teaching of Jewish religion enshrined in the Ten Commandments. *Yeshua* emphasized how deeply one must love God by implying that in comparison, love of parents and family would be hatred.

Logion 101 is an expanded version of Logion 55 in which, like Luke and Matthew, the redactor has attempted to make the saying more understandable. Luke's expansion reads, "If anyone comes to me and doesn't hate his father, and mother, and wife, and children, and brothers, and sisters..." Matthew expands in the same way, but makes the hate hyperbole more understandable by redacting, "Whoever loves father or mother more than me is not worthy of me; and whoever loves son or daughter more than me is not worthy of me."

Matthew, Luke, and *Thomas* Logion 55 all add the following phrase or similar words, which are clearly post-crucifixion Christian redaction and not original with *Yeshua:* "And whoever does not take up the cross and follow me is not worthy of me."[426]

For the Thomasian Syrian Gnostics, this *logion* and Logion 101 probably were understood more literally. They abandoned families to join the Gnostic community. This saying, which pointedly occurs twice in the *Gospel of Thomas,* may have been understood to provide a rationale for leaving parents, wives, and children behind—something that *Yeshua* would have condemned.[427]

---

[426] See commentary for Logion #101.

[427] *Yeshua's* closest disciples travelled with him on his preaching journeys, but they maintained their homes and supported their families. Peter and others are represented in Acts and in the Pauline Epistles as travelling with their wives for Apostolic journeys after the crucifixion.

Logion 56 [Inauthentic Gnostic Saying]

Whoever has come to understand the Kosmos has found [it to be] a corpse, and whoever has found [it to be] a corpse is superior to the world.

COMMENTARY

Like Logion 27, the Gnostic doctrine of this world *(kosmos)* as evil in itself and by nature contradicts the teachings of *Yeshua.* It is true that, when a new disciples asks permission to first return home to bury his father, he says, "Let the dead bury their dead; but you, come and follow me." But that is semitic hyperbole used to make a point. Here in Logion 56, we simply have a Gnostic doctrine put into the mouth of Jesus.

Yeshua did not view the *Eretz* or Earth as evil. His view was that mankind and all the generation of the First Adam were ruled by, or in bondage to, the evil forces of *Shaitan.* Paul explains the view in phrases about the astrological "powers *(dynameis)* and principalities *(archontoi)*" against whom the children of the Second Adam "wrestle."[428] His ultimate mission was to bring about the purification and sanctification of mankind on Earth—not to lead a small contingent of pneumatics up out of the kosmos, leaving it behind to rot in its corruption!

Logion 57

The Sovereignty of the *Abba* is like a man who had [planted] good seed. His enemy came by night and sowed weeds among the good seed. The man did not allow them to pull up the weeds; he said to them, 'I am afraid that you will try to pull up the weeds but pull up the wheat along with them.' For on the day of the harvest the weeds will be plainly visible, and they will be pulled up and burned.

COMMENTARY

---

[428] Cf. Ephesians 6.12, 3.10; Romans 8.38; Colossians 1.16, 2.15. The Pseudo-Pauline Titus 3.1 totally misunderstands Pauline usage and counsels cooperation with the powers and principalities!

This is an independent version of the Parable of the Wheat and the Tares preserved elsewhere only in the special material of Matthew's Gospel.[429]

The semitic *mashal,* which is known to us as a parable, was a simple way of symbolizing complex ideas, but based on familiar events from daily life. The *mashal* might be in the form of an allegory, a simile (X is like Y) or a metaphor (X is Y). *Yeshua* proclaimed *davarim* or divine mysteries in the form of *mashlim.* He specifically used the word *mashal:* "Unto you [the inner-circle disciples] it is given to know the *razim* of the *Malkuth* of God; but unto them that are without, all these things are done in *mashlim.*"[430] In modern biblical criticism, this is a form-critical[431] term.

The *mashlim* were short, memorable stories that lent themselves to accurate oral transmission, but without the interpretive discourse that was given to the inner-circle disciples. They constituted much of his public teaching which, like that of the prophets, was meant to be understood only by those with "ears to hear," that is, spiritual understanding in their hearts.

Matthew connects the saying about "to him who has, will be given" with Isaiah's prophetic charge, "though they hear, they will not understand; though they see, they shall not perceive."[432] Matthew, whose Christian apologetic blamed the entire nation of Israel for rejecting and killing its *Messiah,* further spins this fiction by commenting that "Jesus spoke everything to the [Jewish] multitudes in parables... that it might be fulfilled which was spoken by the prophet, saying, 'I will open my mouth in parables; I will utter things which have been kept secret from the foundation of the world.'"[433] In other words, the Jews were given riddles to condemn them, as Isaiah had supposedly done.

In this case Matthew incorrectly attributes the quotation to a prophet when, in fact, it is from Psalm 78 (Christian numbering), and properly translated says, "I will open my mouth in a *mashal;* I will utter *razim* [hidden mysteries] that we have heard and known, and that our fathers have told us."[434] It was probably part of an early Christian collection of messianic "proof-texts" that were applied to amplify Synoptic Gospel narratives. The assumption was that if an Old Testament passage could be construed as having foretold the mission of Jesus, it must have been fulfilled literally in the life of Jesus.

---

[429] Matthew 13.24-30
[430] Mark 4.11
[431] Form criticism is the analysis of form, structure, and function of conventional oral and literary units used to transmit knowledge—in this case, the semitic *mashal,* which Greek translators rendered as *parabole* and English translators as parable. The term occurs 15 times in the Synoptics Matthew, Mark, and Luke, but not at all in John.
[432] Matthew 6.14, Isaiah 6.9-10
[433] Matthew 13.34-35 incorrectly quoting Psalm 78.2
[434] Psalm 78.2-3

Yeshua expected his disciples to be able to interpret and understand the *mashlim.* Mark follows the previous quotation and telling of the Parable of the Sower with this rebuke: "Do you not understand this *mashal?* Then how will you understand all my other *mashlim?"*[435]

But I disagree with the Synoptic Gospel writers. I do not think that *Yeshua* used *mashlim* to confuse the disobedient Jews, as Isaiah was supposed to have done. Isaiah's mission was to a corrupt and complacent Israel. If that had been so with *Yeshua's Basor,* his mission would have been to the corrupt Temple rulers—not to the villagers and *amme ha-eretz* of Israel.

No, his use of the *mashal* as part of his proclamation of the *Basor* was meant to transmit powerful understandings in a simple way that could be remembered and quickly spread by being repeated to others. He expected his disciples and many of his hearers to understand his *mashlim.* They also served as epitomes and summaries of inner-circle teaching that could be memorized and transmitted. Finally, the *mashlim* were also an effective modality to preach against the religious establishment without risking arrest, as the allegories were open to interpretation in a way that literal accusations were not.

He offered a series of *mashlim* about the *Malkuth*—so-called Parables of the Kingdom. Logion 57 is one of them. He says that the *Malkuth* or manifestation of God's Sovereignty on Earth[436] is like a harvest in which the weeds are separated from the wheat. An enemy has sown weeds in the master's wheat-field, so he allows them to continue growing among the wheat-stalks because when all are ripe, they can be separated without harming the crop.

This is a profound answer to the question of evil. Why to the righteous suffer and the evil flourish? Because this *'olam* is under the domination of evil forces that are so embedded in the social institutions and spiritual constitution of mankind that they cannot be plucked out without destroying the good growth that the entire *'olam* was established to support. Kabbalistically, evil is necessary, as *Yeshua* declares in another saying.[437] Why? Because it tempers, tries, and strengthens the good.[438]

But here *Yeshua* says that the Sovereignty of God is like the master who allows the weeds to grow so that at the end of the season when all is ripe, they can be easily and safely separated from the wheat. We have seen in Logion 21.b.2, the harvest was *Yeshua's* metaphor for the gathering of souls into communities of the *Malkuth.* His disciples were compared to laborers in this harvest, and he said "the fields are white" with wheat for harvest. For *Yeshua,* the great soul harvest was a present—not future—spiritual reality.

---

[435] Mark 4.13

[436] God's *Malkuth* was everywhere, but it was unseen and unperceived by humanity. The coming of the *Malkuth* was the unveiling of the divine *Malkuth* and its *Razim* or Mysteries to mankind, which had been suffering under the spiritual blindness, illusion, and bondage of evil forces since the days of Adam.

[437] Matthew 18.7; Mark 13.7

[438] The Masonic checkerboard floor, white squares alternating with black squares, was designed to symbolize this truth.

In the later churches, however, the harvest was understood as a future eschatological event in which Jesus as the *Messiah ben-David*[439] will swoop down upon the Earth with his troops of angels to save the chosen few from final destruction of the old Earth—i.e., the Pauline so-called Rapture that was back-redacted into the New Testament sayings of *Yeshua*.[440] Christian apocalypticists have been expecting the Second Coming of Jesus, which in Judaism would be the (first) coming of *Messiah*, for thousands of years. The eschatological alarm has been sounded countless times by charismatic church leaders from second-century Montanus to twenty-first century television evangelists.[441]

A correct interpretation of the *davarim* of *Yeshua* about the harvest would seem to be as follows: The time of *Yeshua's* ministry inaugurated both the harvest and the planting of the *Malkuth* on Earth. *Yeshua* called his disciples "fishers of men." The soul-harvest will continue. After death, the *Bar-Enash*, like a Wise Fisherman, will continue to choose the big fish and throw the many small ones back into the sea to grow.

But just as each individual soul will eventually be harvested to be "eaten" or joined with the *Bar-Enash* when ripe or mature after many lives, each soul is also harvested at physical death, when the incarnation has ripened all that its field was capable of producing. In the judgment of each soul after death, the results or weeds of evil works will be removed from each heart and incinerated in the purgatory of the Third heaven. Then the soul will sleep in Paradise until it once again enters the *'olam* of incarnation.

Logion 58

Blessed is the Man of Affliction; he shall find Divine Life.

COMMENTARY

Although this saying is not found in other sources, it is a *davar* that restates the passage in Isaiah 53.3 that is the quintessential text for the *Messiah Ben-Joseph* or suffering *Messiah*. In

---

[439] *Yeshua* specifically opposed the idea of a warrior *Messiah ben-David* in Mark 12.35, as previously explained.

[440] The Marcan Little Apocalypse of chapter 13 was a prediction of the Seige of Jerusalem with the destruction of the Second Temple and the Temple Establishment. It had been fulfilled by the year 70 C.E. However, along with eschatological interpretations of messianic proof-texts excerpted from Isaiah and other prophets, it became the basis for key apocalyptic visions in the Revelations to John, which was not accepted by most churches as authentic until the late fourth century. Even so, it has become the lynchpin for Christian eschatology.

[441] The messianic eschatological crisis has also manifested as distorted revelations about alien beings in space ships coming to save the chosen few before our planet is destroyed in some great cataclysm. As always, the leaders of these movements convince people to sell their possessions, turn the proceeds over to their organization, and await further orders. The prophesied date passes uneventfully, but even so a new date is given and the gullible remain on the hook.

this passage Israel is portrayed as the Suffering Servant of God. In the messianic interpretation familiar to *Yeshua,* it seems to have represented the martyred prophets and saints of Israel, including himself and those who would serve as his disciples.[442]

In Aramaic we find a striking aliteration between the Hebrew word for affliction in the text of Isaiah *(chali)* and for life *(chayyim),* meaning the Divine Life of The *'Olam* here in Logion 58. There is no such connection between possible Greek words, and nothing in Coptic. The Coptic word for affliction is the very general term *hice* which can mean trouble, suffering, disease, confusion, and many other things. Most Coptic scholars translate it as suffer or struggle, but without looking at the probable Aramaic language, they miss the alliteration which is the key to understanding this *logion* as an authentic *davar* of *Yeshua.*

Isaiah 53.3 describes God's Suffering Servant in this way: "He is despised and rejected of men; a man of sorrows, and acquainted with grief." The word for grief is *chali,* and the meaning is "affliction."

Yeshua packs a lot of meaning into his beatitude, "Blessed is the Man of Affliction," which was apparently the messianic title he used for what scholars today know as the Suffering Servant. First, he exhorts his disciples to not be disturbed when they experience rejection and sorrow in their mission. Just as it was to be expected with the saints, prophets, and martyrs of Israel, it is to be expected with them. But, as the description in Isaiah concludes, "He shall see the travail of his soul and be satisfied. By his knowledge my righteous servant shall make many righteous...therefore will I divide him a portion with the great ones...because he poured out his soul unto death."[443] Those who are faithful will be great in Heaven and in the coming *Malkuth* on Earth.

It is likely that the Aramaic-Hebrew imperfect tense was used, such that this beatitude was parallel to the other more familiar ones in the form "Blessed is/are X, because Y." Thus the original meaning in the Hebrew imperfect, which can represent both past and future tenses, could have been, 1. "Blessed was the Man of Affliction, because he found the Life;" or, 2. "Blessed is the Man of Affliction; (because) he shall find Eternal Life." I have opted for a version of the latter in my formal translation.

Scholars have debated the self-consciousness of Jesus. Did he think of himself as the long-awaited *Messiah,* or merely as a prophet of the *Messiah*? Did he literally speak the long sermons in John's Gospel about himself as the Light of the World, or was he more like the prophet of Mark's Gospel who said, "Why do you call me good? There is only one who is

---

[442] Other translations imply that a person who suffers has found true divine life. This is ridiculous. The world is full of suffering people. It isn't suffering that produces sainthood, but the overcoming of it by strength of spirit.

[443] Isaiah 53.11-12

good, and that is God,"[444] quite clearly negating any idea that he "made himself equal to God," as Jewish opponents are represented to have said.

Yeshua's self-consciousness is apparent when we examine his teachings in their own language and thought-world. He saw himself as a messianic prophet like John the Baptist. But unlike John, his understanding of the *Bar-Enash* was not of a warrior *Messiah Ben-David* who would appear as a heavenly being leading armies of angels, as the Essenes thought, or a human warrior who would gather Jewish guerrillas to fight the Romans with heavenly aid, as the Zealots thought. Rather, the *Bar-Enash* or "Son of Man" was a community of saints spiritually generated from the archetypal heavenly New Adam or New Humanity. He saw himself as the first-born of these, whose mission was to proclaim the *Basor,* harvest souls for the *Malkuth,* and teach foundational *halakah* for the New World and the New Humanity.

Yeshua expected opposition and affliction. John the Baptist had been beheaded by Herod. He hoped to prolong his ministry until the foundation had been laid, but he had no illusions about escaping the fate of John. The Man of Affliction would be "cut off from the land of the living."[445] Like the *Messiah Ben-Joseph,* he would fight the greatest of all spiritual battles, be killed, and his legacy would live on to grow and eventually triumph as the *Malkuth* of God became slowly revealed to mankind and in society.

What, then, does the original *davar* underlying Logion 58 mean? Simply that any of his disciples who becomes a faithful member of the messianic corpus will suffer on Earth, but he or she will find the Life of the *'Olam,* both in flesh and in Heaven.

Logion 59

Look unto the Living One while you are alive, lest you die and seek to see Him and have not power to do so.

COMMENTARY

The Gnostic understanding of this *logion* was that Jesus was exhorting his disciples to honor him as the *Messiah* while he was still present with them, because after death it would be too late. Similarities to this interpretation can be found in John's Gospel.[446] But none of these is authentic. *Yeshua* did not demand messianic honors during his ministry.

---

[444] Mark 10.18
[445] Isaiah 53.8
[446] John 7:34 You will search for me, but you will not find me; and where I am, you cannot come.
John 13:33 Little children, I am with you only a little longer. You will look for me; and as I said to the Jews so now I say to you, 'Where I am going, you cannot come.'

Since there is no Gnostic terminology or any other reason to assume this is a Gnostic *logion,* let us examine it as potentially authentic. To understand the potential underlying *davar,* let us first examine the title, "The Living One," in Hebrew. While *chayah* can simply refer to a living person, when it is given the article *Ha-Chayah,* as it appears through the Coptic, it is a Name of God in found Old Testament usage. It can also refer to other living creatures (the *Chayot*) around the *Merkabah* Throne of God. But here it could mean Godhead, with the sense "seek God while you are alive."

However, in kabbalistic usage the Living One *(Chayah)* is the high aspect of a human soul that lives in the *'Olam* of *Atziluth.* The kabbalistic Four Worlds described in medieval literature are probably a later evolution of Hellenistic Kabbalah, but it is instructive to note that the aspects of the soul are attributed as follows: In the World of *Asiah* or the manifest universe, it is *Nephesh;* in the higher World of *Yetzirah* where the seeds of the visible universe pre-exist as invisible forms and the hosts of lower angels abide, it is *Ruah,* in which it is possible to ascend and descend between human and divine worlds; in the even higher World of *Beriah* and the commanders of angelic legions, it is *Neshamah;* in the World of *Atziluth* where Archangels reside, it is *Chayah,* the Living Essence; at the highest level in *Adam Kadmon* it is *Yechidah,* the Monadic or Unique Essence that is a ray of God. *Ruach* binds *Neshamah* to the *Nephesh,* and *Neshamah* is bound by nature to both the individual human being and to Godhead. The highest octaves of the soul, *Chayah* and *Yechidah,* are not bound in any way to the physical body, as the lower psychic aspects are.

Although the kabbalistic doctrine of the Four Worlds may not yet have developed in the Hellenistic period, the five octaves of the soul, which were derived from Egyptian mortuary science, were known in the wisdom schools far before the days of *Yeshua.* When *Yeshua* referred to "looking unto the *Chayah* (Living One)," he would have been using kabbalistic *Merkabah* terminology known to his disciples through his inner-circle teaching.

In that case, the *davar* advises disciples to practice divine communion with the High Self while yet in flesh so that after death they will be able to maintain that communion, which is visionary. The Coptic phrase ϬⲰϢⲦ ⲚⲤⲀ means to "gaze upon" with the eyes, and the corollary ⲈⲚⲀⲨ ⲈⲢⲞϤ denotes seeing in divine vision. In Aramaic the distinction between the two kinds of seeing might be that while in flesh, the disciples should use the *Merkabah* techniques of *shaqad* or meditation to gaze upon the *Chayah,* so that after death they will be able to see their way in *aliyah* or ascent to the High Self.

There are instructions in some of the Egyptian Books of the Dead about the righteous climbing a ladder to the Chariot or Ark of the Sun, which is a light far above the darkness below. In the Enochian scheme, the Seventh Heaven is the abode of the Sun, *Shemesh,* and of all the *Chayot,* or Holy Living Ones around the *Merkabah* Throne of God. This would also have been the abode of the individual *Chayah* that would guide the *tzadikim* to its abode in the Seventh Heaven—as opposed to the Third Heaven, where lesser souls slept until they once again incarnated on Earth. The Enochian Seventh Heaven was comparable to the Hermetic *Ogdoad* or Eighth Heaven, from which the ascended Hermetic saints offered telepathic guidance to incarnate souls.

Because of its kabbalistic terminology and lack of Gnostic themes, I consider Logion 59 to be an authentic *davar* of *Yeshua.* It seems to be an exhortation to persevere in *Merkabah* meditation as a preparation for physical death. A related saying from this New Testament would be, "And what I say unto you I say unto all, keep *shaqad* (vigil, meditation)."[447]

Logion 60-62 [Authentic Sayings with Gnostic Redaction]

60.a [They saw] a Samaritan carrying a lamb on his way to Judea. He said to his disciples, "[Why is] that man carrying the lamb?" They said to him, "So that he may kill it and eat it." He said to them, "While it is alive, he will not eat it, but only when he has killed it and it has become a corpse."

> 60.b They said to him, "He cannot do so otherwise." He said to them, "You too, look for a place for yourself within the *Anapausis*, lest you become a corpse and be eaten."

COMMENTARY

As in Logia #49-53 and 67-69, this is a section that has seen extensive Gnostic redaction woven around authentic *davarim.*

It is likely that the part of the conversation in Logion 60 up to "has become a corpse" is authentic. It follows the "eating" motif that I have discussed earlier with Logion 8, The Wise Fisherman, and Logion 11, "The dead are not alive, and the living will not die. During the days when you ate what is dead, you made it come alive…etc." But like Logion 61 which follows, it is a hybrid saying using part of an authentic *davar* quoted to support an attached Gnostic conclusion—in this case, about the *anapausis.*

---

[447] Mark 13.37 and a host of other references in the Synoptics. Gentile Christianity interpreted these and similar sayings apocalyptically to mean, "keep watch" for the end of the world and the Second Coming of the Lord Jesus. But that is not what we find in the underlying Aramaic, nor is it what *Yeshua* taught.

Yeshua is saying that true and full integration of the soul into the *Bar-Enash* (cf. Wise Fisherman) cannot happen until after physical death. Paul's opposition to the Corinthian Pneumatics or "Perfected Souls," and that the *agon* is not finished until death, reflects this understanding.

61.a Two will recline on a couch: the one will die, and the other will live.

> 61.b Salome said, "Who are you, the man who reclines on my couch and eats from my table?"
> Jesus said to her, "I am he who was generated from the Eternal One.[448] I was given a share in the Sovereignty of my father."
> <...> "I am your disciple."

61.c <...> "Therefore I say, when one [of you] is destroyed [by death], he will be filled with light; but if he is divided,[449] he will be filled with darkness."

COMMENTARY

Again, authentic sayings of *Yeshua* have been used to leverage Gnostic doctrine about Jesus. The prefatory saying of 61.a is an independent version of the *davar* about the division among people that the advent of the *Bar-Enash* will precipitate. In the New Testament it was twisted from its lack of context in Q[450] into an eschatological saying to support the Pauline "rapture."

Here, it was probably linked with 61.c in the original Aramaic dictation, then used here by the redactor as a conclusion to Logion 61. The mnemonic link is established by the idea of two people, one who will spiritually live contrasted to one who will spiritually die. The emphasis in 61.a is the contrast of two people from the same house; that of 61.c is the contrast of enlightened death and one who dies in spiritual darkness.

Logion 61.c is not known from any other source, but it does reflect the kabbalistic teachings of *Yeshua* about establishing singleness of heart (see comments about the heart and the *yetzerim* for Logion 3 and #22). The *davar* declares that after death, those disciples who

---

[448] Coptic (Ⲱ̅ϨⲰ̅) from a root meaning equal, same is a Gnostic term for Godhead as unchanging often found translated with the incomprehensible divine name "the Same." My old Coptic professor Lambdin translates this as "undivided." But in Gnostic usage it means eternal, unchanging Godhead.
[449] In the sense of Greek *dipsychos*, Aramaic *se'eph*, wavering, doubting, not committed to God's ways.
[450] It appears in an eschatological context in Matthew 24:40-41 and Luke 17:34

have become *shalem,* whole, or "single" of heart and soul will abide in divine light or illumination, but those who have not will abide in darkness.

The appearance of Salome is common in early Gnostic writings because she and Mary *Magdala* were considered to be the greatest women disciples of *Yeshua.* The redactor writes them into the text to establish authority for Gnostic doctrine. They are often used to define the ideal of a Gnostic woman as unmarried (or widowed) and without children, which may have been true of both women. They are the Gnostic questioners who ask about the place of women in spiritual life,[451] such as the extant fragment from the Gospel of the Egyptians in which Salome asks how long death would hold sway in the world. Jesus says to her, "So long as women bring forth, for I come to end the works of woman." To this Salome replies, "Then I have done well in not bringing forth."

Salome's appearance in Logion 61 is to ask another question that leads to a teaching about death. Her question to the man Jesus is, "Who are you?" He answers with the Gnostic doctrine about the deity of the eternal Savior: "I am the begotten Son of the Eternal Father, and with him I share Sovereignty over the All." In other words, he is the omniscient and omnipotent Gnostic-Revealer version of the Christian Son of God or Christ, both of whom were variations of the original messianic *Bar-Enash,* with the Christological understanding that the man Jesus himself was the one and only manifestation of the *Bar-Enash.*

Another aspect of the setting of *Yeshua* dining at Salome's couch is the fact that only late in the Roman-Hellenistic era did it become common in some cultures for women to recline with men for dinner. Previously men and women ate separately. That changed in the early Christian church communities. Here in *Thomas* it may indicate that men and women lived and took their meals in common in the Syrian ascetic communities.

How does the Christological question of Salome lead to the *davar* about enlightened death? We can't tell. Worms and microorganisms have eaten holes and removed critical parts of the manuscript, represented in my translation with the symbol **<...>.** This is called a lacuna or Latin "little lake" by scholars. We can often figure out what is missing by counting spaces and filling them with reasonable Coptic or Greek words based on the context. But not here.

Nevertheless, it is interesting to note that while the little buggers ate away at the Gnostic redaction, the authentic *davarim* were preserved. The underlying mnemonic sequence of the two *davarim* has allowed us the better understand them.

The final saying seem to be an authentic *davar* used to conclude this pericope. *Yeshua* declares that when one of his disciples dies ("is destroyed," an Aramaic indiomatic

---

[451] *Thomas* Logion #114, a purely Gnostic creation, uses the issue of Mary *Magdala* to lend credence to the Syrian Thomasian doctrine that women must "become male" or ascetic so they, too, can have salvation and enlightenment.

expression), he will find himself filled with light. But the person who is *se'eph,* "wavering, doubting, not commited to God's ways," which is the opposite of *shalem,* "whole, integrated, unified in will and purpose with God,"[452] will be filled with darkness.

> 62.a It is to those who are worthy of my mysteries that I tell my mysteries.

> 62.b Do not let your left know what your right is doing.

COMMENTARY

These are *logia* that seem to have been adapted or hybridized from authentic sayings, but probably not from the original Aramaic dictation—more likely from other sources like the Christian Gospels.

Logion 62.a seems to be a restatement of the Marcan *logion* that I translate from an Aramaic perspective to emphasize the original *davar,* "To you has been given the *Razim* of the *Malkuth* of God, but for those outside, everything comes in *mashalim.*"[453] In the Thomasian version, the Revealer *Iesous* imparts his secret teachings only to the worthy, i.e. members of the Gnostic community. This implies that the community has received other secret teachings from the Risen Christ through revelations given to its leaders. Most of the extant Gnostic writings from Nag Hammadi and other sources, unlike the *Gospel of Thomas,* consist of long theosophical discourses from the Revealer Christ about the origins, foundations, and heavenly aeons of the All. It is to these that the mysteries of Logion 62.a refer.

Logion 62.b is not a *davar* of *Yeshua,* but the Aramaic expression "do not let your left hand know what your right hand is doing." It means "keep it to yourself, keep it private." The expression appears only in Matthew's special material in conjunction with almsgiving.[454] *Yeshua* advised his disciples not to follow the example of pious Pharisees who publicly proclaimed their charity with the *shofar.* Instead they should keep it private. He advised the same for prayer.

The redactor of *Thomas* has changed the Aramaic expression, which by itself is not a *davar,* into a Coptic Gnostic *logion* in its own right by omitting any reference to left or right hand. That is because in Gnostic thought, the left and right had significance in themselves. The

---

[452] Both are Aramaic terms underlying many of *Yeshua's* teachings in the New Testament.

[453] Mark 4:11, repeated in Luke 8:1 and Matthew 13:11 as "To you has been given the secret(s) of the Kingdom [Sovereignty] of God, but for those outside, everything comes in parables."

[454] Matthew 6.1-3, "Take care that you do not give alms publicly so you can be seen...do not sound a *shofar* before yourself as the self-righteous ones do in synagogues and on the streets...but when you give alms, do not let your left hand know what your right hand is doing."

Coptic of Logion 62.b translates literally, "Do not let your left know what your right is doing."

In the *Hypostasis of the Archons* we find the simplest explanation of left and right: "And *Sophia* (Wisdom) took her daughter *Zoe* (Life) and had her sit upon his[455] right to teach him about the things that exist in the Eighth (Ogdoas, Eighth Heaven); and the angel of wrath she placed upon his left. Since that day, his right has been called Life, and the left has come to represent the unrighteousness of the realm of absolute (astrological) power above."

But in the *Apocryphon of John,* we find detailed astrological rulerships of left and right organs and parts of the human body:

> "And a voice came forth from the exalted aeon-heaven: 'The Man exists and the Son of Man.' And the chief archon, Ialdabaoth,[456] heard (it) and thought that the voice had come from his mother. And he did not know from where it came. And he taught them, the holy and perfect Mother-Father, the complete foreknowledge, the image of the invisible one who is the Father of the all (and) through whom everything came into being, the first Man. For he revealed his likeness in a human form.

> "And the whole aeon of the chief archon trembled, and the foundations of the abyss shook. And of the waters which are above matter, the underside was illuminated by the appearance of his image which had been revealed. And when all the authorities and the chief archon looked, they saw the whole region of the underside which was illuminated. And through the light they saw the form of the image in the water.

> "And he[457] said to the authorities which attend him, 'Come, let us create a man according to the image of God and according to our likeness, that his image may become a light for us.' And they created by means of their respective powers in correspondence with the characteristics which were given. And each authority supplied a characteristic in the form of the image which he had seen in its natural (form). He created a being according to the likeness of the first, perfect Man. And they said, 'Let us call him Adam, that his name may become a power of light for us.'

> "And the powers began: the first one, goodness, created a bone-soul; and the second, foreknowledge, created a sinew-soul; the third, divinity, created a flesh-soul; and the fourth, the lordship, created a marrow-soul; the fifth, kingdom created a blood-soul; the sixth, envy, created a skin-soul; the seventh, understanding, created a hair-soul. And the multitude of the angels attended him and they received from the powers the seven substances of the natural (form) in order to create the proportions of the limbs and the proportion of the rump and the proper working together of each of the parts.

> "The first one began to create the head. Eteraphaope-Abron created his head; Meniggesstroeth created the brain; Asterechme (created) the right eye; Thaspomocha, the left eye; Yeronumos, the

---

[455] Sakla, also called Ialdaboath or Iao (after *Yahweh*), whose Greek named added to 360, the degrees of the heavens. Iao (Ιαω) was the powerful Name intoned in Gnostic ritual and liturgical evocation found in the Greek, Hebrew, and Demotic magical papyri.
[456] The Gnostic Demiurge or Creator God of the Old Testament who mistakenly thought he was Absolute Godhead.
[457] Ialdabaoth.

right ear; Bissoum, the left ear; Akioreim, the nose; Banen-Ephroum, the lips; Amen, the teeth; Ibikan, the molars; Basiliademe, the tonsils; Achcha, the uvula; Adaban, the neck; Chaaman, the vertebrae; Dearcho, the throat; Tebar, the right shoulder; [...], the left shoulder; Mniarcon, the right elbow; [...], the left elbow; Abitrion, the right underarm; Evanthen, the left underarm; Krys, the right hand; Beluai, the left hand; Treneu, the fingers of the right hand; Balbel, the fingers of the left hand; Kriman, the nails of the hands; Astrops, the right breast; Barroph, the left breast; Baoum, the right shoulder joint; Ararim, the left shoulder joint; Areche, the belly; Phthave, the navel; Senaphim, the abdomen; Arachethopi, the right ribs; Zabedo, the left ribs; Barias, the right hip; Phnouth the left hip; Abenlenarchei, the marrow; Chnoumeninorin, the bones; Gesole, the stomach; Agromauna, the heart; Bano, the lungs; Sostrapal, the liver; Anesimalar, the spleen; Thopithro, the intestines; Biblo, the kidneys; Roeror, the sinews; Taphreo, the spine of the body; Ipouspoboba, the veins; Bineborin, the arteries; Atoimenpsephei, theirs are the breaths which are in all the limbs; Entholleia, all the flesh; Bedouk, the right buttock (?); Arabeei, the left penis; Eilo, the testicles; Sorma, the genitals; Gorma-Kaiochlabar, the right thigh; Nebrith, the left thigh; Pserem, the kidneys of the right leg; Asaklas, the left kidney; Ormaoth, the right leg; Emenun, the left leg; Knyx, the right shin-bone; Tupelon, the left shin-bone; Achiel, the right knee; Phnene, the left knee; Phiouthrom, the right foot; Boabel, its toes; Trachoun, the left foot; Phikna, its toes; Miamai, the nails of the feet; Labernioum - .

"And those who were appointed over all of these are: Zathoth, Armas, Kalila, Jabel, (Sabaoth, Cain, Abel). And those who are particularly active in the limbs (are) the head Diolimodraza, the neck Yammeax, the right shoulder Yakouib, the left shoulder Verton, the right hand Oudidi, the left one Arbao, the fingers of the right hand Lampno, the fingers of the left hand Leekaphar, the right breast Barbar, the left breast Imae, the chest Pisandriaptes, the right shoulder joint Koade, the left shoulder joint Odeor, the right ribs Asphixix, the left ribs Synogchouta, the belly Arouph, the womb Sabalo, the right thigh Charcharb, the left thigh Chthaon, all the genitals Bathinoth, the right leg Choux, the left leg Charcha, the right shin-bone Aroer, the left shin-bone Toechtha, the right knee Aol, the left knee Charaner, the right foot Bastan, its toes Archentechtha, the left foot Marephnounth, its toes Abrana.

In both kabbalistic and Gnostic thought, the human soul is a microcosm of the great macrocosm. The *Adam*, or primal *Anthropos* (Mankind), is the divine image reflected in all human souls. Thus, in Logion 62.b, "your left" is the corrupt part of human nature under the rulership of the unrighteous astrological powers (planets)—Plato's Motion to the Left, possibly also influenced by the kabbalistic left-hand evil *yetzer*. "Your right" is the divine, redemptive nature under zodiacal rulership—Plato's Motion to the Right, possibly influenced by the good or divine *yetzer* of the Jewish wisdom tradition.

Logion 62.b advises the Gnostic to keep the powers that rule his corruptible nature in complete ignorance of the divine powers. That is the way Sophia tricked the evil archons into creating Adam, and the method used to protect Adam and Eve in Valentinian myth. The greatest ally of the Gnostic was his secrecy.

CHAPTER NINE: Logia 63-75

Logion 63

There was a rich man who had great wealth. He said, 'I shall invest my money so that I may sow, reap, plant, and fill my storehouse with produce, with the result that I shall lack nothing.' Such were the thoughts of his heart, but that same night he died. Let him who has ears hear.

COMMENTARY

This is an independent telling of the story of the rich man who died in Luke's special material.[458] The Aramaic expressions "thoughts of his heart" and "let him who has ears hear" further verify its authenticity.

This is not an indictment of wealth, rich people, or investing money. In fact, another parable rewards the faithful steward who wisely invests his master's wealth.[459] Rather, it is about

---

[458] Luke 12:16-21

[459] Matthew's Parable of the Talents, 25.14-29, is taken as an endorsement of capitalism and investment, but *Yeshua* strongly upheld the prohibitions in *Torah* against charging interest for loans to friends, family, and other Israelites. This *mashal* is about making profit from trade—not lending money. It reads: "For the kingdom of heaven is as a man travelling into a far country, who called his own servants, and delivered unto them his goods. And unto one he gave five talents, to another two, and to another one; to every man according to his abilities; and straightway took his journey. Then he that had received the five talents went and traded with the same, and made them other five talents. And likewise he that had received two, he also gained other two. But he that had received one went and digged in the earth, and hid his lord's money. After a long time the lord of those servants cometh, and reckoneth with them. And so he that had received five talents came and brought other five talents, saying, Lord, thou deliveredst unto me five talents: behold, I have gained beside them five talents more. His lord said unto him, Well done, thou good and faithful servant: thou hast been faithful over a few things, I will make thee ruler over many things: enter thou into the joy of thy lord. He also that had received two talents came and said, Lord, thou deliveredst unto me two talents: behold, I have gained two other talents beside them. His lord said unto him, Well done, good and faithful servant; thou hast been faithful over a few things, I will make thee ruler over many things: enter thou into the joy of thy lord. Then he which had received the one talent came and said, Lord, I knew thee that thou art an hard man, reaping where thou hast not sown, and gathering where thou hast not strawed: And I was afraid, and went and hid thy talent in the earth: lo, there thou hast that is thine. His lord answered and said unto him, Thou wicked and slothful servant, thou knewest that I reap where I sowed not, and gather where I have not strawed: Thou oughtest therefore to have put my money to the exchangers, and then at my coming I should have received mine own with usury. Take therefore the talent from him, and give it unto him which hath ten talents. For unto every

the impermanence of material riches and the value of spiritual riches. The man follows the impulses of the *yetzer ha-ra,* which mislead him into thinking that he can "lack nothing" if he maximizes his personal wealth. In fact, trust in material wealth is lack of true wealth—in other words, spiritual poverty.

The ironic contrast to the man's intention to create a situation where he "lacked nothing" is implied in *Yeshua's* exhortation, "Let him who has ears hear." The Hebrew-Aramaic word for "hear" also means to understand, comprehend, and obey. The hearer is expected to understand the difference between temporal wealth and spiritual wealth.

For more about *Yeshua* and teachings about "having, lacking," and spiritual wealth, see the commentary to Logion 11.

Logion 64 [Authentic *Mashal* with Gnostic Conclusion]

64.a A man had received visitors. And when he had prepared the dinner, he sent his servant to invite the guests. He went to the first one and said to him, 'My master invites you.' He said, 'I have claims against some merchants. They are coming to me this evening. I must go and give them my orders. I ask to be excused from the dinner.' He went to another and said to him, 'My master has invited you.' He said to him, 'I have just bought a house and am required for the day. I shall not have any spare time.' He went to another and said to him, 'My master invites you.' He said to him, 'My friend is going to get married, and I am to prepare the banquet. I shall not be able to come. I ask to be excused from the dinner.' He went to another and said to him, 'My master invites you.' He said to him, 'I have just bought a farm, and I am on my way to collect the rent. I shall not be able to come. I ask to be excused.' The servant returned and said to his master, 'Those whom you invited to the dinner have asked to be

---

one that hath shall be given, and he shall have abundance: but from him that hath not shall be taken away even that which he hath."

excused.' The master said to his servant, 'Go outside to the streets and bring back whomever you happen to meet, so that they may dine.'

> 64.b Businessmen and merchants will not enter the places of my father."

COMMENTARY

This is a Thomasian redaction of *Yeshua's* Great Supper *mashal* from Q.[460] The version in *Thomas* seems to be closest to the original form of Q, since it provides all common elements of the other two extant versions in Luke and Matthew, which differ from each other.

This is a *mashal* about the messianic Marriage Banquet, which is crucial to understanding *Yeshua's shabbat seder*. He offered his inner-circle teaching to disciples over a Sabbath meal, and perhaps in the context of ordinary meals as well. It was a form of mystical communion with the heavenly Marriage Banquet of *Messiah*—the spiritual, future, or "supersubstantial" sustenance of the Lord's Prayer.[461] This was the historical origin of the Christian Eucharist or Mass—not the legendary Last Supper, which appears only in the Synoptics.

Yeshua's parable is based on the Palestinian custom of inviting a huge company of socially distinguished guests to celebrate the marriage of a son. When the banquet was done, there was still a huge quantity of food, so it was offered to beggars and the poor of the community, who were invited to partake after guests had left. However, *Yeshua's* is an allegory of the messianic Banquet to which the pious religious leaders of the Jerusalem Temple Establishment have been invited, but refused in their rejection of the *Basor* proclaimed by all the prophets up to John the Baptist and *Yeshua*. Therefore *Yeshua*, the prophet and servant of God, is sent forth to invite all those whom the Pharisees and Saducess look down upon—beggars and the *amme-ha-eretz* or common people and villagers.

Luke provides an authentic context by introducing it with these words, "When one of those at the table with him heard this, he said to Jesus, 'Blessed is the man who will eat at the Marriage Banquet in the Kingdom of God.'"[462] Jesus then tells the parable.

---

[460] It appears in Luke 14:16-24 and in abbreviated and highly redacted form in Matthew 22:1-14.
[461] Not "daily bread," is the King James translates. See footnote #254 on *epiousion*.
[462] Luke 14.15. Matthew introduces his abbreviated version with, "Jesus spoke to them again in parables, saying: 'The Kingdom of Heaven is like a king who prepared a wedding banquet for his son.'"

But in the conclusion, Luke has this: "The servant came back and reported this to his master [the refusal of the distinguished guests]. Then the owner of the house became angry and ordered his servant, 'Go out quickly into the streets and alleys of the town and bring in the poor, the crippled, the blind and the lame.' 'Lord,' the servant said, 'what you ordered has been done, but there is still room.' Then the master told his servant, 'Go out to the roads and villages and make them come in, so that my house will be full. I tell you, not one of those men who were invited will get a taste of my banquet.'"

To both Luke and Matthew, it is all Jews who rejected the invitation, and Luke's addition of the phrase about the "roads and the villages" is probably understood as the gentile acceptance of the invitation.

Matthew concludes the parable this way:"'The wedding banquet is ready, but those I invited did not deserve to come. Go to the street corners and invite to the banquet anyone you find.' So the servants [plural] went out into the streets and gathered all the people they could find, both good and bad, and the wedding hall was filled with guests. For I say unto you that none of those who were bidden shall taste of my supper.'" Here "anyone you find" is Matthew's way of representing the gentiles.[463]

The redactor of *Thomas,* who had access to the original *davar,* adds his own conclusion: "Businessmen and merchants will not enter the places of my father." For the ascetic Syrian Gnostic monks, who were totally negative to the cosmos and the human world, Jesus excluded not only the rich from the Kingdom, but all businessmen and merchants! Regardless of what their relationship to wealth, service, and possessions might have been, they could not enter the Sovereignty because they had families, businesses, and were servants of Mammon.

For the Thomas Gnostics, materialists and procreators had taken the place of the religious establishment that *Yeshua* attacked as the enemies of the *Malkuth.*

Logion 65 [An early Christian Adaptation of an Authentic *Mashal*]

There was a good man who owned a vineyard. He leased it to tenant farmers so that they could work it and he would collect the produce from them. He sent his servant so that the tenants might give him the

---

[463] In the Synoptics (Mark, Matthew, Luke) the fact that *Yeshua* preached only to Jews is resolved by having him say that the message must be first preached to all Israel. Paul resolves it with his teachings about salvation coming first to the Jews, then to the gentiles. John's Gospel has a delegation of gentiles sent to *Yeshua* just before his crucifixion, but he does not receive them, implying that only after his death and Resurrection will gentiles have access to him. None of this is historical, but the issue was of concern for the legitimacy of early gentile Christianity in the face of Jewish Apostolic missionaries ("Judaizers") whose preaching contradicted that of Paul, and whose credentials were far more authentic than Paul's.

produce of the vineyard. They seized his servant and beat him, nearly killing him. The servant went back and told his master. The master said, 'Perhaps he [the servant] did not recognize them.' He sent another servant. The tenants beat this one as well. Then the owner sent his son and said, 'Perhaps they will show respect to my son.' Because the tenants knew that he was the heir to the vineyard, they seized him and killed him. Let him who has ears hear.

COMMENTARY

Even though the Parable of the Tenants appears in Mark's Gospel,[464] from which it was copied by Matthew and Luke, it is not clear how much of it is an authentic *mashal* of *Yeshua*. Clearly the servants sent to the tenants refer to prophets whose messages were rejected. The parable was used by the early gentile churches and their Gospels to blame the Jews for killing Jesus. But if the original parable was as transmitted here, what would have been meant by the killing of the son? *Yeshua* had not yet been executed. He would not have spoken about the possibility of coming martyrdom in these terms or in this way. It would have meant nothing to his hearers.

I see two possibilities. The first is that the section about the killing of the son was simply added in pre-Marcan and pre-Pauline Christianity, in which Jesus was interpreted as the *Messiah ben-Joseph* killed by the Jerusalem Temple Establishment. The second is that *Yeshua* spoke of the third prophet as a *bar-Yahweh* or son of god—the Hebrew idiom meaning a *tzadik* or Jewish saint.[465]

Of these two possibilities, the former seems more likely to me. The latter would require a great martyred Jewish saint or prophet preceding *Yeshua* whom he revered. That could have been John the Baptist, but nothing in the phrase about the son points to him. Since the section about the son in the Marcan, Lucan, Matthean, and Thomasian versions emphasize that he was "heir to the vineyard," it clearly points to an early Christian understanding of Jesus as the *Messiah ben-Joseph.* I conclude that even in its early Aramaic form, this parable had been altered.

Here is how we might reconstruct the original *mashal* of the Tenants.

There was a master who owned a vineyard. He leased it to tenant farmers so that they could work it and he would collect part of the produce from them. But

---

[464] Mark 12.1-8

[465] He could not have used it in reference to the *Bar-Enash,* for the Son of Mankind was a heavenly Adam who had not been killed and could not be killed.

when sent his servant so that the tenants might give him produce of the vineyard, they seized him and beat him. The servant went back and told his master. The master sent another servant. The tenants beat this one as well. Then the master sent another servant, and this time they killed him. What then will the master of the vineyard do? He will come and kill those tenants and give the vineyard to others. Let him who has ears hear.

Here *Yeshua* recounts the martyrdom of the prophets, "From the blood of Abel unto the blood of Zacharias which perished between the altar and the temple."[466] He warns that the same is happening today with the "generation of vipers"[467] whose forefathers martyred the prophets—the Jerusalem Pharisees and their interpreters of scripture.[468] The tenants were those to whom the master (God) has given responsibility for tending his fields, i.e, the religious leaders in charge of the Temple and synagogues. In the original *davar* the prophet who is killed by the tenants would have brought the execution of John the Baptist to mind, since he was opposed by the Pharisees and Sadducees of the Jerusalem religious establishment.

Yeshua's conclusion, that the master will kill the unworthy tenants and turn his vineyard over to others, was one of his prophecies against the Jerusalem Temple establishment. When it was fulfilled in the year 70 C.E., the gentile churches interpreted this to mean that they were God's new Israel, and that the blood of Jesus was the sacrificial seal for a New Covenant. The Old Covenant (Testament) had been taken away from the Jews and given to the Christian churches. This became the rubric for interpreting all of *Yeshua's* woe prophecies against the Jewish religious establishment. It guided the way all of his *davarim* and *mashalim* were to be redacted and spun in the Gospels of the New Testament.[469]

---

[466] From Q (Matthew 23.35; Luke 11.51)
[467] Literally "nest of snakes."
[468] Luke 13.34: "O **Jerusalem, Jerusalem**, which killest the prophets, and stonest them that are sent unto thee; how often would I have gathered thy children together, as a hen doth gather her brood under her wings, and ye would not!"
[469] This anti-Jewish spin in the early Greek Christian writings is what scholars refer to as the "anti-semitism" of the New Testament. It was responsible for justifying many atrocities against Jews in medieval Europe.

Show me the stone which the builders have rejected. That one is the capstone.

COMMENTARY

In Mark's version of the Parable of the Tenants, the following proof-text that the *Messiah* would be rejected is integrated into the conclusion. He asks, "Haven't you read this scripture? The stone the builders rejected has become the capstone; the Lord has done this, and it is marvelous in our eyes."[470]

Soon after the crucifixion of *Yeshua,* the early Christians began to search the scriptures to find clues about a *Messiah* who would be rejected, die, and rise again. They found many passages in Isaiah, other prophets like Zechariah, and the Psalms that, when taken interpreted allegorically or kabbalistically, could prophesy the ministry of *Yeshua.* The section from Psalm 118 that is the basis for Logion 66 was connected as a conclusion to the *mashal* of the Tenants before it was received by Mark. It may have been the Apostle Peter who transmitted it to Mark in his notes, or Mark may have taken it from some other source.

Did *Yeshua* quote these lines from Psalm 118? Very possibly so. But for him, it would have been an oft-repeated proverb that he applied to the incompetence of the Jerusalem Temple establishment. *Yeshua* was probably trained as a stone mason.[471] The metaphorical significance of a capstone rejected by builders was something like that of the pious Pharisees who strained gnats from their soup to avoid breaking kosher rules, but "swallowed a camel," whose meat was considered to be far more unclean. They had neglected the basic and essential foundations of religion to construct their own religious house of cards. But God would correct this, for "the stone the builders rejected has become the capstone."[472]

Did *Yeshua* connect this proverb to the *mashal* of the Tenant? Probably not. But since it was a proverb he used, the early Christians connected it to the parable of the Tenants to have

---

[470] Mark 12.10-11 quoting Psalm 118.22 (Christian numeration).

[471] His father was a *teknon* or craftsman in building, wrongly translated as "carpenter" for there was no wood for building anywhere near the village of Nazareth, but lots of stone. He was a stone mason, and as his first-born, *Yeshua* was undoubtedly apprenticed into the trade and initiated into his Jewish masonic guild.

[472] The capstone *(rosh phena),* chief stone, apex-stone, or topstone—not the cornerstone. The cornerstone was the first one placed in the foundation of a new structure—usually the Northeast corner. It had to be stronger and larger than the others. It was also called the foundation stone. It was often inscribed with the date and patron or other dedication, including Masonic markings (Mark Mason). The capstone, by contrast, was the last stone placed. It signified the completion of a building project. It, too, could be inscribed. The Hebrew word also describes the "pinnacle" of Solomon's Temple in Jerusalem where, according to the early Christian *haggadah* about the Temptation of Jesus, he was transported and seated by *Shaitan.*

Jesus foretell his own rejection and martyrdom. That is where the section about the master sending his son (Jesus) was added, and the proverb itself set as a conclusion.

One of the first oral recitations to develop in early Christianity was what scholars call the Passion Narrative. It was constructed following the narration of Psalm 22, *Eloi, Eloi, lama sabachhtani,* "My God, my God, why hast Thou forsaken me?" Mark records in 15.34 that *Yeshua* spoke this from the cross, which may have been so because it refers to the messianic interpretation of the Psalm regarding the death of *Messiah ben-Joseph,* with whom *Yeshua* identified as a scion of the *Bar-Enash.* While Matthew and Luke don't repeat this part of the Marcan narrative, they instead craft their entire narrative from the events of Psalm 22—"not a bone of him broken...cast lots for my garments...pierced my hands and my feet."

This process of memorizing, codifying, and organizing the oral teachings of *Yeshua* using messianic proof-texts that were constantly being discovered as the early churches developed came to full fruition in Matthew's Gospel. The redactor(s) have his family flee to Egypt and return so that Hosea's proof-text can be applied, "Out of Egypt I have called my son."[473]

Mark's version of the Parable of the Tenants serves as a preface to his proof-text from Psalm 118 about the rejected capstone. But in *Thomas* Logion 66, it is not connected to the Parable of the Tenants as a conclusion, but instead simply follows it in order. What kind of order? Mnemonic. The Aramaic dictation connected the two, but as separate sayings of *Yeshua.* In other words, the originally memorized sayings transmitted through *Thomas* had not yet been woven into proof-texts and other narrative contexts.

This kind of evidence, taken with the fact that Q and Mark seem to have been compiled from written Greek sources, suggests that the *Thomas* sayings have an earlier and more authentic derivation than either of these.

Logion 67 [Gnostic Saying]

Whoever knows the All but lacks within himself, lacks the All.

COMMENTARY

The Gnostic jargon of Logion 67 can be related to the teachings of *Yeshua,* but spins them in a very different way. The All means not only the visible, but the invisible *Kosmos* including

---

473 Hosea 11.1; cf. Matthew 2.15

the Pleroma of the Aeons. The term "lack" relates to *Yeshua's* teachings about spiritual wealth (those who "have") as opposed to bondage to material wealth, which is spiritual poverty (those who "lack"). But in Gnostic terms it refers specifically to lacking *gnosis,* the spiritual self-knowledge that was (paradoxically)[474] gained through hearing Gnostic doctrine.

Coptic scholars have translated this saying in several ways. Lambdin attempts a psychological interpretation: "If one who knows the all still feels a personal deficiency, he is completely deficient." Patterson in Robinson's edition paraphrases: "Whoever knows all, if he is lacking one thing, he is (already) lacking everything." Blatz comes closer to a literal interpretation: "He who knows the all, (but) fails (to know) himself, misses everything." Grondin's literal translation reads: "He who knows the All, if he needs himself, needs the place all of it."[475]

To the Gnostic it meant that even if a person were to have all knowledge of the *Kosmos,* if he lacked the interior *gnosis* of his own divine nature, he would lack everything that is real—what the Hermetics called *ta onta,* the things that are really real.

Logion 68-69 [Two inauthentic Beatitudes about persecution]

68.a Blessed are you when you are hated and persecuted.

68.b Wherever you have been persecuted, they will find no place.

69.a Blessed are they who have suffered internally. It is they who have truly come to know the Father.

69.b Blessed are the hungry, for the belly of him who desires will be filled.

COMMENTARY

Logion 68.a is based on a later church expansion of the Beatitude of *Yeshua* in Matthew 5.10, "Blessed are those who are persecuted for righteousness' sake, for the *Malkuth* of Heaven belongs to them." Matthew expands upon this in view of persecution against the early Christian churches in the next verse: "Blessed are you [the persecuted Christian], when men shall revile you, and persecute you, and shall say all manner of evil against you falsely, for my sake." *Thomas* Logion 68.a seems to have developed from Matthew's

---

[474] True philosophical *gnosis* could not be taught—only learned.
[475] See online http://www.geocities.com/Athens/9068/splith.htm.

expansion and was probably interpreted as persecution against the Syrian Gnostic communities. In any case, it is not an authentic Beatitude.

Logion 68.b is a Gnostic Beatitude possibly developed from *Yeshua's* instruction to missionary disciples to ritually shake the dust off their sandals "for a testimony" against the villages who did not receive the *Basor.* It promises that wherever the Syrian Gnostic preachers have been rejected, the villagers will not have a heavenly *topos* or abode in the *anapausis* after death.

Logion 69.a is a Beatitude for those who have adopted not only external asceticism, but the practice of harsh self-examination and continual self-recrimination for their sins. *Yeshua* made self-examination of motives, meaning discrimination between the impulses of good and evil *yetzerim,* fundamental to his *halakah.* But it was not a joyless self-recrimination, as developed in both Gnostic and Christian monastic traditions. Rather, it was more like the Buddhist "mindfulness" discipline of being fully present and aware in the moment. But to the Gnostic ascetic, self-deprivation and internal suffering were the virtues that drew him upward in consciousness and *gnosis* to the *Abba.* In the Hellenistic era, severe asceticism was considered to be the hallmark of a true saint. *Yeshua,* however, was not an ascetic. He was criticized as a "winebibber and a glutton" for his moderation.

The Beatitude of Logion 69.b seems almost identical to the Q *logion* quoted by both Matthew and Luke, "Blessed are you who are hungry now, for you will be filled." Here the Coptic idiom is far more specific than the Aramaic saying as reflected in the Greek Q. The Greek and underlying Aramaic "hunger" and "be filled" can be a simile for having a great desire for righteousness, as in Matthew 5.6, "Blessed are they who hunger and thirst after righteousness, for they shall be filled."

But the Coptic of *Thomas* is speaking literally of physical hunger being satisfied—specifically by filling the belly. This probably had a literal meaning to an ascetic Gnostic, who considered fasting from food to bring spiritual merit in itself.

A glance at Logion 14 may seem to indicate that the Syrian Gnostics didn't fast, "'If you fast, you will bring sin upon yourselves, and if you pray, you will be condemned, and if you give alms, you will harm your spirits." But we know from many sources that they were ascetic. Their interpretation of this *davar* was not that it prohibited praying or fasting or giving alms, but warned to take heed of their intentions in so doing.

Logion 70

When you beget that One you have within your hearts, He will perfect you. If you do not bring forth that One within your hearts, what you have not brought forth within your hearts will kill you.

COMMENTARY

I have translated the Coptic through the lense of Aramaic to better bring out the meaning. The Coptic verb of the first clause is **xΠO**, which means to beget, bring to birth. This is consistent with *Yeshua's* inner-circle teachings about the Birth from Above.[476] The Coptic phrase meaning "inside, within" derives from the Aramaic idiom "within heart." The heart was the abode of the kabbalistic image or *yetzer* of God as well as the evil *yetzter ha-ra,* which was not real, but like a shadow lacking reality. Nevertheless, like a weed it had the power to choke out the divine seed that could become a Tree of Life if carefully germinated and nurtured.

Coptic **ΠH** specifies "that one." I have capitalized One to clarify its meaning. It is the *Bar-Enash,* the Pauline Second Adam or Christ, that must be begotten in the heart. It is the *yetzer ha-tov* or kabbalistic divine spark that has the power to transform self, the human world, and rule in the *Malkuth* or Sovereignty at the right hand of Godhead as the heavenly Son of Mankind.

Logion 70 tells us, If you beget that One in the heart, He will "perfect" you. The Coptic verb is **TOYXϵ**,[477] which occurs only once in the sayings of *Thomas* but represents the Aramaic verb *shalam,* "to be whole, perfect, complete, finished." To become *shalem* or spiritually perfected was the goal of *Yeshua's halakah.* The Aramaic term underlies the Greek word *telios,* which is translated as it was used in the Greek mystery religions of highest-degree initiates, "perfect." For example, "Be ye therefore perfect, even as your *Abba* which is in heaven is perfect."[478]

The next clause, "If you do not bring forth that One," does not repeat the Coptic word for begetting. Rather it is the Achmimic form **TH+,** a very general verb meaning everything from "give, bring" to "pay, go toward, lay upon, fight with, pursue." I used the phrase "bring forth," but it has the sense of "interact with, struggle with" and perhaps best something like "develop, increase." If you do not pay heed to and honor that One, then what you have failed to bring forth [i.e., lack] in your hearts will [spiritually] kill you.

---

[476] Cf. Commentaries on Logia #4 and #22.b
[477] Incorrectly translated by many scholars as he/it will "save" you. The word does not mean "save."
[478] In many places the New Testament renders the original Aramaic word for spiritual perfection *shalem* with Greek *telios.* Luke 6.40b, "...every one that is perfect shall be as his master." John 17.23, "I in them, and thou in me, that they may be made perfect in one [being]." In Luke, Jesus is considered to have become *shalem* by virtue of his crucifixion and Resurrection: Luke 13:32, "And he said unto them, Go ye, and tell that fox [Herod], 'Behold, I cast out devils, and I do cures today and tomorrow, and the third day I shall be perfected.'"

This is consistent with *Yeshua's davarim* such as to those who "have," more will be given. But to those who lack or "have not," even what they have will be taken away. See the Commentary for Logion 41.

Logion 71 [Christian corruption of an original prophecy]

I shall destroy this house, and no one will be able to build it [again].

COMMENTARY

Logion 71 is an independent version of *Yeshua's davar* predicting the destruction of the Second Temple of Solomon that Herod had co-opted and glorified with Roman architecture. *Yeshua* did not say that he would destroy the Temple. Rather, he predicted its destruction. He also predicted God's destruction of the "house" or ruling establishment of the Jerusalem Temple.

It was probably in the context of his final Passover pilgrimage to Jerusalem, when *Yeshua* violently drove away the money-changers with a whip, overturning their tables and animal cages,[479] that he proclaimed the prophecy of destruction against the Temple and its rulers. The act was intended to be provocative, and it was. It galvanized the Pharisees to join Sadducees and Herodians to find a way to silence *Yeshua.*

The Jerusalem Sanhedrin, an uneasy coalition of influential Pharisees and Sadducees, did not have the power to execute *Yeshua*—only to charge him in a religious court. The Romans were not interested in charges of heresy or impiety. But if the High Priest Caiaphas and the rulers of the Temple could find a way to charge him in a Herodian court with treason, the Romans would execute him.

According to Mark's Gospel, they found a charge that would work for both. His prophecies against the Temple of Solomon—that it would be totally destroyed with not one stone standing on another—were twisted to serve: "We heard him say, 'I will destroy this temple that is made with hands, and in three days I will build another, not made with hands.'"[480]

But it is unlikely that *Yeshua* proclaimed himself as the destroyer of the Temple. He probably said something like "the *Abba* will destroy, the Temple and its rulers will be destroyed," or possibly "The Son of Man(kind) will destroy." In Christian memory that would have been tantamount to saying "I shall destroy."

By way of contrast, in Johannine tradition the Temple destruction motif was reinterpreted as a prophecy of *Yeshua's* Resurrection: "Jesus answered and said unto them, 'Destroy this

---

[479] Referred to as the Cleansing of the Temple.
[480] Mark 14:58. Again, redacted to the Christian perspective.

temple, and in three days I will raise it up.'Then said the Jews, 'Forty and six years was this temple in building, and wilt thou rear it up in three days?' But he spake of the temple of his body. When therefore he was risen from the dead, his disciples remembered that he had said this unto them;[481] and they believed the scripture, and the word which Jesus had said."[482]

The Synoptic Gospels place the Cleansing of the Temple at the end of his ministry after the Triumphal Entry into Jerusalem. But John's Gospel begins his ministry with the Cleansing of the Temple at Jerusalem, chapter two. Most scholars agree the Synoptic order makes the most sense historically. [483]It explains the desire of both the Sanhedrin and Herodian authorities to squash *Yeshua's* movement before the Passover crowds could organize messianic violence. It is on that basis that I place it as the setting and context for the historical prophecy of which Logion 71 is one remnant.

Logion 72 [Inauthentic Gnostic logion]

A man said to him, "Tell my brothers to divide my father's possessions with me." He said to him, "O man, who has made me a divider?" He turned to his disciples and said to them, "I am not a divider, am I?"

COMMENTARY

This is a pericope or account of an event—not a prophetic *davar*. In *Thomas* it functions almost as a Gnostic inside joke. The Revealer *Iesous* teaches interior unity, not division (a Gnostic philosophical term for duality). Thus, "I am not a divider, am I?" The phrase "O' man" is used extensively by Paul and in other Greek translations of prophetic literature, but does not constitute an Aramaic idiom. Rather, it is a self-conscious literary idiom found in Greek translations.

This was redacted from Luke's special material in 12.13-15, the only source for a similar pericope: "Someone in the crowd said to him, 'Teacher, tell my brother to divide the family inheritance with me.' But he said to him, 'Friend, who set me to be a judge or arbitrator

---

[481] The disciples' memoires or remembrances differed among themselves, but they were the origin of what was preserved as the teaching of *Yeshua*. Peter's remembrances lie at the root of Mark's Gospel, those of other Apostles at the root of Q, and possibly those of Thomas at the root of the *Gospel of Thomas*. They are remembered differently, but by examining the similarities among them and taking account of bias and spin (Peter was married, Thomas was not, etc.) we can reconstruct many of them with reasonable certainty.
[482] John 2.19-22
[483] The order of events in John's Gospel seems to have been based on lectionary readings for the early Jewish-Christian Church Year, comprising a ministry for Jesus of only one year—not three as in the Synoptics. It is not an attempt to give an historical account, but to organize catechetical sermons.

over you?' And he said to them, 'Take care! Be on your guard against all kinds of greed; for one's life does not consist in the abundance of possessions.'

Note that in the Koine Greek, Jesus hails him as 'friend," not "o' man." Luke may have invented the setting as framework to present the authentic *davar*, "life does not consist in the abundance of possessions." Or possibly *Yeshua,* as a proto-rabbincal authority who would have been asked to judge in disputes, was approached for this kind of legal ruling. If so, he probably declined to do so, as in both Luke and *Thomas.* So the setting may have been historical for Luke, but not for *Thomas.*

In the historical consciousness of *Yeshua* he saw himself as a *Bar-Enash,* thus as a "divider." See my Commentary to Logion 16, "the advent of the Son of Man will bring divisions on the Earth—fire, sword, warfare."

Logion 73

The harvest is great but the laborers are few. Beseech the Adonai,[484] therefore, to send out laborers to the harvest.

COMMENTARY

This is an independent transmission of the Q *logion* found in Matthew and Luke.[485] The only difference is that Q specifies "the lord of the harvest," while *Thomas* simply says "the Lord." Both Coptic and Greek forms translate the Aramaic title of God *Adonai*, although in Q God is called an *adonai* or master of the harvest. In both sources, however, the Master clearly means God because it follows both Greek and Coptic verb meaning to pray. In both sources as well, the harvesters are designated with the Greek word (and loan-word) *ergatai,* field laborers, workers. The Aramaic word was probably from the root *asaph,* meaning laborers who gather the crop and bring it in from the fields.

Yeshua publically proclaimed the *Basor* and sent his closest disciples, of whom there may have been many, out to the villages in pairs to make the same proclamation.[486] It was probably very similar to that of John the Baptist. Mark 1.15 is a summary of the *Basor.* We can reconstruct the Aramaic meaning in paraphrase:

---

[484] Coptic ⲡⳲⲟⲉⲓⲥ "The Master" used of God in Coptic usually represents Greek *Kyrios* from Aramaic *Adonai.* However, *Yeshua's* usage in the New Testament Gospels wasalways *Abba,* which came into Greek as *Pater.* Never-the-less I am assuming an original Aramaic *Adonai* for this *davar.*
[485] Matthew 9:37-38, Luke 10:2
[486] The legendary 70 or 72 were disciples who journeyed and learned from *Yeshua* for several weeks at a time and probably included those we know as Apostles *[mebasrim].* He may have designated them all *mebasrim.*

"The time of *Shaitan's* rule over the world and mankind is coming to an end, and the *Malkuth* [Sovereignty] of God is near. Submit [to God's *Malkuth*] and keep faith with the *Basor* [proclamation of divine birth from the Throne of God]."

Fidelity to the *Basor* meant receiving the *mikveh* or water baptism of John, seeking instruction from *Yeshua,* and keeping the *halakah* he taught. Those whom *Yeshua* sent out were authorized to proclaim the *Basor,* conduct *mikveh,* and demonstrate the power of God's coming *Malkuth* by casting out demons and healing the sick. These were understood to be signs of the coming *Messiah* and God's new world prophesied in Isaiah and other scripture.

Yeshua compared his *mebasrim* [proclaimers of the *Basor*] to fisherman and to workers in a harvest. The latter, which was his most common metaphor, implies that God, the master or owner of the harvest, had other workers to prepare, plant, and cultivate his fields. The work of these Apostles was specifically to harvest the ripened crop of human souls.

Implicit in the saying in which *Yeshua* exhorts his hearers to pray that God will send more harvesters is the concept that each of the *mebasrim* has been sent to *Yeshua* by God. This is vital for an understanding of the New Testament stories about Jesus calling forth and chosing his disciples.

A conventional *rav* in *Yeshua's* day did not solicit disciples, nor did he preach publicly. He taught his own circle from his home or a synagogue. A potential *talmid* or disciple came to him and sought permission for access. All disciples were men. They applied, and he accepted or rejected.

By contrast, *Yeshua* publicly called people to submit to divine Sovereignty and follow his *halakah.* "Follow [*halach*] me!" He did not remain secluded and inaccessible in one place, but journeyed by foot through Palestine proclaiming the *Basor.* He exercised precognition to recognize the signs of a potential *talmid,* whom he called out of a crowd of hearers. And, of course, he accepted women disciples or *talmidoth* (a word that didn't exist in Aramaic). Like John the Baptist, he publicly proclaimed the *Basor.* But unlike John he gave extensive halakic teachings in public—although usually as *mashlim* (parables) and *davarim* (prophetic utterances). John public preaching was apparently based solely on messianic and eschatological prophecy.[487]

---

[487] I know of no evidence that John the Baptist psychically recognized and called disciples, or that he accepted women disciples. He was also inaccessible except when he staged a large public *mikveh* on the Jordan River. *Yeshua* continued John's baptism, but otherwise he was very much his own man and proclaimed his own unique *Basor.*.

Basor and Mebasrim

Logion 73 gives us a glimpse into *Yeshua's* unique attitude toward discipleship and apostlehood. He saw himself as in charge of the training and management of God's workers, whom Heaven would send forth at the end of this long season to harvest the ripened souls of the age.

The term Apostle was used in the early church before Paul—a title that he wished to make his own. During the period when Paul wrote his Epistles there were many Apostles travelling and teaching in the gentile churches that he had founded. Traditionally there were twelve Apostles and seventy or more missionary disciples of *Yeshua*, according to the Synoptic Gospels, but it is likely that all of his missionary disciples held the Aramaic title that underlies the Greek term Apostle.

Greek *Apostolos* of the New Testament means literally "one who is authorized and sent forth on a mission."[488] The Hebrew word for proclamation of a divine message found in key messianic texts is *basor, basorah*. The root means beauty, but a *besurah or besorah* was "good tidings," rendered sometimes as *basor tov*. It was translated in gentile Christianity by the New Testament Greek word *euangelion* or English gospel. One who brings this message is a *mebasor,* as in Isaiah 40.9, 60.6, *et al.* In plural that would be *mebasrim*.

But the key can be found in the messianic passage from Isaiah 61.1-2a[489] read by *Yeshua* in his home synagogue, according to Luke 4.18f.:

> "The Spirit of *Adonai Yahweh is* upon Me,
> Because *Yahweh* has anointed Me
> To preach the *Basor* to the poor;
> He has sent me to heal the brokenhearted,
> To proclaim liberty to the captives,
> And the opening of the prison to *those who are* bound;
> To preach the [long prophecied] Day of *Yahweh's* Favor."

If this was a text that the historical *Yeshua* read, it would have constituted a claim to the same divine authority to preach the *Basor* that the prophet Isaiah had received. The phrase "because Yahweh has anointed me" means that God has authorized me to speak His *Davar* or the Word of God, "Thus saith the Lord."

---

[488] The Aramaic title could have been rooted in *shalach*, "to send." We also find a usage from *berith*, covenant, in which a messenger of a king is called a *malak-berith,* literally a "king covenant." But that refers more to a messenger as a herald announcing the king. There is also a usage from the root *zir,* "to go," that can refer to a messenger. The Prophet Malachi represents the Hebrew word *malach*, which means "one who is sent, a messenger." That would seem to have been a likely Aramaic term used for the Apostles. But it wasn't. *Malach* could have been applied to a prophet like John or *Yeshua*, but not to their disciples.

[489] Trito-Isaiah, the Babylonian prophet of the School of Isaiah.

Followed by *Yeshua's* declaration, "This day is this scripture fulfilled in your hearing," the Pharisaic synagogue authorities would have wanted to drive him away. Messianic proclamations that the Lord's Day of Favor or messianic Age[490] had arrived could only bring trouble. Expectation of the warrior *Messiah Ben-David* of the Zealots was shared by the Baptists and other fringe groups whom the Herodians hunted down and executed to quell popular uprisings. It would have been no wonder that *Yeshua* was driven out of his own village, since his preaching would have seriously endangered the entire population.

Regardless of the historicity of this event, Trito-Isaiah's *Basor* of Chapter 61 was a key text for *Yeshua* and his messianic hearers. Their message was known to them as the *Basor,* and *Yeshua* probably gave his many missionary disciples the Aramaic title of *Mebasrim.* In Greek that title became *Apostoloi,* the basis for Apostolic authority and succession in the churches. Since all the surviving Apostles were Jews, many of them held views on circumcision and kosher laws that Paul and his gentile churches found unacceptable. Many of them were the Judaizers of the New Testament who were opponents of the Hellenists or Greek-speaking diaspora Jews, and became the enemies of Pauline Christianity.

It was in Galatia that the Jewish teachers first invaded Paul's gentile churches to convert them to the ways of the messianic Jewish congregations. Their opposition to Paul resulted in Jewish-gentile conflicts that eventually produced what has been called the anti-semitic bias of the New Testament. By the late first century, there had been complete schism between Jewish and gentile Christians with the extreme rancor we see in the Pastoral Epistles against the "false teachers."

At this point, gentile Christians became totally estranged from their Jewish roots and created the Hellenistic synthesis known as Christianity. Jewish Christianity disappeared from history except in the form of certain Gnostic and Ebionite sects that also eventually disappeared.

Logion 74-75 [Authentic Saying with Gnostic Expansion]

74 O *Adonai*, there are many around the drinking trough, but there is nothing in the well.

> 75 Many are standing at the door, but it is the solitary monk who will enter the Bridal Chamber.

---

[490] There were two Days or Seasons of the LORD *[Yahweh]* proclaimed by the prophets. One was a Day of Wrath, the other a Day of Favor. According to Luke, *Yeshua* read only the first half of Isaiah 61.2, proclaiming this the season of God's favor, i.e., the beginning of the messianic Age.

COMMENTARY

These two sayings belong together as one in *Thomas* because Logion 75 is a Gnostic expansion of Logion 74, which seems to be authentic, although there is no parallel found in other Christian literature.

Logion 74 follows Logion 73.b in which *Yeshua* tells his disciples to pray to the Lord, *Adonai,* to send out more *Mebasrim* to proclaim the *Basor.* In Logion 74, *Yeshua* himself speaks to *Adonai* and observes that there are many people seeking true spiritual teaching (water) through their synagogues and rabbis, but the well of established religion has gone dry.

In fact, at the Council of Jamnia two generations later (the most likely venue), the Pharisees would declare that the Spirit of Prophecy left Israel after the time of the Book of Daniel (second century B.C.E.), after that time there was no more scripture being written, and Judaism would depend upon rabbinic interpretation rather than the inspiration of the *Ruah Ha-Qodesh.* By contrast, messianic Judaism and the early Christian churches considered theirs to be the long-prophesied messianic Age (Dispensation), when the Spirit of God would speak through many.[491] The gentile churches traced the Spirit Age to the Pentacost tongues event recorded in the Book of the Acts and justified glossolalia,[492] which Paul did not encourage. Channeling the Holy Spirit had nothing to do with the historical teachings of *Yeshua.* That was a Post-Resurrection development within Jewish Christianity.

While Logion 74 has a clear mnemonic connection to Logion 73 through prayer to *Adonai,* and is probably part of the original Aramaic dictation, Logion 75 is an expansion of #74 based on a Gnostic interpretation of it. This is obvious from reference to the Gnostic Bridal Chamber. To the Gnostics, those standing around the dry well were probably the proto-orthodox Christians of the second century who lacked the true *gnosis.* Logion 75 expands upon the dry well by observing that "many are standing at the door," i.e. the Christians, but it will be the monk, the "solitary," who will enter the Bridal Chamber.

See the commentary on Logion 22.b for details about the Gnostic Sacrament of the Bridal Chamber and kabbalistic antecedents.

---

[491] Although *Yeshua* says very little about the *Ruach Ha-Qodesh* or Holy Spirit, the New Testament writings are constructed of copious narratives and references to the activity of the Holy Spirit. Pneumatic channelings and spiritual oracles delivered through Christian prophets provided powerful spiritual fuel for the propagation of the early churches.

[492] A phenomenon characteristic of pre-Christian and non-Christian tribal trance rites based in the lower, preliterate cortex of the brain.

CHAPTER TEN: Logia 76-88

Logion 76

The *Malkuth* of the *Abba* is like a merchant who had a consignment of merchandise and who discovered a pearl. That merchant was shrewd. He sold the merchandise and bought the pearl alone for himself. You too, seek his [the Abba's] unfailing and enduring treasure where no moth comes near to devour and no worm destroys.

COMMENTARY

This is an independent transmission of one of the *davarim* about the *Malkuth* that are collected in the thirteenth chapter of Matthew.[493] To this has been added part of another *davar* of *Yeshua* about heavenly treasure.[494]

What was the pearl? It was a powerful symbol of ascetic victory used by the Thomas Gnostics. The *Hymn of the Pearl,* which is preserved in the ascetic *Acts of Thomas,* was originally composed in Old Syriac (related to Aramaic).[495] It seems to have originated in the sect of the Syrian Gnostic Bardaisan sometime before 224 C.E., since it refers to the ruling house of the Parthians, which was overthrown by that date.

The Pearl symbolized the goal of Syrian Christian asceticism. For the Gnostics, it was a treasure that was guarded by a great dragon—a metaphor for flesh and incarnation. The dragon must be lulled to sleep through ascetic practice, chant, and other skillful means, as we shall see below.

---

[493] Matthew 13.45-46: "The Kingdom of Heaven is like a merchant in search of fine pearls; on finding one pearl of great value, he went and sold all that he had and bought it."

[494] See my commentary about the treasures of the heart in Logion #45.

[495] G.R.S.Mead says in his introduction that the poem, which has no title and could as well be called the *Hymn of the Robe of Glory* or the *Hymn of the Soul,* "has evidently nothing to do with the original Greek text of these Acts, and its style and contents are quite foreign to the rest of the matter. It is manifestly an independent document incorporated by the Syrian redactor, who introduces it in the usual naïve fashion of such compilations. Judas Thomas on his travels in India is cast into prison. There he offers up a prayer. On its conclusion we read: 'And when he had prayed and sat down, Judas began to chant this hymn: The Hymn of Judas Thomas the Apostle in the Country of the Indians.' After the Poem comes the subscription: '*The Hymn of Judas Thomas the Apostle,* which he spake in prison, is ended.'"

The Gnostic was a Prince of the Heavenly Royalty (a "Son of God") who had been sent into incarnation with a mission—to return from life in flesh (symbolized by Egypt) in possession of the Pearl. Here are some excerpts from the *Pearl*, which can be found online in several translations. I am quoting from Mead's translation.[496]

> When, a quite little child, I was dwelling
> In the House of my Father's Kingdom,
>
> And in the wealth and the glories
> Of my Up-bringers I was delighting,
>
> From the East, our Home, my Parents
> Forth-sent me with journey-provision.
>
> Indeed from the wealth of our Treasure,
> They bound up for me a load.
>
> Large was it, yet was it so light
> That all alone I could bear it...
>
> And with me They [then] made a compact;
> In my heart wrote it, not to forget it:
>
> "If thou goest down into Egypt,
> And thence thou bring'st the one Pearl --
>
> "[The Pearl] that lies in the Sea,
> Hard by the loud-breathing Serpent --
>
> "[Then] shalt Thou put on thy Robe
> And thy Mantle that goeth upon it,
>
> "And with thy Brother, Our Second,
> Shalt thou be Heir in our Kingdom..."

He finally reaches the land of the Egyptians and,

> Straightway I went to the Serpent;
> Near to his lodging I settled,
>
> To take away my Pearl
> While he should sleep and should slumber.

---

[496] At http://www.gnosis.org/library/hymnpearl.htm

Lone was I there, yea, all lonely;
To my fellow-lodgers a stranger.

He is a "solitary" or a monk, but he is not alone for he is joined by a guide—another Son of Heaven,

I made him my chosen companion,
A comrade, for sharing my wares with.

He warned me against the Egyptians,
'Gainst mixing with the unclean ones.

For I had clothed me as they were,
That they might not guess I had come

From afar to take off the Pearl,
And so rouse the Serpent against me.

VII.

But from some occasion or other
They learned I was not of their country.

With their wiles they made my acquaintance;
Yea, they gave me their victuals to eat.

I forgot that I was a King's son,
And became a slave to their king.

I forgot all concerning the Pearl
For which my Parents had sent me;

And from the weight of their victuals
I sank down into a deep sleep.

Then his Heavenly Mother (Holy Spirit) and Father send him a message that awakens him to his original task, for the words were already written in his heart—i.e., the Gnosis.

I remembered that I was a King's son,
And my rank did long for its nature.

I bethought me again of the Pearl,
For which I was sent down to Egypt.

And I began [then] to charm him,
The terrible loud-breathing Serpent.

I lulled him to sleep and to slumber,
Chanting o'er him the Name of my Father,

The Name of our Second, [my Brother],
And [Name] of my Mother, the East-Queen.[497]

XIII.

And [thereon] I snatched up the Pearl,
And turned to the House of my Father.

Their filthy and unclean garments
I stripped off and left in their country.

To the way that I came I betook me,
To the Light of our Home, to the Dawn-land.

On the road I found [there] before me,
My Letter that had aroused me --

As with its voice it had roused me,
So now with its light it did lead me --

As he dies and strips off his "filthy and unclean garments," i.e., his physical body, and ascends to the highest Heaven and the Throne, his glorious Robe, which is his true Self, rushes to meet him:

My Glorious Robe that I'd stripped off,
And my Mantle with which it was covered...

The Glorious Robe all-bespangled
With sparkling splendour of colours...

[Moreover] the King of Kings' Image
Was depicted entirely all o'er it...

I saw that moreover all o'er it
The motions of Gnosis abounding;

I saw it further was making
Ready as though for to speak.

I heard the sound of its Music
Which it whispered as it descended [?]:

---

[497] These Names would be Father, Son, and Holy Spirit, and *kabbalistic*-Gnostic elaborations of them. The Names of God were understood kabbalistically as 10 *(Sephiroth)*, 32 *(Paths of Wisdom)*, and 72 groups of three-letter Names constituting 216 letter combinations *(Shem-ha-Mephorash)*. They seem to have included Names of Jesus and Spirit as well.

"Behold him the active in deeds!
For whom I was reared with my Father;

"I too have felt in myself
How that with his works waxed my stature."

XIX.

And [now] with its Kingly motions
Was it pouring itself out towards me,

And made haste in the hands of its Givers,
That I might [take and] receive it.

And me, too, my love urged forward
To run for to meet it, to take it.

And I stretched myself forth to receive it;
With its beauty of colour I decked me,

And my Mantle of sparkling colours
I wrapped entirely all o'er me...

He [Jesus] had promised that with him to the Court
Of the King of Kings I should speed,

And taking with me my Pearl
Should with him be seen by our King.

Now that we have a view of what the Pearl was for Syrian Gnostics, we must ask, how did that differ from the Pearl of *Yeshua's davar?* Clearly the Gnostic concept of the Pearl developed from *Yeshua's* kabbalistic symbol. But to that accreted Christian ideas of Heaven as a Kingdom with High Prince (Jesus), Queen (Holy Spirit) and Princes (the victorious ascetic "solitaries" or monks. It is not much different than the vision in the Apocalypse of John of the hundred and forty-four thousand virgins:

"These are they who were not defiled with women; for they are virgins. These are they which follow the Lamb whithersoever he goeth. These were redeemed from among men, being the firstfruits unto God and to the Lamb."[498]

It is important to note that the Book of Revelations, which was not composed by the writer of the Gospel or Epistles of John,[499] was singularly rejected in Syria. The earliest Christian

---

[498] Revelation 14.4.

[499] Even the reader of an English translation can see that the Johannine style so characteristic of the Gospel and Epistles is not used in the Revelation. In Greek the stylistic difference is even more extreme. Authorship of the Revelation was attributed by many church fathers to the Gnostic Cerinthus.

writer to consider Revelations to be authentic was Justin Martyr of Rome in the second century, but the book was omitted from the original *Peshitta* or second-century Syriac New Testament, and Eusebius does not list it as a scripture known to Papias. Its authenticity was denied by many church fathers in second and third centuries, who attributed it to the Gnostic Cerinthus. It was not accepted universally into the New Testament canon until Athanasius and the Church Councils of the fourth century forced its inclusion.

The rejection among the Syrian churches, when taken with the antifeminism of the Revelations ("who were not defiled with women"), lends some credence to a Gnostic or at least monastic source. For our purposes, it is enough to observe that the Thomas Gnostic concept of Heaven as a Kingdom ruled by a King, with Princes (not Princesses) being monastic virgins, exhibits the same later Christian concept as Revelations.[500]

Yeshua's concept of Heaven was quite different. He never taught about Godhead as a King, nor did he teach about a heavenly Kingdom of God. He taught about divine Sovereignty or *Malkuth.* That Sovereignty was universal, but manifest only in Heaven. On Earth and among mankind, it was invisible. In Heaven, the *Bar-Enash* as the collective New Adam sat at the right hand of the *Abba* as Co-Sovereign. But the *Malkuth* on Earth was now only beginning to appear in the consciousness of humanity. The work of the *tzadik* was to sanctify the Earth and humanity through spiritual purity and *halakah,* thereby establishing the divine principles of justice, mercy, beauty, and wisdom among mankind and human institutions.

For *Yeshua* a pearl symbolized the treasure of soul-perfection that was pursued as the highest priority of life (the merchant "sold the merchandise and bought the pearl alone for himself"). It was developed in spiritual *halakah* and communion with Heaven. It is the treasure that accumulates in the heart of each person like the formation of a pearl layer by layer within the soft flesh of an oyster. It was the heart's treasure accumulated by a *tzadik* or saint.

I once had a dream of *Yeshua's* Pearl I'd like to share as an antithesis to the Gnostic *Hymn of the Pearl.* Here is the way I expressed it in my novel, *Astral Man to Cosmic Christ:*

> But, my eyes grew heavy and the lids dropped automatically. I began to dream.
>
> I lay on a deposit of silt, with fish swimming in schools through rocks and coral reefs. The water was a very light blue, and I wasn't very deep. I could feel that it was warm and tropical. Occasionally a large, exotic fish would brush by my half-opened shell.
>
> My shell? What was I—oh, yes. I was an oyster. A very large oyster.

---

[500] There are arguments for an early date of composition, but they are not based on surviving fragments—only tendentious interpretation of textual material.

I felt an irritation on the inner lining of my mother-of-pearl shell. Some-thing—perhaps a grain of sand or a broken piece of shell--had lodged itself within the soft membrane of my lower shell. While it was not extremely painful, it was a constant irritation. I tried to expose it so that bottom currents might wash it free. No luck. I opened and closed my shells, trying to generate enough current to wash it out, as I had managed to do many times before. This time the irritating grain of matter would not budge.

Time passed. The irritant was still with me, but now it had grown. As I tried to protect myself from its sharp pricks, I had lavered it over with layers of the living fluid that weeped from the tiny wounds made by the particle, so that in effect the particle had begun to grow. It had become a cancerous accretion protruding from my inner membrane the size of a small ball bearing. It caused me much physical discomfort and set me apart from the other oysters, who thought me strange and cursed.

As I grew, the lump grew with me. It became the size of a pea, and was still growing.

I prayed to God to remove this thorn in my soft flesh, for it was killing me. I could not bear it any longer, and wished only to die. The burden of this thing was too great.

The only answer I received was more pain from the cancerous lump. I tried to accept the pain.

Several years passed, and again I beseeched God to remove this bulging, hard thing from my flesh. Again my answer was silence. I carried on only because it was all I knew how to do.

Finally I grew old, and the lump had all but pushed me out of my poor shell.Once again I cried out to God.

"Oh, All Mighty God, Thou Who makest the seas to overcome the dry land and bringest dry land up out of the angry waves, hear my ancient plea. I am old and ready for death. Grant me this one comfort—that I may die in peace. For this hard lump that eats me up has made life unbearable all these many years. Remove it, I pray, that my flesh need suffer no longer."

For the first time I heard a reply—a still, small voice coming from within the hard, milky lump itself.The voice said, "MY GRACE IS SUFFICIENT FOR THEE, FOR MY STRENGTH IS MADE PERFECT IN WEAKNESS."

A shadow came between the sun and the waters above. The waters bubbled as a skin-diver intruded into my world. He inspected me carefully through his goggles, and then plucked me from my bed of silt and sand.

I was taken into a boat, where my shells were pried open. Again I cried out to God.

"Oh, Master, do not let me become fish-bait or seagull food! Save me from the boiling pots of these sailors."

At that instant I felt myself being extracted from the shell, and I was held in the hand of a large man who smiled at me and exclaimed,

"Look at the size of this pearl! It's the biggest one we've taken in a month!"

I looked down at my shell. Within the mangled home I'd occupied for so many years beneath the waters I saw the soft, white meat of a dead oyster. A man threw the shell and its contents into the cargo hold, where I heard it rattle as it fell across many other dead oysters.

Then I realized that I was an oyster no more. Instead, I was—a Pearl.

I would be treasured by men, mounted in gold and made immortal. Ages would pass and always I would enjoy safety and plenty. Generations of men and women would love and cherish me, passing me on to their loved ones and guarding me with all their power. Nations and whole civilizations would rise and fall, yet still would I stand immortal.

That in me which had begun as an inconvenient irritation and which had caused me pain and discomfort all my life—that thing was the real me! That which had set me apart from my peers and made me unsightly to them—that thing was the true me! The very thing that had humiliated and crushed me all my life was that which liberated me now, at my death.

The vividness of the dream wakened me.

Logion 77 [Inauthentic Gnostic Christological Doctrine]

77.a It is I who am the light which is above them all. It is I who am the All. From me did the All come forth, and unto me did the All extend.

77.b Split a tree,[501] and I am there. Lift up the stone, and you will find me there.

COMMENTARY

As much as I love the final lines of this saying that I have separated as 77.b, the entire *logion* is later Gnostic Christological doctrine. Logion 77.a probably has its root in the Johannine "I am the Light of the World"[502] sermon and interprets the Christ-Logos as the kabbalistic *Ain Soph Aur* of Creation.[503]

---

[501] The Greek word in the Oxyrhynchus fragment is *zulon*, which in later Hellenistic times meant a live tree.
[502] John 8.12
[503] Based on the emanational or generational *kabbalistic* model, rather than the Christian Platonistic demiurgical model. In Gnostic thought, true Godhead emanated the All, but the Demiurge "created" in the

Logion 77.b may have some relationship to the Christian and Hermetic idea of the guiding deity remaining always with a disciple. "Lo, I am with you, even unto the end of the world," says Matthew's Christ.[504] However, it is more likely that Logion 77.b reflects the proto-Manichaean idea of Christ as the archetypal soul trapped into matter. This is found attached to Logion 30 of the Oxyrhynchus Papari fragments. See my Commentary on Logion 30.

The spirits of trees were thought to abide in their flowing sap, so the translation "split a piece of wood" isn't quite correct. The saying refers to a live tree. Spirits of rocks and the mineral world dwelt near them but not inside, so "lift a stone" is correct.

In Manichaen Gnosticism there were two grades. The Perfect or Elect were unmarried ascetic teachers of the community, and the Hearers or Instructed were young or married community members. It was believed that divine sparks of Godhead were scattered and trapped into matter by the Evil Deity. They were hidden in plants, animals, and among the stones. It was vital for salvation to avoid harming or destroying these spirits, but just to walk or eat resulted in collateral damage.

For the sake of the Elect, the Hearers assumed spiritual responsibility for the harm they caused by walking and eating. Thus the Elect could ascend directly to Heaven after death, and this benefitted the community. The souls of Hearers who had kept piety during life would ascend to the waxing moon, whose increasing light was actually the gathering of their souls. Then after purification they would ascend to Heaven on the waning moon—the decreasing light being the release of souls after purification. This seems to imply that the longest period of Purgatory was thought to have been one lunar cycle.

In any case, primitive animism was alive and well in Hellenistic theories of spirit and matter. In Logion 77.b, we see a prime example.

Logion 78

78.a Why have you come out into the desert? To see a reed shaken by the wind? And to see a man clothed in fine garments like your kings and your great men? Upon them are the fine garments,

---

sense of the Old Testament God. The *Ain Soph Aur* was the *kabbalistic* Light of Emanation that may underlay the Johannine *Logos* Christology: "All things came into being through him (Christ-Logos), and without him not one thing came into being." John 1.3
[504] Matthew 28.20.b

78.b and they are unable to discern the truth.

COMMENTARY

This is an independent transmission of an authentic *davar* known in the Q material of Matthew and Luke,[505] but with a Gnostic concluding phrase. In both Matthew and Luke the *logion* is inserted as a teaching of Jesus about the greatness of John the Baptist after John's disciples have come to him and departed. Interestingly, it is followed in Matthew by the "generation of vipers" *davar* ascribed to John the Baptist earlier in Chapter 3, while in Luke it is followed by the *davar* of *Yeshua* about this generation being like children playing a game. In both cases, it is part of a section denouncing the religious leadership of Jerusalem.

This confusion of John's sayings with those of *Yeshua* indicates a much closer link between the two prophets than is admitted by the New Testament writers. Either *Yeshua* employed some of the language and metaphor of John, indicating that he had been a hearer and probably a student of John, or some of John's remembered sermons were attributed to *Yeshua* because those who transmitted them had been hearers of both men.[506]

Yeshua contrasted the ascetic desert prophet and his camel-hair tunic with his critics, who wore fine garments. The contrast was to show John's strength of character. He was not a "reed shaken by the wind," a semitic expression meaning one who was swayed to compromise his principles by the influence of others. Here he contrasted strength with weakness of character, not the virtues of asceticism with the vices of wealth. But the Thomas Gnostics understood this a different way, as their edited conclusion shows.

The Gnostic conclusion is that the wealthy and powerful—in other words, the antithesis of Gnostics ascetics—are "unable to discern truth." Here the Coptic word ме is used for Greek *aletheia* as found in Johannine language, meaning spiritual and philosophical truth. The underlying Hebrew idea of *emeth* does not mean quite the same. Truth is something that is done and lived—not just said.

The semitic idiom is best illustrated in John 3-20-22: "Everyone who does evil hates the light, and will not come into the light for fear that his deeds will be exposed. [21]But whoever does the truth comes into the light, so that it may be seen plainly that what he has done has been done through God." Here doing truth is contrasted with doing evil. Hebrew truth means doing, thinking, and speaking what is good and right.

---

[505] Matthew 11:7-9, Luke 7:24-26
[506] In my novel, *Yeshua: The Unknown Jesus,* I assume both things were true.

But the Gnostics understood truth as Greek *aletheia,* meaning philosophic *gnosis.* The conclusion that they have added to this *davar* of *Yeshua* implies that the weathy and those who rule society are unable to discern the true *gnosis.* This is what we would expect from ascetic monks who saw merchants and wealthy people as the enemies of Heaven—the Egyptians and unclean ones in the *Hymn of the Pearl.*

Logion 79

79.a A woman from the crowd said to him, "Blessed are the womb which bore you and the breasts which nourished you." He said to her, "Blessed are those who have heard the Word of the *Abba* and have truly kept it.

79.b For there will be days when you will say, 'Blessed are the womb which has not conceived and the breasts which have not given milk.'"

COMMENTARY

This pericope is known in the special Lucan material, "While he was saying this, a woman in the crowd raised her voice and said to him, "Blessed is the womb that bore you and the breasts that nursed you!" But he said, "Blessed rather are those who hear the Word of God and obey it!"[507]

It is similar to the Marcan story, "Then Jesus' mother and brothers arrived. Standing outside, they sent someone in to call him. A crowd was sitting around him, and they told him, 'Your mother and brothers are outside looking for you.' 'Who are my mother and my brothers?' he asked. Then he looked at those seated in a circle around him and said, 'Here are my mother and my brothers! Whoever does the will of God is my brother and sister and mother.'"[508]

The Lucan pericope may preserve an historical Beatitude: Blessed are those who hear the Word of God and do it. The Marcan story may reflect another historical *davar:* Whoever does the will of God is my spiritual kin.

But *Thomas* Logia 79.a and 79.b has redected two unrelated things together. The first is the Lucan pericope, and the second is part of *Yeshua's* prophecy about the coming suffering and

---

[507] Luke 11.27-28
[508] Mark 3.31-35

destruction of Jerusalem. They have been redacted to spin them into a Gnostic saying, first by altering the Word of God to the Word of the Father (the Gnostic reference to Godhead as progenitor). Then the exhortation to obey the Word is changed to "have truly kept." Here "truly" is Coptic "they have watched over it in Truth," the Coptic-Gnostic ME or philosophical *gnosis.* In other words, the blessed are those who have kept the tenets of ascetic Gnostic salvation.

This is concluded by the prophecy, but meaning something quite different. The Beatitude about the "womb which has not conceived and the breasts which have not given milk" means that those who have not had sexual intercourse and borne children—the ascetic monks—will eventually be revealed as the blessed ones. This asceticism, moreover, is implied as the meaning of those who have "truly kept" the Father's Word.

It's just like Fox News. Take a snippet here, another there, and edit them together. Now you have the spin you want to present—not what happened or was said historically, and certainly not any context. Just a sound bite that makes your point! Unfortunately, the ancients, including the redactors of the Gospels, had no more commitment to historical fact than Fox News. The purpose of most religious literature was to persuade, not to record history.

I have divided Logion 79 into two independent Aramaic *davarim* that probably underlay it, then rendered them as they may have been spoken by *Yeshua.*

Logion 80 [Gnostic Logion]

Whoever has known the *kosmos* [i.e., been intimately involved with the material world], has found a corpse, but whoever has recognized [the *kosmos* to be] a corpse, of him the *Kosmos* is not worthy.

ARAMAIC RECONSTRUCTION: He who has recognized the world [for what it really is] has found the body, but he who has recognized the world as only an impermanent body is superior to the world.

COMMENTARY

The only negative language found in the Gospels about Greek *kosmos,* the world, is in the Gospel of John. But Johannine usage is not Gnostic, for Jesus Christ is also the Saviour of the world,[509] and God "so loved the world that he gave his only begotten Son," and sent him

[509] John 4.42

"not to condemn the world, but that the world through him might be saved.[510] The Hebrew concept underlying Greek *kosmos* in the New Testament sayings is "this *'olam*." The world of *Yeshua's Basor* and the messianic visions of Daniel, Enoch, and Trito-Isaiah had been corrupted by *Shaitan,* but it was not evil. It would be redeemed through sanctification and manifestation of divine Sovereignty, the coming *Malkuth,* in flesh and on Earth.

But for the Gnostics, the world or *kosmos* was by definition evil. The goal of Christ was not to sanctify the *kosmos,* but to gather the few elect souls, the hundred and forty-four thousand virgins, and lead them home to Heaven. Thus this Gnostic *logion* says that one who has recognized the *kosmos* for what it is—a mere external body of the true Life and a place of evil and illusion—is superior to the *kosmos.* The one who "has found the body," meaning has realized that earthly reality is merely an external shell of reality, becomes superior to the *kosmos.*

Certainly *Yeshua* taught that life does not consist merely of eating, drinking, and material security. The Life of the *'Olam* was interior. The *Malkuth* of Heaven was "within and beyond." But for Gnostics this world was a hell into which we had all been entrapped. It might eventually be overcome through *askesis* and *gnosis,* and the Gnostic could forever leave it behind.[511]

For *Yeshua,* however, this earthly *'olam* was the proving ground of souls—the field of action where a human soul could be purified, refined, and perfected by trial and sanctification. It was only by one's walk through incarnate life and conduct in this world—his *Halakah*— that a disciple could grow from newly-born child of the *Malkuth* to mature heir exercising the Sovereignty of God.

Logion 80 is a Gnostic teaching developed from the authentic *davar* of Logion 81, as is its corollary in Logion 110. I have rendered it as it may have been spoken in Aramaic by *Yeshua.*

Logion 81

Let him who has grown spiritually wealthy become Sovereign, and let him who possesses worldly power renounce it.

---

[510] John 3.16-17

[511] Much of medieval Christianity had this Gnostic view of the world. The Anglican Book of Common Prayer still exhorts the newly baptized to "overcome the world, the flesh, and the devil." There is no concept of reincarnation in most Christian churches—rather just a striving for "leaving this world behind" at death and returning to the heavenly home.

COMMENTARY

This does not appear in any related sayings of *Yeshua* but there are reasons to accept it as an authentic *davar.* It exhibits no specifically Gnostic vocabulary or concept, but the kabbalistic theme of the *Malkuth* or Sovereignty of the "spiritually wealthy" (*Yeshua's* phrase for those who "have") is familiar from other authentic teachings. Also this is presented in the paradoxical terms we have seen in other *davarim.* "Let him who has grown wealthy rule" is contrasted with "let him who has rulership abdicate it (the Coptic verb ⲁⲡⲛⲁ)." The simple chiastic structure suggests an easily memorized *davar* whose interpretation would be understood by disciples, but not easily apparent to outsiders. My translation clarifies wealth as spiritual wealth and power as worldly power or rulership. Landholders and the wealthy were often known in the Palestinian culture of *Yeshua* as "rulers," and this *davar* exploits that metaphor.

When *Yeshua* is approached by the wealthy young man of the Marcon pericope who is seeking the Life of the *'Olam,* he tells him to sell all his possessions, give the proceeds to the poor, and join his retinue of disciples. The young man sadly walks away and *Yeshua* remarks that it is more difficult for a rich person to find spiritual liberation than it is for a camel to go through the eye of a needle—yet with God, all things are possible.

In this case his advice to the rich young man was exactly that of this *davar*—Let him who possesses worldly power renounce it. This is not advice to abandon all responsibilities and become a monk, as the *Gospel of Thomas* would interpret it. Rather, it is advice to relinquish control over his possessions so that they will no longer have power over him. For those who accumulate much wealth often become slaves to their possessions. "You cannot serve God and Mammon."

Does this advice hold true today in a different culture and society? Paul said that it is not riches, but greed for riches, that is the root of all evil. Already by the third century this pericope was being reinterpreted far more liberally by church fathers like Clement of Alexandria. What about the twenty-first century?

I would argue that it is quite possible for a wealthy person to avoid enslavement to his possessions. Wealthy people who "give back" to society have become the backbone of modern charitable organizations and their activities. Without wealth, a society crumbles. Entrepreneurial talent rightly used benefits all humanity. *Yeshua's* sayings about rich rulers and slaves to Mammon refer to an ancient society exploited by Roman conquerors and Jewish collaborators. They don't apply in the same way to a democratic society ruled by law and the common good.

However his teachings about priorities—spiritual and moral over materialistic goals—are perhaps even more relevant than in his day. The exhortation for the one who is spiritually wealthy to rule as Sovereign, meaning to take his place in the body of the *Bar-Enash* and join in God's work as creator and arbiter of the universe, means that he should contribute conscientiously and creatively in the arts, sciences, economics, government, education, and spiritual life of humanity. He or she should serve as a vinedresser, gardener, and harvestor in the *Pardes.*

Yeshua's exhortation for the one who possesses material wealth and wordly power to renounce them means this today: The only way to conscientiously take responsibility for wealth or to exercise the power of governance is to share it, to work collaboratively, and to renounce all selfish motivation. The key is non-attachment to possessions and personal power in subordination to the greater good.

Logion 82

He who is near to me is near to the Divine Fire, and he who is far from me is far from the Sovereignty.

COMMENTARY

If this were composed in Greek, we would expect the adversative "but" *(alla)* to connect the second clause. Instead we find the "and," which must have been rooted in the Hebrew-Aramaic adversative *vav.* In other words, Logion 82 has an underlying Aramaic construction. Additional, both *Malkuth* (Sovereignty) and *esh* (fire) are part of *Yeshua's* special vocabulary. This seems to be an authentic and previously unknown *davar* of *Yeshua.*

Here the fire is divine fire from Heaven, as discussed in my Commentary to Logion 10, "Behold, I have cast fire upon the world." It is not the Greek *pur* of testing, trial, and alchemical purification. The original meaning of the *davar* made divine fire parallel to *Malkuth* so that those who were disciples of *Yeshua* were near to both.

Interestingly, in Chaldean (Babylonian) cosmology, which greatly influenced Hebrew thought after the Babylonian Captivity, the highest heavens and deities have the nature of intellectual or noetic fire. There had been a large and active Jewish settlement that spoke Aramaic and occupied the city of Babylon since the time of the Babylonian Captivity. They developed the first and oldest Targum, and the community was a major Jewish center at the time of *Yeshua.* Since *Yeshua's* main affinities lie not with Palestinian, but with the Babylonian *Bar-Enash* messianic concepts developed by earlier Babylonian Jews like Trito-Isaiah, the writers of the Enoch school, and those of the School of Daniel, it is useful to compare the Zoroastrian or Chaldean cosmogeny with Jewish kabbalistic emanation as it developed in the early medieval period.

The Kabbalistic Worlds

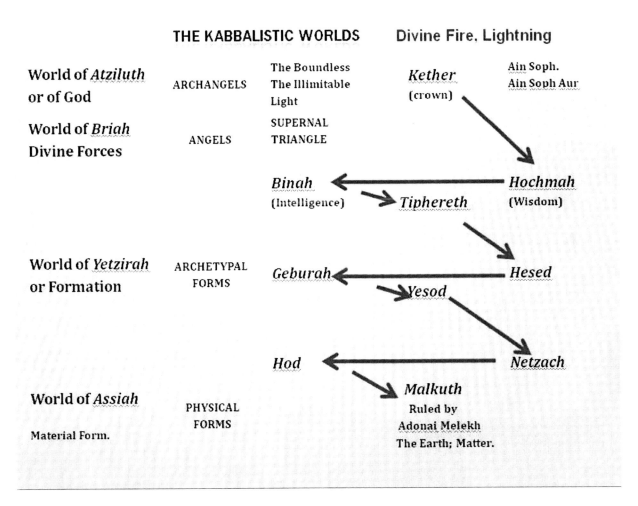

Dating from the second century, the so-called *Chaldean Oracles of Zoroaster* preserve what is probably a Neo-Platonic synthesis of Babylonian and Greek cosmological theories. In his edition of the English translation of *The Chaldaean Oracles*,[512] Sapere Aude includes the following schematic comparison of the so-called Chaldean system and that of the later medieval Jewish Kabbalah.[513] Notice that the Chaldean name for Godhead is Father, meaning Progenitor, One Who Generates or Emanates.

---

[512] From http://www.esotericarchives.com/oracle/oraclez.htm

[513] Kabbalah was orally transmitted in the Jewish Hellenistic world of *Yeshua*, and we can reconstruct much of it from intertestamental source, the second-century *Sepher Yetzirah*, and Talmudic sources. But we can also get insights from the medieval *kabbalistic* writings that were circulated when pogroms had decimated the

The Chaldaean Scheme

The Intelligibles	**The Paternal** *(Fatherly)* **Depth**
World of Supra-mundane Light	**The First Mind**

	The Intelligible Triad **Pater: Mater** *(Father-Mother)* **or Potentia: Mens**
	The Second Mind
Intelligibles and Intellectuals **in the** **Empyræan World**	**Iynges** *(Wheels, like Hebrew Cherubim)*[514] **Synoches** *(Forces that bind together)* **Teletarchæ** *(Initiatic forces that perfect the soul)*
	(The Third Mind.)
Intellectuals **in the Ethereal World**	**Three Cosmagogi** **(Intellectual guides inflexible.)** **Three Amilicti** **(Implacable thunders).**
Elementary World **The Demiurgos of the** **Material Universe**	**Hypezokos** **(Flower of Fire)** **Effable, Essential and** **Elemental Orders** **The Earth; Matter**

A comparison of the two makes it evident that they are interdependent. If we examine a few verses of the *Chaldean Oracles* as preserved among Hellenistic writers, we can get a better idea of the divine fire that *Yeshua* makes parallel to the Sovereignty. They are numbered, and I include the numbers with the verses.

Jewish male population and forced Jewish divines to commit their knowledge to writing in order to preserve it. That is what Sapere Audi (initiatic name) does here. I reproduce it because it is useful for comparison.
[514] Or spirals, wheels like the *Ophanim* of Ezekiel's *Merkabah* vision. In shamanic, Egyptian, and Greek ritual, the "bullroarer" was spun clockwise and anti-clockwise to access the primordial motions of the *Kosmos*.

13. All things have issued from that one Fire. The Father perfected all things, and delivered them over to the Second Mind, whom all Nations of Men call the First *Psellus, 24; Pletho, 30. Z.*

20. The Soul, being a brilliant Fire, by the power of the Father remaineth immortal, and is Mistress of Life, and filleth up the many recesses of the bosom of the World. *Psellus, 28; Pletho, 11. Z.*

22. For not in Matter did the Fire which is in the first beyond enclose His active Power, but in Mind; for the framer of the Fiery World is the Mind of Mind. Proclus in *Theologiam, 333,* and *Tim., 157.* T.

23. Who first sprang from Mind, clothing the one Fire with the other Fire, binding them together, that he might mingle the fountainous craters, while preserving unsullied the brilliance of His own Fire. Proclus in *Parm. Platonis.* T.

24. And thence a Fiery Whirlwind drawing down the brilliance of the flashing flame, penetrating the abysses of the Universe; for from thence downwards do extend their wondrous rays. Proclus in *Theologiam Platonis,* 171 and 172. T.

79. For the Father of Gods and men placed the Mind (nous) in the Soul (psyche); and placed both in the (human) body. *Psell., 26; Pletho, 6. Z.*

80. The Paternal Mind hath sowed symbols in the Soul. *Psell., 26; Pletho, 6. Z.*

81. Having mingled the Vital Spark from two according substances, Mind and Divine Spirit, as a third to these He added Holy Love, the venerable Charioteer uniting all things. Lyd. *De Men., 3.*

Even in the early Babylonian apocalypses of Enoch, the high heavens contain fire-serpents *(Seraphim)* and luminous bodies of fire, including the Phoenix of the Sun. The human essential divine nature was described as a "spark" of divine fire emanating from Godhead. At the firmament or boundary between the Supernal Triad of *Kether-Hochmah-Binah* according to the ancient *Sepher Yetzirah* was the Mother letter *Shin,* associated with *Esh,* Divine Fire.

Logion 82 is translated from a *davar* of *Yeshua* whose meaning would have been understood by his close disciples. Being those of his inner circle, they were "near to the Divine Fire," and thus to the *Malkuth.* Those who opposed, rejected, or chose to remain far from him were also far away from the *Malkuth.*

Logion 83 [Probable Authentic *Davar*]

The *tzelemim* are perceivable by mankind, but the divine light in them remains hidden in the *Tzelem* of the Light (Aur) of the *Abba*. He will be revealed, but his *Tzelem* will remain concealed by his Light.

COMMENTARY

The Gnostics developed special cosmological terminology rooted in Pythagorean and Neo-Platonistic concepts. One of these was of the heavenly *eikon* or image. It seems be an application of the Platonic doctrine of the heavenly *idea,* a word meaning not "idea," but "image, form, pattern." The kabbalistic world of *Yetzirah* or Formation is something like the Platonic World of Form *(Idea).* While the heavenly *idea* of Plato was an invisible "universal" form, the particular images we see of incarnate and material individuals are visible and can reveal the invisible *idea.*

Here, the Gnostic teaching of *Thomas* is that while we see form with our eyes, we cannot perceive the spark or light of the souls, which is hidden in the invisible heavenly form of the Divine Light of the Progenitor-Father. The Father can be revealed, but not to the eyes of humanity.

But on careful examination, we might uncover an authentic kabbalistic *davar* of *Yeshua* underlying this *logion.* The first clue is the Aramaic construction. The two consecutive *vav's,* which were originally rendered into Greek as *kai...kai* and thence into Coptic as ⲁⲩⲱ...ⲁⲩⲱ, "and...and," are a form of semitic adversative. We can translate their meaning as "but...but." I have left them as they would be in Aramaic.

Here the Greek loan word *eikon* probably translated Hebrew-Aramaic *tzelem,* "image." The Divine *Tzelem* was the Image of God embedded in the heart of humanity at its creation. If this were a kabbalistic teaching of *Yeshua* to his inner circle, it would mean that the Image of God is hidden in all the things visible to mankind, but is itself invisible because it is one with the nature of Divine Light *(Ain Soph Aur).*

I discussed the ancient theory of vision by emission of light from the eye that *Yeshua's* teachings reference in my Commentary on Logion 24.b, with details in the footnote. Here, that would be the light through which people see, as opposed to the Divine Light or *Ain Soph Aur* of Creation. The Image of God is not a thing that can be seen by light emitted from the human eye, but is constituted of the *Ain Soph Aur.* Just as we cannot see the surface of the sun because its light overpowers our vision (i.e., the Divine Light prevents the light emitted from our eyes from accessing its surface, according to the operative theory), so mankind cannot see the Image of God, which consists of Divine Light.

Nevertheless, we are told in the *davar,* the time will come when God will be revealed to mankind—in the coming *Malkuth.* But even then, God's Image will remain hidden in Divine Light.

This Divine Light was also considered to be the Glory or *Shekinah* of God, which in *Sepher Yetzirah* was divided into thirty-two Paths of Wisdom or *Hochmah,* which was synonymous with God's (feminine) *Shekinah* or manifestation.

One might ask, why was Moses unable to see any but the "hinder parts" of God's glory? Why was it said that if anyone were to look upon the Face of God, he would immediately die? And why was it that, in spite of all this, the prophets Isaiah and Enoch ascended to the Throne and saw the Image of God?

This *davar* may provide the answer. Moses stood on a mountain, but remained on Earth and saw only with his physical eyes. Peter, James, and John saw Moses and Elijah in the light of their partial ascent with *Yeshua,* but they saw only their *tzelemim,* not the Divine *Tzelem* of God.

However, Isaiah, Enoch, and *Yeshua* ascended to the *Merkabah* in the spark of their own Divine *Tzelemim.* The mechanism of light emission from the physical eyes, as it was understood then, was not operative in that modality. They saw with a divine faculty "to serve as [God's] Eye," as described in Logion 22. Thus even in the coming *Malkuth* on Earth, human eyes will not be able to see God's Image—only His manifestations.

A short saying like Logion 83 could have been transmitted orally, but could kabbalistic concepts like these have survived oral transmission? Usually this process can transmit proverbs, parables, and short metaphors or allegories, but we don't expect sermons or whole teachings to survive memory and oral transmission. When we examine statements in the *Pythagorean Sentences of Demophilus* and others, we do find verses comparable to Logion 83 in complexity of thought. From Demophilus we have these two, which seem to me every bit as complex as the kabbalistic ideas of Logion 83:

> 3. Divinity sends evil to men, not as being influenced by anger, but for the sake of purification; for anger is foreign from Divinity, since it arises from circumstances taking place contrary to the will; but nothing contrary to the will can happen to a god.

> 4. When you deliberate whether or not you shall injure another, you will previously suffer the evil yourself which you intend to commit. But neither must you expect any good from the evil; for the manners of everyone are correspondent to his life and actions. Every soul too is a repository, that which is good, of things good, that which is evil, of things depraved

All things considered, then, with some confidence I identify *Thomas* Logion 83 as derivative from an authentic *davar* of *Yeshua.*

Logion 84

When you perceive your *damutoth*,[515] you rejoice. But when you will perceive your *tzelemim*[516] which came into being before you, and which neither die nor become manifest, how much will you be able to bear?

COMMENTARY

This appears to be a continuation of Logion 83. It concludes with a rhetorical comment typical of rabbinic discourse like that of Logion 11, "what will you do?" Here it is, "how much you will have to bear!" or, "how much will you have to bear?" The point of the comment is to emphasize the transcendant wonder of what has just been said.

In the Commentary to Logion 3, I introduced the kabbalistic interpretation of the formation of mankind in Genesis 1.26ff. found in Hellenistic wisdom school and Talmudic tradition.[517] In order to understand the original terminology of this *logion,* we need to examine the Hebrew words for "image" *(tzelem)* and "likeness" *(damut).*[518]

The Hebrew word that was used to describe the divine image, fire, or spark within mankind was *tzelem.* It referred not to a physical image, but to the essential nature of something—good or evil. The word *damut* "likeness" referred to similarity—again, not a physical similarity, but an essential likeness. The word for a physical form or image seen with the eyes was *to'ar,* which was not used here.

The "image" and "likeness" of Godhead constitutes the *imago dei* or Divine Image. This is invisible. One would refer to a Jewish saint or *tzadik* as a son of Godhead not because of a visible image, but because he shared in the divine nature. That nature was described in the many Names of God such as Crowned Head *(Kether),* Wisdom *(Hochmah),* and Understanding *(Binah)* constituting the Names of the Supernal Triad of the kabbalistic Tree, with others like Justice, Compassion, Beauty. These all described the *tzelem* of Godhead, and as Names each was a *damut* or likeness of Godhead.

The means by which the Divine Image communicated with a person was through motions or impulses in the heart. Taken collectively, they constituted the *yetzer ha-tov.*

---

[515] Personal affinities and likenesses reflected in other people and things outside of you.

[516] Primordial or archetypal and invisible divine forces, energies, and motions; the Images of Godhead.

[517] Then Godhead (the *Elohim*) said, "Let us construct *(asah)* Mankind in our *tzelem*, in our *damut*, and let them rule over the fish of the sea and the birds of the air, over the livestock, over all the earth, and over all the creatures that move along the ground." So Godhead constructed Mankind in his own *tzelem*; in the *tzelem* of Godhead he created him; male and female he created them.

[518] Refer to the Commentary on Logion #3 for an explanation of the good and evil *yetzerim.*

Consequently the good *yetzer* was also identified with the Divine Image, and it was through the *yetzer ha-tov* that the Primordial Light of the *Tzelem* of Godhead could be perceived or envisioned by a person. But in order to have the *visio beatifica* of the *Merkabah* of Godhead, one's heart must be utterly pure, meaning that it operated completely under the motions of the good *yetzer*. *Yeshua* said, "Blessed are the pure in heart, for they shall see Godhead."

Plato's internal motion of the psyche to the right (unity, the way of the philosopher, the *anodos* or ascent to Godhead), as over against the motion to the left (entropy, the *kathodos* or descent into matter and ignorance) was undoubtedly a strong influence in kabbalistic thought about the *yetzerim*. Philo of Alexandria, who was a contemporary of *Yeshua*, was steeped in Platonic philosophy and had synthesized it with his Jewish wisdom tradition. There were undoubtedly many other Hellenistic Jewish philosophers and schools that had developed similar syncretistic ideas that permeated messianic and kabbalistic thought. Many scholars trace the origins of Gnosticism to Jewish sources.

In *Yeshua's* teaching, philosophical speculation seems to have been subordinate to practice or *halakah*. But perhaps that is simply because what Clement of Alexandria referred to as the hierophantic teachings of the Lord were transmitted only to "those who were being perfected" and did not appear except by inference in the public Gospels. What is more, oral tradition can transmit pithy sayings and parables with some accuracy, but discourses cannot be memorized. They are understood and re-discoursed differently by each witness according to his own understanding.

The early Jewish-Christian churches expanded the concept of guidance by the *yetzer ha-tov* into something like the *Bat Kol* of the medieval Kabbalists—the Holy Spirit speaking through Christian prophets to the communities. Nevertheless the *razim* of creation and divine will must have remained much as it was taught by *Yeshua*. Paul's theology was developed from a combination of his rabbinic training and the messianic Kabbalah he learned from his Christian teachers.

We can examine and analyze the divine mysteries expounded by Paul for their earlier roots in the kabbalistic discourse of *Yeshua*. When we do, we find evidence for kabbalistic teachings like those represented in Logia #83-84. Paul's ideas are developed from kabbalistic discourses of *Yeshua* transmitted by Christian teachers in their own terms and understanding of the *Basor*. Thus they can help us recover authentic teachings of *Yeshua* that were too discursive to survive in oral transmission.

For example, Paul told his hearers at Ephesus that God "chose us in Him [Christ] before the foundation of the *Kosmos*." In Christ, God has revealed "the *Raz* of His will, according to His good pleasure which He purposed in Himself," that when the right season has come God will "unify all things in Heaven and Earth under the sovereignty of Christ."[519]

The original Aramaic meaning of these *razim* expounded by Paul was probably something like this:

> All those who are faithful to the *Basor* in these days of the advent of the messianic Age, and who receive spiritual birth into the *Malkuth,* exist as immortal children of the *Bar-Enash.* They share in the Life of God's *'Olam* while yet in flesh. Living as *tzadikim* under the sovereignty of the Divine Image, which is perceived in the motions of the *yetzer ha-tov,* their true nature is that of the eternal *tzelemim* that emanated from Godhead at *Ha-Rosh,* the primordial beginning of creation before the worlds were formed.

In Logia #83-84 we find not a *davar,* but a short kabbalistic discourse. Here is a paraphrase of its meaning:

> We can perceive our own Divine Image through the *yetzer ha-tov,* but the Divine Image of Godhead is hidden to human perception by His glory (cloud *anan* of Primordial Light). When we perceive likenesses, affinities, or reflections of our own nature, we are happy and approve. It is human nature, as *Yeshua* says in another place, for us to love those who love us, and there is no merit in that.[520]

> But how marvelous will it be when you look upon the forces and energies of your own Divine Image in the *'Olam Ha-Ba* or World to come? They pre-existed from the beginning before *Adam Kadmon* was formed. They are immortal, invisible, and do not manifest in form. Yet you will perceive them with divine sight.

In the many *logia* of *Thomas* we find not only authentic *davarim* and *mashlim,* but remembrances of inner-circle kabbalistic teachings of *Yeshua.* These seem to have been a basis for many sayings found adapted and reinterpreted in other Gnostic Gospels. For example, *Thomas* Logion 84 may have underly the following *logion* of the *Gospel of Philip:* "Blessed is he who is before he came into being. For he who exist as a truly real being, has always been and shall always be." However, it could also have developed from the Johannine saying, "Before Abraham was, I AM."[521]

---

[519] Ephesians 1.9-13
[520] Luke 6.32
[521] Greek *Ego Eimi,* an interpretation of the Hebrew Tetragrammaton or Name of God YHVH, "I am that I am."

Adam came into being with marvellous endowments from a great Heavenly Host, and he did not become worthy of you. If he had been worthy, he would not have experienced death.

COMMENTARY

This is not a Gnostic doctrine. The clue is that *Yeshua* declares that his disciples, regenerated in the New Adam, are superior to the original Adam. I am unaware of any Gnostic sect that understood the Christ as *Bar-Enash* or the New Humanity. Rather, from Sethians to Valentinians and even Manicheans, they all regarded themselves to be children of the original Adam whose imperfections caused his fall. Christ came to restore Adam, heal his imperfections, and undo the fall of mankind. But *Yeshua* taught regeneration in the *Bar-Enash* or New Humanity. This distinction is crucial to separating authentic Son-of-Man teachings of *Yeshua* from those advocated by *Thomas* Gnostics.

Logion 85 exhibits semitic structure with consecutive *vav's* carried forward in the Coptic conjunction "and…and." The Greek loan word for power is *dynamis,* which translates Aramaic *chayil* meaning the Host of Heaven in usage contemporary with *Yeshua* as in Daniel 3.20 and 4.22. *Yeshua's* messianic *Bar-Enash* Christology was rooted in the sacred literature of Babylon like that of Daniel and he would have been familiar with this usage.

In accordance with Genesis 1.26ff., which specifies that Adam was "constructed" by consent and activity of the *Elohim,* [522] here *Yeshua* indicates that primal humanity was created from all the energies of the Heavenly Host. The literal Coptic text reads, "Adam came into being out of a great power *(dynamis)* and a great abundance." I have translated it through the lens of Aramaic to read, "Adam came into being with marvellous endowments from a great Heavenly Host." This would be the original meaning.

The kabbalistic concept of *Adam Kadmon* was similar to the Pythagorean-Platonic concept of the human soul as a microcosm, containing within it all the powers and forces of the

---

[522] Hebrew plural of *el* or *eloah,* a god or divine being. The Hebrew deity is known by the Name *Elohim,* which is cognate with Arabic *Allah,* in the Northern Palestinian sources of biblical text and appears as a grammatically singular Name of God in Genesis up to the account of the revelation of God's Name *Yahweh* given to Moses at the burning bush. In the Ras Shamra texts, the *Elohim* is the collective name of the entire Canaanite pantheon of gods. Kabbalistically it seems to have been understood as God and the Sons of God or angelic Host.

macrocosm or manifest *kosmos.*[523]Adam contained within him, to speak kabbalistically, all the Host of Heaven. Such was the "great wealth" that produced the First Adam.[524]

The phrase "but he (Adam) did not become worthy of you" has several implications. It doesn't say "he was not worthy," but "he did not become worthy." In other words, the first humanity did not develop worthiness over time. *Yeshua,* in his dialogue with the Pharisees about the so-called Resurrection, said, "but for those who are worthy of the *Qimah,*" meaning those who have sanctified their lives and purified their hearts. Worthiness is moral and spiritual. It is not something one is born possessing, but earns in life.

The other point is that the old humanity did not become "worthy of you," meaning *Yeshua's* disciples who are being regenerated into the New Adam. This is consistent with another *davar* of *Yeshua* quoted unchanged from Q by Matthew and Luke: "Among those born of women, there has not arisen a greater one than John the Baptist: nevertheless, one that is least in the *Malkuth* of Heaven is greater than he."[525] The term "born of women" means born of flesh in the First Adam. But even the least of those of the *Malkuth* are greater and more worthy.[526]

However, Logion 46 offers an important point. In it, as in the Q saying above, *Yeshua* says, "whichever one of you comes into being as a newly-born will know the *Malkuth* and will become superior to John." In other words, although Logion 85 seems to imply that the disciples are already greater than John, in *Yeshua's halakah* they were in process—not yet superior to John. The wording here, "worthy of you," should not be taken to mean that the disciples are greater than John, but that they have the potential to be so. They are becoming like the "newly-born child of seven days" of Logion 4 (see Commentary), meaning "newly spiritually reborn in the *Malkuth,"* whose wisdom would be sought by the great elders of Israel. But they have not yet achieved that status.

The conclusion of the kabbalistic argument offers proof that the First Adam was not worthy of the blessings of the Second Adam: "If he had been worthy, he would not have experienced death." Like Elijah, he would have been bodily assumed into Heaven so that

---

[523] Plato called *Kosmos* the "Son of God." Thus the human soul as microcosm was, at its essence, an immortal child of Godhead.

[524] In some Gnostic and Arabic theology, *Shaitan* was cast out of Heaven when he refused to obey God's command to bow down to Adam, who represented all of divine creation. In Valentinian theology, Adam is merely a worm constructed by Ialdabaoth until Sophia invokes the Heavenly Light, which elevates primal humanity and makes it greater than the angels. Paul says that the New Humanity will "judge the angels," meaning to have power over them.

[525] Matthew 11.11, Luke 7.28

[526] Cf. Logion #4

Shaitan could not possess even his flesh. Adam's death after living nine hundred and thirty years is described in Genesis 5.5.[527]

The teaching about not experiencing death appears several times in *Thomas*. It seems to be original with *Yeshua*. Paul says many times that in Christ, death ("the last enemy") has been overcome. This does not mean that human bodies won't die, but that consciousness will continue in what Paul calls a spiritual body, and that the faithful will enter the *Qimah*.

The Gnostics, however, interpreted this teaching in many ways. The Docetics said that Jesus did not experience death and suffering on the cross, but stood by watching while a surrogate was crucified. Others said that the flesh of Jesus died, but his spirit survived, and so it would be with all the faithful. Paul said that the body of flesh would transform in death into a spiritual body.

What did *Yeshua* understand about "not experiencing death?" First, his terms life and death did not refer to the flesh. Life was the spiritual Life of the *'Olam,* which could be experienced while in flesh. For him, death meant spiritual death, which was loss of the soul: "For what shall it profit a man, if he shall gain the whole world, and lose his own soul?"[528]

Here the Aramaic word for soul was not *nephesh,* translated *psyche* in the Greek New Testament, since the *nephesh* was understood to dissolve after normal death. It was *neshamah.* This encompassed the higher principles of *ruach, neshamah,* and *yechidah.*

In any case, spiritual death was probably a concept developed from the idea of a person losing his place in Israel if he did not leave posterity behind. That is why the brother of a husband who died childless had the duty to marry the widow and provide her with children.[529] That is not to imply that spiritual death was experienced by those who were sexually infertile! *Yeshua's* teachings were rooted in prophetic justice, not semitic fables and customs.

For him, spiritual death was a consequence of moral abuse, selfishness, and attachment to material rather than spiritual values. It probably meant the *nephesh* had separated itself so

---

[527] Chapter 5 of Genesis is the Book of the Generations of Adam (all the "begats"). He did produce one perfect son, the saint Seth, "in his own likeness, after his image." This implies that the possibility for perfection remained genetically inscribed in all the generation of Adam, despite their failures, but was only rarely realized.

[528] Mark 8.46, Matthew 16.26

[529] The "sin of Onan," who "spilled his seed upon the ground" when having intercourse with his brother's widow in violation of Hebrew law, was that he was cutting his brother off from Israel. Roman Catholic divines have used the passage to condemn masturbation as well as use of condoms or any other kind of birth control, but that sorely misses the point in order to advance Catholic ascetic theology. This is especially onerous when Pope Benedict XVI, formerly head of the Congregation for the Doctrine of the Faith (known in the medieval period as the Inquisition) falsely claims that condom use increases the risk of AIDS in Africa, as he recently preached while visiting Africa. Statistic show exactly the opposite is true.

extremely from its own higher spiritual principles that even the purifications of *Geheena* could not awaken its spirit *(ruach)* or self-consciousness to the *Pardes* of the Third Heaven. The wandering *nephesh* would survive by draining vital force from incarnate beings as a possessing entity until eventually dissolving back into the elements. Thus for a time it becomes an instrument of *Shaitan* and the fallen angels. After the inevitable dissolution of the *nephesh,* the spirit would remain asleep. Any possibility of self-consciousness as a soul or *neshamah* would have been lost in separation from God, Israel, and its higher divine nature.

Logion 86

The foxes have their holes and the birds have their nests, but the *Bar-Enash* has no place on Earth to lay his head and rest.

COMMENTARY

I commented on this *logion,* which is given in Matthew 8.20 and Luke 9.58, in my section on Logion 42. It is a Q saying rendered in each Gospel almost exactly as it is in *Thomas.* To the Gnostic, this and Logion 42 meant that the monk had no true home on Earth. His true home was in Heaven, and until he died the monk would be a passerby.[530] Like the

Yeshua's meaning was somewhat different. "Be ye passersby" of Logion 42 harkens back to the desert wandering of Israel, each family living in a portable *shakan* or tent. It implies non-attachment to specific location—a lesson Jews learned in the Hellenistic Diaspora.

The homelessness of the *Bar-Enash* on Earth was not inteneded to imply that his true home was Heaven and he was merely forced to pass through life on Earth. *Yeshua's* view of the *Bar-Enash* was that of a divine co-sovereign with Godhead whose mission was to overthrow the rule of *Shaitan* and establish the Sovereignty of Heaven on Earth.

When *Yeshua* observed that there was no home on Earth for the *Bar-Enash,* he meant that there was no home as yet. The Son-of-Mankind *Messiah* was foreign to the world. He was entering into a hostile human world. It was neither prepared nor welcoming. Yet he and his *Malkuth* would prevail. Humanity would be purified and sanctified so that the *Malkuth* would manifest in and through mankind. The good will of God would be done on Earth by mankind as it was in Heaven.

---

[530] Cf. the quotation from the *Epistle to Diognetus* at the end of my Commentary on Logion #20.

The Earth and the entire *Kosmos* eagerly await the revealing of the sons of God, as Paul said. It was not just the individual soul of the Elect one, but the entire world that was to be transformed. Paul is transmitting the messianic cosmology he received from historical disciples of *Yeshua* when he declares, "The earnest expectation of the whole universe eagerly waits for the revealing of the children of God. For the world of nature was subjected to corruption, not of its own accord, but by the will of the Maker who subjected it in hope; because all nature itself also will be liberated from its bondage to decay into the glorious freedom of the children of God. For we know that the whole universe groans and labors together in birth pangs until now."[531]

This was quite different from the view of the Gnostic, to whom the Earth was a lost cause, a demiurgical mistake, a fallen world. It was a hellish prison of flesh from whom the Elect were destined to escape to their heavenly home under the leadership of their Revealer and Savior Christ.

Logion 87

The personality of flesh [i.e., the *nephesh*] that clings to flesh *[basar]* will waste away, and the soul *[neshamah]* that is attached to these two will become desolate.

> Literally: Shattered is the body that clings to a body, and shattered is the soul that is attached to these two.

COMMENTARY

The Special Language of this Logion

This is not a declaration of woe in contrast to a beatitude. The Greek loan word in Coptic is ⲗⲁⲓⲡⲱⲣⲟⲛ, which seem to have been derived from Greek λειπω, "to leave behind barren or wretched," and so most translators of *Thomas* render it "wretched is the body." But since this is an authentic *davar,* we need to examine the Aramaic words and concepts underlying it. We find that λειπω was always used to translated Hebrew *pharad,* which means to shatter, scatter, separate, become desolate, dissolve, waste away. It is the same trilateral root used to name the mule—a stubborn animal that would often refuse to move on with a caravan. Thus *pharad* connotes many shades of meaning.

---

[531] Romans 8.19-22

Also, the Greek loan word σωμα is normally translated "body" in *Thomas,* but we find that it was used to translate the Hebrew word *basar,* which means flesh, meat. The distinction between the Greek words *soma* (body) and *sarx* (flesh) was important in Pauline Christianity, since resurrection after death was understood to be of the *soma,* not of the *sarx.* It is only in the late Johannine tradition, with its anti-Thomasian pericope about Thomas putting his hands into the wounds of the risen Jesus, that resurrection of the *sarx* or flesh became an issue. The resurrection of flesh, not *soma* body, finally became Christian doctrine, Paul notwithstanding.

Most translations of Logion 87 render the Coptic verb *ashe,* which is the Sahidic form of *eishe,* with English "is dependant upon, depends upon." The Coptic word denotes something pendent, hanging, or suspended from something else. The general concept is attachment, even clinging.

In the New Testament the word translated as soul is *psyche.* But in Aramaic there were several aspects of soul—*ruah, neshamah, yechidah*—all feminine higher principles that were translated wholesale with the Greek word *psyche.* In *Yeshua's* terminology, the word for soul was *neshamah.* In kabbalistic allegory, the human soul is to Godhead as a bride is to a groom. That is why Paul wrote, "For the husband is the head of the wife, even as Christ is the head of the church."[532] Since this *davar* concerns the kabbalistic concept of spiritual death,[533] which was described by *Yeshua* as loss of the soul *(neshamah),* I translate it with the English word soul.

The Kabbalistic Background

Paul stressed that the *soma* or body of flesh was as different from the body of spirit as the ungerminated seed was from the plant it produced. He referred to the incarnate personality that survives death in as a *psychikos* or mental body.[534] It was like a seed that would dissolve and reveal the spiritual body.

In kabbalistic terms known to Paul, the *psychikos* body was the *nephesh.* The *pneumatikos* or spiritual body was the *neshamah* or immortal soul, which was connected to the mortal *nephesh* by *ruach,* spirit. The soul or *neshamah* served as body to the even higher principle known as *yechida*—the divine soul of the soul. Thus the flesh was body to the mortal mind or personality known as the *nephesh.* The mortal *nephesh* was body to the immortal soul or *neshamah.* And the immortal soul was body to the divine *yechidah.*

---

[532] Ephesians 5.23
[533] See Commentary on Logion #85
[534] I Corinthians 15.42-44: "So also is the resurrection of the dead. The body is sown in corruption, it is raised in incorruption. It is sown in dishonor, it is raised in glory. It is sown in weakness, it is raised in power. It is sown an animal body, it is raised a spiritual body. There is an animal body, and there is a spiritual body."

According to the wisdom schools, the lower form of spirit that connected the *nephesh* to its body of flesh was known as the silver cord.[535] The cord broke after physical death and the *nephesh* would no longer be able to return to its body. Since the *nephesh* was the source of vital force for the physical body, the flesh dissolved and decayed back into its earthly elements. The bodiless *nephesh* would survive for as long as forty days, or six weeks. After this it would die and decay into its elements just as the physical body had done, releasing its immortal soul, the *neshamah*. The soul then experienced a time of purification in the spiritual fires of *Gehenom* in the Third Heaven, which could be as long as a year in the case of souls that had been severely defiled. A true *tzadik* would have already purified his soul in life and would not experience the fires of *Gehenom*. Then the immortal soul would enter into Paradise to sleep until its next incarnation. In the case of a saint, however, the *neshamah* awakened in the *Qimah* and abode in Paradise or higher Heavens. In the case of a fully realized messianic saint of *Yeshua*, I would speculate that his soul served as body to his divine *yechidah*, which now shared the work of Sovereignty with the *Abba* as a member of the new sanctified and fully perfected Heavenly Humanity. Logion 88 may describe that state.

In this *davar*, *Yeshua* applies the Aramaic term *pharad*, "shattered, wasted away, disconnected" to both the flesh or corpse of a dead person and to his *nephesh* or personal self-consciousness that survives death for a time. Both will shatter, i.e. dissolve back into their elements or lose their means of attachment to a body. Using the language and concepts of *Yeshua*, the first line might be translated, "The personality of flesh that clings to flesh will waste away." This was commonly understood. But in the second line he clarifies the meaning of losing the soul. "The soul that is attached to these two will also waste away."

Kabbalistic Teachings Concerning Death

Kabbalistic teachings underlying this *davar* help us to understand its meaning. There were two impulses in the heart: good and evil, light and shadow, real and unreal, eternal and mortal. The *nephesh* or human personality was the builder. When it constructed with the impulses of the *yetzer ha-ra*, accumulating the immortal treasure of good *mitzvoth*, it built a *sullam* or ladder to the higher heavens such that the *ruah* or spirit embodied in the *nephesh* (the soul of the *nephesh*) retained the consciousness of the final personality, which was incorporated into the immortal entity that had originally emanated the incarnation. In other words, the person achieved the *Qimah*.

Jacob's "Ladder" *(sullam,* meaning a stone-cut stairway as leading up the face of a Babylonian ziggurat) appeared to him in a dream while he slept on the place where,

---

[535] "...the silver cord is snapped asunder, and the golden bowl is shattered, and the pitcher is broken at the fountain, and the wheel falleth shattered, into the pit." Eccl. 12.6

according to Midrashic interpretation, the Temple of Solomon would be built in Jerualem many centuries later. The vision came to be interpreted as the vehicle of ascent to the *Merkabah* or Chariot-Thone of Godhead. Philo of Alexandria, a contemporary of *Yeshua,* also interpreted it four ways beginning with the most exalted:

1. a mechanism of reincarnation,

2. the human soul,

3. a rising and falling of virtue in the soul, and

4. the rising and falling of vicissitudes in human life.[536]

A pseudepigraphical text entitled *The Ladder of Jacob* is preserved in Slavonic. It seems to have been originally composed by a messianic Jew shortly after the fall of Masada and destruction of the Temple in 73 C.E. and advocates a warlike *Messiah Ben-David.* The stone steps of the *sullam* lead to the *Merkabah* of God surrounded by *Kerubim* and *Seraphim.*

After physical death the consciousness of a disciple would be filled with light, but those who had not achieved spiritual integrity (become *shalem*) would be lost in darkness.[537] Logion 87 is about the condition of the latter after death. The person whose consciousness has been only of material reality will cling to that after death, even while his flesh is "shattered." Here the Aramaic word *pharad* is the same as used in kabbalistic descriptions of the shattering of the *Sephiroth* or Vessels in the primal creation—just as useless pottery was smashed by a potter, crushed, and re-dissolved into the clay slurry to throw new pottery on the wheel.[538] Flesh was like clay. Corpses were often laid in sealed caves or hewn tombs known in Greek as *sarcophagi,* "flesh eaters," so that the flesh would decay until all that remained was bones, which were then collected and placed in an ossuary or shrine with the bones of past ancestors. Thus the idiom, "gathered to his fathers." This dissolving of flesh back into the elements is what was understood by the term "shattering."

The *davar* says that just as the flesh dissolves after death, so will the soul that clings to flesh as the only form of reality also dissolve. I have used the term soul rather than Hebrew *nephesh* because while the disincarnate personality *(nephesh)* dissolves back into its elements about forty days after death according to kabbalistic theory, it has served as the body of the *neshamah* connected by *ruach.* In the case of a disciple, his consciousness will withdraw into the *neshamah* through the *sullam* or heavenly staircase of *ruach* because spiritual integration has been accomplished in the works of incarnate life. But in the case of

---

536 First Book of *De somniis*

537 Logion 61.c 61.c: "Therefore I say, when one [of you] is destroyed [by death], he will be filled with light; but if he is divided, he will be filled with darkness."

538 Paul used the metaphor of God as a potter forming people in Romans 9.31: "Hath not the potter power over the clay, of the same lump to make one vessel unto honour, and another unto dishonour?" This was a *kabbalistic* allegory of death and rebirth.

one who is "divided" or is *se'eph* (disconnected from his higher realities),[539] i.e. the soul that clings to flesh and the man of flesh ("these two"), the consciousness that has developed in life will dissolve. The soul will be lost—not the immortal *yechiduh,* which will emanate another physical incarnation through the *neshamah.* But the continuity of consciousness that exists for those "worthy" of the *Qimah.*

That is why Peter, James, and John could recognize the ascended saints Moses and Elijah in the so-called transfiguration event. Their spiritual souls were clothed in the temporary *nephesh* or perfected personality of their final incarnation.

The roots of Jewish kabbalistic understanding of death are in Egyptian mortuary science and its seven-fold division of the soul: flesh, *ka, ba,* etc. But very similar teachings can be found in Tibetan Buddhism concerning the *trikaya* or three Buddha bodies—the *Nirmanakaya,* by which a Buddha manifests in form to the human eye and in which the risen *Yeshua* would be understood to have manifested to his disciples while still able to disappear and walk through walls, being equivalent to the emanated and perfected *nephesh* of an ascended Jewish saint.[540]

To paraphrase Logion 87, "The person of flesh-consciousness who depends only upon his simple material reality will find that after death it eventually dissolves, and the soul that clings to the person of flesh and his simple consciousness will also dissolve."

A final selection from the Wisdom of Solomon—a Pharisaic scripture of the Jewish wisdom schools well-known to *Yeshua,* and still part of the apocryphal canon of Catholic and Anglican churches—illustrates the enmity between Jewish materialists (Sadducees, collaborators with the Romans colonizers, who accepted only the first five books of the Old Testament, rejected any form of messianic hope, and rejected the idea of the *Qimah* or afterlife, here named as the "ungody" by the Pharisaic writer) and the Pharisees, who developed mystic, messianic, kabbalistic and rabbinic traditions.

Wisdom Chapter 2

[1] For the ungodly said, reasoning with themselves, but not aright, Our life is short and tedious, and in the death of a man there is no remedy: neither was there any man known to have returned from the grave.

[2] For we are born merely by chance, and after death we shall be as though we had never been: for the breath in our nostrils is as smoke, and mortal spark only in the beating of our heart:

[3] Which being extinguished, our body shall be turned into ashes, and our spirit shall vanish as the soft air,

[4] And our name shall be forgotten in time, and no man shall have our works in remembrance, and our life shall pass away as the trace of a cloud, and shall be dispersed as a mist, that is driven away with the beams of the sun, and overcome with the heat thereof.

[5] For our time is a very shadow that passeth away; and after our end there is no returning: for it is

---

[539] See Commentary on Logion #61.c
[540] The other two bodies of the *trikaya* are *Sambhogakaya* and the *Dharmakaya.*

fast sealed, so that no man cometh again.

[6] Come on therefore, let us make merry with food and wine, and let us indulge in promiscuous debauchery as though we were lusty youths.

[7] Let us fill ourselves with costly wine and ointments: and let no flower of the spring pass by us:

[8] Let us crown ourselves with rosebuds, before they be withered:

[9] Let none of us go without his part of our voluptuousness: let us leave tokens of our pleasurable libertinism in every place: for this is our portion, and our lot is this.

[10] Let us oppress the poor righteous man, let us not spare the widow, nor reverence the ancient gray hairs of the aged.

[11] Let our strength be the law of justice: for that which is feeble is found to be nothing worth.

[12] Therefore let us lie in wait for the righteous; because he is not with us, and he is absolutely contrary to our doings: he upbraideth us with our offending the law, and objecteth to our infamy the transgressions of our traditions.

[13] He professeth to have the knowledge of God: and he calleth himself the child of the Lord.[541]

[14] He was made to reprove our thoughts.

[15] He is grievous unto us even to behold: for his life is not like other men's, his ways are of another fashion.

[16] We are considered by him to be counterfeits: he abstaineth from our ways as from filthiness: he pronounceth the end of the just to be blessed, and maketh his boast that God is his father.

[17] Let us see if his words be true: and let us prove what shall happen in the end of him.

[18] For if the just man be a son of God, he will help him, and deliver him from the hand of his enemies.

[19] Let us examine him with despitefulness and torture, that we may know his meekness, and prove his patience.

[20] Let us condemn him with a shameful death: for by his own saying he shall be respected.

[21] Such things they [the libertine materialists] did imagine, and were deceived: for their own wickedness hath blinded them.

[22] As for the *razim* of God, they knew them not: neither hoped they for the wages of righteousness, nor discerned a reward for blameless souls.

[23] For God created man to be immortal, and made him to be an image of his own eternity.

[24] Nevertheless through envy of the devil came death into the world:[542] and they that do hold of his side do find it.

Wisdom Chapter 3

[1] But the souls of the righteous are in the hand of God, and there shall no torment touch them.

[2] In the sight of the unwise they seemed to die: and their departure is taken for misery,

[3] And their going from us to be utter destruction: but they are in peace.

[4] For though they be punished in the sight of men, yet is their hope full of immortality.

[5] And having been a little chastised, they shall be greatly rewarded: for God proved them, and

---

[541] Son of God, child of God, God is his Father—Aramaic titles and phrases commonly used of Jewish saints, including *Yeshua*.

[542] The Deuteronomic Two Ways doctrine ("I set before you the Way of Life and the Way of Death," said God) developed by way of Zoroastrian dualism (Babylonian Captivity) into the two *yetzerim* doctrine of the intertestamental period and the dualism of moral opposites: life vs. death, light vs. darkness. Death and darkness are associated with *Shaitan* and the dualism of fallen and unfallen angels. This was the moral-spiritual basis for much of *Yeshua's halakah*.

found them worthy for himself.

[6] As gold in the furnace hath he tried them, and received them as a burnt offering.

[7] And in the time of their visitation they shall shine, and run to and fro like sparks among the stubble.

[8] They shall judge the nations, and have Sovereignty over the people, and their Lord shall reign for ever.[543]

Logion 88

The angels and the prophets will come to you and give to you those things you (already) have. And you will reciprocate by offering them those things which you have, and say to yourselves, 'When will they come and take what is theirs?'

COMMENTARY

Logia #83-88 seem to be aspects of *Yeshua's* kabbalistic teachings about death, and Logion 88 refers specifically to the after-death realities that his disciples will discover (possibly also experience in *Merkabah* visions). Here *Yeshua* prepares his disciples for their reception in Heaven after death.

The disciples will be among those who "have" or possess immortal treasure in their hearts after death. To them even more will be given. The message here is that they will be given the power to activate what they already possess—different forms of charism and sovereignty.

The Near Eastern convention of gift-giving and receiving required that a guest entering into another's home be offered gifts—food, drink, hospitality, or other things. He then must reciprocate by offering gifts to the host. But what can the disciples offer when they enter the heavenly *'Olam*? They must offer the treasure they have accumulated in their hearts. But the angels and the prophets of Heaven do not come to accept the reciprocal gifts, so the disciples wonder, "When will they come and take what is theirs?"

---

[543] Online at http://www.earlyjewishwritings.com/text/wisdom.html

The paradox is that unlike human gifting conventions, Godhead and those in Heaven "do not lack." They need nothing because they are *shalem,* spiritually whole, complete, and perfected. You can offer them gifts. They will not be refused, for that would be quite rude! But they never will come to accept them. Why? Because they are givers only.

In the one teaching of *Yeshua* that is directly quoted by Paul in his Epistles he said, "It is better to give than to receive." By this he implied that the giver is whole and lacking nothing, like God. The receiver is in need—unlike God.

Yeshua taught his disciples to imitate God, who causes his sun to shine upon the just as well as the unjust. Be a giver, not a taker. That is the gifting convention in Heaven.

CHAPTER ELEVEN: Logia 89-101

**89.a Jesus said, "Why do you wash the outside of the cup?
89.b Do you not realize that he who made the inside is the
same one who made the outside?"**

**90.a Jesus said, "Come unto me, for my yoke is easy and
my discipline is mild,**

90.b and you will find repose for yourselves."

91 They said to him, "Tell us who you are so that we may believe in
you." He said to them, "You read the face of the sky and of the earth,
but you have not recognized the one who is before you, and you do
not know how to read this season."

92 Jesus said, "Seek and you will find. Yet, what you asked me about
in former times and which I did not tell you then, now I do desire to
tell, but you do not inquire after it."

93 <Jesus said,> "Do not give what is holy to dogs, lest they throw
them on the dung-heap. Do not throw the pearls to swine, lest they
[…] it […]."

COMMENTARY

This group of *logia* is inspired by sayings of *Yeshua* found in New Testament sources, but
they do not transmit authentic *davarim.*

Logion 89 is derived from the Q pericope in Matthew and Luke where *Yeshua* criticized the
Pharisees for ritual *mikveh* before a meal, which was a form of non-essential pious
observation he called the "traditions of men" as opposed to the ways of God. He said rather
that they should give priority to interior purity. "You clean the outside of the cup and the
plate, but on the inside they are full of greed and self-indulgence."[544]

---

[544] Matthew 23.25, cf. Luke 11.39. Notice the change in reference from you to they in Matthew's redaction. It
has been corrected in Luke, but may indicate pre-Gospel redaction already in Q. It is more likely that *Yeshua's*
sermons against Pharisaic self-righteousness were given to his disciples in the third person plural "they,"
rather than strident attacks directly against Pharisaic rulers in the second person plural "you." But they were

The setting is given in Mark 7:4, "When they come from the market place, they do not eat unless they cleanse themselves; and there are many other things which they have received [from human tradition] in order to observe, such as the washing of cups and pitchers and copper pots." But the *Thomas* version has no connection to the setting. Instead, the completely separate saying from Luke 11.40 provides the conclusion: "Foolish ones! Did not He who made the outside make the inside also?"

This may be evidence that the two sayings were linked differently than in Q, at least in the mnemonic dictation from Aramaic, and are clearly independent from Q and the New Testament Gospels.

But my sense is that the two were linked by the redactor of *Thomas* to create Logion 89. He has used the question to frame the idea that God is creator of both the outer and inner worlds, as though the opponent to whom the rhetorical question is addressed has only a gross material understanding. Thus in *Thomas,* two sayings of *Yeshua* are redacted together to attack the materialistic opponents of the ascetic Syrian Gnostics—merchants, wealthy people, and other critics probably including their abandoned family members.

Logion 90 is a rewrite of a Gospel saying. In its original setting, the *logion* found in Matthew's special material was a call for discipleship.[545] The yoke (Hebrew *ol*) was a kabbalistic metaphor for the interpretation of *Torah* that was used by a specific *Rav* to develop his *halakah* or rules of discipleship and living. *Yeshua's* yoke was the spiritual discipline that a student would learn and practice.

The yoke terminology developed out of the Jewish wisdom schools. In the *Wisdom of Jesus Ben Sirach,* which *Yeshua* and his disciples read as scripture, we find: "Come unto me, all ye unlearned, and dwell in the house of learning...Put your neck under the yoke, and let your soul receive instruction...my burden is light and have received much rest."[546]

Here the sage, Jesus ben Sirach, invites the reader to put his neck under the yoke or discipline of *Hochmah,* Wisdom—meaning the kabbalistic study of *Torah.* A yoke, we must understand, was a curved wooden support for jointly carrying a burden that could be shared between two oxen, a man and an ox, or two men. It made the burden half as heavy, i.e., light. An older, more experienced ox would be yoked with a younger one, who would learn his work from the older one. Metaphorically the burden or work was study of the hidden *razim* of scripture. Metaphorically, a disciple was yoked to a sage for the same reason. In Hebrew wisdom tradition, the disciple was called a son of the sage.

Ben Sirach declared, "My burden is light, and I have received much rest." The Hebrew word for rest was *nuach* which developed from the verb *nachah*, "to lead." The idea was that the

---

[545] Matthew 11:28 "Come to me, all you that are weary and are carrying heavy burdens, and I will give you rest. Take my yoke upon you, and learn from me; for I am gentle and humble in heart, and you will find rest for your souls. For my yoke is easy, and my burden is light."
[546] *Sirach* 51.23-27

sage led the disciple into the kabbalistic *Pardes,* which was a transcendent place of *Sabbath* rest in divine instruction, not unlike the Platonic "leisure" for study. It is not the same thing as the Gnostic *anapausis* of Logion 90.

How was the "rest" understood rabbinically? The answer lies in the following passage from the *Mishnah, Avot* 3:6. "Every one who takes upon himself the yoke of the *Torah* removes from his shoulders the yoke of government and daily sorrows. But whoever removes the yoke of the *Torah* will be burdened with the yoke of government and daily sorrows." Spiritual study allows one to be liberated from mundane concerns and find "rest" in the *Pardes* with other sages and students. Rabbinic Judaism even today reserves Saturday not just for cessation of labor, but for fellowship in study of scripture and enjoying the pleasures of *Shabbat* (*Oneg Shabbat*).

In this Gnostic adaptation of Matthew 11.28, which in itself may have been a Matthean composition based on *Sirach* 51.23-27,[547] we find Greek loan words from Matthew's text: *chrestos* (from Hebrew-Aramaic *tov,* "good, pleasant, easy") and *anapausis* (from Hebrew-Aramaic *nuch,* "to sit down, be at rest"), a further indication of its possible source. Logion 90.a seems to be an authentic *davar,* but 90.b is clearly a Gnostic extension.

I paraphrase what the *logion* would have meant to a *Thomas* Gnostic, for whom *Anapausis* was a technical term for the aeonic existence of an ascended monk, and *chrestos* was an allusion to the (Greek) *Christos* or Christ: "Come to me as a monk, for my discipline is Christhood and my rule is gentle, and you will find the eternal *Anapausis* for yourselves."

Logion 91 is a Gnostic composition based on *Yeshua's davar* comparing forecasting weather as an allegory of interpreting the prophetic signs of the advent of the messianic Age found in the Q material of Matthew and Luke.[548] "When it is evening, ye say, It will be fair weather: for the sky is red. And in the morning, It will be foul weather today: for the sky is red and cloudy. O ye hypocrites, ye can discern the face of the sky; but can ye not discern the signs of the times?"[549]

To this the Gnostic writer has added a setting. Those hearing Jesus (not his disciples) ask him to tell them who he is so that they can "believe (*pisteuein*)" in him. Needless to say, *Yeshua* did not preach a gospel about himself as a great being from Heaven, and the issue of "belief" in *Iesous Christos* that later became central to gentile Christian doctrine had no part in his historical teachings—rather, it was the issue of fidelity and faithfulness (Aramaic *emunah*) to God's ways.

This becomes an opportunity for the Gnostic Jesus to declare that if they can read the skies for weather, they should also discern the apocalyptic "season," Greek *kairos* from prophetic

---

[547] The writer(s) of Matthew may have considered specific passages by *Yeshua ben-Sirach* to have been messianic revelations by *Yeshua ha-Mashiah,* such as the "Come unto me, all ye..." of Sirach 51.23f.
[548] Matthew 16.1 ff.; Luke 12.54ff.
[549] Matthew 16.2-3

use of Aramaic *et,* "the proper time, opportunity." Moreover, they should "recognize the one who is before you," i.e. Jesus as the Christ.

Logion 92 is a Gnostic commentary on *Yeshua's davar* from Q, "If you persist in seeking, you will find; if you persist in knocking, it will be opened to you."[550] The Gnostic Jesus explains that he is now ready to teach them the secrets that they have wanted to know. The *logion* implies a community setting in which a Gnostic prophet delivers further revelations from the risen Jesus as Heavenly Revealer.

Logion 93 differs from the authentic *davar* in which *Yeshua* admonishes his disciples to use discretion concerning what and to whom they preach. All three Synoptic Gospels transmit warnings about feeding holy things to "little dogs" or to "swine." Some scholars have speculated these were Aramaic terms of derision for gentiles or Samaritans, but other evidence contradicts, such as the *mashal* of the Good Samaritan. It is more likely that *Yeshua* referred to his intransigent Palestinian religious opponents.

The reason given by *Yeshua* for not giving "pearls" or sacred *razim* to the "swine" is that they will turn around and rip you to pieces. There is no reason offered for not giving holy things to dogs because it was well known that the remnants of sacrificial offerings were prohibited from being thrown to animals.

But in Logion 93, the writer has given a reason: "lest they throw them on the dung-heap." In other words, dishonor them in the worst possible way. That probably means the dogs would turn the holy things into excrement. So the Gnostic understanding of this *logion* was that Jesus forbade offering secret *gnosis* to non-initiates ("dogs"), for they would twist and degrade it into heretical teaching.

Logion 94 [Gnostic Logion]

He who seeks will find, and he who knocks will be let in.

COMMENTARY

Here is the same *davar* that appeared with Gnostic commentary in Logion 92, but this time isolated as it probably was in the original dictation. This indicates that the original collection was expanded and given Gnostic interpretation. Hellenistic scribes were loathe to remove any content, but were happy to expand. Thus many ancient documents contain repetitions of similar material reworked.

---

[550] Matthew 7.7; Luke 11.9

The Greek translation of the original Aramaic *davar* that was transmitted in the Q material uses the present active tense to translate "ask…seek…knock." A correct translation is not "seek and you shall find," but "keep on seeking and you shall find." This reflected an original Aramaic verbal construction that means, "if you persist in seeking, you shall find." The *mashal* about the Importunant Neighbor who wakes up his friend by persistently asking for help is *Yeshua's* metaphor for faithful persistence on behalf of others—he is seeking food for his visitors.

But the Coptic version in *Thomas* has lost its meaning. It simply states that seeking guarantees finding. That was not *Yeshua's* teaching. Spiritual enterprise required great fidelity and perseverance—like the *emunah* of a mustard seed. Just one knock doesn't open the door, although it may have been enough to admit a postulant to the Syrian Gnostic community as Logion 94 implies. See the commentaries to Logia #2 and #20.

Logion 95

If you have money, do not lend it at interest, but give it to one from whom you will not get it back.

COMMENTARY

The Matthean Sermon on the Mount and the comparable Q material in Luke's Sermon on the Plain exhort *Yeshua's* hearers to lend money without charging "usury" or interest. They also teach that if one has money or clothing or other necessities, they should be shared or donated to those in need. These teachings are reflected in the Johannine Epistles: "But whoso hath this world's good, and seeth his brother have need, and shutteth up his bowels of compassion from him, how dwelleth the love of God in him?"[551] These were principles upon which the first messianic communities were formed, where wealth and resources were shared. This "communalism" was not modern communism, but more akin to socialism. The model was used in Buddhist and other religious communities, and survives even in some modern Christian communities. It also became the basis for Christian charity and charitable foundations.

The teachings against usury (making money by lending money), which were consolidated in the Church councils,[552] forced medieval Christian societies to borrow money for

---

[551] I John 3.17

[552] Here is the Wikipedia summary (http://en.wikipedia.org/wiki/Usury): "The First Council of Nicaea in 325, forbade clergy from engaging in usury (canon 17). At the time "usury" meant simply interest of any kind, and the canon merely forbade the clergy to lend money on interest above one per cent per month.
Later ecumenical councils applied this regulation to the laity. Lateran III decreed that persons who accepted interest on loans could receive neither the sacraments nor Christian burial. Pope Clement V made the belief in the right to usury a heresy in 1311, and abolished all secular legislation which allowed it. Pope Sixtus

capitalistic ventures from Jewish money-lenders, since wealthy Christians would invest only in their own ventures—most of which were shipping and trade. King Henry VIII relaxed the laws against usury during his reign, and that resulted in the development of banking systems and more enterprise. But in the eighteen century the Jewish goldsmith Bower inherited his father's business, changed his name to Rothschild, and made a fortune lending money to governments on interest—which was now legal.

Finally the anti-usury laws of Europe, both civil and canonical, were changed to allow for capitalistic lending. That along with the development of corporation law resulted in European imperialism for major economic development. Finally, to assuage the guilty conscience of Christian entrepreneurs and satisfy relaxed church laws, nonprofit corporations were legally defined and developed for charitable purposes and tax avoidance. Today "usury" is understood to be an interest rate that is too high, but there are no laws defining it. Credit card companies can up their rates to 25% and higher with no serious legal consequences.

The economic realities of capitalism and personal wealth have always been opposed to the teachings of *Yeshua.* His idea of social economics was based on sharing and charity—not exploitative accumulation of personal wealth.

Yeshua was not optimistic about any change in world economy or the distribution of wealth anytime soon. He said, according to Mark and repeated in Matthew and Luke, "You have the poor with you always, and whenever you wish, you may do them good."[553] But eventually in the *Malkuth,* there would be no poverty, illness, or crime, just as in the apocalyptic visions of Trito-Isaiah Isaiah and other prophets.

Logion 96-98 [*Mashlim* of the *Malkuth*]

Yeshua's Parables of the "Kingdom" are often collected in one chapter by New Testament writers. In *Thomas* they are scattered throughout, but here we have a section of three authentic *davarim* that probably reflect mnemonic order in the original dictation. Both #96 and #97 concern flour and ingredients for loaves of bread. It is also remarkable that #97 and #98 are not known from any other source.

V condemned the practice of charging interest as "detestable to God and man, damned by the sacred canons and contrary to Christian charity."

Theological historian John Noonan argues that "the doctrine [of usury] was enunciated by popes, expressed by three ecumenical councils, proclaimed by bishops, and taught unanimously by theologians."[2]

553 Mark 14.7 and parallels

The Sovereignty of the *Abba* is like a certain woman. She took a little leaven, <concealed> it in some dough, and made it into large loaves. Let him who has ears hear.

COMMENTARY

This is a version of the Q *logion* found in the thirteenth chapters of Matthew and Luke. Like Parable of the Mustard Seed,[554] tiny but potent seeds are hidden in a matrix and allowed to grow over time, when they become large and serviceable.

The *davar* is addressed to those of understanding with "ears to hear," meaning understanding to properly interpret the prophetic saying. Basically, it tells us that the *Malkuth* of the Father-Mother is hidden so that it can grow over time. When the process is complete, the matrix—which is this *'olam* (human reality and the human world)—will evolve into the desired goal.

The seemingly magical process of yeast causing ground whole-grain dough to rise so that it became edible, rather than hard, flat, and stony, was familiar to all of *Yeshua's* hearers. What would have been unfamiliar to them is the idea of time and evolution required for the advent of God's messianic *Malkuth* on Earth. *Yeshua* made the concept implicit in his parables of the Mustard Seed and the Leaven, but did not expect it to be understood by any but his inner-circle disciples and those who might be ready for discipleship. The public expectation about the *Malkuth* was that a Davidic warrior *Messiah* would suddenly descend from Heaven with armies of angels to overthrow Roman rule and establish Jewish sovereignty over the world.

The only change from previously known parables is the term *Malkuth* of the *Abba*, which is also used in the following *logia.* In the New Testament the reference is to the Kingdom (Greek *Basileion*)[555] of God or of Heaven—with were interchangeable terms for God. Godhead was understood by the *Thomas* Gnostics as a primordial unknown and incomprehensible Patriarch who emanated all things.

---

[554] See Commentary on Logion #20
[555] See the Commentary on Logion #2 for explanations of Greek "Kingdom" vs. Aramaic *Malkuth.*

The Sovereignty of the *Abba* is like a certain woman who was carrying a jar full of meal. While she was walking on the road, still some distance from home, the handle of the jar broke and the meal emptied out behind her on the road. She did not realize the consequences; she did not trouble herself. When she reached her house, she set the jar down and found it empty.

COMMENTARY

The woman carries a jar of meal or flour to make loaves of bread. The grain has already been harvested, winnowed, ground, and apportioned. It is now being transported to the woman's home so that it can be used quickly before it grows rancid to make loaves of bread or other things. But the vessel develops a leak and the meal spills out onto the road where it will be eaten by birds and insects and fouled by dust. It is lost. She makes the discovery only after she sets the vessel down at home, when she finds it empty.

This *davar* warns disciples that simply having gained possession of the keys to the *Malkuth* does not guarantee its fruits. Harvest, winnowing, grinding, and apportionment into a vessel for transport to the home does not guarantee use and nourishment by the bread of the *Malkuth.* Simply hearing, understanding, being baptized and otherwise initiated as a newly-born of the *Malkuth* does not guarantee the Life of the *'Olam.* Discipleship is an ongoing, daily, and conscious growth toward spiritual maturity. If the homeword walk of *halakah* is not done with introspection and self-awareness, the value of all that has been received can be lost.

The literal Coptic reads, "She did not realize; she did not take trouble." It has been incorrectly translated by others as "she did not notice the trouble," but here Coptic *hice* is a verb used with *eime* idiomatically to mean "take trouble, trouble herself. *Yeshua* emphasizes the real reason she lost her treasure. It wasn't because the handle broke and leaked. It was because she didn't realize the importance of her carelessness over time and take steps to remedy it. My teacher Mother Jennie used to say, "It's not the big things that trip us up, but the little things." A few drops of water from a leaky faucet every minute adds up to hundreds of gallons a month. By the same token, ignoring a moral or spiritual problem in oneself can be a game-changer over time.

Paul emphasized that disciples are spiritual athletes who compete in an *agon* or footrace against their old nature, the First Adam, which must be crucified. That is, the old nature must be held accountable by being publically exhibited and deprived of breath so that it cannot crowd out the life of the evolving new nature—that of the Second Adam or *Bar-Enash.* One's unregenerate nature must be exposed to oneself, made conscious and visible, and transformed through mindful awareness and rejection of the evil *yetzer* that guides it. Disciples must be like the man who eats the lion of Logion 7. Spiritual regeneration is an ongoing process. Initiation or spiritual rebirth serves as a starting point, but a newly-born must ripen the empowerment with daily practice or like a seed sown onto a roadway it will be lost to the birds and the worms.

Here they are told that conversion to the *Basor* is not a guarantee of some kind of eternal security. It is only by walking his *halakah* mindfully and with ongoing awareness of interior motivation that the bread of the morrow *(epiousion* = Aramaic *ha ba)* can be baked, eaten, and provide spiritual sustenance.

Logion 98

The Sovereignty of the *Abba* is like a certain man who wanted to kill a powerful man. In his own house he drew his sword and thrust it into the wall in order to practice making his hand strong enough to run it through. Then he slew the powerful man.

COMMENTARY

This *davar* is about interior halakic discipline. Paul reflects this concept when he declares: "Everyone who competes in the games goes into strict training. They do it to get a crown that will not last; but we do it to get a crown that will last forever. Therefore I do not run like a man running aimlessly; I do not fight like a man beating the air. No, I beat my body and make it my slave so that after I have preached to others, I myself will not be disqualified for the prize.[556]

Paul's man "beating the air" is shadow-boxing. An analogy to the swordsman in Logion 98 would exist only if he were swordfighting with his shadow. But he is thrusting against the wall to strengthen his wrist and hand so that he will be able to pierce the body armor of the enemy with his sword—not just practicing his defensive footwork as the shadow-boxer does. Thus what is is doing is analogous to Paul's beating of his body to make it obedient to what he describes in another place as the *Nous* or Divine Mind of Christ within him.[557]

The Coptic translation has not been correctly understood. Most translate it "in order to find out whether his hand would be strong enough/could go through." This implies that he is just testing to see if he has the strength. But the Coptic says literally, "so that he would find,

---

[556] I Corinthians 9.25-27
[557] I Corinthians 2.16: "'For who has known the Mind *(Nous)* of the Lord that he may instruct him?' But we have the Mind *(Nous)* of Christ."

namely, his hand would be strong to go through." This means "in order to practice making his hand strong enough to run it through." *Yeshua's* teaching was to "always pray and not give up…[558] keep on asking/seeking/knocking…always keep vigil *(shaqad)*."[559] It was to continually practice spiritual discipline, not just make a one-time test.

How is the Sovereignty of the *Abba* like a swordsman strengthening and preparing for mortal battle with an enemy? Again, the *Malkuth* does not manifest upon the Earth at one time or in one place. It is a process of evolution. It exists on Earth, but is invisible to mankind. Its "coming" means that it appears within and unto humanity. Its manifestation, like that of the kabbalistic Mustard Tree of the *Pardes* in the messianic Age, comes by growth and cultivation in the human heart, for it is "within you and beyond you."[560]

Furthermore, the Sovereignty of the *Abba* on Earth appears and manifests to humanity through a process of spiritual battle. As Paul correctly said, "We do not wrestle against flesh and blood, but against principalities, against powers, against the rulers of the darkness of this age, against spiritual hosts of wickedness in the heavenly places."[561] That warfare, taught *Yeshua,* is not external, but internal. The enemy is not Rome, for example, but the dark forces that guide and animate the evil that Roman rulers and institutions wage against humanity. The Romans and all humanity act out of spiritual blindness and ignorance. According to the Lucan source, *Yeshua* is reported to have prayed on the cross, "*Abba,* forgive them [the Roman soldiers], for they know not what they do."[562]

That enemy is internal to all of us. Thus the swordsman practices piercing the wall of his own home. This is the core of spiritual *halakah*—clear-sighted self-examination that pierces through the walls of defense one has erected that blind him to his own faults. Beyond the wall lies the concealed enemy.

In this *davar, Yeshua* reveals to his disciples that the newly-borns must train to be spiritual warriors. Again, Paul reflects this with his well-known exhortation in Ephesians 6.13-18:

> Therefore take up the whole armor of God that you may be able to withstand in the evil day, and having done all, to stand.[563] Stand therefore, having girded your waist with truth, having put on the breastplate of righteousness, and having shod your feet with the preparation of the gospel of peace; above all, taking the shield of faithfulness with which you will be able to

---

[558] Luke 18.1; Luke

[559] Luke 21.36. The *shaqad* was both a form of *Merkabah* meditation and daily halakic vigilance over one's own interior motivations and feelings.

[560] See Commentary and notes on Logion #3

[561] Ephesians 6.12

[562] Luke 23.34. One could argue that if *Yeshua* forgave those who crucified him, then no one, not the "Jews" or the Romans or all humanity, should be held guilty of Christ-killing—a lesson lost on the Lucan author!

[563] This repetition of the Greek word "stand" reflects the Aramaic word for Resurrection of the saints, *Qimah,* "the state of standing forth in uprightness after physical death," from which the Gnostics derived their term Standing One.

quench all the fiery darts of the wicked one. And take the helmet of liberation, and the sword of the Spirit, which is the Word of God; praying always with all prayer and supplication in the Spirit, being watchful to this end with all perseverance and supplication for all the saints.

Here as in many Hebrew and Aramaic sources, especially apocalyptic writings known to or contemporary with *Yeshua,* the "sword of God" is a metaphor for the prophetic Word of God. The *Messiah ben-Joseph* will slay the enemies of Godhead with the sword of his tongue.[564] Thus Logion 98 seems to reflect a *davar* exhorting *Yeshua's* disciples to become proficient in knowledge and use of scripture for battle with the Enemy—*Shaitan.* Practice driving a sword through a wall to strengthen the arm for battle with a heavy sword is probably analogous to developing scriptural muscle for persuasive debate, preaching, and teaching—the work of an Apostle.

Logion 99

The disciples said to him, "Your brothers and your mother are standing outside." He said to them, "Those here who do the will of our *Abba* are my brothers and my mother. It is they who will attain unto the Sovereignty of our *Abba.*"

COMMENTARY

This is the Marcan pericope, repeated by Matthew, of the time early on in *Yeshua's* first Galilean ministry when his mother and family tried to stop him. They probably feared that Herod would kill him as he had John the Baptist. They stood outside and protested that he was insane—the only legal excuse for treason, which the preaching of the messianic Age was considered to be in the case of Galilean zealots. His family was probably trying to protect him. Whatever the case, it was on this occasion that *Yeshua* declared, "Whoever does the will of God is my family."

---

[564] Origin of the messianic Sword of God's Word: Isaiah 49:1-3: "Listen to me, you islands; hear this, you distant nations: Before I was born YAHWEH called me; from my birth he has made mention of my name. He made my mouth like a sharpened sword, in the shadow of his hand he hid me; he made me into a polished arrow and concealed me in his quiver. He said to me, "You are my servant, Israel, in whom I will display my splendor." Developed in Trito-Isaiah: Isaiah 66:16 "For by fire (of God's Word) and by his sword (of his mouth) will YAHWEH plead with all flesh: and the slain (in the spirit) of YAHWEH shall be many." In the Christian Revelation to St. John: Revelation 1:16 In his right hand he held seven stars, and out of his mouth came a sharp double-edged sword. His face was like the sun shining in all its brilliance. Revelation 2:16 Repent therefore! Otherwise, I will soon come to you and will fight against them with the sword of my mouth. Revelation 19:15 Out of his mouth comes a sharp sword with which to strike down the nations.

The Meaning of "entering into the Kingdom"

In Logion 99 we have an independent version of this pericope that is concluded with a phrase that appears in several of the New Testament *logia* in reference to those who will "enter into" the *Malkuth.* But the Greek *eiserchomai* "to come into," which is consistently employed for this usage in all three Synoptics and John, translates Hebrew-Aramaic *ba* from *boa.*

This semitic verb had special meaning in Jewish eschatological usage, as in the *'Olam Ha-Ba,* the World that Has Come/Will Come. While *boa* could mean to enter into a specific place, in reference to the *Malkuth* (which was not a location but a state of being) it meant to come upon, come as far as. It had the sense of sense of "coming into" an inheritance. Inheritance is, in fact, a metaphor constantly used in early Christian writings because many of *Yeshua's davarim* for "coming into" the *Malkuth* require the Greek verb *kleronomeiv,* "to receive as one's lot, to inherit,"[565] or the noun *kleronomia,* "inheritance."[566]

Hebrew *boa, ba* also carried the meaning "to bring, bring unto, bring forth." In view of such *mashlim* as the Mustard Seed, the Sower, the Wise Fisherman, and those with various harvest motifs, the phrase could be translated "to bring forth, develop" the *Malkuth.* In this case the concept of spiritual evolution, adoption, or rebirth as a royal heir is also implied.

Both of these concepts are implied in many of the *Thomas logia.* However the core concept in *Thomas* is that of spiritual attainment. For example, in Logion 22 the disciples ask, "When will we, being newly-born ones [into the *Bar-Enash*], attain the *Malkuth?*" They have received spiritual rebirth as children of Godhead, and as such they are heirs of the Sovereignty of the Son of Mankind, but when will they begin to co-rule?

The task of spiritual growth and maturation that lies ahead of them, says *Yeshua,* must be worked out in his *Halakah,* which in itself is initiatic and will eventually make them *shalem,* like the angels. When the disciples have become *shalem,* then they will attain the Sovereignty,[567] just as a royal heir begins to co-rule and apprentice the monarch's work when he becomes of age.

The disjuncture between *Yeshua's* meaning of "attainment" and the second-generation Christian understanding of "entering into" occurred at the point where the oral Aramaic

---

[565] Matthew 5.5,
[566] Acts 20.32, Galatians 3.18, *et al.*
[567] The Coptic wording for this phrase, which usually appears in New Testament Greek as "enter into the Kingdom," is ⲃⲱⲕ ⲉϩⲟⲩⲛ, an idiomatic use of verb and preposition meaning to "go in, enter," taken directly from the lost Greek version of *Thomas* that underlies the Coptic using *eiserchomai.* But *Yeshua's* Aramaic usage probably meant to "approach, attain" the *Malkuth.*

dictation was translated and written down in Koine Greek sometime before 50 C.E. Aramaic *ba*, meaning to journey unto, attain to, or even "come forth, become" qualified and worthy for Sovereignty, was understood as Greek *eiserchomai*, to physically "enter into" a kingdom.

Gentile Christianity understood Hebrew messianic *Malkuth* as Greek *Basileion*, Kingdom. It expected the return in glory of Jesus as a Davidic *Messiah* to establish a kingdom or new Jerusalem on Earth. For this reason, the teachings of *Yeshua* about attaining the Sovereignty were understood as entering into a kingdom. The *Malkuth* or Sovereignty entrusted to the *Bar-Enash* or coming messianic humanity was understood eschatologically and in a gross physical way as a place that could be entered. All this in spite of *Yeshua's* many teachings that the *Malkuth* of God/Heaven was not "lo here, lo there," and that it existed in the human heart (Greek *entos humon*, inside of you(plural) from Aramaic within your hearts).

As I said in an earlier chapter, the *Malkuth* was not a place, but a community like Israel. Membership in Israel was by birth, circumcision, and rites of passage. Membership in the community of the *Malkuth* was by divine rebirth and the halakic path of spiritual maturity. The entrance was not physical, but initiatic.

This idea, which was not part of *Yeshua's* teaching, may have developed first in post-Resurrection messianic Judaism, where the ancient greeting *Maranatha* originated. This could be interpreted as either the invocative prayer *Marana Tha*, "Our Master, Come;" or the original Christian creed[568] *Maran Atha*, "Our Master has/will Come."[569] To the original Jewish Christians, it was an invocation of *Yeshua's* presence in the context of the messianic banqet *seder* he used as a vehicle for teaching his inner-circle.[570] But to the later gentile

---

[568] Scholars have speculated that the Koine Greek title *'Iesous Christos* "Jesus Christ" used and promoted by Paul was the original Christian creed. It affirmed that "Jesus is the Christ," the *Messiah*. But *Maran Atha* must be more ancient, being Aramaic. It affirms that *Yeshua*, whose title as a teacher would have been *Mar* "Master," known to his disciples as *Maran* "Our Master," had appeared on Earth. Aramaic *Mar* was misunderstood to mean *Adonai*, "The Lord," a title of God, which in Greek was *Kyrie*, and in the Pauline identification of Jesus as an aspect of Godhead the titles *Kyrios 'Iesous* "Lord Jesus" and *Kyrios Christos* were also applied to *Yeshua* in the New Testament. This in spite of *Yeshua's* clear statement that he did not claim to be equal to God, transmitted in Mark and Luke: "Why do you call me good? There is only one that is good, and that is God alone." Mark 10.18, Luke 18.19

[569] The Aramaic verb forms, imperative *tha* "come" and *atha* "has come" did not have the sense of the verb *ba*, which could mean both past and future "has come/shall come."

[570] To the Apostles it may have been both an invocation of the Risen Lord ("Our Lord, Come"), but an affirmation that the messianic Age has already arrived—"Our Master has Come," in the form of the "realized eschatology" taught by the Jesus of history as reflected in the *Gospel of Thomas*, Logion 113: "The *Malkuth* of God is spread out upon the Earth, but men to not see it."

Pauline Christians it was a prayer for the return of Christ in victory as well as an invocation for the presence of Christ in the Eucharistic elements.[571]

The Hebrew-Aramaic word *Malkuth* used by *Yeshua* in his proclamation of the *Basor* meant rulership, sovereignty, kingship. Also, *Yeshua* referred to the *Abba* or our *Abba*, but not "my *Abba*." That would have been contrary to his best-known teaching about correct prayer, the Lord' Prayer which begins, "Our *Abba*." In Christian and Gnostic literature, Jesus is seen as the only Son of God and is represented as using the phrase "my Father." But there is a preponderance of evidence that he used the Aramaic word *Abbaoon*, Our *Abba*, which is a single word in Hebrew and Aramaic.

Thus the best translation of the concluding phrase of Logion 99 is "Those here who do the will of our *Abba*...will attain/come into/inherit the Sovereignty of our *Abba*."

Logion 100-101 [Altered *Davarim*]

100.a They showed Jesus a gold coin and said to him, "Caesar's men demand taxes from us." He said to them, "Give Caesar what belongs to Caesar, give God what belongs to God,
> 100.b and give me what is mine."

101.a Whoever does not hate his father and his mother

> 101.b in my way

101.c cannot become a disciple to me. And whoever does not love his father and his mother in my way cannot become a disciple to me. For my mother [...], but my true Mother gave me Aeonic Life.

COMMENTARY

Logia #99-#101 are all authentic *davarim* that have been redacted in various ways, again probably from the New Testament Gospels. Many of the logia in the last section of *Thomas*

---

[571] *The Didache (Teaching) of the Twelve Apostles*, late first century document that was part of the earliest New Testament canons but later excluded: "Let grace come, and let this world pass away. Hosanna to the God (Son) of David! If anyone is holy, let him come; if anyone is not so, let him repent. *Maranatha. Amen.*"

seem to have adaped from the Christian Gospels in the first Greek composition of this Gnostic Gospel. Thus many of them are not part of the original Aramaic kernel *davarim*.

Logion 99 was constructed by joining two previously unconnected sayings of *Yeshua*. Since there is no specific Gnostic alteration I have presented it separately as I do with other authentic *davarim*. However, Logia #100 and #101 have been redacted to reflect Gnostic interpretation in various degrees, so I present them together but unscramble the Gnostic phrases from those that are authentic.

Logion 101.a appears first in Marcan (Petrine) tradition, then is repeated in Matthew and Luke.[572] It is the well-known "render unto Caesar" story in which *Yeshua* was challenged by Pharisees and Herodian opponents to make a rabbinic ruling on the controversy of paying taxes to the Romans. How did he interpret the guidance of scripture regarding the issue?

This was a trap. He was opposed to the Roman occupation, as were the people watching. But if he made a ruling against paying taxes, he would be accused of publicly advocating treachery and rebellion, as did the zealots, and the Herodians would have an excuse to arrest him. But if he ruled the other way, he would oppose his own conscience and lose the respect of his hearers.

Tiberian Silver Denarius

He told his opponents to produce a Roman coin, since it would have been blasphemous to pay Roman taxes with a Jewish coin. Here is a photo of the coin they produced. It was a *denarius* worth about $20 in current U.S. currency. This event occurred during the reign of Tiberius, whose image was engraved upon one side. The inscription read, *"Ti[berivs] Caesar Divi Avg[vsti] F[ilivs] Avgvstvs"* or "Caesar Augustus Tiberius, son of the Divine Augustus." This would have been blasphemous to *Yeshua* and his hearers as it claimed that Augustus Caesar was divine.

Yeshua held up the coin and asked, "Whose image is inscribed on this coin?" The opponents answered, "Caesar's image." He then made a rabbibical ruling that was really a non-ruling. "Render unto Caesar the things that belong to Caesar, and to God the things that belong to God."

His opponents were trumped. This could not be interpreted in a court of law as advocacy of tax resistance, but neither could it be understood by his Jewish hearers as a ruling in favor of paying Roman taxes. The interpretation of his ruling was thrown back upon the hearers and hinged upon their understanding of what belonged to Caesar and what belonged to God. If one understood that "the Earth is the LORD's, and the fullness thereof," as the Psalm

---

[572] Mark 12.17, Matthew 22.21, Luke 20.25

taught, then one could justify tax resistance. But that was an individual matter. *Yeshua's* clever non-ruling could not be prosecuted, nor could it be interpreted as capitulation to the Romans.

The *Gospel of Thomas* presents a radically altered version of the story. It does imply a vestigial setting by saying, "They showed Jesus a gold coin," but doesn't identify "they." The coin described as gold was not a Roman *denarius,* which was silver. A golden quinarius of the time would have been worth far more. No one would have been carrying one in a purse to show to *Yeshua* any more than we would carry a $500 bill in a pocket. In other words, there is no historical setting or *sitz im leben* associated with Logion 100. Rather, it is understood simply as a saying or Greek *logion.* The Gnostic conclusion is added, "and give to me [Jesus] what is mine." This parallelism to "what belongs to God" inserts into the saying a concept of Jesus as self-proclaimed divine Redeemer, not unlike the redactions in John's Gospel.

Was this saying part of the original Aramaic dictation? Probably so. It is transmitted like a *davar* rather than a pericope with setting, an abbreviation resulting from mnemonic oral transmission. The Aramaic genitive "give to God what is to God" may underly the Coptic "give to God of God's" with consecutive genitive ‏נ‎-, as in Hebrew-Aramaic consecutive genitive ‏ל‎-. The change in the narrative from silver to gold coin may reflect an Aramaic-speaking Galilean disciple's lack of familiarity with Roman coinage. What is more, the entire point of the pericope has been lost, which would not have occurred if the saying were taken from a Gospel narrative.

Logion 101 appears to be another orally transmitted *davar* that has been severely redacted to make sense to a Gnostic. The underlying *davar,* which is preserved in Luke and Matthew in differently redacted forms taken from Q, is probably most authentically given in Luke 14.26: "If any man come to me, and hate not his father, and mother, and wife, and children, and brethren, and sisters, yea, and his own life also, he cannot be my disciple." This means that true disciples must love God more than any human or temporal attachments. It seems the most authentic extant version to me because it employs the characteristic hyperbole known in rabbinic sources from the period, and that characterizes several other sayings of *Yeshua.*[573] Biblical literalist might take it as an injunction to hate their parents (!), but

---

[573] For example, "It is more difficult for a rich man to attain to the *Malkuth* than for a camel to go through the eye of a needle." (Mark 10.25, Matthew 19.24, Luke 18.25) People have tried to explain this hyperbole (gross exaggeration) in many ways: 1. There was an entrance to a city through a narrow gate called the needle, where camels had to be unpacked to pass. But such a place never existed; 2. Aramaic *gamel* can also mean a camel-hair rope (Lamsa), so the story was told wrong and should have said "rope" through the eye of a needle. But in fact, *Yeshua* employed the camel hyperbole elsewhere: "Strain at gnats and swallow camels." Also, we find similar hyperbole about huge animals passing through the eye of a needle in rabbic stories from the contemporary Babylonian Talmud: "an elephant going through the eye of a needle" (Babylonian Talmud, *Berakoth,* 55b); "who can make an elephant pass through the eye of a needle?" Only God, concludes

rather it is a semitic way to emphasize the vital importance of *hesed* or covenantal love for God's justice, compassion, and all the other divine attributes above all earthly attachments.

The writers of Matthew were troubled by the hyperbolism of the *davar*, which they were afraid their readers would not understand, and so paraphrased it, "Anyone who loves his father or mother more than me is not worthy of me; anyone who loves his son or daughter more than me is not worthy of me."[574] This rendering assumes a developed gentile church tradition centered upon worshipping and loving the Christian divine Jesus .This attitude is associated with Christian worthiness. So it is a later interpretation than is found in Luke's version of what must have been a *logion* from the original Q material shared by both Gospels.

Now we come to the even later redaction done by the writer of the *Gospel of Thomas* that reads, "Whoever does not hate his father and his mother in my way cannot become a disciple to me." This seems to derive from the original Aramaic dictation, "Whoever does not hate his father and his mother cannot become a disciple to me," with the insertion of "in my way" for clarification—Christians knew that Jesus loved and honored his parents. The Coptic ⲚⲀⳘ "to me" for genitive "my disciple" reflects the original Aramaic genitival idiom ‏לִי‎ "to me."

But for further clarification the redactor adds, "And whoever does not love his father and his mother in my way cannot become a disciple to me." This was not part of the original hyperbolic *davar*. Pricked by his Gnostic conscience, the redactor adds the part about the true Mother and Father being God, "For my mother [...], but my true Mother gave me Aeonic ("Eternal") Life." Filling in the lacuna, it probably said something like, "For my [human] mother gave me birth in flesh, but my true Mother gave me the Life [of the Aeon]."

That part of the *logion*, too, has its roots in a saying of *Yeshua*. "Call no man your *ab* (father)upon the earth, for you have only one *Abba*(Father-Mother), who is in heaven."[575] This appears only in Matthew's special material. In *Thomas,* however, the reference is to receiving true Life from God as Mother. Since the original *davar* is redacted quite differently in Matthew than in Luke, which is much closer to the *Thomas* version, yet

---

the *Rav* (Babylonian Talmud, *Baba Mezi'a*, 38b). Here also *Yeshua* continues his *davar*, "But with God, all things are possible." See Jonathan Went's excellent analyses at
http://www.biblicalhebrew.com/nt/camelneedle.htm#1 where he observes, "The camel was the largest animal seen regularly in Israel, whereas in regions where the Babylonian Talmud was written, the elephant was the biggest animal. Thus the aphorism is culturally translated from a camel to an elephant in regions outside of Israel." To this I would add that *Yeshua's* messianic Son-of-Man concepts were all rooted in Babylonian Judaism—not Palestinian. These parallel hyperbolisms all occur in the Babylonian Talmud. For reasons like these, in my novel *Yeshua: The Unknown Jesus* I place *Yeshua* in the Jewish community of Babylon for his "lost years."
[574] Matthew 10.37
[575] Matthew 23.9

the final phrase of Logion 101 has its only rough parallel in Matthew, it seem logical that like Logion 100, this was also material from the original Aramaic dictation that has been heavily redacted, rather than having been derived from two separate canonical Gospels.

CHAPTER TWELVE: Logia 102-114

Logion 102

Woe to the Pharisees, for they are like a dog sleeping in a cattle manger, for neither does he eat nor does he let the cattle eat.

COMMENTARY

There are no parallels to this saying in the New Testament or other sources. However it exhibits authentic Semitisms. The "for...for" from Greek *hoti...hoti* reflects Aramaic *gi...gi* (from Hebrew *chi...chi*). "Woe" is an Hebrew-Aramaic loan word transliterated into Greek and from Greek into Coptic ογοει.

Aesop's fable about the dog who lay in a manger[576] and would not allow the cattle to eat was proverbial throughout the Hellenized world and may have been known to *Yeshua.* But this *davar* does not run parallel to Aesop's fable, where the dog lay upon the hay that he could not eat, but ferociously kept the cattle from eating it. The moral given was, "People often begrudge others what they themselves cannot have."

However, the scenario in which a mean dog lay on hay fodder and growled when cattle tried to eat would have been well known to *Yeshua's* Palestinian hearers. Dogs roamed village streets scavenging food and were often a nuisance. The situation in Logion 102 is consistent with other familiar themes and motifs *Yeshua* draws upon for his *mashlim.* The reason Aesop wrote his fable about the dog in the manger five-hundred years earlier in Greece is that it was so common in any village.

Yeshua's Pharisaic Opponents

The Pharisees, though only a small sect, controlled most of the synagogues in Palestine and the Galilee. A Pharisee often served as *Chazzan*[577] or Ruler of a Synagogue—a precursor to what later developed as the office of ordained Rabbi. He had trained and studied with other *Ravs* and scriptural experts, or worked as a scribe and learned scripture by copying and discussing it. He was often acknowledged as an expert in the knowledge and interpretation of *Torah* or the five books of the Law. He might be consulted for rulings on situations and issues not covered by literal biblical law. These ruling would be based on allegorical and

---

[576] Barn or enclosed area where domestic animals slept and grazed on harvested hays and grains.
[577] In modern Judaism the *Chazzan* is the Cantor.

typological extensions of existing scriptural law. The entire body of these traditions was transmitted through lineages of proto-rabbinical schools, such as that of Gamaliel with whom Paul (Saul) had studied, or Hillel and Shammai.

But Pharisaic tradition had developed as the heart and soul of pious Judaism ever since the strict reformers Ezra and Nehemiah returned in the fifth century B.C.E. with colonizers from Babylonian exile. The institution of the synagogue had become the center of village Jewish life, with occasional Passover pilgrimages to the Temple in Jerusalem. Pharisaism had produced the wisdom schools, apocalyptic scriptures, and "remnant"[578] desert communities like the Essenes, the Zodokites, and the Damascus community.

In both Babylon and Palestine, Pharisaism had been the source of messianic and kabbalistic interpretation, *halakah*, and *haggadah*. It also lay at the root of Galilean zealotism, but after zealot uprisings had resulted in extermination of whole villages, such as Sepphoris which Herod rebuilt as his Roman capital city, Pharisees generally rejected zealotism and all other messianic movements.

The Pharisees accepted not only the *Torah*, but the Books of the Prophets and those called the Writings (Psalms, Proverbs, wisdom books) as inspired scripture. Pharisaism was the religious matrix in which *Yeshua* had been raised. But from Jerusalem, where they shared Sanhedrin power with the Sadduccean Temple elite, the Pharisees tried to rule conforming synagogues with their school traditions. These "traditions of men," which *Yeshua* disdained and contrasted with the "laws of God," constituted the core of Pharisaic religion that *Yeshua* opposed.

The Jerusalem Pharisaic leadership and the Sadducean Temple establishment collaborated with the Herodians[579] against John the Baptist and *Yeshua* because they feared the social and economic disruption of Jewish messianic movements. Most specifically, the guerilla warfare waged against Roman occupiers by zealot *sicarii* (assassins) and paramilitary groups had brought swift and vicious reprisal that most people wanted to avoid. The Jerusalem establishment was content to live at peace with the Roman occupiers because arrangements for mutual benefit enriched them and ensured their safety. Consequently Pharisaic interpretations of *Torah* had become increasingly void of justice and lost sight of the basic divine principles demanded by the prophets. This was one of the issues that *Yeshua* targeted in his attacks on the Jerusalem Pharisees.

---

[578] The "remnant" was a small group of faithful or observant Jews that God would use to rebuild Israel in the messianic Age, according to prophecy.

[579] Jewish Roman citizens loyal to Herod and committed to Hellenistic rather than traditional Jewish culture and values. Paul was a Jewish Roman citizen, a Pharisee, and perhaps could have been identified as an Herodian. His mission to deliver legal documents for the arrest and imprisonment of messianic Jews in Damascus would have allied him with Herodians, as would his tacit participation in the stoning of Stephen.

The other issue was Pharisaic self-righteousness. The New Testament term is "hypocrisy," but there was no word for that in Aramaic. *Hypokritos* was a term from Greek theater meaning "play actor, pretender." But there was no tradition of theater among the Jews. The Greek word for hypocrite translated the Aramaic phrase *nasa beaph* "take nose," which meant to turn up the nose, or look down the nose, at some one.

The thing *Yeshua* disliked most about Pharisaic piety was its disdainful self-righteousness. Pharisaic tradition required all kinds of peripheral ceremonial and ritual observances, but abandoned the primary principles of justice and compassion. The wealthy Pharisees of Jerusalem esteemed themselves as true children of God and Abraham, but regarded the non-observant Jews and villagers of the Galilee to be little better than heathen. The Pharisees were saints, all other were sinners.

There are as many "woes" declared by *Yeshua* against the Pharisees as there are beatitudes in the New Testament Gospels. Logion 102 declares woe upon them because they are like a dog in a manger who lies upon fodder he cannot eat, but refuses to allow the cattle to even approach it.

By the hay or fodder, *Yeshua* refers to the spiritual food of messianic and kabbalistic scriptural interpretation that had been developed in the Pharisaic wisdom schools, but was withheld from synagogue and public study. This was based on the scripture that I have called the Bible of *Yeshua* and his messianic communities of disciples: the Enochian books, Daniel, Deutero- and Trito-Isaiah, the kabbalistic study of Genesis, the messianic study of the Prophets and Writings, the *Testaments of the Twelve Patriarchs, Odes of Solomon,* and a host of other writings that form what is today known as the Apocrypha and Pseudepigrapha of the Old Testament. These were the sources for understanding the messianic *Basor* proclaimed by John and *Yeshua,* but opposed by the Pharisees.

Instead of teaching the great and weighty principles of the Prophets, who fulminated against the ritualistic Temple religion of their days that was devoid of justice and vision, the Pharisees nit-picked ritual *mitzvoth.* They established rabbinic rulings such as the *Qurban,* which allowed wealthy children to avoid supporting their aged parents by ritually donating their wealth to the Temple, while actually retaining control of it.

So the fodder that was withheld from the cattle in the manger also refers to suppression of the essential teachings of justice and compassion that were emphasized by the Prophets. They were not only suppressed, but neglected and misunderstood by the religious establishment.

The comparable *davar* known from the special Lucan material at Luke 11.52 reads: "Woe unto you, Torah experts! For you have taken away the key[580] of knowledge *(gnosis = manda)*. You did not attain to it yourselves, and you hindered those who were attaining it."

Logion 103

Blessed is the man who knows where the thieves will enter, so that he may get up, gather defenders for his domain, and put on his armor before they invade.

COMMENTARY

This is a corollary to Logion 21, where my Commentary discusses the halakik practice of defense from *elilim* or obsessing entities and the evil *yetzer*. Here, however, the issue is not when they will invade, but where. In other words, the disciple who has carried out self-examination through *shaqad* and other forms of vigilance has seen and understood his weaknesses. They are "where" the invaders will try to enter.

We find two parallel sayings from the New Testament. The first was sourced from Q and refers to when, like Logion 21: "If the master of the house had known in what part of the night the thief was coming, he would have stayed awake and would not have let his house be broken into."[581]

The second is Marcan and refers to where, i.e., character flaws that constitute weaknesses that will be exploited by dark forces: "If thy hand offend thee, cut it off. It is better for thee to enter into life maimed, than having two hands to go into Purgatory, into the relentless fire...and if thy foot offend thee, cut it off. It is better for thee to enter lame into life than having two feet to be cast into Purgatory... and if thine eye offend thee, pluck it out. It is better for thee to enter into the Sovereignty of God with one eye, than having two eyes to be cast into Purgatory, where their worm[582] dieth not and the fire is relentless."[583]

---

[580] A kabbalistic term for the root allegorical or typological metaphor used in interpretation. This would not include numerical methods like *notaricon* or *gemmatria*.

[581] Matthew 24:43, Luke 12:39

[582] Isaiah 66:23-24, "And they shall go forth, and look upon the carcasses of the men that have transgressed against me: for their worm shall not die, neither shall their fire be quenched; and they shall be an abhorring unto all flesh." Greek *skolex* from Hebrew-Aramaic *tola*, root *tala*, designating a worm that self-generates from putrifying organic matter. It was associated with the color scarlet because this kind of worm produces a dye that can be obtained for royal garments and use with blue and purple in the Temple sanctuary. But in Hebrew usage the worm was the lowest and most unclean form of life, as in Psalm 21: "But I am a worm, and no man; the reproach of men, and the outcast of the people. All they who saw me have laughed me to scorn." The idiomatic phrase "their worm dieth not" means the scorn that Heaven and Earth have for their acts of wickedness will never change, as in Isaiah 66.24.

[583] Mark 9.43-47, repeated in Matthew chapters 5 and 18

Hands, feet, and eyes represent openings for forces of the *yetzer ha-ra.* Hands represent powers and actions, feet represent places one choses to go, and eyes represent the source of good and evil light, as explained in earlier comments on the evil eye and the Hellenistic theory of vision.

Logion 103 tells us that the person who knows his weaknesses is blessed because he can be prepared when they provide openings for tests against his soul. But the weaknesses must be addressed and repaired. In the hyperbole of *Yeshua's davar,* "If thy right eye causes offence, pluck it out!"

Logion 104 [Gnostic *logion*]

> They said to Jesus, "Come, let us pray today and let us fast."
> Jesus said, "What is the sin that I have committed, or wherein have I been overcome [by evil]? But when the Bridegroom leaves the Bride Chamber, then let them fast and pray."

COMMENTARY

We come to a section of Gnostic redactions from Christian Gospels as well as Gnostic compositions with no basis in Christian sayings. These may have been originally composed in Coptic—not translated from Greek—even though some Greek loan words appear, as they do in all Coptic. These are Logia 104, 105, 107, 108, 109, 110, 111, and 114. If so, they may have been composed or redacted in late second- or third-century Egypt and added to the manuscript.

Logion 104 is a Gnostic composition based on Mark 2.18-20, but with no understanding of its meaning. The first phrase supports the Gnostic idea that Jesus, unlike the disciples, was sinless and had no need for prayer and fasting. Yet we know that *Yeshua* resorted to prayer and fasting in his forty-day fast ("Temptation") in the Judean desert and the many other times he withdrew, and also as revealed in his advice to disciples on difficult exorcisms: "This kind [of demon] can be exorcized only by prayer and fasting."[584] Logion 14 also seems to denounce fasting, but it represents extreme hyperbole. Clearly the Thomasian ascetics were not only unmarried, sexually abstinent, and isolated from family and society, but as monks practiced prayer and fasting.

In contrast, *Yeshua* was often challenged for laxity in discipline. He was accused of being a "winebibber and a glutton." He responded to such accusations with rhetorical questions about new wine and old wine skeins, new unshrunk patches on old garments, and here in Logion 104, the example from Jewish nuptial customs

---

[584] Mark 9.29, Matthew 17.21

In the Marcan pericope, which is embellished in the versions redacted in Matthew and Luke, the Pharisees ask, "'Why do the disciples of John and of the Pharisees fast, but your disciples do not fast?' Jesus answered them, 'Can the sons of the bride chamber fast while the bride groom is with them? As long as they have the bride groom with them, they cannot fast. But the days will come, when the bride groom shall be taken away from them, and then shall they fast in those days.'"

In traditional Jewish nuptial ceremonies of *Yeshua's* era, the bride groom came in procession with the "sons of the bride chamber" or groomsmen at night to kidnap the bride. The procession followed them to the bride chamber, or room where the marriage would be consummated. When the bride groom reappeared to exhibit the bloody sheets as proof of the Bride's virginity, the revelry and the marriage feast began—sometimes lasting a full week. No fasting was involved, and to fast would have been a deliberate insult to the families.

The Original Bridechamber *Davar* and the Messianic Self-Consciousness of *Yeshua*

In the original *davar, Yeshua* compares himself to a bride groom and his disciples to groomsmen. In John's Gospel the writers present John the Baptist as the chief groomsman or best man ("friend of the brideroom") and Jesus as the bride groom, meaning the *Messiah*, because "He that has the bride is the bride groom."[585] This appears immediately following the section about Nicodemus and initiatic rebirth, so the context is that of Jewish mysticism.

In rabbinical *haggadah,* the theme of the Marriage of *Messiah* was derived from such scripture as Psalm 45, a love song for the wedding of the king's son. In Pauline Christianity the Church was the Bride, but in *Yeshua's davar* the disciples (prototype of the Church) are the groomsmen, not the Bride. The Church as bride of Christ was a later Christian idea. But who was the bride of *Messiah* in Jewish thought?

First, let us note that *Yeshua* compared himself to a bride groom in the Marcan *davar* as an answer to why his disciples didn't fast. He compared his presence with the disciples on Earth to the celebration and feasting of bride groom, groomsmen, and all who had been invited to a marriage feast, when it would be inappropriate to fast. This occurred after the consummation of the bride chamber. In other words, the bride groom was now a newly married man and the order of the day was feasting and celebration.

According to Hosea 2:19-20, a scripture used in messianic speculation and known to *Yeshua*, the Bride of God was Israel. By the same token, the Bride of *Messiah* seems to have been a reformed and purified remnant of Israel for the Essenes of Qumran. In the Great Isaiah Scroll from Qumran, Isaiah 61.4-5, we read: "You shall no more be termed

---

585 John 2.29

abandoned; neither shall your land any more be termed Desolate: because you shall be called *Hephzibah, my desire is in her,* and your land *Beulah, married,* because YHWH desires you, and your land shall be married. Because as a chosen youth marries a virgin, your sons will marry you; and as the bride groom rejoices over the bride, your God will rejoice over you."

In other words, the bride of *Messiah* would be a faithful remnant of Israel. This is the rabbinic basis of Paul's idea of the Church as the Bride of Christ. Later gentile Christianity would consider themselves to be the true remnant of Israel, but would considered the messianic Jews or Jewish Christians to be "Judaizers" who, like the non-messianic Jews, had no part in the New Israel.

Second, let us realize that *Yeshua's* instructed his inner circle of disciples in the context of a sacred meal developed from the Friday *Shabbat seder.* He also offered teachings during meals in host homes on other nights of the week. But his *Shabbat seder* was messianic. He offered the cup of blessing and broke bread, they all ate and asked him questions about the *Malkuth* and the *Bar-Enash*, then he led them in spiritual song and ended the meal with the final cup of blessing. This messianic *seder* was a mystical participation on Earth and in flesh of the great Marriage Banquet of *Messiah* in the coming *Malkuth.* It was a communion with Heaven and the Living Ones—the Marriage Banquet of Heaven. It was this meal, and not the legendary "last supper," that provided the basis for the Christian *Agape* that Paul transformed into a mystery religion sacrament.[586] See Appendix Two.

After his crucifixion, *Yeshua* continued to make himself known in the messianic meal. We are told in Luke's Gospel that his Uncle Cleopas and another disciple met a stranger on the road from Jerusalem to Emmaus after the crucifixion. He walked with them expounding messianic scripture, then sat with them for supper. During the meal he blessed and broke bread and suddenly they recognized the stranger as *Yeshua,* who then disappeared. But he was recognized by them "in the breaking of the bread."[587]

At this point the resurrected *Yeshua* personified the *Bar-Enash* or Son-of-Man *Messiah* to his disciples. But before the resurrection appearances he was considered to be a teacher, prophet, and messenger of the Son of Man. He was not worshipped as an aspect of Godhead, nor did he consider himself to be God.

---

[586] I Corinthians 20-29: "When ye come together therefore into one place, this is not the proper way to eat the Lord's Supper. For in eating every one taketh before other his own supper: and one is hungry, and another is drunken...For I have received of the Lord that which also I delivered unto you, that the Lord Jesus the same night in which he was handed over took bread: And when he had given thanks, he brake it, and said, Take, eat: this is my body, which is broken for you: this do in remembrance of me. After the same manner also he took the cup, when he had supped, saying, this cup is the new testament in my blood: this do ye, as oft as ye drink it, in remembrance of me. For as often as ye eat this bread, and drink this cup, ye do shew the Lord's death till he come...."
[587] Luke 24.35

But *Yeshua's davar* about groom and bride chamber give us a glimpse into his messianic self-consciousness, for in it he presents himself in the role of groom and his disciples as groomsmen. The reason they don't fast is that they are celebrating his Marriage Feast. Whom has he married?

This indicates that *Yeshua* had achieved a unique spiritual status. He was the first son of Adam to have become one with the archetypal heavenly *Bar-Enash.* He was the spiritually first-born[588] of the New Adam, and thus the messenger, teacher, and initiator for those who would follow him in spiritual regeneration. The Greek Johannine term *monogenes huios,* which has been interpreted as "only begotten Son" of god, also means "first-begotten, especially beloved son." This Greek term translated Hebrew usages like Psalm 22.20, "deliver my soul from the sword, my "darling" [*yechid,* highest aspect of the femininine soul or *yechidah,* translated into Greek *monogenes*] from the power of the dog." In late Hellenistic times *yechid* was a kabbalistic term for the highest and masculine aspect of the soul. The earliest Jewish Christians considered *Yeshua* to be not only a son of God (i.e., a *tzadik*), but the greatest of the *tzadikim,* thus the *Yechid* of the *Bar-Enash.*

There can be no doubt that this was part of *Yeshua's* messianic self-consciousness. He personified the incarnate Son of Man in his ministry. He shared divine Sovereignty with the *Bar-Enash.* His Son-of-Man sayings were originally *davarim* or sermons about the coming of *Bar-Enash,* as we find them in John's Gospel. But they also referred at times to his own self-consciousness, as for example in the Q saying transmitted independently in *Thomas* Logion 86, "The foxes have their holes and the birds have their nests, but the *Bar-Enash* [in His incarnation through *Yeshua*] has no place on Earth to lay his head and rest." This saying reminded his disciples that they, too, as members of the *Bar-Enash,* will find that they must "become passersby," for the world is not yet prepared to receive the emissaries and exemplars of the Coming One. They must live the paradox that while the Earth is to become the home of the New Humanity, it will be won only through great spiritual struggle and sacrifice. Until then, their only true home will be in Heaven.

The original bride chamber *davar*[589] reveals something of *Yeshua's* messianic self-consciousness. But he did not consider his Messiahship to continue in perpetuity as

---

[588] Greek *monogenes*

[589] This saying may underlie Matthew's Parable of the Ten Virgins, which was clearly not an authentic *mashal* of *Yeshua.* Here, however, disciples are compared to "virgins" (meaning young unmarried women) in a midnight procession. They would have followed bride and groom to the bride chamber, but the parable indicates that the virgins are supposed to be admitted to the place where the groom is. That would have been quite a party, since bride and groom were supposed to be secluded in the bride chamber! Clearly Matthew's parable knows nothing of Jewish wedding customs, but instead confuses the midnight procession with that of a Greek mystery religion and apparently the bride with the ten virgins! But in the context of the later Sacrament of the Bride Chamber known through the Gnostic *Gospel of Philip,* the Parable of the Ten Virgins may have represented the Pauline "mystery" of the marriage of Christ and his Church after which the Gnostic sacrament was designed.

something unique to only him. His work was to facilitate the spiritual rebirth of other souls so that they would become members of the Messianic Body and would eventually participate in the Sovereignty (*Malkuth,* wrongly "Kingdom") of Godhead on Earth.

With this understanding we have an answer to our question, Whom had *Yeshua* married? For what bride was he the groom? In kabbalistic mysticism, the highest union that a human being could aspire to achieve with Godhead was that of *Yechid* (one's root sonship as an emanation of Godhead) and *Yechidah* (the highest aspect of the human soul). The marriage of *Yechid* and *Yechidah* was a union of Godhead and a human soul.[590] *Yeshua* was considered by his disciples to be one whose feminine soul had been made perfect *(shalem)* by virtue of his interior union (cf. Logion 22), and thus to have accomplished this.

But as masculine *Yechid* (Greek *Monogenes*) of the Son-of-Man *Messiah, Yeshua* was also bride groom to the *Yechidah* or highest aspect of the soul of the New Humanity. As first-born of the New Humanity, he stood in the position of Groom to the souls of the New Humanity as they became worthy to be joined to the Sovereignty. He probably saw himself in a light not unlike that of a Hindu *guru,* through whom illumination and initiation into immortality could come. But *Yeshua's* status in the eyes of his disciples after the resurrection event became identical with Godhead. "If you have seen me, you have seen the *Abba.*"[591]

The Marcan pericope adds the following conclusion to the saying about *Yeshua* as messianic bride groom: "But the days will come, when the bride groom shall be taken away from them, and then shall they fast in those days." If this saying is historical, rather than a later Christian extension, it implies that *Yeshua* was aware that he would eventually be executed. Good arguments could be made for either possibility.

The Bridegroom in Logion *Thomas* 104

Logion 104 is ignorant of Jewish nuptial customs. In it Jesus says, "When the Bridegroom leaves the Bride Chamber, then let them fast and pray." That has no more basis in Jewish custom than Matthew's Parable of the Ten Virgins. It is inauthentic.

Then to what Bride Chamber does the Logion refer? Probably the Gnostic Sacrament of the Bride Chamber. For details see my Commentary on Logion 2 in the section on *Malkuth* as well as the Commentary on Logion 22. Here Logion 104 seems to indicate that after the

---

[590] That was the metaphorical meaning of the Wise Fisherman choosing one large fish and eating it in Logion 8.

[591] John 14.9. Scholars doubt that this was an authentic saying of *Yeshua.* It follows a long train of Johannine doctrine in the Gospel beginning with "No man hath seen God at any time, but the *monogenes* Son, who is in the Heart of the Father, he hath declared him (1.18)," continuing through statements like "Not that any man hath seen the Father, save he which is of God, he hath seen the Father (6.46)," leading up to, "I and my Father are one (10.30)." These are quite antithetical to the authentic teachings of *Yeshua* in Q and the Synoptics.

Gnostic Sacrament of the Bridal Chamber[592] was complete, the initiate was expected to pray and fast.

But in the *Gospel of Philip,* the Father unites with the Bride, derived from Jewish kabbalistic *Matronit,* who is an aspect of *Hochmah* and *Shekinah.* She descended upon the crucified Jesus and her Light illuminated and led him to the Bridal Chamber. His Resurrection Body was born in the Bridal Chamber.

The writer of *Philip* says in Logion 82, "Since it is allowed to me to reveal this mystery, I say: the Father of everything united (in the Bridal Chamber) with the Bride Who afterwards came down (to crucified Jesus), and the Light illuminated Him then. And He (leaving that place) came to the Great Bridal Chamber. Therefore, His body, which

Nuns in Bridal Gowns for their Marriage to Christ

appeared in next days, came out from the Bridal Chamber. This body was similar to a body born from a unity of husband and wife (i.e. similar to a normally born body). Jesus made in it (in His new body) everything similar to the image (of a usual body).[593]

"It is necessary that each disciple enter the Chamber of the Father."[594]This was the ritual in which each Gnostic monk became a Bride of the Father, thus made a vow of celibacy and was "married" to God.

This would have been comparable to the final commitment of a Catholic nun to celibacy when she becomes a "Bride of Christ." This Gnostic idea underlies the modern practice.

If *Thomas* Logion 104 is based on some version of the Gnostic understanding of the Bride Chamber, it would consider the Father to be the Groom—not Jesus, who is a "child" of the Bridal Chamber. When the Father leaves the Bridal Chamber at the conclusion of the sacrament, then the disciples would fast.

Another possibility is simply that the Gnostic redactor of *Thomas* has simply conflated the original *davar* of *Yeshua* with Marks's conclusion, "But the days will come, when the bride

---

[592] Although the Sacrament was merely an initiation into the greater divine reality understood as the Bridal Chamber.

[593] Translated by Anton Teplyy and Dr.Mikhail Nikolenko © Antonov V.V., 2002 http://teachings-of-jesus-christ.org/gospel-of-philip.shtml

[594] The *logion* in Philip ends with the comment that each disciple must enter the Chamber of the Father, i.e. the Bridal Chamber. This seems to have been rooted in Matthew's Parable of the Ten Virgins.

groom shall be taken away from them, and then shall they fast in those days." Thus it reads, "But when the Bridegroom leaves the Bride Chamber, then let them fast and pray."

Logion 105 [Gnostic *logion*]

> He who knows the Father and the Mother [i.e. Jesus] will be called the son of a harlot.

COMMENTARY

We don't know of any accusations that *Yeshua* was the son of a whore from New Testament sources. But they were made later in the first century by Jewish opponents of Christianity and have been preserved in the Talmudic literature, which was contemporary with second-century Gnosticism.

"Jesus was a bastard born of adultery." (Yebamoth 49b, p.324). "Mary was a whore: Jesus (Balaam) was an evil man." (Sanhedrin 106a &b, p.725). "Jesus was a magician and a fool. Mary was an adulteress". (Shabbath 104b, p.504).

This famous piece of ancient graffiti depicting a crucified ass is from approximately 30 years after *Yeshua's* crucifixion, found scratched in the wall of a Roman barracks in the *Pædagogioum* near to Nero's Golden House on Palatine Hill in Rome. The text says, 'Alexamenos worships god'.

The accusations against Jesus were made after he was crucified—not before. Thus Logion 105 must have originated after that time and could not have been a *davar* of *Yeshua*. In this Gnostic saying, "he" is Jesus who "knows the Father and the Mother." These were attributions of Godhead that meant something quite different in Gnostic theodicy than in the original Jewish kabbalistic interpretation.

Yeshua was called *ben Pantera,* the bastard son of a Roman soldier named Pantherus. His mother *Miriam* was called a hairdresser and a harlot. A great many of the allusions to *Yeshua* in the *Mishna* and early Talmudic literature were edited to make them unrecognizable to the Christians who confiscated Jewish books, or else they were simply removed to protect the Jewish community. We know about them from many sources and some of them remain. Among other things, the Talmudic literature tells us that Messianic Jews survived separate from gentile Christianity for several centuries, and that they were allied with Pharisaism.[595]

Logion 106

---

[595] For more information see *Jesus in the Talmud* by Peter Schafer, http://www.amazon.com/Jesus-Talmud-Peter-Schafer/dp/0691129266

When you make the two one, you will become the *Bar-Enash*, and when you say, "Mountain, move away," it will move away.

COMMENTARY

Most of the Commentary on Logion 22 applies to this authentic *davar*. When the disciples, who are spiritual newly-borns, achieve the goals of *Yeshua's Halakah* and become *shalem* or spiritually perfected, they will become one with the *Bar-Enash*. Another metaphor would be brides of *Messiah*, since each *Yechidah* would be married to the *Yechid* of the New Adam.

Once that is achieved, they will participate as heirs in the Sovereignty or *Malkuth* of God. Then they will rule with Godhead and rightly exercise divine power as represented by the kabbalistic phrase conventionally used to represent the power of prophets and sons of God, "You will say, 'Mountain, move!' And the mountain will move."[596]

Logion 107 [Gnostic Redaction]

> The Sovereignty is like a shepherd who had a hundred sheep. One of them, the largest, went astray. He left the ninety-nine sheep and sought after the one until he found it. After all this trouble, he said to the one sheep, "I am more pleased with you than the ninety-nine."

COMMENTARY

There is no way to tell whether Logion 107 was redacted from the Q Parable of the Lost Sheep of Matthew and Luke or from an independent version of the saying. In any case, as it stands it is Gnostic.

The original *mashal* reads in the Matthean version, "What do you think? If a shepherd has a hundred sheep, and one of them has gone astray, does he not leave the ninety-nine on the mountains and go in search of the one that went astray? And if he finds it, truly I tell you, he rejoices over it more than over the ninety-nine that never went astray."[597] It conveys the same information in the longer and more elaborated Lucan version, who adds that "I say unto you, that likewise joy shall be in heaven over one sinner that repenteth, more than over ninety and nine just persons, which need no repentance."

In both cases, the message is that *Yeshua* as God's shepherd of Israel seeks out the lost sheep of Israel. It is an answer to the same question posed by the observant Pharisees, who

---

[596] Used by *Yeshua* to illustrate the power of *emunah*, faithfulness or fidelity to God's ways, but incorrectly applied in Gospel redaction to the power of *pistis* "faith" or credal belief.
[597] Matthew 18:12

questioned his attention to the non-observant *amme-ha-eretz*. He answered, "Those who are well have no need of a physician, but those who are sick."[598]

But Logion 107 has been redacted to tease out a message that is quite the opposite. It specifies that the sheep who strays is the largest one. It is written to indicate that the shepherd loves the one biggest sheep more than all the others, and will abandon the others and go to much trouble (Coptic hice) to seek him out. The shepherd doesn't rejoice because he has found a lost sheep, but says to the sheep, "I am more pleased with you than the ninety-nine."

Just as the Pharisees believed that God preferred the small number of observant Jews to the many non-observant, the Gnostics believed that Heaven loved their "one out of a thousand"[599] and cared not for the non-monastic majority of society.

Logion 108 [Gnostic *Logion*]

> Whoever drinks from my mouth will become like me. I myself shall be born within him, and the things that are hidden will be revealed to him.

COMMENTARY

This beautiful Gnostic *logion* is based on the same ideas that produced Logia 1 and 13. There is not a Hebrew idiom for "drink from my mouth," although there are many idioms relating eating to learning. This has has close relation to Logion 13, "I am not your teacher because you have drunk deeply from the bubbling fountainhead which I have poured out, and you have become divinely intoxicated."

The idea of Christ coming to birth within a disciple as a development of *Yeshua's* original teachings on the rebirth from above is a Gnostic interpretation of Pauline thought. "I am again in the pains of childbirth until Christ is formed in you[600] ... this mystery, which is Christ in [or among] you [plural], the hope of glory[601] ... we have the mind (*nous*, divine mind) of Christ."[602] *Yeshua's* teaching was about spiritual regeneration in the *Bar-Enash* or New Adam. Paul's metaphors were drawn from rabbinic mysticism—mystical union in death, in divine marriage, as the Body of Christ. But he did not use kabbalistic metaphors of lover and beloved—the rabbinic mysticism based on the Song of Songs. Gnostic interpretation , however, went beyond "putting on the perfect Man" to the mystical union of the Bridal Chamber, drinking from the mouth of the Risen Christ, and finally merging with Christ.

---

[598] Mark 2.17 repeated in Matthew and Luke.
[599] Cf. Logion 23
[600] Galatians 4.19
[601] Colossians 1.27
[602] I Corinthians 2.16

Logion 109 [Gnostic Parable]

> The Sovereignty is like a man who had a hidden treasure in his field without knowing it. And after he died, he left it to his son. The son did not know (about the treasure). He inherited the field and sold it. And the one who bought it went plowing and found the treasure. He began to lend money at interest to whomever he wished.

COMMENTARY

This is yet another Gnostic parable that starts with an authentic *mashal* of *Yeshua* and redacts it to make it relevant to them—and in so doing absolutely misses or distorts the original message.

The authentic *mashal* is found only as part of Matthew's special material. It reads, "The Sovereignty of heaven is like treasure hidden in a field, which someone found and hid; then in his joy he goes and sells all that he has and buys that field."[603]

It means that the *razim* of Heaven are treasures hidden in the *Malkuth,* which is compared to a field. Personal revelation of a *raz* such as the *Basor,* which might come through hearing or study of apocalyptic scripture, awakens a disciple of *Hochmah* to the reality and immanence of the *Malkuth.* His response is to "sell all that he has" and invest in the field, meaning to make the *Malkuth* his top priority over all else. *Yeshua* emphasized love of God and his Sovereign ways—justice, compassion, love, beauty—over all other forms of love and loyalty, often using extreme hyperbole: "If you do not hate father and mother, you cannot be my disciple." Paul transmitted the the same teaching and used the same extreme hyperbole when he said, "I have given up everything else and count it all as shit *(skybalon)*."[604]

But Gnostic Logion 109 makes a different point. First, the treasure has been hidden generations ago and the field is already in possession of the family. It does not have to be purchased. The treasure *(gnosis)* is already in their possession, but unknown to them. That is a major Gnostic tenet.

Second, the heir sold it to another person. It was lost to the family. In other words, the Jews gave up their birthright to the gentile Christians, who "went plowing" (i.e. began to work the field of the *Malkuth)* and discovered the *raz,* which is *gnosis.*

Third, the Gnostic now begins to "lend money at interest" to whomever he pleases. Red flag! *Yeshua* hated usury (cf. Commentary on Logion 95: "If you have money, do not lend it at interest, but give it to one from whom you will not get it back.").[605] While we find making

---

[603] Matthew 13:44
[604] Philippians 3.8 Yes. Paul said "shit!"
[605] Luke 6:35 "Lend without expecting to be paid back."

profit by trade used as a positive example in the Parable of the Talents, charging interest on loans *("usury") was uised only in negative examples in other *mashlim.* This parable starkly contradicts his others.

To the Thomasian monks, "to lend money at interest" meant to profit spiritually from adding to their converts. The phrase "to whomever he wished" referred to the right of the monastic community to accept or reject petitioners for admission.

Logion 110 [Gnostic *Logion*]

> Whoever finds the world and becomes rich, let him renounce the world.

COMMENTARY

This is a Gnostic corollary to Gnostic Logion 80, which was a Gnostic interpretation of the authentic *davar* of Logion 81. See the Commentary to Logia 80 and 81. "Renunciation" was an ascetic monastic practice.

Logion 111 [Gnostic *Logia*]

> Logion 111.a The heavens and the earth will be rolled up in your presence. And the one who lives from the Living One will not see death.

> Logion 111.b Does not Jesus say, "Whoever finds himself, of him the world is not worthy?"

COMMENTARY

We do not find any words of *Yeshua* describing the conventional Jewish apocalyptic image of heavens and Earth being rolled up like a scroll. The earliest that we find this image used in Christianity is in the second-century Book of Revelations after the Sixth Seal is opened.[606]

The imagery used by the writer of Revelations did not come to him in an independent vision as presented, but was drawn from earlier Jewish apocalyptic writings. Many of these were produced in the first century after the time of *Yeshua.* The Old Testament sources

---

[606] Revelation 6.12-14: "And I beheld when he had opened the sixth seal, and, lo, there was a great earthquake; and the sun became black as sackcloth of hair, and the moon became as blood; And the stars of heaven fell unto the earth, even as a fig tree casteth her untimely figs, when she is shaken of a mighty wind. And the heaven departed as a scroll when it is rolled together; and every mountain and island were moved out of their places."

include Isaiah, Jeremiah, Ezekiel, Daniel, Zechariah, Joel, Amos, Hosea, and others. He also used the *Testament of Levi, 1 Enoch,* and the *Assumption of Moses* as well as the Gospels of Matthew and Luke.

The image of heavens rolled up like a scroll seems to enter apocalyptic imagery in this later period, and we find it also used even later in the Koran. But it does not appear in the language and apocalyptic imagery of *Yeshua.* This alone removes Logion 111.a from *Yeshua's* historical time and setting. Coupled with the Gnostic phrase "one who lives from the Living One" and the lack of Aramaisms,[607] there is nothing to identify 111.a as authentic. It is a product of late first- and second-century apocalyptic speculation.

Logion 111.b claims to be a *davar* of *Yeshua,* but it is not found among the authentic sayings in other literature, and the phrase "find himself" was not used by *Yeshua.* He spoke of losing one's soul. The "find" true divine self relates to the Jewish concept of the indwelling *yetzer ha-tov,* but here it refers to the *gnosis* of the immortal soul. It is a Gnostic concept.

Finally, the phrase "of him the *kosmos* is not worthy" repeats a common Gnostic doctrine.

Logion 112

Woe to the flesh because it depends upon the soul; but woe to the soul if it depends upon the flesh!

COMMENTARY

Literally, "Woe to the flesh that depends upon the soul; and woe to the soul that depends upon the flesh."

This is the authentic *davar* from which Gnostic Logion 29 was created.[608] As I pointed out, it exhibits the kind of paradox that we find in many authentic teachings of *Yeshua* such as Logion 7, and contains the semitic parallel construction of contrasting phrases "woe to X because Y, but woe to Y if X."

The meaning has been explored in the Commentary to Logion 29.

Logion 113

His disciples said to him, "When will the Sovereignty appear [on Earth]?" <Jesus answered,> "It will not appear

---

[607] "Not see death" is used in late first-century Greek New Testament writings, but the Aramaic idiom employed by *Yeshua* was "not taste death."

[608] The scholar might say, "Woe to the Gnostic saying that depends upon an authentic *davar;* but woe to the *davar* that depends upon a Gnostic saying!"

by waiting for it. It will not be a matter of saying 'it is here' or 'it is there.' Rather, the Sovereignty of the *Abba* is spread out upon the Earth, but mankind does not see it."

COMMENTARY

As I said in the first page of Chapter Two and in the Commentary to Logion 2, this is the end of the authentic *davarim* of *Yeshua* in the *Gospel of Thomas* and the logical conclusion to the original Aramaic dictation upon which the Greek text was based. It began with Logion 2, which summarizes the path of the disciple, and ends here with the revelation that the *Malkuth* and the *'Olam Ha-Ba* is eternally present. It is mankind who is blind to its realities.

When Will the *Malkuth* Appear?

In this saying, the disciples pose the same wrong question that Pharisaic and messianic Judaism asked: "When will the *Malkuth* appear?" His answer incorporates an independent version of the saying in Luke 17.21: "The *Malkuth* of God comes not by observation. Neither shall they say, Lo it is here! or, Lo, it is there! For, behold, the *Malkuth* of God is within you." In other words, the coming of the *Malkuth* is not a matter of where or when, but of how.

The Marcan version of the "Lo, here, Lo there" *davar* is repeated in Matthew, but it concerns the question of when *Messiah* would appear on Earth. The two appearances were separate apocalyptic events in Jewish eschatology, but were conflated into one event along with the prophetic concept of the Day of *Yahweh* in popular messianic and Christian interpretation.

According to the Babylonian Son-of-Man wisdom tradition of *Yeshua,* the *Malkuth* or Sovereignty of God was universal and omnipresent. However it had been hidden from the consciousness of mankind by *Shaitan,* who ruled human hearts and governments through his host of fallen archons, principalities, and powers. But the season of *Shaitan's* illegitimate sovereignty, brought in by the fall of the Old Adam, was coming to an end. God's Sovereignty was to be established in the hearts of the New Humanity. The spiritual ignorance and moral blindness of humanity was to come to an end. The old world was to pass away.

The Book of Daniel, a major source of the Son-of-Man tradition, describes this vision of the *Malkuth* of God manifesting on Earth. The Beasts represent oppressive governments like the Roman Empire. This imagery was developed in the Christian Book of Revelations:

> As I looked, thrones were placed,
> and the Ancient of Days took his seat;
> his clothing was white as snow, and the hair of his head like pure wool;
> his throne was fiery flames; its wheels were burning fire.

> A stream of fire issued forth and came out from before him;
> a thousand thousands served him, and ten thousand times ten thousand stood before him; the court sat in judgment, and the books were opened.

> I looked then because of the sound of the great words that the horn was speaking. And as I looked the beast was killed, and its body destroyed and given over to be burned with fire. As for the rest of the beasts, their dominion was taken away, but their lives were prolonged for a season and a time.

This is the Babylonian messianic interpretation of the prophetic Day of the LORD *(Yahweh)* or Day of Judgement. Immediately following is related Daniel's prophetic dream about the *Bar-Enash* or "one like unto a son of mankind" who would inherit co-sovereignty with God:

> I saw in the night visions, and behold, with the clouds of heaven
> there came one like unto a son of man *(bar-enash)*,[609]
> and he came to the Ancient of Days and was presented before him.

> And to him was given dominion and glory and sovereignty *(malkuth)*,
> that all peoples, nations, and languages should serve him.
> His dominion is an everlasting dominion, which shall not pass away, and his sovereignty one that shall not be destroyed.

The figure became the Son of Man or archetypal *Bar-Enash* of the Enochian and other subsequent apocalyptic and messianic literature.[610] The Enochian scroll preserved at Qumran, which would have been the version known to *Yeshua,* says this about the messianic interpretation of the Son of Man:

> "This is the *Bar-Enash,* who hath righteousness, with whom dwelleth righteousness, and who revealeth all the treasures of that which is hidden *(razim)*, because the Lord of Spirits [messianic designation for God] hath chosen him, and whose lot hath the pre-eminence before the Lord of Spirits in uprightness for an aeon *['olam]* of aeons *['olamim]* ..."[611]

Since the vision of the Son of Man appears in Daniel after the vision of the Day of the LORD, kabbalistic interpretation determined that the Son-of-Man *Messiah* would commence his sovereignty after God's destruction of *Shaitan's* rule. Even so,

> "As for the rest of the beasts, their dominion was taken away, but their lives were prolonged for a season and a time."

Evil forces would remain for a longer period, probably until they eventually died out, but they would have lost their sovereignty under the rule of the *Bar-Enash.*

The survival of evil forces appears in the Book of Revelations as the thousand-year reign of the saints, when *Shaitan* and his host are bound and cast into the bottomless pit. After this,

---

[609] In contrast to the beasts that had hitherto ruled on Earth.
[610] See Commentary on Logion 2, "The Gospel Publically Proclaimed by *Yeshua*"
[611] See Commentary on Logion 2 for a complete translation and documentation of the text.

"*Shaitan* shall be loosed out of his prison and go out to deceive the nations."[612] Satan is then defeated, cast into the lake of fire and brimstone with all his cohorts, and tortured forever. The new heavens and Earth appear, and the New Jerusalem descends from Heaven "prepared as a bride adorned for her husband."[613]

However, Revelations inserts the Second Coming of Christ—the Christian interpretation of the appearance of Jesus as the victorious *Messiah ben-David*—before the Day of the LORD. In Christian thought, Christ will return victorious to conquer *Shaitan* and prepare the Earth for divine Judgment.

Yeshua and the Son-of-Man tradition, however, taught differently. The Little Apocalypse of Mark 13 is probably the earliest surviving example of the Christian interpretation of *Yeshua's* prophecies about the Day of the LORD and coming of the *Bar-Enash*—even earlier than the Pauline teachings. It has been thoroughly redacted to reflect gentile Christian ideas.

For example, Jesus is made to say, "And the Gospel must first be published among all the gentiles."[614] But *Yeshua* did not preach to gentiles. In his words, the *Basor* would not be preached to all of Palestine before the *Malkuth* began to appear, and there were some standing before him who would not taste death "until they see the *Malkuth*"[615] or "until they see the *Bar-Enash* coming in his *Malkuth*."[616]

While the prophetic tradition underlying messianic thought envisioned gentiles worshipping at the Mountain of the LORD in the *'Olam Ha-Ba*, *Yeshua* himself did not preach to gentiles or send out his Apostles to convert them. The inclusion of gentiles began with Peter on his missionary journeys to Jewish synagogues after the Resurrection, according to the Book of Acts, and was promoted and carried forward later by Paul. Thus the Marcan statement about the Gospel being first preached to all the gentiles before the coming of the Day of the LORD was not part of *Yeshua's* teaching.

Nevertheless the Marcan order of apocalyptic events is based on the Son-of-Man order taught by *Yeshua,* which differs from later Christian teachings and that of the Book of Revelations. In this order, when the *Malkuth* begins to appear it is accompanied by the Birth Pangs of *Messiah*, or what in early Christianity was known as the Tribulation. These immanent times of trial were the subject of most of *Yeshua's* prophecy—the destruction of Jerusalem and the Temple being foremost.

---

[612] Revelations 20.7-8

[613] The New Jerusalem was understood by the Christian writer to be the Church—the Pauline Bride of Christ. Catholic theology developed the concept of the Church Militant (the faithful on Earth), Church Suffering (the faithful in Purgatory), and Church Triumphant (the faithful in Heaven). The New Jerusalem would have been a *coniunctio* of all three forms.

[614] Mark 13.10

[615] Lucan redaction of the Q saying at 9.27

[616] Matthean redaction of the Q saying at 16.28

"And then if any man shall say to you, Lo, here is Christ; or, lo, he is there; believe him not. But take ye heed: behold, I have foretold you all things"[617] Into this the Marcan redactor inserts, "For false Christs and false prophets shall rise, and shall shew signs and wonders, to seduce, if it were possible, even the elect."[618] This was the period that the early churches believed themselves to be experiencing.

And then, even though *Yeshua's* prophecy has ended ("Behold, I have foretold you all things"), the redactor adds, "But in those days, after that tribulation, the sun shall be darkened, and the moon shall not give her light, and the stars of heaven shall fall, and the powers that are in heaven shall be shaken, and then shall they see the Son of Man coming in the clouds with great power and glory. And then shall he send his angels, and shall gather together his elect from the four winds, from the uttermost part of the earth to the uttermost part of heaven."[619]

These lines are quoted word for word, but out of context and with no scriptural attribution, from prophecies of Isaiah 13.10 and 34.4, followed by lines from Daniel's *Bar-Enash* vision at 7.13-14 . They were delivered not by *Yeshua,* but by the Marcan redactor.

Even with much redaction, the Marcan apocalypse still follows the Son-of-Man order in which only <u>after</u> the Birth Pangs of *Messiah* and the Day of the LORD does the *Bar-Enash* come "in the clouds," that is, in the *razim* of Heaven, with great power and glory.[620]

In view of all this, the answer to "when" the *Malkuth* will appear must be, "It is spread out upon the Earth, but men do not see it." But if the question concerned when the *Messiah* would appear on Earth, that was a *razim.* Daniel said that the Son-of-Man *Messiah* approached the Throne in the *annani* (mysteries, obscurations, "clouds") of Heaven. The early Christians interpreted that to mean Christ would descend to Earth from the sky riding on the physical clouds. But in his historical teachings, *Yeshua* does not suggest the mode by which the *Bar-Enash* will appear on Earth. More important, in the messianic eschatology of *Yeshua's* tradition, the appearance of the *Bar-Enash* could not occur until <u>after</u> the Day of the LORD. The *Bar-Enash* was not a Davidic warrior, but a Solomonic Sovereign.

Logion 113 is a summary of quintessential kabbalistic *manda* about the advent of *Malkuth* and *Messiah* that *Yeshua* revealed to his inner-circle of *talmidim.*

---

[617] Mark 13.21, 23
[618] Mark 13.22
[619] Mark 13.24-27
[620] The addition of the verse about sending out his angels to the four corners of the Earth is taken from

Logion 114 [Inauthentic Gnostic *Logion*]

Simon Peter said to him, "Let Mary leave us, for women are not worthy of The Life." Jesus said, "I myself shall guide her in order to make her male, so that she too may become a living spirit resembling you males. For every woman who will make herself male will enter the Kingdom of Heaven."

COMMENTARY

Peter as adversary of Mary *Magdala* is a theme known in other Gnostic documents, such as the *Gospel of Mary*. This *logion* is replete with Gnostic terminology and the originally Pythagorean dichotomy of male-divinity, female-mortality found in other Gnostic fragments like one extant from the lost *Gospel of the Egyptians*, where Jesus is reputed to have declared, "I came to destroy the works of woman." Godhead was male and all that was temporal and corruptible was female.

In Logion 114 the Coptic words for male and female are the same as for man and woman. The phrase could be translated "every woman who will make herself a man will enter the Kingdom." In other words, "every woman who makes herself divine," or of the same substance as Godhead.

The issue of women as disciples and what authority they might have was resolved originally by *Yeshua,* whose hosts, hearers, and inner circle of disciples included many women. More than a third of the people that Paul greets as leaders of the early churches by name in his Epistles were women, including travelling teachers who would have carried the title Apostle.

Mary *Magdala* travelled with *Yeshua* and the male disciples, and after his execution preached the Gospel in cities of the diaspora. Mary the Mother of *Yeshua* was not a disciple, but Mary *Magdala* and John were inner-circle disciples. She did not undertake earlier journeys when *Yeshua* sent disciples out in pairs to preach the *Basor* as women were not acceptable in the role and she would have been in danger. But early legends tell of her later Apostolic travels, including the miraculous egg she produced for Emperor Tiberius—basis for the Eastern and Russian Orthodox painted Easter eggs.

There are very late legends about Mary as penitent prostitute that originated in eleventh-century Europe, such as the Golden Legend that placed her in France. However, the only credible legend about her life is that she journeyed with Mary the Mother of Jesus and John to Ephesus in Asia Minor and established the churches there, where she would have been a mentor to the young John and best friend of Mother Mary. Orthodox legends portray her as the most virtuous of women (not a prostitute, as in later Roman Catholicism). She and

Mother Mary died in Ephesus of old age, leaving John as Apostolic head of the churches in Asia Minor.[621] Her relics were later brought to Constantinople.

Several scholars have speculated that Mary *Magdala* was the "beloved disciple" of John's Gospel—gender changed to preserve secrecy. Certainly as the disciple to whom the resurrected *Yeshua* first appeared, she was one of his most spiritually astute and talented students. It is likely that much of what we know as Johannine tradition developed in the context of her mentorship of the young John son of Zebedee after they journeyed to Asia Minor. Perhaps it would be more accurate to refer to Johnanine tradition as Magdalenic.

The Gnostic fascination with Mary *Magdala* and Johannine tradition probably did not originate with the Syrian *Thomas* monks, but in later Gnostic schools. As the archetypal witness to the Risen Savior, Mary seems to have been a kind of patron saint of Gnostic revelation—as opposed to charismatic and pneumatic Spirit revelation. Gnostic revelation always involved an appearance of the Risen Christ as with Mary, not a glossolalia or a pneumatic prophecy séance.

Logion 114 was the last saying added to the *Gospel of Thomas.* We don't have any Oxyrhynchus or other fragments or quotations like it from the original Greek version. Like many of the final *logia* it may have been composed in Coptic, not translated from an earlier Greek. Thus it may reflect an issue in the Egyptian *Thomas* community about the admission and status of female monks. The resolution was that they must become like the widows and virgin of the gentile churches—totally ascetic.

Sexual asceticism was the authentic sign and gold standard of sainthood in Roman-Hellenistic Syria. This was the practice of the unmarried Apostle Thomas and the main spiritual theme of his preaching, at least in Thomas literature and tradition.[622] It was probably also the practice of the Egyptian *Thomas* Gnostics.

---

[621] The fiction that Jesus and Mary were spouses or lovers, which appeared and was promulgated in the mid-twentieth century, assumes that Jesus went for older women—i.e., the age of his mother!

[622] This and the docetic teachings about Jesus and Resurrection current with his Syrian followers put them into direct conflict with the Johannites such that they portrayed Thomas as the "doubter"—the spiritually weakest of the Apostles—in John's Gospel.

CONCLUSION:
THE MEANING OF *YESHUA'S* TEACHING FOR CONTEMPORARY HUMANITY

The Master *Yeshua* was both a man of his times and the prophet of a new humanity. His message was both simple and highly complex. He spoke in simple and often incomprehensible ways to his own age through the limitations of language and culture. But the complex realities that were impossible to be properly understood and transmitted in his age have ripened and become comprehensible to twenty-first century humanity.

Our keys to understanding are these:

> 1. Separate the *Basor* and teachings of *Yeshua* from the doctrines and traditions of Christianity.

> 2. Examine them in the light of their historical Jewish spiritual, linguistic, and social context so we can understand them on their own terms.

> 3. Draw valid parallels to our own spiritual, linguistic, and social context so we can see how *Yeshua's* teachings might illuminate us—the evolving New Humanity of his prophecies.

We have already taken steps one and two in our study of the *davarim.* To help organize what we have learned into a bigger picture, I have listed the authentic sayings according to topic in an appendix that you will find worth your time to examine.

Yeshua's Message and the End of the Ancient World

Yeshua's mission was to sow the seeds that would begin the process of overthrowing the sovereignty of evil on Earth and establish the Reign of God in the consciousness and social institutions of mankind. The seeds were his words and his *Halakah* which, like those of Gautama Buddha, have endured regardless of how poorly they were understood.

The Reign of God was the rule of Justice, Compassion, and all the Names or attributes of Godhead. It was fidelity to the Way of God in human life, because the problem of evil was rooted in the human heart. Therefore the heart, which had inscribed within it from its very creation an innate knowledge of the ways of God, must be taught to develop its divine nature. Selflessness must overcome selfishness. The spiritual voices of the heart must be given heed in preference to the grossly material and ignorant cries of a lower, less mature nature. The walk of life must be in awareness, beauty, and service that cause the doer to grow, mature, and evolve—not in blindness or ignorance of one's ultimate dependence upon all beings and unity with all human beings.

Yeshua taught that the New Humanity, the *Bar-Enash,* was within all people. "Inasmuch as you have done it to the least of these, my brothers and sisters, you have done it unto me." Yet it must be brought to birth, and that process was one of trial and testing—the Birthpangs of the *Messiah.* Thus all human suffering could lead ultimately to spiritual transformation when rightly endured. "Blessed is the Man of Affliction; he shall find Divine Life."

Mankind was to come of age and inherit Co-Sovereignty with God. *Yeshua* established a new consciousness of the *Malkuth.* Even though the Son of Man had nowhere on Earth to lay his head, he was able to lay the foundations for the *Malkuth* on Earth. The kabbalistic mustard seed of Divine *Malkuth* that he planted has already grown into the great tree of the Messianic Age. But the tares still grow among the wheat.

The Sovereignty and the New Humanity Two Millennia Later

So how has humanity changed over two thousand years? Has the *Malkuth* come? Has the *Messiah* appeared? *Yeshua* would say yes, in part. The Sovereignty of God is spread out upon the Earth, and now men are starting to see it. Democratic government and institutions are triumphing over the oppressive "beast" monarchies of the Old Adam. Women are triumphing over male oppression. Race and culture wars are mitigating as through intermarriage and intercultural exchange as the Earth becomes one world for all.

We live in a far better world than the Roman Empire. Medicine, technology, science, art, education—all aspects of the Way of God—dominate human enterprise. We exemplify many aspects of the New Humanity prophesied by *Yeshua* and envisioned by the Jewish sages of his day. We are creating a new Heaven and a new Earth. We are becoming Co-Creators with Godhead and stewards of our world, and one day will be stewards of our solar system.

But like the *davar* of the Wheat and the Tares, the human heart and its world are checkerboards of black and white, battlegrounds of virtue and vice. Ongoing warfare rages between the Old Humanity and the New over issues like race, culture, religion, science, and the environment. All too often conservative forms of religion and other social institutions fight to preserve not their wisdom, but their destructive "traditions of men"—the Old Adam.

The Roman Catholic hierarchy doggedly maintains socially regressive opposition to birth control and abortion while virtually ignoring the problems of many of its ascetic male clergy with child molestation and alcoholism. Certain Islamic brotherhoods fund and promulgate violent *jihad* against rival religions and culture. Many Orthodox Jews agitate for violence against Islamic Palestinians. Muslim extremists continue to attack Israeli cities and settlements. And yet these same institutions support laudable charities and social work.

The Adolescence of the New Humanity

Yeshua taught us that we are all to become Gods. We are to take responsibility for ourselves and our world in ways that are far beyond the imagination of any religion. The material, secular world is to be transformed into a Paradise by a New Humanity—the spiritual heir of the Old Humanity, the *Bar-Enash,* the Offspring of Adam.

Why was the man born blind? Was it because of his past-life sins or those of his parents? *Yeshua* answered that the man was born blind so that the glory of God would be revealed in his healing. What does that mean? Yes, life and the world are replete with illness, injustice, and unfinished business. But there is no constructive benefit in looking backwards to lay blame. Life and the world are still in the process of divine formation. They are like partially made clay pots. The design can be inferred, but we must complete the process with our own hands. To glorify God means to value and implement the attributes of Godhead in life, like justice, healing, compassion, wisdom, beauty.

As humanity comes of age, it is not only its privilege, but its responsibility, to give sight to the man born blind. It is our responsibility to develop science, education, medicine, art. It is our responsibility to work with God and nature to make our planet into a place of justice, beauty, and greenery for all interdependent species.

Whenever religion opposes conscientious science, the advancement of human rights, or the leadership of wise politicians, on the basis of outworn doctrines that are designed to keep humanity in bondage to guilt and all the ways of the Old Adam, the true teachings of *Yeshua* are being denigrated.

The Teachings of *Yeshua* Illuminate our Lives in the 21st Century

Human souls stand at as many levels of readiness for spiritual knowledge as there are grades from kindergarten to graduate school. Some are still self-indulgent children at heart, others wise old souls, with every stage in-between. *Yeshua's* teachings address all levels.

Most of Christianity is able to use *Yeshua's* simple moral teachings at what we might call a grade school level. Parables like the Good Samaritan reinforce basic charitable impulses, and sayings from the Sermon on the Mount help people to become somewhat aware of judgmental flaws. But this is all mixed with regressive church doctrines about hell, damnation, and false religions—including other denominations of Christianity.

People of these grades in Christianity and other traditions are often religious fundamentalists who are committed practitioners of daily ritual. They stick rigidly to foods prescribed by priests, rabbis, or other religious authorities, and attach themselves fixedly to gurus and other religious teachers. Much of their spiritual practice has to do with purifications and warding off evil. They donate or tithe their money only to their own religious institutions.

Guilt, fear, and social pressure—ultimately rooted in the impulses of the *yetzer ha-ra*—are major forces that produce their ugly fruits of self-righteousness, false humility, blindness to one's own vices, and intolerance for other spiritual ways. This level of spirituality usually allies with conservative political views and is opposed to positive change. It is anti-feministic, anti-scientific, and open or secret disrespecters of other religious traditions. In other words, these are cases that produce the very manifestations of Pharisaism that *Yeshua* bitterly criticized.

In the spiritual high-school grades, human souls of the New Humanity experience the highs and lows of spiritual adolescence. Christians have rebelled against their churches to become agnostic, gone church-hopping, or are exploring different religions. They often experience many kinds of emotional and physical suffering and addictions that periodically drive them regressively back into their rejected religious havens for security. This is part of an experience of the Birth Pangs of *Messiah*, because ultimately they will stabilize and begin to make progress toward spiritual maturation.

At the spiritual college level, human souls have achieved a great deal of individuation. They begin to develop spiritual practices of various sorts that they find meaningful—but that might be as varied as Buddhist Tantras or wilderness trekking. They are no longer "religious," but spiritual. They have often developed a personal spiritual synthesis of ideas and practices from different religious and non-religious sources, including New Age spirituality. They often seek spiritual peers but are disappointed—they have become too unique to find others like them. They have a lot of spiritual integrity. Life can still knock them down and bring them deep suffering, but it can also cause them to experience bliss and joy beyond what the lower spiritual grades can bring.

What about graduate school? The higher degrees? That is where the kabbalistic *Halakah* of *Yeshua*—many aspects of which are found in the *Gospel of Thomas*—can be understood and put into practice. For one thing, they transcend Christianity and Judaism. In one place they suggest Buddhist practices, at another Hindu practices, at another those of Shamanism, and at another those associated with Jungian and other psychological systems. That is because they reflect universal principles of human spiritual evolution.

Again, the kabbalistic teachings and *Halakah* of *Yeshua* are not prescriptive. They are suggestive. The disciple is committed to a grand spiritual do-it-yourself project with benchmarks and goals, but no external guidance. He or she must use *manda, gnosis.* The operative methodology is persist and "know for thyself."

But this cannot be successful if it is an uninformed enterprise, merely feeding one's own presets and defaults into the way *Yeshua's* teachings and practices are implemented. As I said at the outset, too many readers of *Thomas* and other sources of *Yeshua's* teachings such as the New Testament blissfully create their own interpretations oblivious to which portions are authentic, which are later interpolations, and what the original Aramaic *davarim* of *Yeshua* really taught.

This little volume is my best attempt to provide raw materials for understanding the authentic teachings and *Halakah* of *Yeshua.* They are not offered by any Christian church or other religious institution. My presentation of them is, without doubt, quite flawed.

But it is my hope that one day Christian institutions will make serious attempts to improve upon what I have done—to reconstruct, study, and practice the teachings of *Mar Yeshua.* It will be a great day when Christianity cleans its slate of all church dogma and goes back to the drawing board with the best tools of scholarship to re-examine and re-establish its foundation in the *halakah* and teachings of the Master Jesus.

This doesn't mean that Christmas and all the beautiful traditions of Christianity must be sacrificed. They simply must be reinterpreted. For example, the Advent and Christmas legends are archetypal. They celebrate the birth of Christ in the heart of humanity. Why not teach them that way in the churches?

The Apostolic charge of the Master was to proclaim the *Basor*—not the Gospel of Paul or the doctrines of Calvin or Rome. The basis for that *Basor* is not the Bible. The Bible is a great tool, but only one of many that can be used.

Rather, the basis is the historical Word spoken by *Yeshua.* It tells us *what mankind is and can become.* It invites us to become Christs. When we finally have a valid understanding of his Word, then we can begin to develop true and useful spirituality for the developing New Humanity of the twenty-first century.

APPENDIX ONE: The *Ma'aseh Merkabah*

The Work of the Chariot *(Merkabah)* based its meditative visualizations on the biblical accounts of Isaiah's ascent to the heavenly court of *Yahweh,*[623] Ezekiel's vision of God seated in his *Merkabah* or Throne-Chariot,[624] and the ten-heaven astrological scheme of the apocalyptic ascent of Enoch.[625]

Also Jacob's vision of the stairway or "ladder" connecting Heaven and Earth,[626] which was the theophany upon which the sacred temple of Israel at Beth-El (House of the *Elohim*)was founded, was later understood as a *Merkabah* event. A late first-century Greek Christian pseudepigraphical writing entitled *The Ladder of Jacob*[627] interprets all the experiences of the patriarchs as *Merkabah* events.

According to the Gospel of John, Jesus says to Nathanael, whom he calls a true Israelite without guile (i.e., he is already a saint), *"Amen, amen, I say unto you, you will see the Heavens opened and the angels of the Elohim ascending and descending unto the Bar-Enash."*[628]

Here follows a summary of the origins and development of the *Ma'aseh Merkabah* reproduced from PowerPoint slides I created for my multimedia lecture-seminar on the Pre-Christian Teachings of *Yeshua.*

---

[623] Isaiah, chapter six

[624] Ezekiel, chapter one

[625] II Enoch or the Secrets *(Razim)* of Enoch. Significantly, it was in the Babylonian Jewish exile community that *Merkabah* and other apocalyptic mysticism developed. The extant sayings of *Yeshua* use the language and concepts of Babylonian messianic mysticism. He must have lived and studied in Babylon.

[626] Genesis 28.11-19

[627] The Greek book was lost, but extant in a Slavonic translation. It was preserved only by Christians—not Jews.

[628] The Greek pronoun *epi* is translated "upon," but the Aramaic *al-* that may underlie the saying if it is authentic suggests ascent up to the heavens. The image in John's Gospel is that of a disciple witnessing a *Merkabah* event with angels ascending and descending upon Jesus. But if authentic, *Yeshua* could have said either that he would show Nathanael the vision of the heavens, as he did for James, Peter, and John in the so-called Transfiguration event, or that he would transmit to Nathanael the *Ma'aseh Merkabah* so that he would be able to attain the vision himself.

RAZIM: EVOLUTION OF THE *MERKABAH* ASCENT

- **PRE-EXILIC:**
    - JACOB'S DREAM Stairs with angels ascending and descending
    - ISAIAH: Vision or dream in the Night-Heaven (two *Shamayim*) above Firmament (no series of Heavens)
    - Assumed bodily into Heaven in Chariot instead of death ENOCH, ELIJAH
- **POST-EXILIC:**
    - EZEKIEL'S VISION OF YHWH ON HIS THRONE-CHARIOT *(MERKABAH)*
    - Vision or dream in Day or Night Heaven, Throne descends or Prophet ascends PAUL, ETC.
- **Riders of the Chariot *Ma'aseh Merkabah* "Work of the Chariot"**
    - WISDOM SCHOOLS (Alexandria, Palestine, Babylon):
        - Meditation techniques and contemplation of Ezekiel's *Merkabah* images; Night-Heaven ascent in Chariot
    - ENOCHIAN APOCALYPTIC SCHOOLS (Palestine, Babylon):
        - Ascent with Great Angel and/or Chariot, Babylonian-Greek astrological models of 7-10 Heavens, Great Sea; CHRISTIAN BOOK OF REVELATIONS

    - RABBINIC SCHOOL OF AKIBA (Palestine):
        - Contemplation of Ezekiel's *Merkabah* images, Great Sea, and addition of *Hekhaloth* or Hallways to Palace of YHWH
    - *HEKHALOTH* MYSTICS:
        - Contemplation using Akiba's method, but with greater and detailed elaboration of Heavenly Palace and its Hallways
- **Yeshua's Traditions**
    - BABYLONIAN WISDOM SCHOOL TRADITION:
        - Techniques Developed for Enochian Ascent through the Heavens: *Book of Parables* with all the Messianic, Danielic "Son of Man" and *Enoch-Metatron* (little YHVH) "Prince of this World" from Babylonian archives.
    - JOHN THE BAPTIST AND QUMRAN TRADITION:
        - Enochian Ascent through the Heavens: *Book of Watchers* and other fragments found at Qumran

- **Yeshua's Probable Method of *Merkabah* Ascent**
    - **MYSTERIES OF THE *MALKUTH* OF THE *SHAMAYYIM* :** Wisdom school Enochian techniques of Night-Heaven meditation, prayer, contemplation of *Merkabah*, , ascent in a *Merkabah* in context of a midnight *Mishqad* or Vigil

MERKABAH ASCENT: THE THRONE-CHARIOT [MERKABAH] VISION OF EZEKIEL

•Babylon during Captivity
•Same images in Near Eastern, Egyptian, and Solomon's Temple
•Chariot-Throne [Merkabah] had wheels like that used by a king in battle as his traveling war-throne.

> •Significance DIVINE OMNISCIENCE: YHWH is mobile, omniscient, omnipotent—can be everywhere at once
> •Chariot-Throne or Merkabah made of many angels being driven by the "Likeness of a Man," or YHWH.

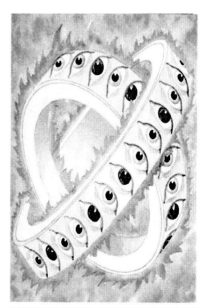

•Four angels form the basic structure of the Merkabah. These angels are called the Chayot (חיות lit. "living creatures"). The bodies of the Chayot are like that of a human being, but each of them has four faces, corresponding to the four directions the chariot can go (North, East, South, and West). The faces are that of a man, a lion, an ox (later changed to a child or cherub or kerub) and an eagle. Since there are four angels and each has four faces, there are a total of sixteen faces.
•The angel with the face of the man is always on the east side and looks up at the "Likeness of a Man" [YHWH] that drives the chariot.
•Each Chayot angel also has four wings. Two of these wings spread across the length of the chariot and connected with the wings of the angel on the other side. This created a sort of 'box' of wings that formed the perimeter of the chariot. With the remaining two wings, each angel covered its own body.

•Below, but not attached to the feet of the Chayot angels, are other angels that are shaped like wheels. These wheel angels ("wheels within wheels"), are called Ophannim אופנים (lit. wheels, cycles or ways). These wheels are not directly under the chariot, but are nearby and along its perimeter. Each wheel is full of eyes. DIVINE OMNSCIENCE
•The "Likeness of a Man" sits on a throne-seat made of sapphire.

JEWISH TALMUDIC ACCOUNTS FROM 2ND CENTURY C.E.

- "The *Ma'aseh Merkabah* should not be taught to any one except he be wise and able to deduce knowledge through wisdom ('gnosis') of his own" (Ḥag. ii. 1).
- "R. Eleazar ben 'Arak was riding on a mule behind R. Johanan b. Zakkai, when he asked for the privilege of being initiated into the secrets of the *Merkabah*. The great master demanded proof of his initiation into the *manda (gnosis)*, and when Eleazar began to tell what he had learned thereof. R. Johanan immediately descended from the mule and sat upon a rock.
- "'Why. O master. dost thou descend from the mule?' asked the disciple. He answered. 'Can I remain mounted upon the mule when the telling of the secrets of the *Merkabah* causes the *Shekinah* [feminine "Glory" of YHWH: God as Mother-Teacher] to dwell with us and the angels to accompany us?' Eleazar continued. and, behold, fire descended from heaven and lit up the trees of the field. causing them to sing anthems. and an angel cried out. 'Truly these are the secrets of the *Merkabah*.' Whereupon R. Johanan kissed Eleazar upon the forehead. saying. 'Blessed be thou. O father Abraham. that hast a descendant like Eleazar b. 'Arak!'
- "Subsequently two other disciples of R. Johanan b. Zakkai walking together said to each other: 'Let us also talk together about the *Ma'aseh Merkabah*'; and no sooner did R. *Yeshua* begin speaking than a rainbow-like appearance [Ezek. 1. 28] was seen upon the thick clouds which covered the sky. and angels came to listen as men do to hear <u>wedding-music.</u> On hearing the things related by R. Jose. R. Johanan b. Zakkai blessed his disciples and said: 'Blessed are the eyes that beheld these things! Indeed I saw myself in a dream together with you. seated like the select ones [comp. Ex. 24. 11] upon Mount Sinai: and I heard a heavenly voice saying: <u>"Enter the banquet-hall and take your seats with your disciples and disciples' disciples. among the elect. the highest ('third') class."</u>
- Messianic mysticism themes: Wedding Banquet. "elect." marriage of Heaven and Earth
- Tosefta Hagigah 2:3-4: Four entered the Orchard (*Pardes*): Ben Azzai. Ben Zoma. Akher and Rabbi Akiba. One peeked and died: one peeked and was smitten: one peeked and cut down the shoots: one ascended safely and descended safely.
- Great danger of insanity or death
- Study descriptions in *Yeshua: The Unknown Jesus*

APPENDIX TWO: The Messianic Banquet *Seder:* Original Life-Setting of the Inner-Circle Teachings of *Yeshua*

The Original Sacred Meal of *Yeshua*

The Christian Mass did not originate in the legendary Last Supper or Passover recounted in the synoptic gospels. It was an adaptation of the Jewish *Shabbat Seder. Yeshua* used the *seder* as a mystic vehicle for teaching his disciples, and especially for transmitting kabbalistic teachings to his inner circle.

It seems to have been modeled on the Jewish *Shabbat* gathering of kabbalistic sages to discuss the *razim* and mysteries of Heaven. When they convened for sacred studies, they entered a place of timeless joy known as the *Pardes*—the Paradise from which mankind had been expelled, but which could be experienced and partially realized by God's *tzadikim.*

Yeshua's messianic version of the *Pardes* was understood to be a foretaste of the Marriage Banquet of Messiah, symbolizing restoration of divine communion with the *Abba* or Father-Mother Godhead in the Messianic Age-to-Come, the *Olam Ha-Ba.* In the *Seder* of *Yeshua,* Heaven and Earth were united. The Bread of Heaven or divine kabbalistic teachings were shared and discussed among the disciples or sages. The Wine or spiritual joy of Eternal or Life (the spiritual life of the divine *'Olam*) was shared. These were understood to be the Body and Blood of the Son-of-Man Messiah, the *Bar-Enash* or corporate New Humanity. The Blessing, distribution, and partaking of bread, fish, or other food symbolized membership in the Body of Messiah, and the wine symbolized the sanctified Life of Messiah.

Exploring the Evidence

The Book of Acts describes the original Jerusalem Christians living communally and breaking bread together, or sharing a messianic meal. The later Antiochene community combined Jewish and gentile members who shared the meal, but at separate tables. This was later understood in the context of Hellenistic tradition to be an *agape* meal or "love feast," which was an annual banquet-gathering of friends of the deceased to remember and honor him. The original messianic meaning was transformed into *anamnesis,* "remembrance." However this was a magical remembrance that was understood to evoke the spiritual presence of the Lord Jesus.

Luke-Acts is a late Greek document reflecting Pauline theology and gentile Christian antagonism against Jewish Christianity. It presents Peter as the leader of the Jerusalem Church when, in fact, James the Brother of *Yeshua* was leader. Peter is also represented as an advocate of the gentiles, having admitted gentiles into the Church and received a vision to negate the Jewish kosher food laws as Paul and his gentile congregations wanted.

However, in spite of the tendency to project current gentile Christian practice anachronistically back into the early Church, Acts describes the early Christian Eucharist as a *full meal* instead of the sacramental mass instituted by Paul. When a writer includes information that runs counter to his practice or bias, that is considered by scholars to constitute strong evidence for its historicity. The earliest Jewish-Christian Eucharistic gatherings were full-meal community banquets.

Luke-Acts also provides another clue. After the crucifixion of Jesus, his Uncle Cleopas and another disciple are walking on the road to Emmaus. They are confused and sorrowful because they know that Scripture said a crucified man ("who is hung upon a tree") is accursed of God. The Pharisaic rabbis seem to be right that Jesus was not a saint or messiah. He was a criminal heretic.

They are joined by a stranger who walks with them. He interprets many kabbalistic allegories from the Old Testament Scripture that show the Messiah was to be rejected, crucified, and raised from the dead—like Jesus. That evening they sit down with him for a meal. The stranger performs the Blessing of bread and wine, and suddenly the disciples realize they are in the presence of the risen Jesus. The stranger then disappears.

How did they recognize him? "He was known to them in the breaking of the bread," we are told. Why did his recitation of his unique Blessing *seder* make him recognizable? Because the most common venue for *Yeshua's* teaching was a *Shabbat* or other meal where he led the *seder*, performing the initial breaking and blessing of the bread and the cup. He celebrated and framed the meal as a foretaste of the Marriage Banquet of the Messianic Age, using it innovatively as a venue for teaching. The stranger of Luke-Acts did all this in the unique way that *Yeshua* always had. That is how Cleopas and the other disciple recognized him.

In other words, for the earliest Christians it was in the Eucharistic meal—the messianic banquet—that the presence of the risen Jesus could be accessed. See Appendix Two.

Yeshua was known in Aramaic as *Mar Yeshua,* the Master *Yeshua.* The earliest Eucharistic meals of the Christians always included the Aramaic invocation quoted by Paul, *Maranatha.* This can be translated *Maran* (Our Master) *Atha* (Come), similar to the invocation of the

Holy Spirit later used in gentile Christianity.[629] The invocation "Our Master, Come" was used at the common full meal celebrated by the original Jewish Christians before Paul reformed the Eucharist to become what we know as the Mass. For the original Jewish Church, it was in the fellowship meal that the Risen Christ was present.

It was this Christian banquet meal that Paul, who never knew or studied with *Yeshua,* sought vigorously to reform, as he declared in I Corinthians 11:

> [20]**When you come together, it is not the Lord's supper that you eat.** [21]**For in eating, each one goes ahead with his own meal. One goes hungry, another gets drunk.** [22]**What! Do you not have houses to eat and drink in? Or do you despise the church of God and humiliate those who have nothing? What shall I say to you? Shall I commend you in this? No, I will not.**

> [23]**For I received from the Lord what I also delivered to you, that the Lord Jesus on the night when he was handed over took bread,** [24]**and when he had given thanks, he broke it, and said, "This is my body which is for you. Do this in remembrance of me."** [25]**In the same way also he took the cup, after supper, saying, "This cup is the new covenant in my blood. Do this, as often as you drink it, in remembrance of me."** [26]**For as often as you eat this bread and drink the cup, you proclaim the Lord's death until he comes.**

> [27]**Whoever, therefore, eats the bread or drinks the cup of the Lord in an unworthy manner will be guilty concerning the body and blood of the Lord.** [28]**(Let a person examine himself, then, and so eat of the bread and drink of the cup.** [29]**For anyone who eats and drinks without discerning the body eats and drinks judgment on himself.** [30]**That is why many of you are weak and ill, and some have died.**

As late as Paul's time (A.D. 50-60), the gentile churches were celebrating the Christian Eucharist as an anamnestic *agape* meal. It was the gentile cultural adaptation of a full-meal banquet, but celebrated weekly rather than annually. Paul objects vigorously to abuses of the banquet. He declared, "I received from the Lord," meaning he had received a personal revelation from the risen Jesus Christ, that the Christian Eucharist was *not* to be a full-meal banquet to satisfy hunger. Rather, it must be a sacramental meal like that of the Greek mystery religions (i.e. the bread-and-wine sacrament of Mithraism, in which the sacrament was understood to be the Body and Blood of the world savior Mithra). Paul justified his view by referring to the legend of the Last Supper, which he claims to have received orally from earlier Christians. Significantly, however, Paul does not refer to it as a Passover meal—simply as the *Deipnon Kyriakon,* Lord's Supper. It is only later in Mark's Gospel that the Lord's Supper is understood to have been a Passover *seder.*

---

[629] It can also be translated *Mara* ([The] Master) *Natha* (Comes/Will Come) as a credal statement of belief in a Second Coming. But that would be anachronistic, as the Second Coming doctrine developed later in the gentile churches.

The Last Supper: Passover Meal or Not?

The Last Supper is terribly problematic for scholars because the Gospel accounts indicate origins in legend rather than history. The original version in Mark, which was later elaborated in Luke and Matthew, tells the Pauline "body and blood" story, but framed as a Passover *seder*. (Paul's account is more historical because it reflects a *Shabbat seder* in which *Yeshua* offers a second Cup of Blessing *after* the meal.) But the account of the Last Supper in John's Gospel is not a Passover *seder,* and it makes no mention of the "body and blood." Instead it tells the story of the foot-washing lesson rather than the institution of the Eucharist.

Moreover, The Pauline and Johannine versions both represent *Yeshua* as being crucified at the time the Passover lambs were being slaughtered—the sacrificial "Lamb of God" that provides the central tenet of Paul's interpretation of the execution of Jesus as a cosmic sacrifice that expiated the sins of mankind. It was such a powerful magical act that all who merely believe in Jesus as Messiah will be redeemed. Therefore in the Pauline and Johannine sacrificial accounts, Jesus was crucified *before* the Passover meal was eaten, when the Passover lambs were being slaughtered.

Here's the dilemma: How could Jesus eat a Passover Last Supper if he was already crucified? Who is right—the synoptic Gospels, or Paul and John's Gospel?

Mark was written about A.D. 50 perhaps contemporary with Paul, but without strong Pauline influence. The writer of Mark's Gospel didn't try to show Jesus as being crucified at the time the Passover lambs were being slaughtered. Instead, he presented the Last Supper as a Passover meal *after* the lambs were slaughtered. Why? Because for Mark, the Lord's Supper was instituted by Jesus as a reinterpretation of the Passover *Seder.* It originated at the final Passover.

It is important to remember that the writer of Mark's Gospel was a gentile who was totally unfamiliar with Palestine and Judaism. Examples: His geographical sequences make no sense; his description of the roof from which the paralytic is lowered for Jesus to heal is a Roman-style tile roof—not the type of roof found in Palestine; etc. Mark handed down the gentile interpretation that Jesus was a magical Passover sacrifice, but without the Jewish understanding of sequence—slaughter of the lambs.

Luke saw the dilemma, wanted some kind of reconciliation with the Pauline view, so edited the Marcan Last Supper account to have Jesus say, "I have earnestly desired to eat this Passover with you, but I tell you that *I will not eat it until it is fulfilled in the Kingdom of God.*" In other words, Luke represented Jesus as not eating the Passover meal as a sacrificial vow. Nevertheless, Luke presented the Last Supper as a Passover meal, blithely glossing over the timeline contradictions. Matthew wrote, "...I will not eat it *again* until it is fulfilled in the Kingdom...," meaning that Jesus did eat the Passover meal. But in all three cases, the

Lord's Supper is understood to have been instituted in the context of a Passover *seder,* which is simply a-historical, i.e., legendary.

John's Gospel seems to be uncharacteristically historical in this case. It did not interpret the Last Supper as a Passover meal, but as a final inner-circle teaching venue that included parables and the foot-washing. Significantly it was also not a *Shabbat seder. Yeshua's* Messianic Banquet was not limited to *Shabbat.*

In John's Gospel, the Last Supper seems to occur the night before Passover, so that Jesus would have been crucified on a Friday while the lambs were being slaughtered for the "High Holy *Shabbat,"* since Passover fell on Friday evening *Shabbat.* Thus Jesus never ate the Passover with his disciples. This agrees with Paul's interpretation of Jesus as having been crucified at the time the lambs were being slaughtered, and may explain Luke's confusion about presenting Jesus as refraining from eating the Passover meal with his disciples.

We can't have it both ways. Either Jesus was crucified while the lambs were being slaughtered before the Passover meal, or the day after the Passover meal. Matthew, Mark, and Luke try to have it both ways, which is historically impossible and thus is rooted in legend. Most scholars agree that the Pauline-Johannine timeline is historical, and thus there was no Passover Last Supper.

The implication is that the Lord's Supper originated in a messianic *seder* that *Yeshua* often led while travelling with his disciples—and not necessarily limited to *Shabbat.* In addition to large public venues for teaching, such as those of the Sermon on the Mount and Sermon on the Plain, the Gospels offer many accounts of Jesus teaching his disciples privately at meals. This must have been the context of the original "institution" of the Lord's Supper.

In the Markan legend, an account of the Last Supper seems to have been conflated with a bread-and-wine blessing allegorizing the disciples as Body and Blood of the Son-of-Man Messiah *(Bar-Enash)* that *Yeshua* probably taught in his Messianic *Seder.* This provided the basis for Paul's Eucharistic Body and Blood of Jesus Christ, since in Paul's understanding Jesus (not the disciples) was the Messiah. The disciples or church then comprised his Body.

In the Liturgy of the Messianic Banquet that I have composed, we as disciples all constitute the Body and Blood of Christ, faithful to the original Eucharistic meal of *Yeshua.*

From Messianic Banquet to Christian Mass

When did the Body and Blood of the Lord Jesus transform the meaning of the original Messianic Banquet of *Yeshua?* I have suggested that membership in the Body and Blood of the Son-of-Man Messiah, the *Bar-Enash,* was originally symbolized by *Yeshua* in the food and drink Blessings for private meals with his inner-circle of disciples. That would have been the original version of the Body and Blood of Christ.

But the post-resurrection transformation of Jewish *Mar Yeshua* into Greek gentile *Kyrios 'Iesous,* the divine Lord Jesus, changed the understanding of Messiah from the corporate Second Adam in which all disciples were mystically included to the deity Jesus Christ, whose body was the Church. Jesus became the one and only *Bar-Enash,* the Christ. By mid-first-century, the Eucharistic bread and wine had been understood in the Hellenistic context of Mithraic mysteries as the magical flesh and blood of a deity.

In his Epistle to the Romans c. A.D. 110, Bishop Ignatius of Antioch, writing while a prisoner on his way to martyrdom, said, "I desire the Bread of God, the heavenly Bread, the Bread of Life, which is the flesh of Jesus Christ, the Son of God, who became afterwards of the seed of David and Abraham; I wish the drink of God, namely His blood, which is incorruptible love and eternal life."

How did this idea that the Eucharist was the flesh and blood of Jesus arise? To understand this, we must begin with the crucifixion of *Yeshua* on Passover.

Herod probably chose to execute *Yeshua* by crucifixion because, as any observant Jew knew, scripture declared that "one who hangs upon a tree is accursed of God." Crucifixion was the most effective way to utterly destroy *Yeshua's* public credibility as saint or messiah. That is why Paul later referred to the crucifixion as a "scandal" for Jews.

Yet the disciples of *Yeshua* knew that he was, indeed, a great saint. How could God allow him to be crucified? The answer lay in the technique of allegorical, kabbalistic interpretation of scripture and events that the Master had always used. *Yeshua* was crucified at the same time the sacrificial lambs of Passover were being slaughtered by Temple Priests. That was highly significant. *Yeshua's* execution was not a rebuke by God. Rather, it was the greatest of all sacrifices. He was the sacrificial Lamb of God.

Using allegorical analysis of Scripture, the Jewish-Christian predecessors of Paul had discovered many proof-texts and prophecies that they could interpret as pointing to a crucified Christ. Paul built upon this to develop his sacrificial Christology and sacramental theology of the Eucharist.

As a Pharisaic disciple of R. Gamaliel, Paul knew that observant Jews could never accept the idea of a crucified Messiah. Since his only experience of Jesus was his vision of the Risen Christ, and the early church was based on pneumatic revelation received from the "Holy Spirit" or directly from the Risen Jesus, Paul prided himself on receiving everything through personal revelation. He downplayed the traditions he had learned from previous Christian teachers.

Paul knew very little of the historical *Yeshua* and his teachings. But in the light of his personal vision of the Risen Christ and his rabbinic training, he focused on the theological meaning of *Yeshua's* death and resurrection. For Paul, the Lord Jesus was the World Savior whose death was offered as a sacrifice to expiate the sins of mankind. "You are baptized into the death of Jesus," he often taught. "I proclaim the gospel of Christ crucified!" he declared. Thus Pauline Christology determined the way that Christian Eucharistic liturgy would develop.

Because Christianity derived the Mass or Eucharist from a legendary account of the Last Passover in which Jesus instituted the Lord's Supper, the Anamnesis of the Mass quotes Paul's transmission of the Words of Institution: "On the night he was handed over,[630] the Lord Jesus took bread and blessed it saying, 'This is my Body, which is given for you.' Likewise after supper he took the Cup saying, 'This is my blood...drink this in remembrance of me.'" That was the final evolution of *Maran Atha*.

The idea of "remembrance" (Greek *anamnesis*) was the basis for the gentile interpretation of the Mass as an *agape* meal. This was rooted in the earlier Jewish-Christian magical invocation *Maran Atha* to evoke the spiritual presence (Real Presence) of the risen *Yeshua* at the Eucharist. "Wherever two or three are gathered together in my Name, there am I in your midst." (Matthew 18.20)

---

[630] The legend of Judas Iscariot the betrayer of Jesus (not Judas the Twin, and not Judas the brother of Jesus) does not appear in Paul's letters, even though the King James version translated the verb "handed over" as "betrayed," assuming betrayal. Judas, which means "Jew," as the betrayer of Jesus probably came into the oral legend scholars have named the Passion Narrative in the gentile churches after the time of Paul (50-60 C.E.) and before the time Mark's Gospel was written. It reflects the conflict between Jewish and gentile Christians that produced the anti-semitism of the Christian Gospels.

APPENDIX THREE: The Authentic *Davarim* listed by Topic

CONCERNING THE SOVEREIGNTY *(MALKUTH)*

3. If those who try to exert spiritual influence over you say, "Behold, the *Malkuth* will descend from the sky," then the birds of the sky will be greater than you in the *Malkuth*. If they say to you, "Behold, the *Malkuth* will arise from the sea," then the fish will be greater than you. But the *Malkuth* is within your heart and beyond your understanding.

4.b Many who are regarded as masters of Israel will take the lowest seats at the Marriage Banquet of *Messiah*.
> **4.b [Literal Translation]**
> **Many who are greatest shall become least.**

113 His disciples said to him, "When will the Sovereignty appear [on Earth]?" <Jesus answered,> "It will not appear by waiting for it. It will not be a matter of saying 'it is here' or 'it is there.' Rather, the Sovereignty of the *Abba* is spread out upon the Earth, but mankind does not see it."

REGENERATION AS A CHRIST *(BAR-ENASH)*

22.a *Yeshua* saw babies being suckled. He said, "Those who will attain the *Malkuth* are like these newly-begotten ones at a mother's breast."

22.b His disciples asked, "Then shall we, being spiritually newly-begotten ones, attain the Sovereignty [*Malkuth*]?" *Yeshua* replied, "When you make the inner as the outer, and the outer as the inner; and the above as the below; and when you make the male and the female into a single unity, so that the male will not be [merely] masculine, and the female [merely] feminine; and when you make [human] eyes to serve as [God's] Eye, and a [human] hand to serve as [God's] Hand, and a [human] foot to serve as [God's] Foot, [and]

a human image to serve as [the Divine] Image; then you shall attain the Sovereignty.

46 Among those born of women, from Adam until John the Baptist, there is no one so superior to John the Baptist that his eyes should not be lowered (in his presence). Yet I have said, whichever one of you comes into being as a newly-born will know the *Malkuth* and will become superior to John.

KABBALISTIC MYSTERIES *(RAZIM)* OF THE SOVEREIGNTY *(MALKUTH)*

5.a Know what is in your sight, and the *Razim* will be revealed to you.

5.b There is no *Raz* that will not be brought into the light.

4.a A spiritual master of Israel will not hesitate to ask a newly-reborn saint of the *Malkuth* about the *Razim* concerning the Abode of the Living Ones, and he will also become a Living One.
     4.a [Literal Translation]
     An old man will not hesitate to ask a newly-born child of seven days about the '*Olam* of Life, and he will become alive.

11 This heaven and the one above it shall pass away. The spiritually dead are not alive, and the spiritually alive shall not die. In the days when you ate dead things, you made them alive. But when you enter into the Eternal Light, what will you do? On the day when you were one, you became two. But now that you are two, what will you do?

18 The disciples besought *Yeshua,* "Tell us about our ultimate future." *Yeshua* replied, "Then have you uncovered *Ha- Roshit* that you are now qualified to inquire about *Ha-Acharit?* For where the *maqom* of the Beginning exists, that will be the End. Blessed is he who is able to stand at the Beginning, for he shall know the End; and he shall never taste death."

19.d There are five Trees in the *Pardes* which are unmoved in summer or winter and their leaves never fall. Whoever has knowledge of them will not taste death.

48 If two were to make peace with each other in this one house, they will say to the mountain, 'Move away from here,' and it will move away.

70 When you beget that One you have within your hearts, He will perfect you. If you do not bring forth that One within your hearts, what you have not brought forth within your hearts will kill you.

83 The *tzelemim* are perceivable by mankind, but the divine light in them remains hidden in the *Tzelem* of the Light of the *Abba*. He will be revealed, but his *Tzelem* will remain concealed by his light.

84 When you perceive your *damutoth*,[631] you rejoice. But when you will perceive your *tzelemim*[632] which came into being before you, and which neither die nor become manifest, how much will you be able to bear?

85 Adam came into being with marvelous endowments from a great Heavenly Host, but he did not become worthy of you. If he had been worthy, he would not have experienced death.

81 Let him who has grown spiritually wealthy be Sovereign, and let him who possesses worldly power renounce it.

82 He who is near to me is near to the Divine Fire, and he who is far from me is far from the Sovereignty.

PARABLES *(MASHLIM)* OF THE SOVEREIGNTY *(MALKUTH)*

20 The *Malkuth* can be compared to a mustard seed, which is smaller than all other seeds. But when it falls onto properly prepared soil, it produces a large branch and becomes shelter for the birds of Heaven.

57 The Sovereignty of the *Abba* is like a man who had good seed. His enemy came by night and sowed weeds among the good seed. The man did not allow them to pull up the weeds; he said to them, 'I am afraid that you will try to pull up the weeds but pull up the wheat along with them.' For on the day of the harvest the weeds will be plainly visible, and they will be pulled up and burned.

76 The *Malkuth* of the *Abba* is like a merchant who had a consignment of merchandise and who discovered a pearl. That merchant was shrewd. He sold the merchandise and bought the pearl alone for himself. You too, seek his unfailing and enduring treasure where no moth comes near to devour and no worm destroys.

---

[631] Personal affinities and likenesses reflected in other people and things outside of you.

[632] Primordial or archetypal and invisible divine forces, energies, and motions; the Images of Godhead.

96 The Sovereignty of the *Abba* is like a certain woman. She took a little leaven, <concealed> it in some dough, and made it into large loaves. Let him who has ears hear.

97 The Sovereignty of the *Abba* is like a certain woman who was carrying a jar full of meal. While she was walking on the road, still some distance from home, the handle of the jar broke and the meal emptied out behind her on the road. She did not realize the consequences; she did not trouble herself. When she reached her house, she set the jar down and found it empty.

98 The Sovereignty of the *Abba* is like a certain man who wanted to kill a powerful man. In his own house he drew his sword and thrust it into the wall in order to practice making his hand strong enough to run it through. Then he slew the powerful man.

BEATITUDES

19.a Blessed is the one who existed before he was emanated into existence.

54 Blessed are the poor, for theirs is the Sovereignty of Heaven.

58 Blessed is the Man of Affliction; he shall find Divine Life.

103 Blessed is the man who knows where the thieves will enter, so that he may get up, gather defenders for his domain, and put on his armor before they invade.

CONCERNING THE SON-OF-MANKIND MESSIAH *(BAR-ENASH)*

8 The *Bar-Enash* is like a wise fisherman who cast his net into the sea and pulled it up full of small fish. Among them he found one good, large fish. That wise fisherman threw all the small fish back down into the sea without regret, but chose to keep the large fish. Whoever can understand my *mashal*, let him apply it to his own life.

9 [Reconstructed from Authentic *Mashal*] Behold, a Sower went forth, filled his hand, and scattered seeds. A few fell on the road, but the birds came and ate them. A few fell on stone, could not strike root into the earth, and did not produce ears of grain. And a few fell on thorns. They choked the seedlings and the worms ate them. But most of the seed fell onto good soil, and it brought forth good fruit. It bore from sixty to one hundred per measure.

16.a People may think that the *Bar-Enash* will come to bring peace to the world, but they do not realize that the advent of the Son of Man will bring divisions on the Earth—fire, sword, warfare.

16.b For there shall be five in one home; three shall be against two, and two against three; the father against the son, and the son against the father.

17 The *Bar-Enash* shall give you that which no eye has ever seen, no ear has ever heard, no hand has ever touched, and which has never arisen in the human heart.

37 His disciples asked, "When will the *Bar-Enash* be revealed to us, and when shall we see him?" Jesus answered, "When you disrobe without being ashamed and take up your garments and place them under your feet like little children and tread on them, then will you see the son of the living one, and you will not be afraid."

86 The foxes have their holes and the birds have their nests, but the *Bar-Enash* has no place on Earth to lay his head and rest.

106 When you make the two one, you will become the *Bar-Enash*, and when you say, "Mountain, move away," it will move away.

THE KABBALISTIC DISCIPLINE (HALAKAH) OF YESHUA

2. Let the seeker keep on seeking until he finds, and when he finds, he will experience the fear of God, and in that consciousness he will ascend, and he will share Sovereignty with God over all things.

6.a His disciples questioned him and asked, Do you want us to fast? and how should we pray,? and should we give alms? and what diet should we observe? Jesus answered, Do not fabricate a lie, and do not do what you hate others doing. For all deeds are manifest before the Face of God.

7 Happy is the lion whom the man eats, for the lion will become man; but utterly destroyed is the man whom the lion eats, for the lion will become man.

14.a If you do a religious fast, you will beget sin for yourselves; if you pray, you will come under judgment; if you give alms to the poor, you will do evil things to your spirits.

14.c For what goes into your mouth will not defile you, but rather what comes out of your mouth—that is what will defile you.

21.b.1 "Therefore I say, if the head of the house knows that a thief is coming, he will remain awake until he comes and will not allow him to tunnel through [the walls] into his sovereign home to carry away his treasure. You must keep vigil from the very foundations against the world and gird up your loins with great power, lest those who break into homes find a way to penetrate into you, because they will always discover your weakness.

21.b.2 "May there be a perceptive person of understanding among you: When the fruit splits open with ripeness, one comes quickly with sickle in hand to harvest it."

25 Honor your neighbor like your own heart, and protect him like the pupil of your eye.

26 You see the speck in your brother's eye, but you do not see the beam in your own eye. When you cast the beam out of your own eye, then you will see clearly to remove the speck from your brother's eye.

31 No prophet is accepted in his own village; no resident physician practices healing upon those who know him.

32. A city built on a high mountain and fortified cannot fall, nor can it be hidden.

33. Proclaim from your housetops what you will hear in your ear. For no one lights a lamp and puts it under a bushel, nor does he put it in a hiding place, but rather he sets it on a lampstand so that everyone who enters and leaves can see by its light.

36 Do not worry from morning until evening and from evening until morning about what you will wear.

39.b Be as wise as serpents and as pure as doves.

42 Become passers-by.

55.a Whoever does not hate his father and his mother cannot become a disciple to me.

79.a A woman from the crowd said to him, "Blessed are the womb which bore you and the breasts which nourished you." He said to her, "Blessed are those who have heard the Word of the *Abba* and have truly kept it.

AFTER *YESHUA* WILL BE MARTYRED

12 The *talmidim* said to *Yeshua,* "We know that you will disappear from our sight. Who is the one that will succeed you as our *Rav?*" *Yeshua* replied, "From whatever place you may be, you shall go to James the *Tzadik*, for whose sake Heaven and Earth came into being."

38.a Many times you have desired to hear these *davarim* that I am revealing to you, and you have no one else to hear them from.

DISCIPLESHIP AND APOSTOLIC MINISTRY

10 I have cast a sacred flame onto the world and behold, I am tending it until the whole world is ablaze.

14.b When you go into any region and enter into the district villages, if they welcome you, eat what they set before you and heal the sick among them.

19.b-c If you become my true disciples, and put my words into practice, these very stones will minister to you.

23 The *Bar-Enash* shall select you, one out of a thousand, and two out of ten thousand; and you shall stand immortal as a Single Being.

24.b Whoever has ears, let him hear. There is Divine Light within a Man of Light and he enlightens the whole *Kosmos.* When it does not shine, there is spiritual darkness.

73 The harvest is great but the laborers are few. Beseech the Lord, therefore, to send out laborers to the harvest.

90.a Jesus said, "Come unto me, for my yoke is easy and my lordship is mild.

94 He who seeks will find, and he who knocks will be let in.

95 If you have money, do not lend it at interest, but give it to one from whom you will not get it back.

99 The disciples said to him, "Your brothers and your mother are standing outside." He said to them, "Those here who do the will of the *Abba* are my brothers and my mother. It is they who will attain unto the Sovereignty of the *Abba*."

100.a They showed Jesus a gold coin and said to him, "Caesar's men demand taxes from us." He said to them, "Give Caesar what belongs to Caesar and give God what belongs to God.

101.b Whoever does not hate his father and his mother cannot become a disciple to me.

47.a It is impossible for a man to mount two horses or to stretch two bows. And it is impossible for a servant to serve two masters; otherwise, he will honor the one and treat the other contemptuously.

CONCERNING HUMAN DEATH AND LIFE IN THE *'OLAM* OF GOD

21.a *Miriam* asked *Yeshua,* "What are your disciples like?" He said, "They are like small children who are dressing up and playing house with property they don't own. When the owners of the property come upon them, they will say, 'Give us back what we own.' They strip naked and give everything back to them.

41 Whoever has, will receive more; but whoever lacks will be deprived of even what little he has.

59 Look unto the Living One while you are alive, lest you die and seek to see Him and have not power to do so.

63 There was a rich man who had great wealth. He said, 'I shall invest my money so that I may sow, reap, plant, and fill my storehouse with produce, with the result that I shall lack nothing.' Such were the thoughts of his heart, but that same night he died. Let him who has ears hear.

87 The personality of flesh [i.e., the *nephesh*] that clings to flesh [*basar*] will waste away, and the soul [*neshamah*] that is attached to these two will become desolate.

88 The angels and the prophets will come to you and give to you those things you (already) have. And you will reciprocate by offering them those things which you have, and say to yourselves, 'When will they come and take what is theirs?'

112 Woe to the flesh because it depends upon the soul; but woe to the soul if it depends upon the flesh!

CRITICISM OF THE RELIGIOUS ESTABLISHMENT

34 If a blind man leads a blind man, they will both fall into a pit.

39.a The Pharisees and the scribes have taken the keys of spiritual knowledge [manda] and hidden them. They themselves have not entered, nor have they allowed those who wish to enter.

40 A grapevine has been planted without the Abba, but because it is corrupt, it will be pulled up by its roots and destroyed.

44 Whoever blasphemes against the Abba will find release, and whoever blasphemes against the Bar-Enash will find release; but whoever blasphemes against the Ruach Ha-Qodesh will not find release in this 'olam.

47.b No man drinks old wine and immediately desires to drink new wine.

47.c New wine is not put into old wineskins, lest they burst; nor is old wine put into a new wineskin, lest it spoil it. An old patch is not sewn onto a new garment, because it will split apart.

65 [Reconstruction] There was a master who owned a vineyard. He leased it to tenant farmers so that they could work it and he would collect part of the produce from them. But when sent his servant so that the tenants might give him produce of the vineyard, they seized him and beat him. The servant went back and told his master. The master sent another servant. The tenants beat this one as well. Then the master sent another servant, and this time they killed him. What then will the master of the vineyard do? He will come and kill those tenants and give the vineyard to others. Let him who has ears hear.

64.a A man had received visitors. And when he had prepared the dinner, he sent his servant to invite the guests. He went to the first one and said to him, 'My master invites you.' He said, 'I have claims against some merchants. They are coming to me this evening. I must go and give them my orders. I ask to be excused from the dinner.' He went to another and said to him, 'My master has invited you.' He said to him, 'I have just bought a house and am required for the day. I shall not have any spare time.' He went to another and said to him, 'My master invites you.' He said to him, 'My friend is going to get married, and I am to prepare the banquet. I shall not be able to come. I ask to be excused from the dinner.' He went to another and said to him, 'My master invites you.' He said to him, 'I have just bought a farm, and I am on my way to collect the rent. I shall not be able to come. I ask to be excused.' The servant returned and said to his master, 'Those whom you invited to the dinner have asked to be excused.' The master said to his servant, 'Go outside to the streets and bring back whomever you happen to meet, so that they may dine.'

66 Show me the stone which the builders have rejected. That one is the capstone.

74 O Lord, there are many around the drinking trough, but there is nothing in the well.

78 Why have you come out into the desert? To see a reed shaken by the wind? And to see a man clothed in fine garments like your kings and your great men? Upon them are the fine garments.

79.b There will be days when you will say, 'Blessed are the womb which has not conceived and the breasts which have not given milk.'"

89.a Jesus said, "Why do you wash the outside of the cup?

89.b Do you not realize that he who made the inside is the same one who made the outside?"

102 Woe to the Pharisees, for they are like a dog sleeping in a cattle manger, for neither does he eat nor does he let the cattle eat.

EXORCISM

35 It is not possible for anyone to enter the house of a strong man and take it by force unless he binds his hands; then he will ransack his house.

45 Grapes are not harvested from thorns, nor are figs gathered from thistles, for they do not produce fruit. A good man brings forth a good thing from his storehouse; an evil man brings forth evil things from his evil storehouse, which is in his heart, and says evil things. For out of the impulses of the heart he brings forth evil.

CPSIA information can be obtained at www.ICGtesting.com
Printed in the USA
BVOW04s0132250216

438033BV00001B/1/P